To Vivian —

One time student
all time friend!

Best of luck —

Stu Knee

The Concept of Zionist Dissent in the American Mind 1917-1941

by Stuart E. Knee

The Concept of Zionist Dissent in the American Mind 1917-1941

By Stuart E. Knee

ROBERT SPELLER & SONS, PUBLISHERS
New York, New York 10010

© 1979 by Stuart E. Knee
ISBN 0-8315-0177-4
Printed in the United States of America

To Sonya

Table of Contents

Introduction

Over the past one hundred years the Jewish people of Erez Israel, or what the Romans and Britons used to call Palestine, have shown the world that Zionism works. Again and again in a multitude of human endeavors they have proven that Jews can be farmers, soldiers, factory workers, engineers, as well as professors, bankers, merchants and artists. Since the rebirth of the State of Israel in 1948 that same Jewish people has brought new life to a land ravaged by interminable warfare of one empire against another. But despite all this, Zionism and the right of a Jewish State to exist is presently being challenged as it was some 30, 50 and even 100 years ago. Among the challengers are the empire spokesmen, industrial and oil interests, Arab leaders, missionary groups, and even educators. As in the past, there are some Jews among the detractors and challengers. They are consumed with the fear of being considered and identified as Jews. They reject fellow Jews who are not afraid to identify with their culture, religion and nationality.

In this unique book, Dr. Stuart M. Knee has given us a definitive study of Zionist dissent in America from 1917 to 1941. He has carefully examined the anti-Zionist thinking of State Department officials, missionaries, selected educators, socialists and communists, Arab Americans, advisors to such Presidents as Woodrow Wilson and others. At times their anti-Zionism reflected an ingrained racism, and not just an anti-Zionism. What is most difficult to fathom is the anti-Zionism evident among some American Jews. Some of these Jews were so preoccupied with being accepted as

Americans that they could not stand to see Jews in America who openly maintained their traditions. The presence of Jews who maintained their traditions was most distracting to these assimilationists and they did everything possible to either help assimilate the newcomers or by encouraging restrictive immigration so as to keep the "Jewish" Jews in Europe. They were thunderstruck when many of the newcomers became Zionists. Dr. Knee gives us a careful history of the reaction of some of these establishment Jews and their organizations. He tells us for instance how the Joint Distribution Committee went so far as to set aside millions of dollars to help Russian Jews resettle in the Crimea rather than in Palestine or America. Little came of this experiment, but nevertheless it was tried and it reflected the fear of some establishment American Jewish organizational leaders that they might be regarded as Jewish-Americans and not just Americans. They did not want Zionism but then they were not so sure about Judaism either.

The division within the American Jewish community held back the progress of Zionism in America. Not until after World War II would American Zionism be strong enough to give support for the recreation of the Jewish State in Israel. That inability to unite, that weakness contributed to the destruction of European Jewry at the hands of Hitler from 1933 to 1945. They were not united and strong enough to demand of their American Government that it help rescue the Jews of Europe, that it make good the Balfour Declaration promises which President Woodrow Wilson helped draft.

As you read through these pages you will see the very same anti-Zionist arguments that contemporary opponents of Zionism make today. We owe Dr. Knee a debt of gratitude for unearthing this history for us so that we can see our own time a bit more clearly.

Herbert Druks, Ph.D.
Professor, Judaic Studies & History
Brooklyn College

Preface

THIS BOOK takes a somewhat different approach to American Zionism than have its predecessors. To be sure, Yonathan Shapiro's *Leadership of the American Zionist Organization 1897-1930* and Melvin I. Urofsky's *American Zionism From Herzl to the Holocaust* are significant and thorough. This, however, is a detailed study of anti-Zionism, non-Zionism and economic Zionism, all of which are variations on the major theme of Jewish nationalism and were amply represented in American society during the interwar period of the 1920s and 1930s. In offering what I believe to be a significant amount of new information about the personalities, currents and factions within the American Jewish and non-Jewish communities, I have stressed a topical study for the most part rather than a purely chronological one. It appeared to me that some separation of the several critiques would serve to distinguish individuals far more clearly than would the constant mixing and mingling of their ideas which, sometimes, confuses and mislabels important spokesmen and their philosophies.

My work is not anti-Zionist, non-Zionist or Zionist in its outlook, although it contains elements of all three. It is the history of an idea which evolved not in a vacuum but in clear response to such larger concerns as the postwar peacemaking at Paris and in the Middle East, the era of illusory prosperity and collective security in the 1920s, the isolation of the United States from active participation in world affairs, and tensions wrought in America from the incompatibility of dual ethnicity and ''pure'' Americanism, the melting pot and cultural pluralism, realpolitik and idealism and modern nationalism and the racist variety of Germany. As a battleground for ideas in American society, there is no better field of study than Jewish nationalism, for the concept was altered, rearranged, criticized and assaulted during the years 1917 - 1941 to fit certain individual and group psychological, emotional, political and social needs. Although a valid criticism of the following pages may be that they do not relate the internal United States situation more effectively to the external European-Middle Eastern one, I might respond that I did not intend to. My primary focus is the exploration of an idea, Zionism, and its progress and durability in the American environment through two unsettled, disturbing decades in this country's history.

I am grateful to many people and institutions for their aid and encouragement. I would first like to thank Professor David M. Reimers of New York University who helped me explore the subject in all its ramifications, offering much of himself, his time and his effort. I am also indebted to Professor Stanley P. Hirshson of Queens College of the City University of New York who, through the years, has unstintingly supported my various academic endeavors, offering me nothing but the best advice. More recently, Professor Herbert Druks of Brooklyn College has reviewed and discussed the work with me and has provided many useful ideas for revision.

During many months of research in the manuscripts and newspaper divisions of the New York Public Library, I was treated by the staff with the utmost consideration and courtesy. I would also like to thank several archivists and librarians who forwarded to me manuscript materials relating to William Yale, Albert Lybyer and the Paris Peace Conference of 1919. They are Judith Schiff, Chief Research Archivist at the Sterling Library of Yale University, Paul Heffron of the Library of Congress Manuscript Division, Milton O. Gustafson of the National Archives and Records Service and Maynard Brichford, University Archivist at University Library, the University of Illinois at Urbana-Champaign. Once again in New York City, I appreciate the kindness of those at Columbia University's Butler Library and School of International Affairs, the Zionist Archives, the American Jewish Committee Archives, Tamiment Institute and Jewish Theological Seminary who permitted me to use the papers of Eleanor Robson Belmont, Louis D. Brandeis, Nicholas Murray Butler, the Carnegie Endowment for International Peace, Israel Friedlaender, *State Department Record Group 59,* Morris Hillquit, Herbert Lehman, James G. McDonald, Edwin R.A. Seligman, Baruch C. Vladeck, Henry White and William Westermann. I am expecially appreciative of the aid I received at the Bund Archives, where I was privileged to interview Yaakov Shalom Hertz, Emanuel Scherer and

May Bromberg. Librarian and archivist Hillel Kempinski performed above and beyond the call of duty when, for a month, he patiently and painstakingly translated Yiddish newspaper and biographical sources to me. For service such at this, a simple thanks seems woefully inadequate.

Finally, to all my friends who listened to my endless discussions on this topic, thanks for not being bored. There are no words of gratitude which can express the warm feelings I have for my wife, Sonya, who was and is unfailingly loyal to me and my project. She listened, understood and helped me in both good times and bad. Of course, I stand alone in accepting full responsibility for any mistakes or interpretive deficiencies recorded herein.

The Concept of Zionist Dissent in the American Mind 1917-1941

by Stuart E. Knee

The Foundation
Of Zionist Criticism in America

AS AN ORGANIZED MOVEMENT, modern Zionism dates from 1897, when the first Zionist Congress was convened at Basel, Switzerland. Zionism, however, was by no means an exclusively nineteenth century product or an ultimate solution to anti-Semitism. Theodor Herzl did not invent Jewish nationalism at the Dreyfus trial nor was it his whim or sudden fancy. Herzl's "revelation" was a revival and modernization of a venerable concept, as old as the Jewish people itself. The prophet Isaiah, who lived in the last third of the eighth century B.C., witnessed the decline and fall of the Jewish State but did not yield to utter dispair. He envisioned exile for the people but offered them these cryptic words of consolation: "A remnant shall return (*Isaiah*, X:20-22)." What this meant no one deigned to say, but nearly three thousand years of debate clothed the statement in mystic garb. The will to fight for Palestine was manifested in the Maccabean revolt and the insurgency of Bar Kochba; the impulse toward nationalism and self-determination, even outside the Holy Land, culminated in the founding by converts of the Khazar State in the seventh and eighth centuries A.D.

Harried in England, France and Spain in the Middle Ages, victims of the Crusades and the Inquisition, the Jews finally found a measure of safety in the New World, and probably more would have come had not the French Revolution intervened. The disabilities they had suffered under were wiped away in pre-Napoleonic France, and other "enlightened" Western European nations followed suit. The ghetto disappeared but anti-Semitism lingered. For some liberated Jews in the arts, science, finance and politics, the burden of light discrimination bore more heavily on their minds than centuries of isolation; many Jews would settle for nothing less than full freedom. The year 1848 was one of national revolution. In 1861, Italy had achieved the goal of unification; ten years later Germany did the same. Significantly, Jews participated in all the great revivals, but had won precious little. Now, some of them thought seriously of initiating a drama of their own.

The German Socialist Moses Hess wrote the first modern Zionist work, *Rome and Jerusalem,* in 1860. Leo Pinsker, a Russian physician, equaled the feat in 1881 with his *Auto-Emancipation.* Thus, two wings out of East and West, one responding to the anti-Semitism of a liberal milieu and the other in the throes of medieval oppression, arrived at analagous conclusions. Russian born, though living in London at the turn of the century, Chaim Weizmann perceived the needs of Russian Jewry and undertook the Zionist struggle on their behalf. Herzl was the Western innovator; it was his concept of nationalism that was carried to America by Jacob de Haas and presented to Louis D. Brandeis in 1910.

In Zionism's formative years, 1898 to 1917, the Eastern and Western movements paralleled each other in their efforts to remedy the Jewish plight, although they did not always precisely agree on solutions. Securing Palestine was vital to both (less so to Western European Zionists), but discussion on the strategy to be employed after the goal was attained was regarded as premature. As long as future plans remained amorphous, cooperation was possible. The Balfour Declaration of 1917, however, signified that a fundamental debate on the nature of Zionism could no longer be deferred. Then and only then did actual Zionist critics emerge: Reform Jews who, prior to 1917, were the only definable opposition group were soon complemented by Brandeis's criticism.[1] This statement does not

---

[1] Toward the end of the nineteenth century, the anti-Zionist spokesmen for Reform Judaism in the United States were Kaufmann Kohler of Temple Beth-El, New York City, Rudolph Grossman of Temple Rodeph Shalom, Philadelphia, the Honorable Meyer S. Isaacs and the *American Hebrew.* By the Pittsburgh Platform of 1885, the Reform Jewish faith in the United States was transformed into a religion of service, enjoined to "participate in the great task of modern times, to solve on the basis of justice... the problems presented by the contrasts and evils of the present organization of society." See Julius Haber, *The Odyssey of an American Zionist: Fifty Years of Zionist History* (New York, 1956), pp. 115-116; Nathan Glazer, *American Judaism* (New York, 1957), pp. 151-152.

intend to imply that the two groups, one anti-Zionist and the other Zionist, were allied: it simply acknowledges the presence of disparate forces in American Jewry and the pressure exerted upon Zionism from within and without the movement. Rabbi Samuel Schulman's political criticism of all Zionism was poles apart from Brandeis's censure of the social and economic methodology of Weizmann: it is the difference between changing the rules of the game or not playing at all.

Where were the other critics: non-Zionists, Socialists, Arab-Americans, missionaries and non-Jewish liberals and why was the year 1917 one of confluence for their varied modes of thought? Understanding the year is pivotal. From 1878, the year of the founding of *Petach Tikvah*, the first Zionist agricultural settlement, to 1914, Jewish nationalism, or the return to Zion in force, was unrealistic. For one thing, Turkey would not surrender Palestine. For another, some of the *kibbutzim* were subsidized by Edmond de Rothschild and were somewhat dependent upon his bounty. Finally, East European refugees did not choose to scrape out a livelihood in the desert when the United States was accessible. Orthodox Jewish villages and institutions of learning continued to subsist in the Holy Land as they had in ages past, upon the *Chalukah*, or dole, of worldwide Jewry. The somber visage of Palestine was vividly portrayed in 1868 by an American traveler, Mark Twain: "Palestine sits in a sackcloth and ashes. Over it broods the spell of a curse that has withered its fields and fettered its energies."[2]

The four phases of Zionism crystallized with the Balfour Declaration and the Brandeis-Weizmann controversy. *Social Zionism* reflected the Weizmann philosophy, a primary concern with Jewish exiles and facilitating their removal to Palestine with all due haste. It grew as a result of the Russian May Laws of 1881 and the pogroms of the ensuing two decades which compelled large numbers of Jews to emigrate from the "Pale of Settlement" in Poland. Weizmann understood the need of these Jews for immediate domicile in Palestine. It did not matter to him whether such Jews were professionals, skilled workers or common laborers; whether they could support themselves or not. A Social Zionist was cognizant of a single overriding truth: the Jews must leave the countries of oppression,

---

[2] As quoted in "How Many People Can Palestine Maintain?" *Palestine*, (January, 1944), p.5.

and they must leave immediately. If they were unable to earn a livelihood, it was the task of world Jewry to sustain them until they could. *Economic Zionism* was to be the field of Brandeis's work and the point of departure between Weizmann and the West. Its emphasis was Palestinian industrial and agricultural development. Brandeis, Julian Mack, Stephen Wise and Jacob De Haas, just to name a few of this philosophy's advocates, were entirely sympathetic with the needs of Jewish refugees. But this did not prevent them from taking issue with Weizmann on the crucial order of priorities: Why they asked, must Jews in Palestine rely on world Jewish charity for their survival? Is it not better to prepare the land and its people for an independent life? Their solution was to control immigration while industry and agriculture remained in their first stages of growth. After a specified number of years, emigration to Palestine would be permitted to increase gradually, in accordance with the absorptive capacity of the country. *Cultural Zionism* was more at home in Eastern Europe than in America. It encompassed literature, art, education, language and the key, religion. The latter was the overriding interest of messianic, traditional, Orthodox Jews, and they guarded their prerogatives jealously; they could be Zionists or not but either way, exhibited no desire to compromise on matters of faith. *Political Zionism* may be classed as a mortar, a binding and setting solution, a motive for the first three, the author which established the fate of the players and maneuvered them toward the Balfour denouement. "Political Zionism" meant the establishment of a Jewish government in Palestine and the support of that government through immigration. In short, the creation of a Jewish State Whenever this phrase appears in the text, this is the meaning it conveys.

At this stage, a clarification of terms is in order. One who dissents from or criticizes Zionism may not be an anti-Zionist. In other words, "anti-Zionists" and Zionist "critics" are not synonymous. It is not a question of semantics but a concept upon which the following study is constructed. Anti-Zionism was the opposition to a Jewish Government in Palestine supported by a large Jewish immigration there. Conceivably, then, one could be anti-Semitic without necessarily being an anti-Zionist. Such a person, if he resided in America, would favor Jewish departure from there to Palestine or anywhere else on the map. In the case of American foreign correspondents Vincent Sheean and Albert Viton the opposite was true.[3] The Socialists and non-Zionists introduced further modifications in terminology. Though both groups were critical of Zionism, neither one could be properly called anti-Zionist. A Zionist critic may reject any one, some or all four of Zionism's phases. The most common forms of criticism were aimed at the alleged political and religious motives.

Brandeis is an interesting and relevant case in point. Why, one might ask, might he appear in the following chapters? Is he not a Zionist? Does he not promote the Jewish national interest? How, then, can he be a critic in the regular use of the word? Again, let us say that ''anti-Zionist'' and ''critic'' are a pair of terms which may be misleading if they are used interchangeably. Among all ''critics,'' it was the unique role of Brandeis to postulate a constructive alternative to Central European Zionism by adapting American progressivism,[4] individual initiative and technology to the Herzlian, Western Zionist program. The American Zionists of the Brandeis persuasion were unique in their sensitivity to the diverse ideas inherent in a ''national home.'' A different insight will naturally be derived from the ''critic'' who, by failing to draw a distinction between Brandeis and Weizmann, launches upon a blanket attack of both leaders and the two forms of Zionism. That latter motif is indicative of the anti-Zionist who may either be self-serving, unsophisticated as to the numerous implications of Zionism-nationalism or careless enough to think that any and all Zionist distinctions are hairsplitting irrelevancies. With the exception of the Brandeis-Mack group, some Socialists, some liberal Jews of the 1930s and non-Zionists after 1918, critics did not distinguish between American and European Zionism, perhaps because of innate Jewish prejudice or self-hatred, as in the case of pre-1935 liberal Jews, who were more intensely American than they were Jewish. But this is not

[3] Vincent Sheean was a foreign correspondent and freelance writer whose interest in freedom movements had taken him to Morocco, China and Russia during the 1920s. He landed in Palestine in the summer of 1929 and shortly discovered that Jewish Nationalism was inimical to the Marxian Philosophy he revered. Sheean, however, as his later writings after the Evian Conference illustrate, was neither anti-Semitic, nor anti-Jewish, but anti-Zionist and anti-British. See Vincent Sheean, *Personal History* (Boston, 1969), pp. 83-161, 260-303, 333-398, and several articles he wrote for *Asia* magazine (December 1929 and January 1930, for example) and *Commonweal* (May 21, 1930). See also his *Not Peace But A Sword* (New York, 1939) and *The Eleventh Hour* (London, 1939). Vitor, also a journalist and correspondent wrote for *Asia, The Nation* and *Christian Century* throughout the 1930s.

[4] For a more complete discussion of Brandeis's efforts to reconcile Zionism and Americanism, see Melvin I. Urofsky, *American Zionism From Herzl to the Holocaust* (Garden City, New York, Doubleday, 1975).

to say that it is advisable to forget that certain intragroup differences occurred and that defenders of Jewish nationalism were capable of rejecting a form of Zionism but not the entire ideology. In this respect, the inclusion of Brandeis here serves an eminently useful purpose: by not being an anti- or non-Zionist, by being critical of Zionism from within the movement itself, his assertions and convictions provide a counterpoise, a sense of equilibrium, to the wholly political exposition. In sum, an explanation of the Brandeis-Mack philosophy and its significance adds another dimension to Zionist criticism.

A persistent, albeit slight, controversy surrounding Zionism emerged after 1897, when the political phase of the movement was attested to at Basel and more precisely after 1903 when the Uganda project was rejected. As a result, the World Zionist movement divided, the contending parties being Herzl's and Weizmann's. The former may be called undiluted politicals for it was their intention to settle Jews anywhere, even Africa; the latter, including De Haas, Nahum Sokolow and Menachem Ussischkin were religio-politicals and were interested only in Palestine. It was the second rather than the first interpretation which proved most durable.

In 1914, however, Zionism had yet to enter what Brandeis later called its "propagandistic" era. It was not taken seriously because it was not unified. All the components were present, but Palestine was still a Turkish possession and legally unattainable. Some focus was required for economics to have it proceed beyond mere dilettantism, religion to have its proceed beyond Messianism and Palestinian Jewish society to have it proceed beyond pastoralism. But how to capture the Jewish imagination? This was a problem which European and American Zionists were pressed to solve and, without benefit of a concrete, practical program, it was a nearly impossible task. In the United States, Jewish nationalism was undergoing a painfully slow metamorphosis. The initial Zionist influence came from Russian immigrants who arrived in America between 1881 and 1898. American Zionist societies were modeled on the *Chovevei Zion,* "Lovers of Zion," and the moving spirits were Joseph Bluestone of Odessa and several West European rabbis, including Pereira Mendes, Benjamin Szold (father of Henrietta and Robert), Aaron Wise (father of Stephen), Gustav Gottheil (father of Richard), and Marcus Jastrow, all of whom were touched by the plight of Russian Jews. The Dreyfus Affair spurred Americans to revamp the movement and, in accordance with the anti-Semitic urgency and the knowledge of Herzl's work abroad, a more efficient transatlantic apparatus was constructed in 1898, the Federation of American Zionists (F.A.Z.)

Impressive on paper, the membership and structure of the F.A.Z. was disappointing in nearly every other way. Its three central organizations were the Hadassah, women's branch, founded in 1912 by Henrietta Szold; the Order of the Sons of Zion, presided over by Joseph Barondess, and Young Judea, the creation of Israel Friedlaender. Printed materials on Palestine and the nature of Zionism abounded but the success of the promotional campaign was doubtful: approximately three million, three hundred thousand Jews resided in the United States in 1914 but less than ten percent were enrolled Zionists. There had been a Reform statement at Pittsburgh in 1885 and another by Isaac Mayer Wise in 1897, but they were hardly necessary: Zionism was not yet considered a rival.

World War I, however, disturbed the status quo existing between Jewish nationalism and its as yet undefined critics. By entering the conflict, Turkey gambled with her empire and proved to be its inadequate protector. Hence, Zionism arrived at the forefront, no longer a philosophic debate but an imperative. Seizing the moment, American Zionists acted. Established on August 30, 1914, the Provisional Executive Committee for General Zionist Affairs was, at the outset, commanded by Louis Brandeis. His very name lent dignity and stature to the Jewish national cause in the United States. The organization raised large sums of money for the relief of Jews in Europe and Palestine. Julian Mack, Felix Frankfurter, Eugene Meyer, Jr., Harry Cutler and Louis Kirstein congregated beneath the standard which was now held by Brandeis. In the meantime, the American Jewish Committee, peopled by Henry Morgenthau, Louis Marshall, Jacob Schiff, Julius Rosenwald and Felix Warburg proved that one could be of service to Jews without gathering under a nationalist banner. Early in 1915, the American collier *Vulcan* arrived at Jaffa with nine hundred tons of food for the people of Palestine. Zionists and the American Jewish Committee collaborated on the project but there was some unpleasantness when the American Jewish Committee refused to let the ship fly the flag of Zion beside the Stars and Stripes because it feared the charge of dual allegiance.

Dual allegiance. When the stigma first arose is uncertain, but in 1915 it thrived. For some of America's Jews, the fear was enhanced by the attempted formation of an exclusively Jewish army for the liberation of Palestine. The presumed leaders of such an enterprise would have been Europeans, Joseph Trumpeldor and Vladimir Jabotinsky, later the President of the New Zionist Revisionists. The suggestion of a Jewish fighting force organized as a unit of the English army to participate in the conquest of Palestine was eventually vetoed by British officials in Cairo. Instead, they offered to let the Jews form a body of muleteers to carry food and ammunition to the soldiers who manned the trenches in the ill-fated Gallipoli campaign. The overture was reluctantly accepted but the agitation for a Jewish army was resumed after the Gallipoli campaign was abandoned in March, 1916.[5]

Obviously, then, Jewish nationalism was no longer a shimmering phantom vanishing in the desert sun. Russian Jews were in need of asylum and Americans had joined the Zion Mule Corps. To what end? This question was asked by the American Jewish Committee which was shortly to divide into anti- and non-Zionists. The problem was considered by Jewish Socialists, Reform rabbis, Protestant ministers and several Arab-Americans. Liberal periodicals and Gentile intellectuals were also in the process of reevaluating their basic attitudes on nationalism. Herzl's platform had called for a "political solution" to the "Jewish Question" and the time of such a solution's feasibility was rapidly approaching.

It was not surprising that Brandeis was initially to underestimate his opposition; ironically, the P.E.C.G.Z.A. chairman was soon to become a critic himself, but his criticism was founded on economics rather than politics.[6] In this, however, his disapproval was unique. Politics was uppermost in the minds of other Zionist critics and remained so for twenty-four years. They were unconvinced that Jews should be the ultimate determiners of their fate. The essential issues of Zionism to all critics save Brandeis were nationalism, the incompatibility of the Jewish homeland concept with the course of Jewish history and the recrudescence of anti-Semitism. The anger American Reform Jews felt for Zionism was manifest in January, 1916, when Rabbi Samuel Schulman of New York City authored his first of a succession of anti-Zionist articles.[7] Apparently, Chaim Weizmann's work, to some roughly equivalent to Don Quixote's

---

[5] Rufus Learsi, *The Jews in America: A History* (New York, 1954), pp. 230, 246-250.

[6] Leonard Stein, *The Balfour Declaration* (New York, 1961), p.584.

[7] Samuel Schulman, "Why American Jews Consider Zionism Undesirable," *Outlook*, CXII (January 5, 1916), 40-42; "Outlook's Opinion" (editorial), *Outlook,* CXII (January 5, 1916), 42.

fighting of the windmills, suddenly assumed a concrete, if not vaguely malevolent, meaning.

The situation was further complicated by the European powers, principally England and France, and the United States, all of whom appeared determined to share in the development and utilization of oil and other natural resources of the Middle East. To this end, they acquired a foot-hold in the area by offering the native peoples several "freedom doctrines." For the Arabs, Britain dispensed the Husain-McMahon correspondence and offered up the Declaration of the Seven. Only when it was too late did the Arab leaders realize that a third document, the Sykes-Picot Agreement, contradicted both the aforementioned pacts. An equivalent promise was extended to the Jews, the Balfour Declaration.

It has recently been postulated that, as "a Zionist instrument, the Balfour Declaration is vastly overrated."[8] There is some truth in this assertion as the English pledge was not really a "Zionist instrument" but an instrument through which Zionists had to work, and there is a great deal of difference between the two. As it developed the Arabs and Zionists, though dependent on the Western powers in 1917, were, within thirty years, to turn their backs on Britain and risk the consequences of speaking out in favor of Palestinian self-determination. They were aided by their ethnic counterparts on the Continent and in the United States.

At first, though, Arabs and Jews failed to comprehend the implicit danger in trusting Europe and the United States. Due to the urgency of their situation, they may have had no choice but to trust; avowed American ideals may have made them feel justified in their trust. However, the passage of one decade and then another did not translate this trust into firm Congressional or presidential action on behalf of either ethnic group. The Zionist Organization of America and the Revisionists awakened to Britain's failings in the mid and late 1920s. The Arabs were even more tardy for, until 1936, the bulk of their case, as the following chapters will indicate, was founded on the King-Crane Report of 1919.

The King-Crane Commission, sent out by the Peace Conference in June 1919, warned against Zionist machinations in Palestine, and proposed an American trusteeship in Syria (including Palestine) or, failing that, a British one. It was crucial because it determined the scope and influence of the anti-Zionist political argument until

---

8 Samuel J. Goldsmith, "Creation of Israel As A State Traced To Zionist Congress 75 Years Ago," *The Jewish Week*, January 20, 1972, p.7.

World War II. At one time or another, every Zionist group made use of it. It gained rather than lost advocates during the interwar period and it is a model upon which the political critique is based. Its importance as an anti-Zionist instrument for certain Jewish and non-Jewish interest groups demands consideration, and it is to this commission, its formation and its findings, that I will first direct my attention.

II

The King-Crane Commission: The Articulation of Political Anti-Zionism

The idea of an "equitable" Near East settlement had long been on the mind of America's Chief Executive. The twelfth of Wilson's Fourteen Points favored popular sovereignty for resident subject nationalities within the Ottoman Empire with appropriate opportunities for their development. However, there were disturbing reports about certain portions of Turkey. American observers reported the duplicity of Great Britain as an occupying power in Palestine; it appeared that English officials were permitting Zionist propaganda to flourish but, at the same time, were employing repressive measures to muzzle the Arab populace. It was rumored that Britain encouraged the situation "in order to attain certain political and military aims." The Department of State received many communiques suggesting that "in the Southern zone of Palestine, violent hatred of the Jews and Zionists and general dissatisfaction with British administration" would lead to civil war.[1]

Meanwhile, there had been a British pledge to the Jews in the form of the Balfour Declaration. On November 2, 1917, His Majesty's Government, through Lord Balfour, had looked with favor upon the "establishment in Palestine of a national home for the Jewish people ...."[2] If there had been promises made to the Arabs,[3] there were

---

[1] Initialed memorandum to the State Department, William Yale Papers, Edward M. House Collection (hereafter abbreviated WYP, EMHC), No. 176, December 18, 1918, folder 122, Sterling Library of Yale University, New Haven.

certainly promises made to the Jews as well. In most instances, however, the promises to the two people were regarded as unequal. To one American negotiator, the Balfour Declaration represented a change in British policy "granting" to the "insistent Zionists" the Palestinian homeland.[4] But, in the opinion of President Wilson and the various state legislatures which endorsed it, the Declaration was an "open covenant fought for in the open."[5] Among knowledge-able Americans, then, there existed a difference of opinion on the Balfour Declaration. Each of the opposing views was to be represented at Versailles.

In January, 1919, the delegates of the Great Powers converged upon Paris. Among the first to begin work was an American, William Linn Westermann, who was to play a key role in the Near East peace settlement. He was a regional specialist for Western Asia and a professor of Ancient History at the University of Wisconsin. He had been attached to the Inquiry, an organization formed by Colonel House in the autumn of 1917 to collect information about the future peace.[6] In January, 1919, the Inquiry was absorbed by the

[2] For the full text of the Balfour Declaration, see for example, Frank P. Chambers, *This Age of Conflict* (New York, 1962), p. 833 or Israel Cohen, *A Short History of Zionism* (London, 1951), p. 74, also Harry Louis Selden, *5,000,000 Jews Without a Country — What is the Answer: A Digest of The Rape of Palestine by William Ziff* (New York, 1940), pp. 20-21.

[3] Pre-1917 British policy with regard to the Near East and Palestine is contained within two documents. The first was the Husain McMahon correspondence, a series of exchanges between Sharif Husain and Sir Henry McMahon, High Commissioner for Egypt, occurring between July 1915 and January, 1916. The second was the Sykes-Picot Agreement. The first agreement guaranteed Arab independence but left the fate of Palestine unclear. The second document agreed to a parceling out of Ottoman territories among the Allies, the establishment of an independent Arab state or confederation of states and for internal control of Palestine. See Howard Morley Sachar, *The Course of Modern Jewish History* (New York 1958), pp. 370-374; George Antonius, *The Arab Awakening* (new York, 1965), pp. 163-185, 248-254, 413-430.

[4] Esco Foundation for Palestine, *Palestine: A Study of Jewish, Arab and British Policies*, 2 vols. (New Haven, 1947), I, 251.

[5] *Ibid.*

[6] The members of the Inquiry were Sidney Mezes of City College of New York, Director, Walter Lippmann, Secretary, David Hunter Miller, attorney and Trea-surer, Dr. Isaiah Bowman, then of the American Geographic Society, Chief Territorial Specialist, James T. Shotwell of Columbia University, Librarian and Specialist in History and William Westermann. *Ibid.*, p. 244.

American Commission to Negotiate the Peace.

Westermann, however, was no longer associated with the Inquiry. A few days after his arrival in France, he assumed control of the West Asia Division of the American Commission to Negotiate the Peace.[7] His mood toward the Balfour Declaration was pessimistic. Writing to William Bullitt, Chief of the Intelligence Reports Section of the American Commission, Westermann conveyed his grave misgivings. He thought that the Near Eastern situation, as it was presently unfolding, denied Wilson's views on self-determination. Jewish national ambitions, he felt, were misguided. The Zionists were looking forward to the establishment of a Jewish *state* and, therefore, he was troubled by the plight of the Arabs. He believed that if Palestine became a Jewish State the Balfour Declaration's promise of protecting Arab rights should be guaranteed. Finally, he averred that the Sykes-Picot Agreement ought to be scrapped in favor of the Commission proposal suggested by the American missionary and President of the Syrian Protestant College at Beirut, Howard Bliss. This plan called for the sending of an inter-Allied commission to Syria to determine the actual desires of the people. In Westermann's estimation, the Bliss idea embodied the Wilson principle of self-determination.[8]

At its inception, Westermann admired the "undoubted idealism" of the Zionist movement but at the Peace Conference came to regret its descent into the realm of international politics.[9] Before formal negotiations began, he met and took an immediate personal dislike to Chaim Weizmann.[10] The following week, he dined with Colonel T.E. Lawrence and Emir Faisal. He was so impressed with both men that he proclaimed his immediate conversion to the Arab cause.[11]

[7] Frank E. Manuel, *The Realities of American-Palestine Relations,* (Washington, 1949).

[8] *Ibid.*, pp. 222-223.

[9] Westermann to Marvin M. Lowenthal, April 12, 1944, Westermann Mss., Box 2, Butler Library, Columbia University. Hereafter, the William L. Westermann Manuscript Collection will be abbreviated as WLW.

[10] The meeting with Weizmann took place on January 12, 1919. Unpublished *Personal Diary of William Linn Westermann* kept aboard the S.S. George Washington from December 4, 1918 to circa July 4, 1919 (hereafter abbreviated *PDWLW*), p. 18, Butler Library, Columbia University.

[11] *Ibid.*, January 20, 1919, pp. 19, 25.

Early in February, Westermann met William Yale, a man who probably knew more about the condition of the Near East than any other American at Paris. [12] Yale had recently been released from his duties as United States observer in Cairo, where he was attached to the British Expeditionary Force. In an atmosphere saturated with idealistic talk concerning America's postwar role as a Near East guardian, Yale managed to remain immune. At Versailles and again in Syria, Yale spoke against a proposed American mandate or political involvement in the Near East. After sixteen months in Egypt and Palestine, he had become anti-British and pro-French and was optimistic as to the ultimate reconciliation and eventual co-operation between antagonistic Arab and Jewish nationalisms. [13] Later, Yale was to disagree with King and Crane on these very points.

Discussions began in earnest only when the President and his immediate staff were settled. [14] The experts surrounding Wilson knew and cared little about Near Eastern affairs. Secretary of State Robert Lansing was convinced that America should remain aloof from European intrigue in the Near East. He feared lest the Allies attempt to ensnare the United States into assuming a protectorate in either Armenia or Palestine. [15] Henry White, the designated but uninfluential Republican on the Commission was opposed to Jewish autonomy in Palestine. General Tasker Bliss had little interest in

[12] *Ibid.*, February 12, 1919, p. 35. In ensuing years, Yale was a history professor at Boston University and at the outbreak of World War II held the same position at the University of New Hampshire.

[13] Although Yale proved to be much more equitable in his judgment of the Zionists than King or Crane, it must be emphasized that he was consistently pro-Arab and, if not openly opposed, he was always suspicious of Zionism and its leaders. Westermann to Harry N. Howard, September 6, 1940, Westermann Mss., Box 1; PDWLW , February 12, 1919, p. 35; William Yale to State Department, *Zionism and the Arab Movement*, Report No. 19, March 18, 1918 and Yale to State Department *Arrival of the Zionist Commission,* Report No. 20, March 25, 1918. William Yale Papers, Library of Congress, Peace Conference 1918-1919. Acquisition 2206 (hereafter abbreviated WYPLC); E.H. Byrne *Report on the Desires of the Syrians,* October 7, 1918, WYP, EMHC, folder 74, p. 90, Sterling Library of Yale University, New Haven.

[14] Formal deliberations were not held until January 12, 1919; the first plenary session convened on January 18. Actually, Wilson arrived at Brest in December, 1918 but spent about three weeks touring France, England and Italy before commencing work at Paris. Thomas A. Bailey, *Woodrow Wilson and the Lost Peace* (Chicago, 1963), pp. 110-114.

Zionism, although the few allusions he made were hostile.[16] The last of Wilson's team, Colonel Edward M. House, conducted an interview with Faisal two days before the Arab leader's scheduled appearance before the Council of Ten. House, who had wide experience with American Zionists, noted in his diary that he felt kindly disposed toward the Arabs and "my influence will be thrown in their direction whenever they are right."[17]

On February 6, Emir Faisal, officially heading the Hejaz delegation and claiming to be spokesman for the entire Arab people, appeared before the Conference. He demanded hegemony over Asia Minor, excluding Palestine. Lansing was entranced with his dignified appearance and forceful presentation. He was "swept off his feet" by Faisal's bold affirmation "that one hundred thousand men had joined his revolt"'during the war. William Yale, though, "had estimated this glorious insurgent army at 2,000."[18] Exactly three weeks later, the Zionists advanced their case before the Council. The fact that there were no American Jews on the Zionist commission may have reenforced the idea in the minds of the American negotiatiors that the movement was essentially foreign. In any event, Lansing was exposed to two opposing philosophies: the political Zionism of Weizmann and the non-nation vision of the culturalist, Sylvain Levi. The Secretary of State was aware of Jewish division on the Zionist issue in America and sought to stay clear of what he believed to be purely Jewish concerns. He felt that the testimony he had heard at Paris vindicated his old position.[19]

Not until March did the Great Powers decided to send a commis-

[15] Laurence Evans, *United States Policy and the Partition of Turkey 1914-1924* (Baltimore, 1965), p. 64; Manuel, pp. 4, 217. During the Paris Peace, the Standard Oil Company kept Lansing apprised of its interests in Palestine. Apparently they effectively communicated their misgivings to the State Secretary. Nadav Safran, *The Unites States and Israel* (Cambridge, Mass., 1963), p. 37.

[16] Manuel, p. 216

[17] Evans, p. 122.

[18] Manuel, pp. 202, 227; Evans, p. 125.

[19] Paris Peace Conference, 180.03101/48, Minutes of Meetings, Council of Ten, February 15-June 17, 1919, United States, Department of State, Papers Relating to *the Foreign Relations of the United States* (hereafter abbreviated as *USFR*); *The Paris Peace Conference 1919* (hereafter abbreviated PPC) IV, 159, 161n., 1699-170.

sion to Syria. An investigation was not seriously considered until both sides had spoken. Besides, the thought of self-determination in an area whose fate had been secretly decided upon during the war was unacceptable to France and Great Britain. Neither of these nations had ever discussed the project with much enthusiasm.

Pressure groups, including anti- and non-Zionists, missionaries and Arab-Americans played a significant role in converting the American negotiators to favor the dispatching of a commission. These lobbies, their activities at Versailles and their subsequent endeavors, will be separately discussed. Suffice it to say that they considered the Arab case more justified than the Jewish and they mounted a resistance in 1919 which, although not united, was as powerful, as well informed, and as aggressive as was Zionism in the pursuit of its objectives.

During February and March the peacemakers of the United States, including President Wilson, decided to take unilateral action. Wilson was close to the Zionist movement in America; he knew its leaders as well as its detractors. If he held Zionism in high esteem, a point about which there is little disagreement among historians, why did he authorize the selection of a group of men to question the Arab peoples concerning their desires? No scholar has shed any light on the subject. It appears that two hard to reconcile ideas existed simultaneously in the President's mind: one dealing with Jewish redemption in Palestine and the other with self-determination of the Arab peoples. Perhaps in order to satisfy both requests and to justify his own sense of morality, he sent the Commission to ascertain the wishes of the native peoples, and by employing a great deal of self-deception, persuaded himself that their aspirations would coincide with his own unique vision.[20]

By mid-March, Wilson was accepting suggestions for commissioners. Ray Stannard Baker suggested William Westermann but he declined.[21] On March 20, no commissioners had yet been designated, although Wilson had publicly acknowledged his sponsorship of an Allied, or mixed, commission.[22] The search for two qualified Americans, conducted only in Paris, was to bear fruit

---

[20] A good summary and analysis of Wilson's attitude toward Zionism is contained in Selig Adler, "The Palestine Question in the Wilson Era," *Jewish Social Studies*, X, (October 1948) 303-334. Other parts of this study will offer a more systematic consideration of Wilson and Zionism.

[21] Harry N. Howard, *The American Inquiry into the Middle East: King-Crane Commission* (Beirut, 1963), p. 36.

within a week.

The President had stated the requisite credentials for commission leadership. He wanted two men with liberal backgrounds and no previous contact with the Near East. He also desired that the choice be made from candidates who were then in Europe; hence, the preoccupation with haste narrowed the field considerably. As to the identities of the men, he had not a clue.[23]   On March 23, Westermann approved the suggestion of British Intelligence official Gertrude Bell, who said that a thorough survey of the area by an inter-Allied commission would "take at least six months: that the men chosen must be of high political standing, whose positions will carry great weight." Westermann proposed that Henry Cabot Lodge be one of those men.[24]

On March 27, the final selection was announced. Senator Lodge was not one of those chosen. The President's choices were revealed by Henry White before a meeting of the American peace commissioners.[25] Wilson thought that Henry Churchill King and Charles R. Crane were particularly qualified because "they knew nothing about" Syria; also, they were "absolutely disinterested." Crane, in particular, was "a very experienced and cosmopolitan man."[26]

Wilson's misjudgment of these two men, their backgrounds,

[22] Esco Foundation, I, 214; Suleiman Mousa, *T.E. Lawrence: An Arab View*, trans. Albert Butros (London, 1966), p. 225.

[23] Esco Foundation, I, 215. It appears that the importance of "ready availability" among candidates was of greater moment than their abilities.

[24] *PDWLW*, March 23, 1919, pp. 46-47; Mousa, p. 8.

[25] Parris Peace Conference, 184.00101/39, Minutes of Daily Meetings, Commissioners Plenipotentiary, march 27, 1919, *USFR: PPC*, XI, 133; Howard, p. 451.

[26] Paris Peace Conference, 184.00101/39, Minutes of Daily Meetings, Commissioners Plenipotentiary, March 27, 1919, *USFR: PPC*, XI, 133; Paris Peace Conference, 180.03041/22 1/2, Minutes of Daily Meetings, Council of Four, May 22, 1919, *USFR:PPC*, V, 812. Woodrow Wilson later mentioned to Lloyd George that the Commission was unequivocally disinterested. Manuel, p. 245. M'Uarrokh al-Thawret al-Arabiyyeh, historian of the Arab revolt, offers an interesting commenatary on the part played by Mrs. Wilson in the President's final decision to send a commission to the Near East: "Mrs. Wilson was in Paris when Emir Faisal arrived for the first time. She met him there and admired him ... and later wrote him several letters. She used to say that his face reflected the picture of Christ ... I believe that she was instrumental in bringing about the decision to send out the King-Crane Commission to Syria." Mousa, p. 226n.

abilities and incentives, was nearly total. One explanation for this inexcusable lapse in judgment appears to refut e previous scholarship which generally affirms that Wilson selected the commissioners for the reasons he gave.[27] Another hypothesis, which has yet to be explored, is that, in fact, Wilson chose neither King nor Crane nor anyone else on the nine-man Commission. That they were actually selected by other highly interested individuals or groups and their appointment was merely seconded by the President is not only plausible but provable. Finally, these two men were not, nor had the ever been disinterested. Both had easily discernible prejudices and it is, assuredly, because of these prejudices that they were chosen.

Henry Churchill King had three important sponsors, Ray Stannard Baker, Colonel House and the State Department. In 1919, King was Director of Religious Work for the division of the Y.M.C.A. serving the needs of the American Expeditionary Force, with headquarters in Paris. The year before, while in Rome, he met Ray Stannard Baker "who later recommended him to President Wilson for the Commission on Mandates in Turkey. Wilson's acquaintance with King seems to have been slight.[28] It is also evident that Colonel House exercised some influence on King's behalf. House favored the sending of the Commission and chafed at Wilson's lack of action. He

[27] The King-Crane Report was suppressed for three years before it was finally made public in 1922, with the aid of Ray Stannard Baker. The Report became a symbol of bankrupt american idealism and received a favorable, alomst sensational, coverage by the American press. Historiographically speaking, until the present time, there has never been anything unfavorable written about it that was well documented. For an in-depth survey of the King-Crane Report and the commentary on it from 19191-1972, the following ought to be consulted: Ray Stannard Baker, *Woodrow Wilson and the World Settlement*, 2 vols. (New York, 1923), II, 213-216; Henry C. King and Charles R. Crane, *Recommendations of the King-Crane Commission with Regard to Syria, Palestine and Iraq*, in George Antonius *The Arab Awakening*, pp. 443-458. The entire Report is printed in *USFR: The Paris Peace Conference, 1919*, 13 vols. (Washington, 1947), XII, 745-863. See all of the following: Harry N. Howard, *The American Inquiry into the Middle East: The King-Crane Commission;* Harry N. Howard, "An Experiment in Peacemaking: The King-Crane Commission," *Moslem World*, XXXII (April 1942), 122-146; Antonius, p. 288-300; Manuel, pp. 236-255; Adler, *Jewish Social Studies*, X, 323-328; Evans, pp. 135-149; Mousa, pp. 225-234; Richard P. Stevens, "Colonization By Proxy: Two Franchising Ventures of the Home Office," *The Arab World*, XVIII (March-April 1972) 18-25. For some interesting contemporary comment, see *Editor and Publisher*, December 9 and 22, 1922; "Harmony For A Jewish Homeland in Palestine," (editorial) *The Denver Jewish News*, VIII (October 25, 1922), 4; and two editorials entitled "The Crane-King Report," one from *The New York Times*, August 20, 1922, p. 4 and the other from *The American Hebrew*, III (August 25, 1922), 341, 360.

believed Felix Frankfurter's fears about the Commission stripping the Jews of Palestine to be utter nonsense.[29] On March 23, the same day he saw Frankfurter, he interviewed King and apparently had the final say.[30] The State Department "wired Oberlin, transmitting a cable from Colonel House which asked whether the College would release its President for a service which ... would be ... uncertain duration." The College gave President King leave to act as he desired and he accepted the nomination.[31]

Henry Churchill King's qualifications for his assignment should now be critically examined with the following thoughts in mind: first of all, did he fulfill Wilson's specifications and secondly, was he sensitive or responsive enough to Middle Eastern problems to shape the destiny of the Jewish and Arab peoples, given the sum of his experiences in 1919?

Prior to his selection, King had been to the Near East.[32] Obviously, then, Wilson's assertion that the men chosen should be novices was sidestepped. Furthermore, President King was unfamiliar with the Jewish National idea and maintained friendships with the missionary Protestants who opposed it.[33]

The fact that King was well-disposed to the missionary element at Versailles is understandable. The year that he was a freshman at

[28] Donald M. Love, *Henry Churchill King of Oberlin* (New Haven, 1956); Henry Churchill King (1858-1934) — Congregationalist; liberal theologian; President of Oberlin College, 1902-1927. Oberlin had had at least two anti-Zionists on its staff, Kemper Fullerton, professor of Semitics and a traveler in Palestine in 1917, and Albert Lybyer, whose career to 1919 is described later in this chapter. The College had also a well-known missionary alumnus, James Barton, about whom more will be said in Chapter VII. For Fullerton's insights, see Kemper Fullerton, "Zionism," *The American Hebres,* 104, (May 2, 9, 1919), 657, 667-669, 692-693, 698-699; "Professor Fullerton on Zionism" (editorial), *The American Hebrew,* 104 (May 2, 1919), 654-655.

[29] Ezekiel Rabinowitz, *Justice Louis D. Brandeis: The Zionist Chapter of His Life* (New York, 1968), p. 97; Howard, p. 37.

[30] Rabinowitz, p. 97.

[31] Love, p. 215.

[32] Howard. p. 39.

[33] Morton Tenzer, "The Jews," *The Immigrants' Influence on Wilson's Peace Policies,* ed. Joseph P. O'Grady (n.p., 1967), p. 313; *USFR:PPC,* XXI, 749-750, 785, 792, 859.

Oberlin, 1877, the College still occupied a distinctive position for its commitment to missionary work. In February, 1884, Oberlin's President wrote that the institution "represents not so much a kind of theology as a kind of aggressive Christianity."[34] President King's "early religious life was of the intense, evangelical type" and he maintained his deep faith until he died. At the turn of the century, Professor King was a major religious thinker and liberal theologian whose ideas were in harmony with post Darwinian progressivism. He advocated not an unknowable God but a man-centered religion which emphasized a personal faith rather than sterile ceremony. King's biographer, Donald M. Love, further stresses the similarity in ethical thought of King and the first Oberlin President, Charles Grandison Finney.[35]

King's concern with missionary activities never abated. In the early 1880s, he was interested in being a missionary in China but then reconsidered and continued his studies at Oberlin.[36] In 1906 and 1907, he continued his membership on the American Board of Commissioners for Foreign Missions. In 1909-1910, he took a leave of absence and, under the auspices of the American Board spent four months observing missionary work in the Orient, including China, Burma, Ceylon and Japan. In 1912 and 1913, President King made twenty-three miscellaneous addresses, "educational and missionary..." In 1920, after his work in Palestine ended, he served as President of the American Missionary Association.[37]

When it began, neither President King nor Oberlin College was interested in World War I. King probably regarding the hostilities as a strictly European affair, did not encourage a better understanding of the issue on the part of his students. During the War, King evolved toward a position of internationalism "through the universal application of moral principles" and by 1917 had become an interventionist, but on purely moral grounds, that is, German culpability.[38]

[34] Love, pp. 3-4, 20.

[35] *Ibid.*, pp. 169-170, 187-189.

[36] King was partial to the writings of Paul and to the Gospels in general. *Ibid.* pp. 27-28.

[37] *Ibid.*, pp. 165-166, 228.

[38] *Ibid.*, pp. 191, 194-196, 203-206.

Testimony in the *Congressional Record* suggests that the second Wilson appointee, Charles R. Crane, was a political choice of the Democratic Party.[39] In the eyes of the Democrats, Crane's past services merited his appointment. He was a progressive, an associate of Wilson's rather than a personal friend, and Vice Chairman of the Finance Committee of Wilson's 1912 campaign.[40] In 1909, Crane was appointed minister to China "although the appointment was cancelled by Secretary of State Knox because of an 'indiscreet speech' in which Mr. Crane had predicted war with Japan on the eve of his departure for China."[41] In 1920, he was once again nominated and this time served as minister to China.

Early in the 1890s, Crane had visited some of the Russian-held portions of the Ottoman Empire.[42] Before World War I, he had journeyed extensively throughout Turkey and had many Near Eastern interests. He was on the Board of Trustees of the Constantinople College for Women and treasurer of the Armenian and Syrian Relief Committee which was organized in the United States in November, 1915.[43] Far more significant than his charitable works as a determinative factor of his state of mind was his lifelong devotion to Arab lore and the Arab people. Crane was of the Unitarian faith and in an undated correspondence to a friend, Mrs. Augusta Belmont, had admiringly called the Arabs "Unitarians of the desert."[44]

For days following Wilson's announcement of his choices, the fate of the Commission was in jeopardy. It became increasingly apparent that France would not participate. Britain had already chosen its commissioners but demurred at the last moment because

[39] U.S. Congress, House, *Establishment of a National Home in Palestine, House of Representatives, Committee on Foreign Affairs, Sixty-Seventh Congress, Second Session, on H. Con. Res. 52 Expressing Satisfaction at the Recreation of Palestine as the National Home of the Jewish Race*, April 18, 19, 20, 21, 22, 1922 (Washington, 1922), p. 69.

[40] James L. Barton, *The Story of Near Eastern Relief 1915-1930* (New York, 1930), pp. 6, 381; Joan Eisner, "American Policy Toward Palestine 1916-1948" (Unpublished M.A. essay, New York University, 1955), p. 9; Manuel, p. 236. When Wilson revealed his appointees to Lloyd George, he mispronounced Crane's name, calling him "Craig" instead. *USFR:PPC*, V, 812. Crane (1858-1939) was a millionaire valve manufacturer from Chicago.

[41] Howard, *American Inquiry*, p. 39.

[42] Westermann to his wife, April 27, 1919, *PDWLW*, p. 68.

[43] Barton, pp. 6, 381.

of Clemenceau's refusal to participate. The Inter-Allied Commission on Turkish Mandates thus became a purely American enterprise.[45] William Westermann, who had initially favored the sending of an international commission was now frankly opposed, probably because he disliked the possibility of identifying unilateral American participation with the European imperialist game.[46] Another possibility is that his position toward Zionists, if not Zionism, had softened. He had always admired the romanticism of Aaron Aaronsohn and, while at Paris, was interested in the thoughts of the Italian Zionist, Bianchini, and those of the Americans, Felix Frankfurter and Julian Mack.[47]

Immediately upon the selection of King and Crane, no adverse response was forthcoming from the Zionists. Frankfurter had even

[44] Charles R. Crane to Eleanor Robson Belmont, August 30 (n.y.) Belmont Collection, Special Mss., Butler Library, Columbia University. Crane never cared for Jews and documentary evidence in the Nicholas Murray Butler Papers, Butler Library, Columbia University, may be presented to substantiate the allegation that, by 1933, Crane was rabidly anti-Semitic and pro-Arab. His mild dislike for certain Jews changed in 1917, when he served as a member of Wilson's special commission to Russia. At the height of the Bolshevik Revolution he was there, probably observing those Jews who led the insurgency. Apparently, Bolshevism and Judaism were henceforth linked in his mind. After visiting the Hejaz, Yemen and Syria in the 1920s as an Arab philanthropist and informal economic adviser, he became convinced that the Arabs, with no "external interference" by Western powers, would finally and absolutely solve their Jewish problem. In the 1930s he was pro-Hitler and felt the Jews were running the world with their atheistic Communism. See all of the following: Crane to Mrs. Augusta Belmont, February 20, June 24 and July 21 (n.y.); Crane to Mrs. Belmont, September 21, 1925, May 11, a927 and January 30, 1929, Belmont Collection; Crane to Nicholas Murray Butler, March 19, 1928, June 6, 1933 and May 21, 1938, Nicholas Murray Butler Papers; Memorandum by William Westermann, December 5, 1938, WLW, Box 2; William Yale, *The Near East* (Ann Arbor, 1968), pp. 337, 362; Sydney N. Fisher, *The Middle East: A History* (New York, 1960), pp. 532-544; "Crane Forcasts Settlement of Jewish-Arab Conflict," *Christian Science Monitor*, August 26, 1929, p. 2; Elie Kedourie, *The Chatham House Version and Other Middle Eastern Studies* (New York, 1970), p. 337.

45 The official name of the King-Crane Commission was the American Section of

45 The official name of the King-Crane Commission was the American Section of the Inter-Allied Commission on Turkish Mandates.

[46] Westermann to Harry N. Howard, September 6, 1940, *WLW*, Box 1; Westermann to Robert J. Kerner, November 13, 1941, *WLW*, Box 2.

[47] *PDWLW*, May 7, 1919 and May 17, 1919, pp. 71, 76-78.

wired Louis Brandeis to congratulate Crane officially, "assuming of course...that he will...consult with the United States in detail as to the Zionist bearings of the problem."[48]   There is no record of Crane's consulting with any Zionists or obtaining any Zionist opinion. On April 4, Westermann noted that Crane "does not seem to be interested and is said to be loath to go because he is interested in the Bulgarian matters."[49] To offset Crane, Westermann submitted two names of his own choosing and both were approved for Commission membership.[50]

The first of these was George Montgomery, a Ph.D. from Yale and a Protestant missionary who had resided in the Near East for a number of years.[51] The second man was William Yale, whose views Westermann shared and whose experience with the Allied Forces had very recently taken him to Egypt and Palestine for a long tour of duty. From 1915 to 1917, Yale was the representative of Standard Oil Company in Palestine. On August 17, 1917, he was appointed special agent of the State Department and ordered to Egypt.[52] There, he was attached to Allenby's forces as an American observer and intelligence reporter in Cairo. From then until January, 1919, when he arrived in Paris, Yale remained in the Middle East and spent six months in Palestine.

Yale's understanding of Near Eastern politics was shrewd and his insights into Jewish and Arab nationalism penetrating. His most interesting belief was that Jews and Arabs were capable of cooperation in Palestine.[52] In his opinion, this goal was realizable if the Jews mollified Arab fears concerning the Balfour Declaration.[53] After

---

[48] Frankfurter to Brandeis and Brandeis to Crane, March 29, 1919, Brandeis Papers, Zionist Archives, New York City (hereafter abbreviated *LDB*).

[49] *PDWLW*, April 4, 1919, pp. 54-55.

[50] Westermann to Harry N. Howard, September 6, 1940, Westermann Mss., Box 1; *PDWLW*, April 23, 1919, p. 67; Howard, *American Inquiry*, p. 40.

[51] Howard M. Sachar, *The Emergence of the Middle East 1914-1924*, (New York, 1969), p. 266.

[52] Yale to State Department, *The Zionist Commission and the Syrians in Egypt*, Report No. 22, April 8, 1918 and Yale to State Department, *Arrival of the Zionist Commission*, Report No 20, March 25, 1918, *WYPLC*.

[53] Yale to State Department, *Zionism and Palestine*, Report No. 24, April 22, 1918, *Ibid*.

conversing with Chaim Weizmann, he became convinced of the Zionist leader's sincerity;[54] he was equally sympathetic to the Arab view as presented by T.E. Lawrence, whom he had also met.[55] Yale felt certain that neither the Jewish religion[56] nor the imported radicalism of young Zionists from Russia was important to the Jewish future in Palestine.[57] Both would have to be curbed if the trust of the Arabs was to be gained. He was heavily influenced by the Cairo Syrians who favored a French mandate and was opposed to the British because of their intransigent response to Arab supplications after the promulgation of the Balfour Declaration.[58] Yale's dispatches usually reflected his concern for the native populations and his suspicion of the Zionists and the Allies.[59]

Upon his arrival at Paris, Yale was opposed to a Zionist state but not to immigration. He became angered with what he interpreted to be a Zionist attempt to include Transjordania, a purely Arab inhabited territory, within the boundaries of Palestine. This, in addition to the Brandeisian features of public ownership of utilities and public works which, to him, smacked of Russian Socialism, resulted in the destructive attitude he adopted toward a proposed mandate scheme drawn up by Felix Frankfurter at the Peace Conference.[60]

King and Crane secured the approval of some individuals they had suggested.[61] King personally selected Professor Albert Howe Lybyer and for secretary-treasurer chose Captain Donald M. Brodie. President King had labeled Lybyer an "expert" in Balkan affairs.[62] Dr. Lybyer was, in 1919, a history professor at the University of Illinois. Woodrow Wilson may have known of him because he was a graduate of Princeton Theological Seminary. There is reason to believe that he was not a random choice of King because Lybyer's

---

[54] Yale to State Department, Reports Nos. 20 and 22, *Ibid.*

[55] Byrne, pp. 75, 84, 89, *WYP, EMHC*. Yale's exact words were that "Major Lawrence knew his onions." See also O.J. Campbell, *A Report on Zionism,* Addendum, p. 10, marginal note, folder 143, *WYP, EMHC*.

[56] Yale to State Department, Report No. 24, WYPLC.

[57] Byrne, p. 84, *WYP, EMHC.*

[58] *Ibid.,* pp. 75, 89-90.

[59] Yale to State Department, *Zionism and the Arab Movement,* Report No. 19, March 18, 1918, *WYPLC.*

teaching career included an assignment at Oberlin. Lybyer had also been an instructor at an important missionary institution at Constantinople, Robert College. Before his appointment to the King-Crane Commission, he served in Westermann's West Asia Division. Upon his selection, Westermann questioned the wisdom of Dr. King's choice of experts. Lybyer, he said, "did not know much about Syria."[63]

Unlike Crane, whose boredom Westermann had noted, King displayed an ardent interest in his assignment. He worked hard to increase his understanding of the Near East and was a daily visitor at Westermann's office to receive additional material.[64] Accumulation of data, however, is a poor substitute for experience. Prior to 1919, there is little evidence that President King had any contact with Jews, although he had known American missionaries to the Arabs.   At Paris, he was influenced by the highly persuasive but biased arguments of anti-Zionist Henry Morgenthau.[65] Eventually, King began

---

[60] The Frankfurter mandate proposal, as conceived, was impressive because it had been "handled, perfected and amended by so many people." Yale red-penciled it until it was unrecognizable: (1) the words "historic title of the Jewish people" were questioned, (2) in a provision which read " 'it is the wish of the inhabitants of Palestine and the Jews that the government be conferred upon Great Britain as mandatory,' " the words " 'of the inhabitants of Palestine' " were deleted, (3) section II of the Frankfurter proposal began with the words, " 'The establishment of Palestine as the Jewish National Home...' " Yale and his unnamed assistant rephrased it so it would read precisely according to the Balfour Declaration phraseology, "a national home" for the Jews in Palestine (4) section IIa, committing the mandatory power to promoting immigration was cut out, presumably because of Yale's belief that Jewish immigration into Palestine should be the sole concern of the Jews (5) section IIe and f, relating to public ownership of utilities, public works, land and natural resources, all part of the Brandeis program adopted at Pittsburgh in 1918, was marked " 'socialization of land on the lines of Zionist social views' " (6) Yale wanted an entire subsection omitted which dealth with cooperation of a Jewish agency with the mandatory (7) He underlined the section involving the introduction of Hebrew into Palestine as an official language (8) he questioned the desirability of permitting Jews free access to certain Moslem Holy Places containing venerated, historic Jewish relics and remains. Manuel, pp. 232-233; Howard, *American Inquiry*, p. 101.

[61] Paris Peace Conference, 184.00101/58, Minutes of Daily Meetings, Commissioners Plenipotentiary, April 26, 1919 *USFR: PPC*, XI, 165.

[62] *PDWLW*, April 15, 1919, p. 60; Love, p. 283.

[63] *PDWLW*, April 15, 1919, p. 60; Adler, *Jewish Social Studies,* X, 325.

[64] *PDWLW*, April 4, 1919, pp. 54-55.

to think that Morgenthau was what he had erroneously presented himself to be: spokesman for the overwhelming majority of America's Jews.

By April 23, it was certain that no one was going to Syria except the Americans. The King-Crane Commission might have left immediately if they had not been told to wait. "King said that the British stated openly that Faisal must have two weeks to prepare the ground in Syria."[66] If Westermann's quotation of President King is an accurate one, the meaning of Faisal's hasty departure from Paris is obviated: it (Faisal's departure) was planned by the anti-Zionist English officers in Palestine and American missionaries at Versailles as soon as they were positive that the Commission would depart. It was expected that the Arab leader would activate Syrian nationalism for the benefit of the Americans.

The fact that the other Allies were not going to participate in the survey of Palestine made the American negotiators uneasy. The fear that the United States was going to be entrapped in the maze of European politics was pervasive. Tasker Bliss and Henry White felt it was inadvisable to send a solely American body to Syria because it might create the idea of a special United States interest in that area.[67] The Zionists, now better informed on the personalities and interests of King and Crane, sought personal reassurances from Wilson. Felix Frankfurter volunteered to go to Palestine to ease the apprehensions of the Jewish population. The President believed that Frankfurter's misgivings were unfounded, but, nevertheless, reaffirmed his support for the creation of a Jewish National Home.[68] It was also at this time that Wilson conveyed assurances to Emir Faisal that the Commission would definitely be sent.[69] The confusion was heightened by the assertion of William Westermann to Howard Bliss that he thought the King-Crane Commission without British and French representation could only cause harm.[70]

[65] On April 25, King had "rather long talks with Mr. Morgenthau...." Quoted from *King Diary*, kept while President was abroad in war service in 1918 and 1919, by Love, pp. 285-286.

[66] *PDWLW*, April 23, 1919, p. 67.

[67] Howard, *American Inquiry*, p. 49.

[68] Tenzer, *The Immigrants' Influence on Wilson's Peace Policies*, p.314; Howard, *American Inquiry*, pp. 73-74.

[69] Mousa, p. 226.

The drifting which preceded the Commission's departure was dramatically halted by Colonel House. On May 20, he advised the President that the Commission would depart the following week and the next day, Wilson announced in the Council of Four that his men were leaving for Syria.[71] Preparatory to his quitting Paris, Henry Churchill King met with the Syrian Commission. It "instructed" King to fight against a Zionist State.[72] It seems that President King made no parallel attempt to ascertain the wishes of the Zionists. At the time of its departure, the King-Crane Commission was staffed by a total of nine people. Aside from the leaders there were Dr. Albert Lybyer, technical adviser, Dr. George Montgomery, expert on the northern regions of the Ottoman Empire, William Yale, expert on the Southern regions, Captain Donald M. Brodie, U.S. Army, secretary and treasurer, Dr. Sami Haddad, instructor at the School of Medicine, Syrian Protestant College, physician and interpreter, Mr. Laurence S. Moore, business manager and Major Paul Toren, stenographer.[73] The character of the Commission was thus established: three seminarians, an Arab and a possible political appointee began a six week journey which, by a conservative estimate made to Westermann in March, should have taken six months. William Yale was the lone dissenter from the prevailing mood of the King-Crane Commission. Jews and Zionists were unrepresented.

[70] Esco Foundation, I, 215; Zeine N. Zeine, *The Struggle for Arab Independence,* (Beirut, 1960), p. 219n. 4; Howard, *American Inquiry,* p. 48.

[71] Evans, p.146.

[72] The exact citation is as follows: "Kg. (King) and advisers" met "with the Syrian Commission, less Rihbany (an American Arab) who went home. They do not want

[72] The exact citation is as follows: "Kg. (King) and advisers" met "with the Syrian Commission, less Rihbany (an American Arab) who went home. They do not want a Zionistic State — no instructions beyond." It seems that the Commission had been "instructed" to fight against a Zionist State; there is no other apparent interpretation for Lybyer's strange but meaningful phrasing. It opens the possibility that by the time of their departure, the commissioners were nothing more than a rubber stamp for Arab opinion and that their findings were predetermined days before they left. *Albert Lybyer Diary* (unpublished, hereafter abbreviated as *ALD*), May 28, 1919, University Library, University of Illinois, Urbana-Champaign.

[73] Manuel, p. 245; Howard, *American Inquiry*, p. 40; Esco Foundation, I, 215; *USDSPRFRUS: PPC, XXI, 752.*

On June 10, 1919, the King-Crane Commission landed at Jaffa.[74] Crane's enthusiasm for Islam provided some of the shipboard diversion, especially for Albert Lybyer, who was apparently not as well versed on the subject.[75] The evening they arrived, the group dined with the American Consul in Jerusalem, Reverend Otis Glazebrook, and a Red Cross official, Captain Logan. Glazebrook, a Protestant minister who had been won over to Wilsonian progressivism in 1910, outlined his own plan for the Turkish domain during the course of the meal.[76] He favored unity of the Ottoman Empire under a United States mandate and decried the plans and capabilities of the Zionists.[77] Later, a discussion of American missionary influence will reveal that Dr. James L. Barton had advocated Glazebrook's plan in 1918. The project envisioned not national sovereignty for any people but the transformation of the late Turkish Empire into a vast theater for American missionary enterprise; it was never undertaken or seriously considered by any of the chief negotiators at Versailles.

What direct effect Glazebrook had on the findings of the Commission cannot be precisely determined. Some circumstantial evidence, (including references in Chapters II and III to King's discussions with Henry Morgenthau and the Syrian Commission at Paris), however, can be brought to bear in support of the contention that the Consul had confirmed what had been believed by King and Crane before they ever sailed. After it was shown that they would meet no resistance, the two leading commissioners dropped the veneer of impartial inquiry and conducted an opinion poll which reflected the attitudes of neither Arabs nor Jews but of the Christian population resident in Palestine.

After a single day in the Holy Land, King and Crane dispatched a telegram to Paris which said that it would be impossible to carry out the Zionist program without the presence of a large army.[78] It was

---

[74] *Evans, p. 153; Howard, American Inquiry,* pp. 88-89.

[75] *ALD*, June 6, 1919. Crane's fascination for Islam is further elucidated in the next decade. For example, see Crane to Mrs. Belmont, August 9, 1926, Belmont [76] Otis A. Glazebrook was born in Richmond, Virginia in 1845 and participated in missionary work in Virginia before he finally settled in Elizabeth, New Jersey as a church pastor. "It was while tending his flock in the latter city that he made ... an impassioned prayer at the convention which nominated the President of Princeton as the Governor of New Jersey." In 1914, Glazebrook was appointed Consul at Jerusalem. Adler, *Jewish Social Studies,* X, 331.

[78] Esco Foundation, I, 216; Howard, *American Inquiry,* p. 92.

hardly likely that the Commission had conducted a careful inquiry in twenty-four hours. The fact that until June 12, the only official they spoke to was Glazebrook confirms their lack of impartiality at the time of their arrival. Upon hearing of this cablegram, Yale, still unconvinced, instantly cabled Westermann to discount its alarming features.[79]

After June 13, when the Commission spent the greater part of the day visiting Zionist agricultural settlements on the way to Jerusalem almost nothing is recorded of further Jewish encounters.[80] In Jerusalem, on June 16, the King-Crane Commission interviewed a Zionist deputation. Among the American contingent, there were four important Zionists: Dr. Harry Friedenwald, a Baltimore ophthalmologist, Dr. David De Sola Pool of the Spanish-Portuguese Synagogue in New York City, Shearith Israel, E.W. Lewin-Epstein of New York and a Brandeis lieutenant, Robert Szold, of Washington, D.C. The statement of Zionist aims presented to Messrs. King and Crane was essentially what the Zionist Commission had advanced at Versailles.[81] The response of the Commission to the Zionists is unknown.

Over a period of two weeks, the King-Crane Commission attended a number of anti-Zionist gatherings and, in an informal party-dinner atmosphere, socialized with anti-Zionist British officers, Arab nationalists and resident Christians. After calling on King and Crane that morning, Glazebrook entertained them on the evening of June 14 at a "twelve course dinner, where the principal guests were a Frenchman who favored a unified Turkey" and two anti-Zionist British officials, Sir Ronald Storrs, military governor of Jerusalem and General Arthur Money, military governor for Palestine. The sentiments they conveyed were sucessfully implanted in the minds of the Commissioners. Albert Lybyer for one recorded his view on the Zionists: all of them were unscrupulous and "all Americans and Britons oppose them." He wrote this after having been in Palestine only four days.[82] In another six days, Lybyer approved of a constitution for Palestine prepared by a British colonel which modified Zionist demands in the "direction of fairness."[83]

[79] Howard, *American Inquiry*, p. 93.

[80] *ALD*, June 13, 1919.

[81] Howard, *American Inquiry*, p. 96.

[82] *ALD*, June 14, 1919.

On June 20, the first of three official reports to the American peace delegation was transmitted. It read, in part: "Here, the older inhabitants, both Moslem and Christian, take a united and ... hostile attitude toward any exclusive Jewish immigration or toward any effort to establish Jewish sovereignty over them. We doubt if any British or American official believes that it is possible to carry out the Zionist program except through the support of a large army."[84] On June 21, King, Crane and Lybyer dined with the English and Lybyer sat near the anti-Zionist, anti-French Colonel Watson. The people at dinner were "nearly all Moslems...."[85]

Before departing the Holy Land, Charles R. Crane befriended General Money and the anti-Zionist John Huston Finley, then supervisor of American Red Cross work in Palestine.[86] On June 27, King and Crane held an informal interview with Frederick Bliss, son of the American Protestant College's missionary President.[87] Now, having concluded their business in Palestine, they sped to Damascus, reaching that city in time for the opening session of the Syrian National Congress.

King and Crane seemed to have agreed with the Congress resolutions. On July 11, they sent another telegram to Paris, describing the " 'unexpectedly strong expression of national feeling in Syria opposing both a French mandate and Zionist plans in Palestine.' " Both King and Crane manifested an outright sympathy for a Great Arab Kingdom under Faisal with an American protectorate.[88] They "announced that he (Faisal) even seemed willing to allow the establishment of an American women's college in forbidden Mecca. No zealous missionaries could have asked for more.... With the French and Vatican beaten and the Jews out of the way, their

[83] *Ibid.*, June 20, 1919.

[84] Crane and King to the Commission to Negotiate the Peace, Paris Peace Conference, 867N/91 telegram, June 20, 1919, *USFR: PPC*, XII, p.748.

[85] *ALD*. June 21, 1919.

[86] Arthur Money to John Huston Finley, August 5, 1920, John Huston Finley Papers, Box 75, New York Public Library, (hereafter abbreviated *JHF*). Interesting reference is made to Charles Crane and the members of "his" commission. Arthur Money to Finley, May 1, 1920, *Ibid.* The idea that Crane's influence on the Commission was predominant has also been advanced by the military official subordinate only to Money, Sir Ronald Storrs. John Noble, "American Imperialism Turns to Zionism," *The Jewish Voice*, I, (May 1941), 15-16.

[87] *ALD*, June 27, 1919.

missions would flower in the desert under American protection."
The third and last of the reports to Paris demanded strong curbs on
Jewish immigration, the erection of a unified Syrian State including
Palestine and the administration of the Holy Places by an inter-
national commission. [89]

Montgomery and Yale disagreed with the majority report of King,
Crane and Lybyer. Montgomery suggested that Palestine be placed
under a separate British mandate, that Lebanon be autonomous under
a French mandate and that Syria be governed by a joint Anglo-French
mandate with Faisal as king. He further claimed that, at least with
regard to Palestine, Arab antagonism was to be expected but that
eventually, the arrival of Jewish industry would benefit the Near
East. Jews, however, should not be led to believe that a Palestinian
homeland would solve the world-wide problem of anti-Semitism, an
issue which was still being discussed at Paris by the Christian
nations. [90]

The experience with the King-Crane Commission profoundly
altered Yale's attitude. [91] As the weeks passed, he became increasingly disillusioned with the Commission's work and mode of
inquiry. It must be remembered that the avowed purpose of the
Commission had been to ascertain the political wishes of the Near
Eastern peoples. Instead, the reverse occurred. By mid-July, 1919,
King and Crane were not only accepting petitions but also "investigating certain industrial quesitons" in Syria. [92] Thus, for the second
time in a month, the commissioners had been unable to maintain
Wilson's high standard. In Palestine, they were compromised by a

[88] Crane and King to the Commission to Negotiate the Peace, Paris Peace
Conference, 181.9102/3 telegram, July 10, 1919 *USFR: PPC*, XII, 750. Included
in this telegram is a confirmation of their previous Zionist assessment. The people
"vigorously oppose Zionistic plan and Jewish immigration" and were protesting
against the Balfour Declaration. For a complete statement of the Damascus
Congress Resolutions, see Antonius, pp. 292-294, 440-442.

[89] Manuel, p. 248.

[90] Esco Foundation, I, 216; Adler, *Jewish Social Studies,* X, 327; Howard,
American Inquiry, pp. 100-101.

[91] Westermann to Harry N. Howard, September 6, 1940, *WLW,* Box 1.

[92] William T. Ellis, "Impossible to Give Palestine to the Jews," *American
Hebrew,* 105, (July 18, 1919), 231. They had not been charged to do this either by
Wilson or by any of the Allies. They had clearly overstepped the bounds of their
investigation.

manipulative Anglo-American clique; in Syria, they were again diverted. It was at this time that Yale authored his Minority Report, which was an attempt to disengage himself on the one hand from the findings of the King-Crane Commission and on the other to outline a plan that would effectively deal with the social and political realities of the Near East as he conceived them.

The arrival of the Commission in Palestine and Syria had aroused a strong national sentiment.[93] Yale was astounded by the inability of the King-Crane Commission to see the hand of Britain in the Arab rising of 1919. Realizing that Britain did not want Syria to fall into the hands of the French, he perceived that Britain must have had a hand in the encouraging of the "spontaneous Arab nationalism" of 1919 for a unified Syria under an English rather than a French mandate.[94] It was Yale's impression that the Arabs did not want a national home for the Jews in Palestine but that Arab nationalism was too recent to be anything but "artificially cultivated." He believed that the promise of the Balfour Declaration ought to be kept since the entire Near East would benefit through Jewish enterprise. Great Britain, he concluded, would be the best mandatory for Palestine, which should be separated from Syria and developed in conformity with the wishes of the Zionists. He stated that there was no reason for United States participation because England, the nation most responsible for the Balfour Declaration, should now be charged with the obligation of carrying it out. Yale recommended the following divisions: To France, Lebanon, to a joint English-French protectorate, Syria, to Britain, Palestine, and nothing for the United States. He believed that through his solution, everyone — Jews, Moslems, Christians, France and England had been taken into consideration. The wisest course for the United States was to withdraw, since assigning her a mandate would result in unnecessary strife with the European powers.[95]

[93] Yale, p. 336.

Adler, *Jewish Social Studies*, X, 328.

[95] Eisner, p. 10; Esco Foundation, I, 216; William Yale, *Recommendations As to the Future Disposition of Palestine, Syria and Mount Lebanon, July 26, 1919*, WYP, EMHC, folder 130. Yale began to adopt a more sympathetic stand toward Zionism because he had arrived at the conviction that Palestine would be developed on a Western model, in accordance with American ideals. He thought that the biggest contributors toward the renascence of Palestine would be the American Jews, to whom he had recently taken an increased liking. Ben V. Cohen to Brandeis, September 12, 1919, Brandeis Papers. By October, 1919, Yale thought

Shortly after submitting his report, Yale resigned from the Commission.[96] King and Crane, undaunted, moved on with the assistance of a grant from the State Department for additional salaries and expenses.[97] By August 16, however, their work had also been concluded.

The findings of the King-Crane Commission were not shrouded in secrecy. On August 28, their Report was submitted to Undersecretary Polk who was then head of the American peace delegation in Paris.[98] Within forty-eight hours of his return to America, Charles R. Crane had personally cabled Wilson as to the contents of the Report.[99] By August 30, both King and Crane had spoken to representatives of the *New York Tribune* and the *New York Herald*; they discussed their findings with Associated Press reporters, and mentioned the "overwhelming desire (of the Arab people) for the United States as mandatory in most of the Near East." The only portions of the Report not discussed were the specific mandate recommendations for certain areas of the Ottoman Empire. Aside from that, the contents of the Report were entirely revealed in 1919, including references to Syrian opposition to a Zionist state.[100]

Donald M. Brodie arrived at the White House with the text of the King-Crane Report on September 27. At this time, Wilson was

---

that Zionism's vital force was waning and, consequently, they would have to accept the idea of a "limited Palestine," less the Hauran, the Valley of the Litany and Transjordan. In the future, he felt that the fate of the Jews would be dependent on a British mandate under which Palestine would be established as a national home for the Jewish people. Zionism, he implied, no longer had the stature to self-determine its fate. William Yale, *The Significance and Import of the Clemenceau-Lloyd George Agreement*, October 21, 1919, WYP, EMHC, folder 125; Adler, *Jewish Social Studies*, X, 329.

[96] Howard, *American Inquiry*, p. 101; Manuel, p. 254.

[97] American Commission to Negotiate the Peace, Minutes of Daily Meetings of Commissioners Plenipotentiary, July 31, 1919, Henry White Papers, Butler Library, Columbia University. King and Crane were originally commissioned to examine the non-Arabic portions of the Ottoman Empire as well. Before their return, they had taken surveys in Mesopotamia, Armenia, Cilicia and Greece.

[98] Evans, p. 153.

[99] Zeine N. Zeine, *The Struggle for Arab Independence*, (Beirut, 1960), p. 220 n2.

[100] "American Mission Finds East Wants American Mandate," *New York Herald*, August 30, 1919, Sec 2, p. 2; "Urge Broad U.S. Mandate in Turkey," *New York Tribune*, August 30, 1919, p.1.

stumping through the country, trying to arouse support for the League and fell ill before his return to Washington. The Report's overt hostility to the French necessitated its deliberate exclusion from the Paris Peace Conference. There is a strong possibility that Wilson never saw the Report. Except for personal correspondence and eyewitness accounts,[101] it remained outside the public eye for three years.

Charles Crane, who was in the Near East at the time, wrote to Woodrow Wilson on January 23, 1923, that the Report "is looked upon as a serious, careful and sympathetic effort to apply the principles you had enunciated and for which America went to war."[102] Though admirable, Crane's candor regarding the report does not stand up to intensive scrutiny.

The Commission's findings were not a scientific survey but pieces of political propaganda remarkably coinciding with the program of Howard Bliss and the Syrian nationalists.[103] Some of the very obvious irregularities were apoliogized for at the outset. First, the number of petitions was not proportional to the respective populations. For example, in Palestine, the area designated as Occupied Enemy Territory Administration (O.E.T.A.) South, [104] a total of two hundred sixty petitions were submitted from political, economic and religious groups combined but in O.E.T.A. East, Syria, more than four times that number were submitted although the latter population was only slightly greater than twice that of the former. Second, the number of petitions from different religious groups was not pro-

---

[101] "What About Syria," Frederick Jones Bliss, *North American Review*, CCXI, (May, 1920), 597-599); Howard, *American Inquiry*, p. 262.

[102] At the Exercises in honor of President King at Oberlin, on June 20, 1927, Donald M. Brodie read a statement prepared by Crane and quoted the latter as saying the following: "...The high hopes of the Arab people...have been disappointed... all the Arab.... into the remotest oasis...revere that report...(The King-Crane Report)"; Howard, *American Inquiry*, pp. 315, 319-320.

[103] Esco Foundation, I, 218.

[104] O.E.T.A. North was Cilicia, O.E.T.A. East was Syria, O.E.T.A. West was Lebanon and O.E.T.A. South was Palestine, including Acre, Beersheba, Haifa, Jaffa, Jenin, Jerusalem, Nablus, Nazareth, Safed, Tiberias, Rishon Le Tzion and Tel Aviv. The South was under British military administration, the North and West were under the French and the East was controlled by the Arabs. Paris Peace Conference, 181.9102/9 *Report of the American Section of the International Commission on Mandates in Turkey*, August 28, 1919, *USFR: PPC, XII, 756*.

portional to the numerical strength of the religious faith. In more precise terms, as will be seen shortly, this means that the total number of petitions received from Moslems fell far short of the total number of petitions received from Christians, although nearly three-quarters of the Near East peoples under consideration by the Commission were of the Moslem faith. This inordinate recognition of Christian primacy was tied to the missionary interest of the Commissioners who were only casually committed to the fate of the majority population. Third, a number of petitions displayed the influence of organized propaganda through the similarity of phrasing and identical wording. Fourth, many of the petitions were fraudulent. Last, the value of a petition was not necessarily determined by the number of signatures. In terms of public opinion, King and Crane assumed, arbitrarily, that a petition signed by thousands of villagers may have had less value than one signed by a municipal council. With characteristic gloss, the commissioners asserted that the "great majority of the irregularities offset one another."[105]

The charts and tables presented by the Commission in support of its findings are deceptive. Under the first Roman numeral, political groups, there are no Jewish organizations listed. Significantly, Jews are cited only under the third Roman numeral,[106] religious groups. In addition, throughout the entire one hundred eighteen page Report the Balfour Declaration is only mentioned five times. The reason behind this near omission is unclear; because of it one might assume that neither King nor Crane viewed Zionism in political terms, but this is untrue. There are no religious or social arguments leveled against the Jews, although they are not represented as a political group they are attacked in none other than political terms. They are, in the estimate of King and Crane, a people with a "Zionistic" scheme: "an aggressive, imperialistic people" who would not be content with hegemony over Palestine." The manner of description in these pages is conspiratorial and probably received its inspiration from Crane, a man with preconceptions concerning alleged "Jewish plots." The Jews were subjecting the Arab population to Zionist immigration plans and "steady financial and social pressure to surrender the land.... The Zionists look forward to a complete dispossession of the... non-Jewish inhabitants of Palestine."

[105] *Ibid.*, 763-764.

[106] There is also no listing for Jews under petitions received from economic groups. See tables, *Ibid.*, 756-757.

Furthermore, the Jews could not be entrusted to guard the Christian and Moslem Holy Places because "they are not only not sacred to the Jews but abhorrent to them...."[107]

In the O.E.T.A. South, (Palestine) lived the fewest people. 79.4 per cent were Moslems and it is significant to note that Jews outnumbered Christians by two thousand five hundred. Yet of all the petitions collected and tabulated under category III, Religious Groups, (they were given right into the hands of King and Crane by the interested parties), only fourteen (16.4 per cent) were from Jewish delegations while fifty three (nearly 60 per cent) were from Christian organizations. The Moslems, nearly four-fifths of the population, were represented on only eighteen (20.5 per cent) of the total of eight-eight petitions under this subheading. The suggestion of Albert Lybyer, that "because of the numerous sub-divisions of the Christians... it was inevitable from the beginning the Commission would give a disproportionate number of interviews and amount of time to them" is unsatisfactory. This is a bold admission of the overriding importance to King, Crane and Lybyer of Christian opinion in the overall solution to the Near Eastern problem, an importance entirely out of proportion to the numerical population.[108]

The concern with Christian sensibilities was also paramount in O.E.T.A. East and O.E.T.A. West. In the former, a total of 56 per cent of the petitions were from Christian sects, although they comprised but 8.3 per cent of the population; 38.1 per cent of the petitions were from Moslems, though they totaled five-sixths of the population and only three petitions were collected from Jews. In the latter, where Christians totaled 36 per cent of the population, they turned in 54 per cent of the requests; Moslems were 54 percent of the population and submitted 35 per cent of the total number. Of

---

[107] The Zionist "scheme" was accurately delimited but the phrasing made it sound particularly unsavory, e.g. (1) "....Palestine....to be set aside at once as a 'national home for the Jews.' " (2) Sooner or later, the political rule of the land "will become organized as a 'Jewish Commonwealth' " (3) "The Great Powers of the world have declared in favor of the scheme which merely awaits execution" (4) In reference to the ancient Jewish mode of life which the writer fears may be restored, such words as "exclusivism and particularism" are employed. *Ibid.*, 773, 792-794.

[108] See tables on population estimates and religious groups, *Ibid.*, 756-757, 771. For the number of petitions per group and percentages, calculations are based only on table III, or religious groups. If economic and political groups (tables I and II) were also included the imbalance would be even more striking with reference to the Jews.

equivalent importance to the King-Crane Commission were the Jews and the Nusairiyeh religious sect: from both were collected five petitions.[109]

The outspoken missionary character of the document seems, in no small part, to have been lent by President King, especially the assertion that the United States ought to be the recipient of a mandate because of the spirit of American educational institutions in Syria, notably "the College of Beirut." The morality and rhetoric of Wilson, acquired by King when he became an interventionist, is laced through the Report.

> In the first place...the Syrian people (recognize) that at the foundation of the common life of America were to be found certain convictions... They saw that she had a passion for peace... and that to bring righteous peace nearer she entered the war. They saw she had a passion for democracy... they knew too that with a high religious idealism, America... combined a belief in the separation of Church and State... for the highest good of (the) religious unit... (and) the State.[110]

The Syrian people, he continued, believed in the unselfish motives of the United States which she had espoused upon entering the war; America did not seek the spoils of war but the fruit of peace. "It may be doubtful...if America could do anything so significant for the human race today as to prove she has not forgotten her own high ideals" by undertaking the Syrian mandate.[111]

There was little left to be said for the Jews because only they "supported the Zionistic scheme. The Jews are distinctly for Britain as a mandatory power because of the Balfour Declaration, though many think that if the scheme goes ahead, American Jews will become its chief promoters..." The final recommendations of the King-Crane Commission on Zionism were predicated on the assumption that the historic claims of the Jews were invalid and that any influx of their co-religionists into Palestine would be granted to them as a privilege rather than a right. The idea of a Jewish State would have to be abandoned and immigration severely limited. The commissioners claimed that they had begun their study "as

[109] Refer to table III — Religious groups, *Ibid.*, 757.

[110] *Ibid.*, 844-847.

[111] *Ibid.*

favorable to Zionism" but had been "driven to the reverse view."
They were aware of Zionist achievements in Palestine but, in
accordance with the Balfour Declaration, the "extreme Zionist
program" would have to modified. The rights of the non-Jewish
communities in Palestine, they concluded, should not be trampled
upon. Credence was lent to the idea of aroused Arab nationalism
taking a sanguinary path against the Jews to ameliorate its frustra-
tion.[112]

The petitions presented to the King-Crane Commission in reference
to the implementation of the Zionist program are misleading. In
O.E.T.A. South, two hundred twenty-two of the two hundred sixty
total petitions[113] (or about 85.3 per cent) were opposed to the Zionist
program, but these figures do not necessarily reveal the climate of
opinion of the majority Moslem population, since as has already
been observed, most of the petitions originated from Christian
denominations. In O.E.T.A. East ninety per cent (one thousand
forty petitions) were against Zionism but fifty-six per cent of the
entreaties were from Christian sects and only thirty-eight per cent
from Moslem. Again, it must be noted that Christians composed
only eight per cent of the total Syrian population.[114]   Thus,

---

[112] *Ibid.*, 779, 792-794. In a report written for the Inquiry at the close of 1918,
Howard Crosby Butler claimed, as had William Yale, that Arab nationalism hardly
existed. Butler had been to the Near East and averred that "it would be impossible
to apply any theory of self-determination...because it would be impossible to
discover what any large number of these peoples desire and even if this were
possible, it might easily turn out that they desired something which would be
disastrous to their well-being." Excluding Syria proper, the Arab peoples "have no
real national consciousness. Particularism...takes the place of nationalism...."
Howard Crosby Butler, *Report on the Proposals for an Independent Arab State or
States,* WYP, EMHC, folder 142, p. 37. William Yale recounts an incident in
which Crane asked the Arabs of Hebron whom they wished as mandatory. They
replied that "all governments were evil." A moment after they told Crane to return
to Paris and "tell the Peace Conference and your President we want Allah to rule
over us."   These replies fail to demonstrate the presence of a viable Arab
nationalism but on the contrary, serve to reinforce Butler's conclusion. Yale,
p. 337.

[113] the two hundred sixty petition total represents all the petitions collected in
O.E.T.A. South, from Categories I (political groups), II (economic and social
groups), III (Religious groups) and miscellaneous delegations.

[114] See "Petition Summaries," subheading "E" in *USFR: PPC*, XII, 758, 760-
762.

to say that the wishes of the majority Moslem population were presented in the King-Crane Report is fallacious.   There was also too little contact with Jews and Zionism to validate their contention that the movement was "pernicious" and that Jewish immigration ought to be restricted.

Only the Christian population remains to be considered.   A *New York Times* correspondent and critic of Zionism commented that "Palestine Christians are more bitterly against the mandate... than the Moslems...."[115] The accuracy of this statement would lead to the conclusion that King and Crane drew their anti-Zionist consensus from a vindictive minority population.. Far from being an "experiment in peacemaking,"[116] the King Crane Report was a pro-Christian document.   Its findings were suppressed in America for three years because they were thought to be inimical to Allied objectives in the Near East.   Had the United States Government known that it had nothing to fear from France or Britain, the King-Crane Report probably would have been published in 1919.   As it developed, the palpable tragedy of the King-Crane Commission was not its failure to cause an impact at Paris but that the legendary aura surrounding its members and findings had no substance.   Nevertheless, during the interwar period, the chimera of King and Crane continued to exercise its influence over those American interest groups which decried Zionism and its policies.

[115] *Ibid.*, 749-750, 785, 792,859; T. Walter Williams, "Palestine Still a Land of Problems," *New York Times,* July 10, 1921, Sec. 2, p. 3.

[116] Harry N. Howard, "An Experiment in Peacemaking: The King-Crane Commission," *Moslem World*, XXXII (April, 1942), 122-146. In the 1930s Howard was an Anglophobe and purveyor of the "international Jewry" mystique. See Harry N. Howard, *The Partition of Turkey* (New York, 1966), p.. 197.

III

Jewish Anti-Zionism:
The Converted Wing

Between 1917 and 1941, Reform Judaism in the United States altered its opinion on Zionism. From 1917 to 1921, there existed among a majority of these Jews an opposition to all forms of Zionism and a militant resistance movement arose grounded on a faith in democratic progress, gleaned partly from European antecedents but to a greater degree from the American experience. From 1921 until 1929, Reform Judaism became more friendly with Brandeis Zionism but also courted Weizmann. During the 1930's, some anti-Zionist Jews even participated in the Jewish Agency for Palestine, an organization founded for the purpose of promoting the economic well-being of the Yishuv.[1]

With the rise of Hitler and in response to the Holocaust, the Central Conference of American Rabbis (C.C.A.R.) relaxed its unfavorable stand on increased Jewish immigration to Palestine.[2] Prior to 1935, Reform Judaism failed to view mass immigration to the Holy Land with much enthusiasm; before 1921, it had also looked askance at the great numbers of Jews arriving in America. Both of these important migrations were regarded as incompatible with the Reform philosophy which stressed that the solution to the

---

[1] The Yishuv refers to the Jewish settlement in Palestine prior to 1948. Sachar, *The Course of Modern Jewish History,* p. 369.

[2] David Philipson, ''Central Conference of American Rabbis 1889-1939,'' *American Jewish Yearbook* (hereafter abbreviated *AJYB*), ed. Harry Schneiderman, 73 vols. (Philadelphia, 1940), XLII, 203.

Jewish problem must be found in the countries where Jews resided.[3] After the issuance of the White Paper in May, 1939, the transformation of the mainstream of Reform to the Zionist cause was complete.[4] A splinter group remained outside the pro-Palestine movement and coalesced into the American Council for Judaism. It was this dissident minority that carried with it an inability to accept the premise of the Balfour Declaration,[5] an overriding concern with "one hundred per cent Americanism,"[6] and a fear of nascent anti-Semitism.[7]

[3] "Shall the Anti-Zionists Be Silent," *The New Jewish Chronicle,* I (November 1918), 17; M.R. Werner, *Julius Rosenwald: The Life of A Practical Humanitarian* (New York, 1939), p. 221; "Asserts Jewish Problem is World's Problem," *The Jewish Review and Observer,* XLVI (August 13, 1920), 1, 4; "Thinks Palestine Fails As Panacea," *New York Times,* April 6, 1925, p. 22; Sol Bloom, *The Autobiography of Sol Bloom* (New York, 1948), pp. 295-297.

[4] The White Paper of May, 1939, was the last word of the British Government on all its negotiations, investigations and conferences during the preceding three years. In it, the English declared unequivocally that Palestine should not become a Jewish State and that the original Balfour Declaration had never intended it to be so. The White Paper envisioned "the establishment within ten years of an independent Palestine State" in treaty relationship with Great Britain. During this period, land sales were to be restricted. Some fifty thousand Jewish immigrants would be authorized to enter Palestine during the ensuing five years together with an above quota twenty-five thousand Jewish refugees as a "contribution" toward the settlement of the Jewish problem in Europe — a grand total of seventy-five thousand. Thereafter, Jewish immigration would cease unless the Arabs of Palestine were prepared to acquiesce to it. Chambers, pp. 199-200; Israel Cohen, *A Short History of Zionism,* pp. 148-151.

[5] "We owe this to the Memory of the Late Rabbi Levy" (editorial), *The Jewish Criterion,* 49, (November 16, 1917), 8; "Boruch Atah B'voecho" (editorial), *The Jewish Tribune,* XXX (December 21, 1917), 18; Moses Rischin, "The American Jewish Committee and Zionism 1906-1922," *Herzl Year Book,* V (1963), 76-77. In June, 1918, the C.C.A.R. said, in effect, that they did not oppose Jewish immigration to Palestine to escape persecution, just as they did not oppose Jewish migration anywhere in the world. What they objected to was the supposed unique status the Jews were to have in the Holy Land under the national home provision of the Balfour Declaration. David Philipson, *The Reform Movement in Judaism,* 2nd ed. (New York, 1967), pp. 362-363; David Philipson, *My Life as an American Jew: An Autobiography* (Cincinnati, 1941), p. 301; "The Central Conference and Zionism" (editorial), *The Jewish Criterion,* 49 (July 5, 1918), 10.

[6] Henry Moskowitz, "Palestine Not a Solution of Jewish Problem," *New York Times,* June 10, 1917, Sec. 6, pp. 10-11; Samuel Hirschberg, "Judaism and Assimilation," *The Jewish Review and Observer,* XLIII (August 10, 1917), 4; Ralph P. Boas, "Zionist Program and Jewish Unity," *The American Hebrew,* 102

   Neither the Reform philosophy itself nor its spokesmen were localized in one particular area of the country. Lay leaders were found in a variety of highly regarded professions, from newspaper editors to stage and screen personalities[8] to company executives[9] to American ambassadors.[10]   The major Reform newspapers, mainly weeklies, were located in St. Louis, San Francisco, Pittsburgh, Chicago, Cincinnati, Baltimore and New York.[11]   The spiritual leaders of Reform were also drawn from the North, the South, the Midwest and the Far West.[12]   In terms of numbers, "liberal" Judaism, as Reform was often called, was the smallest of the existing

(December 28, 1917, 254. Israel Friedlaender to Ralph P. Boas, March 2, 1919, Israel Friedlaender Papers (hereafter abbreviated IF) Jewish Theological Seminary, New York City; "The Program of Zionism as a Menace to Jewish Unity," *Current Opinion*, LXIV (February 1918), 121-122; "New York and Zionism" (editorial), *The Modern View*, 37 (September 13, 1918, 3.

[7] Liberals...regarded racialist anti-Semitism as a major nuisance...a rearguard action by the retreating forces of reaction...American liberals were above all concerned with the political implications of Zionism." Walter Laqueur, "Zionism and Its Liberal Critics," *Journal of Contemporary History*, VI (1971), 163.

[8] Among these were P.J. Wolfson, David Belasco, Eddie Cantor and Daniel Frohman. "Cross-Currents in American Judaism," *Current Opinion*, LXVI (May 1919) 314-315; "Prominent Jews Protest Against Zionism," *The Jewish Review and Observer*, XLV (March 14, 1919), 1,4; Raymond Dannenbaum, "Eddie Cantor Confides Beliefs in Exclusive Interview — Cites Need for Judaism," *Jewish Journal*, III (October 15, 1930), 3, 10; David Weissman "P.J. Wolfson," *Jewish Community Press*, IV (March 26, 1937), 32-33.

[9] "Prominent Jews Protest Against Zionism," *Jewish Review and Observer*, XLV (March 14, 1919) 1, 4.

[10] *Ibid.*

[11] *The Jewish Criterion* (Pittsburgh), *Emanu-El* (San Francisco), *The B'nai B'rith Messenger* (San Francisco), *The Modern View* (St. Louis, *The Israelite* (Cincinnati), *The Reform Advocate* (Chicago), *Jewish Comment* (Baltimore), and *The American Hebrew* (New York) are the best known.

[12] Rabbis Edgar F. Magnin and Irving Reichert, both of California, represent the Far West. Cincinnati boasted of David Philipson and Kaufmann Kohler, President of Hebrew Union College. Rabbis Leo Franklin of Detroit; Gerson B. Levi and Emil G. Hirsch of Chicago and Louis Wolsey of Cleveland round out the Mid-West. The Eastern wing was represented by Rabbis Isaac Landman, Samuel Schulman and Henry Berkowitz, the former two from New York and the latter from Philadelphia. Four well-known Southerners were Rabbis Charles A. Rubenstein, William Rosenau and Morris Lazaron, all of Baltimore and Rabbi Edward Nathaniel Calisch of Virginia. The Southwest claims Rabbi Henry Cohen of Galveston.

American Judaisms[13] but it boasted a vocal press, several influential officials to whom the State Department was responsive[14] and valuable connections within the non-Jewish community.

On November 9, 1917, "liberal" Judaism was placed in an anomalous position. Never before had it been called upon to defend its assimilationist attitude. The absorption of Jews into the non-Jewish environment seemed to have been a natural phenomenon, begun a century before in Western Europe and culminating in America. Its end result was clearly an increased tolerance for the Jews on the part of the Christian community and an eventual loss to the Jew of his past identity in all save religion. Reform doctrine stated that, in fact, it was the unique religious heritage of Judaism that had preserved the Jew intact for five thousand years.[15] After the destruction of the Second Temple, the Jews ceased to exist as a viable national entity[16] and became dispersed, henceforth charged with a universal mission: they were to be witnesses to God among the Christian nations, illuminating a path reaching up from the darkness to redemption. Their duty was to promulgate moral and ethical concepts as a preliminary to realizing a world brotherhood of man.[17]

---

[13] In 1917, the *AJYB* estimated that three million three hundred thousand Jews resided in America. Glazer, p. 164. Of these, perhaps seven or eight per cent were affiliated with Reform Judaism as organization or congregation members.

[14] Simon Wolf, Henry Morgenthau, Sr., and Abram I. Elkus were all Ambassadors to Turkey and Samuel Edelman was Vice-Consul at Jerusalem. They all served in the State Department between 1907 and 1920.

[15] Actually, Reform theology is a little more complicated as it is the entire liberal philosophy. According to liberals, both European and American, the emancipation of the Jews was not based on subjective factors but on historical, socio-economic trends and on the irresistable progress of civilization. American liberals in particular were concerned with the political implications of Zionism upon their loyalty and citizenship in the United States. When Jewish nationalism first appeared on the American scene, it was regarded as "the momentary inebriation of morbid minds," a movement arresting the march of progress and tolerance, an obstacle to "Jewish adjustment in a Christian environment." "Ziomania," as the movement was called, was thought not merely to be reactionary in character but a menace to Jewish security. Laqueur, *Journal of Contemporary History,* VI, 163-164, 171, 178-179; Naomi Wiener Cohen, "The Reaction of Reform Judaism in America to Political Zionism, 1897-1922," *The Jewish Experience in America,* ed. Abraham J. Karp (New York, 1969) pp. 159-160, 175n; "Editorial" (editorial) *American Jewish World,* VI (July 5, 1918), 736.

[16] Solomon Zeitlin, "The Jews: Race, Nation or Religion — Which?" *The Jewish Quarterly Review,* ed. Cyrus Adler, XXVI (April, 1936), 337-338, 341, 347; David Philipson, *Centenary Papers and Others* (Cincinnati, 1919) p. 268.

Nationalism, locked in a shadowy, dead past was an enigma to them. Apparently, it was safe enough for Greek-Americans, Polish-Americans, Irish-Americans and even Arab-Americans, but it was deadly for the Jew. Behind nationalism there lurked separatism, particularism and ghettoism. Intermarriage was tacitly acknowledged as the way Reform Judaism would penetrate Christian society.[18] Disloyalty to the country of one's birth, advocacy of a church-state union and Jewish solidarity was the avenue of the Zionist.[19] There was no meeting ground between the prince of light, liberalism, and the prince of darkness, nationalism.[20] The credibility of Reform was endangered by the Balfour Declaration, as the movement was thrown back upon itself to seek a rationale for its very being.[21]

[17] Kaufman Kohler, *Jewish Theology: Systematically and Historically Considered* (Cincinnati, 1943), 390-391, 395-396; "The Open Forum," *Jewish Comment,* XLVIII (March 16, 1917), 529; "Zionism and Bible Exegesis" (editorial, *The American Jewish World,* VI (December 28, 1917), 288; Kaufmann Kohler, "Ordination Address," *Union Bulletin,* VIII (June, 1918), 12-13.

[18] Jews often defended the right of other national groups to exist and to support the freedom movements in their ancestral lands. "We Don't Intend to Bore You," *The New Jewish Chronicle,* II (January, 1919), 55; "Most Jews Oppose Zionism, Says Kahn," *New York Times,* March 9, 1919, p. 9; Maximilian Hurwitz, "The Strange Case of Mr. Weil," *The Jewish Tribune,* 39 (October 20, 1922), 3, 16. An excellent defense of intermarriage may be found in Archibald Hillman, "Zionism — The Other Angle," *Journal of Race Development,* VIII (January, 1918) 319; David Philipson, *Israel, the International People* (n.p. January 15, 1917), 15pp.; Philipson, *Centenary Papers,* pp.11, 52-53, 59, 277-278; Robert T. Marx, "Cincinnati Letter," *Jewish Comment,* LI (January 19, 1917), 348; Eli Mayer, "Judaism and Zionism," *Jewish Comment,* LI (May 17, 1918), 172.

[19] For a more detailed explanation of these phenomena during the years of their widest acceptance, see "Message of the President" (editorial), *The Jewish Tribune,* XXX (July 20, 1917), 4, and "A Jewish State Would Be A Misfortune for Israel" (editorial), *American Jewish World,* VI (July 19, 1918), 769.

[20] The organizations whose pronouncements set the tone of anti-Zionist protest were the C.C.A.R. and its lay arm, the Union of American Hebrew Congregations, "The Union of American Hebrew Congregations and Zionism" (editorial), *Jewish Comment,* XLVIII (February 9, 1917), 418; Horace J. Wolf, "Central Conference of Rabbis," *The American Hebrew,* 101 (July 6, 1917), 226, 240; Israel Abrahams, "Palestine and Jewish Nationality: A Reply," *The Hibbert Journal,* XVI (April 1918), 465; Naomi Cohen, *The Jewish Experience in America,* p. 154; *Central Conference of American Rabbis Yearbook* (hereafter abbreviated *CCARY*) XXVII (Cincinnati, 1917), 132; Philipson, *AJYB,* XLII, 198-199; Philipson, *The Reform Movement in Judaism,* p. 362; Stephen Wise to Louis D. Brandeis, July 6, 1917, LDB.

As much as oppressed Jews from Eastern Europe, Reform Jewry in America was engaged in a struggle for life. Every issue affecting Judaism in 1917 and 1918 was weighed and measured by liberals for its ultimate bearing on the pivotal issue of nationalism. The American Jewish Congress, an organization opposed by non-Zionists and anti-Zionists alike was bludgeoned out of existence until war's end through the concerted efforts of the Anglo- or Reform Jewish press, the Reform rabbinate and Henry Morgenthau.[22] Morgenthau's efforts on behalf of anti-Zionism were supposed to lead

[21] A complete explanation of the arguments and where they are to be found would fill many pages. For a sampling, see Jacob De Haas to Louis Brandeis, December 12, 1917, LDB, Stephen Wise to Louis Brandeis, September 13, 1917, LDB; De Haas to Chaim Weizmann, December 12, 1917, LDB; "City," *Jewish Voice,* LXIII (December 14, 1917), 3; "America or Palestine — Which" (editorial), *The Modern View,* 35 (December 7, 1917), 1,4; "Jerusalem" (editorial), *The Jewish Criterion,* 49 (December 14, 1917), 10; Henry Morgenthau and French Strother, *All in a Lifetime* (Garden City, N.Y., 1922), pp. 289-292; Henry Morgenthau, "Palestine and the American Jews," *The American Hebrew,* 102 (December 14, 1917), 178. For some outstanding discourse on anti-Zionism and an elaboration of the various facets of anti-nationalism, including dual loyalty, hyphenism, anti-Semitic fear and nationalist regression, see H.G. Enelow, *The Allied Countries and the Jews* (New York, 1918), pp. 63-77, 98; Henry Berkowitz, "Balfour on Zionism," *Jewish Comment,* L (November 16, 1917), 178; "Why Pervert the Truth?" (editorial), *The Jewish Tribune,* XXX (August 3, 1917), 4.

[22] "Under the leadership of Stephen Wise, a campaign was inaugurated to elect an American Jewish Congress. Such an assembly, presumably, would represent the will of the entire Jewish community at the Peace Conference, and would endorse the programs of autonomism and Zionism." Originally, liberal Judaism was to have taken part in the Congress, but its suspicion of Wise and fear that the body was Zionist inspired (which it was) resulted in the resignation of individuals and organizations from the Executive Committee of the Congress. Campaigns were begun in New Jersey and New York to stop the Congress and the body, itself, was calumniated by the well-known Jews, for example, Simon Wolf, Simon Rosendale, former Attorney General of New York State and Dr. Henry Moskowitz. By May, 1917, the Union of American Hebrew Congregations, C.C.A.R., B'nai B'rith and the Council of Jewish Women refused to participate in the projected Congress. Eighteen months later, the Congress met without them and was adjourned for good in 1920. J. Walter Freiberg to Harry Cutler, undated (probably April 24, 1917), LDB; S. Marcus to Bernard G. Richards, April 26, 1917, LDB; Wise to Brandeis, October 5, 1917, LDB; De Haas to Brandeis, October 14, 1917, LDB; Sarah Kussy to Joseph Barondess, May 21, 1917, Joseph Barondess Papers (hereafter abbreviated JB), Box 4, New York Public Library; Simon Rosendale to Harry Cutler, May 22, 1917, LDB. In his missive, Rosendale castigated the Congress movement as a form of "reprehensible Jewish nationalism," whose symbols were the "Zionistic flags and songs." The separate national existence of Zionism meant hyphenism for American Jews. See also Tamar De Sola Pool to John Huston Finley, JHF, Box 74.

him to Turkey, where it was hoped he would conclude a separate peace with the Ottoman Empire, thereby knocking her out of the war and rendering Palestine unavailable to the Zionists.   Through Secretary of State Lansing, Morgenthau appealed to Brandeis to postpone the first meeting of the American Jewish Congress, scheduled for September. The former Minister to Turkey felt that the motive for his journey would be compromised by American Jewish nationalism if the Congress was convened. The State Department camouflaged the actual intent of the mission which seemed to be either simple war relief for the Jews of Turkey or the division of the Central Powers with an eye toward isolating Germany. The cloak and dagger tactics proved unnecessary because the mission was aborted five days after it left America.[23] The Congress movement was further blunted by the Russian Revolution which, to "liberal" Jews, signaled the crumbling of the last fortress barring the road to Jewish emancipation.[24]

At the close of 1917, the cry for unity was raised in the liberal camp. "Organize or die" was the popular slogan of Pittsburgh's *Jewish Criterion*.[25] Heretofore, Reform Judaism had engaged the spectre of Zionism rather than its substance. Now, it was confronted with a written British promise, that Palestine was to become a

[23] Brandeis was not supposed to know that Morgenthau was behind the appeal. Morgenthau to Lansing, 867N.01/13 1/2, June 15, 1917, *General Records of the Department of State: Record Group 59, Decimal and Numerical File* (hereafter abbreviated *GRDS:RG 59*) Zionist Archives, New York City; Manuel, pp. 156-157; "Morgenthau's Mission," *The Jewish Tribune*, XXX (June 29, 1917), 1. Although the Zionists were not well-informed as to the purpose of the mission, Chaim Weizmann had correctly guessed it and asked the permission of the British Government to intercept Morgenthau before he reached Turkey. Weizmann was successful in restraining Morgenthau and the mission never proceeded beyond Gibraltar. Richard Ned Lebow, "The Morgenthau Peace Mission of 1917," *Jewish Social Studies*, XXXIII (October 1970), 267-286.

[24] "Sees Zionism's End in Russian Revolt," *New York Times*, April 5, 1917, p. 13; Henry Moskowitz, "Palestine Not A Solution of the Jewish Problem," *The Jewish Review and Observer*, XLIII (July 20, 1917), 4, 8; "New Russia and the Jews" (editorial), *Jewish Comment*, XLIX (March 30, 1917), 8; Gerson B. Levi, "Another Year," *Reform Advocate*, LIII (August 4, 1917), 853-854. Even the *New York Evening Post* believed that the Russian Revolution was the herald of freedom. "Zionism and the Russian Revolution," *The New York Evening Post*, May 10, 1917, p.10.

[25] Charles Joseph, "A Serious Question," *The Jewish Criterion*, 49 (December 28, 1917), 10. A similar exhortation was given by Gerson B. Levi, "Editorial Notes," *Reform Advocate*, LVII (February 8, 1919), 7.

national home for those Jews who wished to emigrate there. The word "state" was hammered at by liberal Jews throughout 1918 as the fully developed Reform argument emerged.[26] Neither Brandeis nor Weizmann, however, had uttered the word "state" in their own deliberate appraisals of Zionism. The possibility of a Jewish commonwealth coming into existence in Palestine if the Jewish population there should ever exceed the non-Jewish, was not ruled out. However, the primary thrust of Zionism was, at this time, not directed at securing political ends. A Jewish urban and agricultural life was to be established by immigrants in a convivial atmosphere of flourishing Jewish culture. In 1918, it was a reasonable assumption that Jews needed homes to replace the ones from which they were driven. Neither the United States nor Europe were able to accommodate the tragic waves surging out of Russia, Hungary, Poland and Rumania. After 1921, restrictive immigration legislation declared American unwillingness to receive Southern and Eastern Europeans, including Jewish, refugees. Huddled Jews seeking refuge in the United States were a blight upon the name of Reform Judaism. The movement was ambivalent toward Jews in Eastern Europe who needed immediate assistance. In this respect, Palestine was regarded by Reform Jews as a mixed blessing. Liberals may have disavowed it as a place of recrudescent foreign nationalism but, at least, a critical upsurge of anti-Semitism in the United States might be avoided through the diversion of unwelcome immigrants somewhere else. Since several Reform Jewish philanthropists, among them Julius Rosenwald, found it difficult to reconcile exclusive support of Palestinian Jewish immigration with American loyalty, they emphasized the importance of returning Jews to Russia, where there were vast areas of unused land on which refugees could earn a livelihood.[27] A great deal of financial support was proffered to the Crimean resettlement plan but for several reasons colonization of this type never proved to be as popular as Zionism and Palestine. For one thing, Russian-Jewish refugees had little desire to return to a rule which was oppressive; for another, anti-Jewish feelings in the

---

[26]Charles Israel Goldblatt, "The Impact of the Balfour Declaration in America," *American Jewish Historical Quarterly*, LVII (June 1968), 459-464; *CCARY*, XXIX (Cincinnati, 1918) pp. 95, 134.

[27] "Prove Your Sanity (editorial), *The Jewish Tribune*, XXX (September 28, 1917), 4; Goldblatt, *American Jewish Historical Quarterly*, LVII, 487. Werner, pp. 173, 221, 249-252.

Soviet Union intensified as the leadership of Lenin and Trotsky was replaced by that of Stalin.

In September, 1918, the organizational theme was pressed after Zionism received a fillip from American congressmen, senators and President Wilson. Moreover, democratic elections for the American Jewish Congress eliminated the possibility of liberal control of that body.[28] The preceding year, organized Reform Judaism withdrew from the Congress arena to conduct a silent, but nevertheless effective, campaign to vitiate the nationalist position.[29] Now, retreat through silence was no longer a realistic alternative. Zionism, it contended, had intruded itself upon American idealism and had to be combatted publicly. Ironically, the method adopted by "liberal" Jewish assimilationists turned them into something they had never aspired to become: a coordinated, noticeable, ethnic pressure group desirous of achieving certain goals within the American society through the formation of lobbies and appeals to government officials.[30] Since these goals could not be directly related to the enlightened mission of Reform Judaism, some other

---

[28] The majority of Jews in America at this time were unassimilated East Europeans. As for Congress, a letter was circulated by Zionists to representatives and senators requesting that they state their feelings on the erection of a Jewish national home. Most were favorably disposed. Wilson announced his approval of the Balfour Declaration in an open letter to Stephen Wise, August 31, 1918. Alpheus Thomas Mason, *Brandeis; A Free Man's Life* (New York, 1956), p. 455; Adler, *Jewish Social Studies,* X, 313-314; "Sees Danger in Zionism," *New York Times,* September 14, 1918, p. 7; Philip Bregstone, *Chicago and Its Jews* (n.p. 1933), pp. 272-273; "Protest to Wilson on Zionist Message," *New York Times,* September 6, 1918, p. 9; "Let Us Nail Our Colors to the Mast" (editorial), *The Jewish Criterion,* 49 (August 26, 1918), 10; "The American Press on Zionism," *The American Jewish World,* VII (September 27, 1918), 67.

[29] As late as October, 1917, a forecast of the coming Balfour Declaration by Jacob De Haas created no excitement and no opposition. Thus, the anti-national campaign was initially diluted by an unwillingness to view Zionism as anything but a distasteful, shadowy presence. Jacob De Haas, *Louis D. Brandeis: A Biographical Sketch* (New York, 1929), p. 92. In the New York City Mayoralty election of November, 1917, Edward Lauterbach, Chairman of the Board of Trustees of City College of New York and Senior Director of the Hebrew Orphan Society of New York, privately corresponded with other Jews on the large Jewish vote received by Socialist-pacifist candidate Morris Hillquit. Like many others, Lauterbach was anxious to lump Zionism with such subversive activities as "anarchism ... pacifism ... Socialism and Kehillaism." Lauterbach to Joseph Barondess, November 7, 1917, JB, Box 4. It was claimed that all Jewish newspapers run by native Americans were openly anti-Zionist. Naomi Cohen, *The Jewish Experience in America,* p. 156.

explanation for them must be advanced. By acting in concert, Reform Jews demonstrated a lack of faith in the ability of American society to diminish their ethnic visibility. Though reluctant to admit to a group consciousness, Jewish solidarity among assimilationists grew as did the need to defend themselves against such solidarity before the inquiring gaze of non-Jews. Such was the vicious circle enclosing liberal Jews in the United States and England, where the first group had been established to contend with Zionism and what appeared to be a concomitant rise in international anti-Semitism.[31]

The League of American Jews was modeled on its British counter-part, the Anglo-Jewish Association. The accepted leader of the American anti-Zionists was Rabbi David Philipson of Cincinnati, dean of American Reform and heir apparent to the mantle worn by Isaac Mayer Wise. The League of American Jews was discussed at the C.C.A.R. Convention in June, 1918 and a committee of seven, later expanded to thirteen, was appointed to investigate the matter further.[32] The corresponding secretary for the organization, Max Senior, was distressed by the lack of positive response, especially from non-Zionists, with whom it was believed anti-Zionists shared a community of interest. Louis Marshall and Jacob Schiff, both non-national but not opposed to Jewish immigration or to cultural revival in the Holy Land, scored Senior's overtures as harmful and divisive

---

[30] The first response to the Balfour Declaration was, typically, as individuals. Adler, *Jewish Social Studies*, X, 312, 318. Two of the most influential reporters were Vice-Consul Edelman from Jerusalem and Switzerland and the American philanthropist, Oscar S. Straus. Secretary of State Lansing was sufficiently swayed to order a general State Department inquiry into the feelings of American Jews toward the Balfour Declaration. In England, Ambassador Walter Hines Page was told to "discreetly" investigate the reasons for the Balfour statement "relative to a Jewish State in Palestine." Adler, *Jewish Social Studies*, X, 313; Manuel, pp. 170-171; Naomi Wiener Cohen, *A Dual Heritage: The Public Career of Oscar S. Straus* (Philadelphia, 1969), pp. 266-267; Lansing to Page, 867N.01/2a, December 15, 1917 and Page to Lansing, 867N.01/2, December 21, 1917, Supplement Two: The *USFR, 1917, Supplement Two: The World War*, 2 vols. (Washington, 1932) II, 473, 483; Rabinowitz, p. 9.

[31] "League of British Jews" (editorial). *The Jewish Criterion*, 49 (February 15, 1918), 10.

[32] "Rabbis Preach on Lessons From War," *New York Times*, September 8, 1918, p. 12; Zionist Organization of America, *Correspondence on the Advisability of Calling a Conference for the Purpose of Combating Zionism* (New York, 1918) p. 3; Laqueur, *Journal of Contemporary History*, VI, 179; Naomi W. Cohen, *The Jewish Experience in America*, pp. 154-155.

to American Jews as well as refugee Jews who needed an immediate shelter. Because their membership demands were directed only at wealth the League did not appeal at all to the uncommitted majority of Jews in the United States. A minimum contribution of fifty thousand dollars was solicited from those who "valued" their American citizenship.[33] Consequently, a combination of the two factors, the coldness of non-Zionists to the project and fiscal patricianism among anti-Zionists, contributed to the movement's speedy demise.[34]

The second and more impressive display of militant Reform Judaism was the dual presentation of the Kahn petition at Versailles and Washington the following March. By January, 1919, the American Jewish Congress had met and had selected a body of men to attend the Paris Peace Conference. The contingent was instructed by the Zionists and non-Zionists to deal exclusively with the minority rights of Jews living in Europe.[35] A separate Zionist cadre, unconnected with the American Jewish Congress group was to deal with the problem of Palestine. Liberal Judaism remained outside both of these delegations, preferring a course which would in no way identify it with the American Jewish Congress or the pro-Balfourite non-Zionists.[36] The idea that had most recently caught the fancy of the liberals was internationalizing Palestine and it was at the suggestion of a well-known Jewish political figure that the second anti-Zionist campaign was inaugurated.[37]

Julius Kahn, after whom the Kahn petition is named, was of German parentage and held membership at Temple Emanu-El, a

[33] Memorandum of Max Senior, October 16, 1918, American Jewish Committee Archives, New York City (hereafter abbreviated AJC).

[34] Ben Halpern, *The Idea of a Jewish State* (Cambridge, 1961), p. 197; Elmer Berger, *The Jewish Dilemma* (New York, 1945), p. 135.

[35] Solomon Grayzel, *A History of Contemporary Jews from 1900 to the Present* (New York, 1969), pp. 83-84; Janowsky, pp. 290, 303-308; Lawton Kessler, "American Jews and the Paris Peace Conference," *Yivo Annual of Jewish Social Science,* 14 vols. (New York, 1947/48), II, 231-235; Goldblatt, *American Jewish Historical Quarterly,* LVII, 487.

[36] Rabbi Joseph Silverman of New York accused American Zionists of suppressing a cable sent by Weizmann to the Congress, stating that it would be unjust for Jews to ask for a Jewish State. The European leader further suggested Great Britain as Mandatory. "Palestine Proposal Sent to Zionists," *New York Times,* December 23, 1918, p. 6.

large, affluent Reform congregation in San Francisco. He was a Republican congressman from California who was out of sympathy with the Balfour Declaration and Wilson's pro-homeland statements.[38] He was aided by Rabbi Henry Berkowitz, founder of the Jewish Chautauqua Society and Morris Jastrow, Jr., Professor of Semitics at the University of Pennsylvania. A lively correspondence ensued between Jastrow and influential Jewish liberals, for example, E.R.A. Seligman, a Professor of Political Economy at Columbia University and, in 1919, President of the New York based Ethical Culture Society.[39] Both Jastrow and Berkowitz prevailed over Seligman's doubts[40] and the latter assented to be one of those comprising an honorary committee which was to hand the petition to Wilson at the White House on the same day Congressman Kahn was to present it at Paris to the American Commission to Negotiate the Peace.[41]

---

[37] Samuel Goldenson to John Huston Finley, November 19, 1918, JHF, Box 74; Abram Isaacs to Finley, November 29, 1918, JHF, Box 74; Henry Woodrow Hulbert to Finley, December 14, 1918, JHF, Box 74; Morris Jastrow, "Constructive Program for Zionists and Non-Zionists," enclosure in a letter from Edward Lauterbach to Finley, November 18, 1918, JHF, Box 74; "A Solution of the Palestine Problem," *The American Hebrew,* 106 (April 9, 1920), 696, 708; "The Case Against Zionism," *Literary Digest,* 61 (June 14, 1919), 30-31; Philipson, *My Life,* p. 278. The first to propose this solution was Samuel Edelman. Edelman to Louis Marshall, March 28, 1915, AJC.

[38] "Kahn Opposes Zionism," *New York Times,* February 6, 1919, p. 24; Harry Schneiderman, "Julius Kahn," *AJYB,* XXVII (New York, 1925), 238, 242.

[39] Felix Adler, *Nationalism and Zionism* (New York, 1919), pp. 2-14; Elisha M. Friedman, "America and the Israel of Tomorrow," *Israel of Tomorrow,* ed. Leo Jung, 2 vols. (New York, 1949), II, 486.

[40] Jastrow assisted in the in the preparation of the Kahn petition. His friends included Christian anti-Zionists like Herbert Adams Gibbons. Typical of anti-Zionists at this time, he detested Brandeis Zionism because of its "unhistorical approach" to Judaism which effaced two thousand years of Judaism. Jastrow to Edwin R. A. Seligman, January 6, 1919, E.R.A. Seligman Papers (hereafter abbreviated ERAS), Box 34; Jastrow to Seligman, January 18, 1919 and July 23, 1919; Berkowitz to Seligman, February 17, 1919, *Ibid.*

[41] "Protest to Wilson Against Zionist State," *New York Times,* March 5, 1919, p. 7. Although most anti-Zionists gave cursory recognition to opening Palestine as a refuge haven, an important liberal minority would have absolutely nothing whatever to do with it, even if the question were raised by influential non-Jews, Richard T. Ely to Seligman, June 28, 1919, July 19, 1919 and October 19, 1919, ERAS, Box 8.

The Kahn petition aimed to impress qualitatively rather than quantitatively.[42] Recruiting a man of Seligman's stature to the cause was deemed of greater moment than the signature of a thousand average citizens. In all, two hundred ninety-nine signatures were acquired from Jews in thirty-one American cities. The list of names appended to the petition read like a Who's Who of American Jewry: rabbis, playwrights, theatrical producers, judges, diplomats and bank presidents gladly signed the document[43] which was said to have defined the position of "the overwhelming majority of American Jews."[44] A glance at the professional categories reveals that this was not the case. Fifty per cent of the petition signers were businessmen, attorneys, rabbis, medical doctors, college professors and city officials; one-fifth of the aggregate of signers were from New York and Cincinnati.[45]   As was anticipated, the Zionist reaction was defensive rather than belligerent. Although politics was not an issue for Zionists at Paris, a further affirmation was made to the American Jewish public that Zionists had indeed forsworn a political solution.[46] Stephen Wise questioned the President on the

[42] The intention was to "limit ourselves" to one hundred names. Berkowitz to Seligman, February 17, 1919, *Ibid.,* Box 34.

[43] Aside from influential Reform rabbis like Henry Cohen of Galveston, Henry Berkowitz of Philadelphia and Isaac Landman of New York, the best known signers were George Oakes-Ochs, editor of *Current History Magazine,* Henry Morgenthau, E.R.A. Seligman, David Belasco, and Daniel Frohman. *The New York Times,* edited by Adolph Ochs, gave the petition wide coverage. "Cross-Currents in American Judaism," *Current Opinion,* LXVI (May 1919) 314-315; Max Berkowitz, *The Beloved Rabbi: An Account of the Life and Works of Henry Berkowitz* (New York, 1932), p. 92; Morgenthau, *All in a Lifetime,* p. 350; For a complete list of signers, see "Prominent Jews Protest Against Zionism," *The Jewish Review and Observer,* XLV (March 14, 1919), 1, 4.

[44] A reproduction of the document may be found in Morris Jastrow, *Zionism and the Future of Palestine: The Fallacies and Dangers of Political Zionism* (New York, 1919), pp. 151-159. The main provisions of the Kahn petition were the following: (1) it objected to the segregation of the Jews as a national unit (2) it protested against the Zionist reversal of a Jewish historical trend toward emancipation (3) it claimed that Zionism annulled minority rights for Jews in the lands of their birth (4) it said that Palestine was physically unsuited to be a Jewish homeland (5) it proclaimed the dangers of hyphenism, dual allegiance, disloyalty and anti-Semitic revival.

[45] "Prominent Jews Protest Against Zionism," *The Jewish Review and Observer,* XLV (March 14, 1919), 1, 4.

[46] "Zionism is Dead! Long Live Judaism!" (editorial), *The American Hebrew,* 104 (February 7, 1919), 315.

issue of the Kahn petition and received an encouraging reply. Wilson did not favor it and made his position abundantly clear to the Zionists.[47]

The Kahn forces were offered a respite with the arrival at Versailles of Isaac Landman and Henry Morgenthau. The petition had been well-received among anti-Zionists at Paris and experienced wide publicity in the United States.[48] Rabbi Landman, editor of the *American Hebrew*, had come to kick off an anti-Zionist propaganda campaign.[49] Morgenthau's purpose was to link anti-Zionism and State Department objectives in the minds of the peacemakers. Lines of communication between Jews and the American Commission to Negotiate the Peace were opened before Morgenthau's arrival and served to smooth his way.[50]

[47] Wise asked the President about the Kahn protest "and his answer was, 'Has the gentleman protested?' Then I said: 'What will you do, Mr. President, when the protest comes?' His answer was: 'I will accept it.' Then I asked, 'What will you say, Mr. President?' to which he replied, 'I will say nothing.' " Carl Herman Voss, ed., *Stephen S. Wise: Servant of the People Selected Letters* (Philadelphia, 1969), p. 89.

[48] The Kahn insurgency was neither small nor isolated. His cause was championed by an impressive selection of Jews and Christians. A steady stream of anti-national speeches and writings demonstrated that the movement was daily becoming more popular. "Jewish Boys Won Deathless Glory, Says Congressman," *The Jewish Review and Observer*, XLV (February 28, 1919), 1, 4; "The Plain Truth" (editorial), *The American Jewish World*, VII (March 21, 1919), 477; "Editorial" (editorial), *The Hebrew Standard*, LXXII (February 28, 1919), 8. The *Standard* was an Orthodox journal. "Jewish Territorial Sovereignty" (editorial), *The Modern View*, 37 (March 7, 1919), 2; "Arabs Oppose Zionism" (editorial), *The American Hebrew*, 104 (March 28, 1919), 467; "Asserts Split Among Jews is Danger," *The Jewish Review and Observer*, XLV (April 18, 1919), 1, 4; Morris Raphael Cohen, "Zionism, Tribalism or Liberalism," *Zionism Reconsidered: The Rejection of Jewish Normalcy*, ed. Michael Selzer (London, 1970), pp. 65-73; Horace Kallen, *Judaism At Bay* (New York, 1932), pp. 111-112.

[49] Rabinowitz, p. 10. *The American Hebrew*, had become a clearing house for more emotional anti-Zionist stories, penned by *New York World* correspondent Herbert Bayard Swope, *Newark News* reporter Cecil Dorrian, Palestinian war correspondent and member of the so-called "missionary clique" of the *New York Herald*, William T. Ellis and a young journalist for the *New York Globe*, Marion Weinstein. See the *Hebrew* for the following dates: March 14, 1919, March 28, 1919, June 6, 1919, July 4, 18 and 25, 1919, August 29, 1919 and October 22, 1920.

[50] A letter bearing the protests of Morris Jastrow and Simon Rosendale was presented to William Westermann by Professor Herbert Adams Gibbons. Wallace Murray to Judge Moore, 867N.01/469, May 28, 1937, *GRDS: RG 59*.

Along with Abram I. Elkus, Bernard Baruch and Jacob Schiff, Henry Morgenthau had been a supporter of Wilson in 1912.[51] His active membership in the Democratic Party may have been a factor in Wilson's cautious approach to the Zionist issue.[52] During World War I, Morgenthau was Vice-Chairman of the American Committee for Relief in the Near East and was a member of the American Red Cross War Fund Committee.[53] Privately, Morgenthau had written against Zionism to Wilson[54] and had resigned the Presidency of New York's Free Synagogue over Zionist differences with Rabbi Stephen Wise.[55]

At Paris, Morgenthau hedged little in his advocacy of the missionary proposals of Glazebrook and Barton, both of whom he knew.   [56] In a discussion with William Westermann, Morgenthau

[51] Adler, *Jewish Social Studies,* X, 304.

[52]Morgenthau was probably as friendly with Wilson as was Brandeis. Furthermore, Morgenthau was an expert on Near Eastern affairs, having served as Ambassador to Turkey from 1913 to 1916. He was quoted as an authority by Walter Hines Page, American Ambassador to England and, in early 1918, was giving anti-Zionist reports to the French Ambassador in America, Jusserand. Known as a Kahn supporter, Morgenthau's influence in official circles appears to have equaled Brandeis's. Chaim Weizmann to Brandeis, January 16, 1918, LDB; *Summary of Dispatches From the Peace Conference,* March 27, 1919, LDB: Leonard Stein, *The Balfour Declaration* (New York, 1961), p. 358; Burton J. Hendrick, *The Life and Letters of Walter Hines Page,* 3 vols. (Garden City, N.Y., 1923), II, 350-351; David Philipson, "The Late Ambassador Walter Hines Page on Zionism," *The American Hebrew,* 113 (October 12, 1923), 572; Morgenthau, *All in a Lifetime,* pp. 294-295; Manuel, p. 237; "Jews Will Honor Dr. Wise's Memory," *New York Times,* March 11, 1919, p. 5.

[53] Manuel, p. 172.   Although Morgenthau resigned as Vice-President of the American Committee for Relief in the Near East in 1920, he remained on the Board of Trustees into the 1930's. It will be remembered that Henry Churchill King was also a trustee and Charles Crane was the organization's secretary. The Jewish composition on the American Red Cross War Fund Committee is enlightening. Of the nine Jews inscribed on the letterhead only one (Stephen Wise) was a Zionist, two were non-Zionist and six were anti-Zionist. H.C. Jacquith to Albert Shaw, May 7, 1920 and Barclay Acheson to Shaw, November 30, 1932, Albert Shaw Papers, Near East Relief Correspondence 1919-1944, New York Public Library. The letterhead from the Red Cross War Fund Committee may be found on any of the official correspondence of John Huston Finley, JHF, Box 80.

[54] Manuel, p. 172

[55] Haber, p. 59; Morgenthau, *All in a Lifetime,* p. 293; "Quit Because of Zionism," *New York Times,* March 7, 1918, p. 18.

bestowed credit upon Colonel House for suggesting the plan of a unified Turkey under an American trusteeship. When Westermann pointed out that perhaps the establishment of a national home in Palestine would serve to alleviate the social inferiority of the Jew, Morgenthau shot back that the Jews of Great Britain and America felt no such inferiority; American Jews would not go to Palestine and the "real power which would save the oppressed Jews of Eastern Europe lay in American ideals" and protection of these Jews by United States assumption of the mandate for Constantinople. Colonel House had suggested that Morgenthau become Governor General of Constantinople and that American warships be stationed in the Black Sea so that they could look after the Jews of Rumania and Russia. Westermann was aghast: "Talk of the power of the Jews in American politics today. This is my first real knowledge of it and of its cool realization...." Morgenthau then proceeded to outline the boundaries of the Constantinople domain on both sides of the Straits and asked whether the peace commissioners' plan for the Asiatic side coincided with his own. Later, Westermann commented that "the scheme has Zionism beaten in a dozen ways."[57] Westermann dined again with Morgenthau who, for the second time in their brief acquaintance proclaimed that he was not strongly anti-Zionist if the Balfour Declaration was not stretched "too far."[58]

On April 25, Morgenthau conversed with Henry Churchill King and made a deep impression on him.[59] May, 1919, was the month of peak strength for the anti-nationalists; they were never closer to union than at that time. The spark was kindled and rekindled in the United States. The Union of American Hebrew Congregations (U.A.H.C.), the lay arm of the C.C.A.R., declared in favor of Jewish rehabilitation in Palestine but would have nothing to do with either the Balfour Declaration or the Zionists.[60] *The American*

[56] Morgenthau had made a party for Glazebrook. "Honor Dr. Glazebrook," *The American Hebrew*, 102 (December 14, 1917), 178; Simcha Berkowitz, "Felix Frankfurter's Zionist Activities" (unpublished D.H.L. Dissertation, Jewish Theological Seminary, 1971), p. 103.

[57]*PDWLW*, March 27, 1919, p. 50.

[58] Despite the fact that he disliked Morgenthau, Westermann was heavily influenced by the ex-Ambassador's view of the Balfour Declaration. *PDWLW* April 18, 1919, p. 64.

[59] Love pp. 285-286.

Hebrew applauded the various anti-Zionist events at Paris;[61] *The Israelite* scoffed at Zionism as having dwindled to a mere colonization project.[62] Liberal Judaism recalled the words of the late Theodore Roosevelt, that Zionism was incompatible with "good Americanism." Ex-President Taft publicly expressed his doubts as to the wisdom of establishing a Jewish State.[63] Secretary of State Lansing, a Versailles negotiator, had misgivings concerning the compatibility of Zionism and self-determination,[64] but he also believed that Wilson was practically committed to Jewish nationalism. Although, Lansing consistently carried out the

[60] Isaac Landman to Israel Friedlaender, July 9, 1919, IF; "Discuss Problems Confronting American Judaism," *The Jewish Review and Observer*, XLV (May 23, 1919), 1, 6; "Union of Hebrew Congregations Opposes Jewish State," *The Jewish Review and Observer*, XLV (May 30, 1919), 1, Naomi Cohen, *The Jewish Experience in America*, pp. 171-172; "Events in 5679," *AJYB*, XXI (Philadelphia, 1919), p. 185.

[61] "Zionists! Wake UP!" (editorial), *The American Hebrew*, 105 (June 27, 1919), 153-155; "Cross-Currents in American Judaism," *Current Opinion*, LXVI (May 1919), 314.

[62] Naomi W. Cohen, *The Jewish Experience in America*, p. 177. An American Rabbi, Emil Gustav Hirsch, editor of the *Reform Advocate*, until his death in 1923 was a universalist for whom Zionism had no appeal. He told his congregation that he had no objection to the founding of "a" homeland in Palestine as long as it was not "the" homeland. He declared America "and no other" to be his home. Besides, being militantly American, Rabbi Hirsch stressed "our Zionism," the Zionism of the spirit of loyalty to the country of birth and of "social and international justice." Hirsch's thought made a considerable impact on the American Jewish community. Emil G. Hirsch, "Address to the Confirmation Class at Sinai Temple," *Reform Advocate*, LVII (May 31, 1919), 396; "Rabbi Hirsch Returns to Chicago Pulpit," *The Jewish Review and Observer*, XLV (May 9, 1919), 1, 5; Emil G. Hirsch, *My Religion* (New York, 1925), p. 221; S.D. Schwartz, "Emil Gustav Hirsch," *AJYB*, XXVII (Philadelphia, 1925), pp. 230, 235.

[63] "Theodore Roosevelt on Zionism," *Council News*, II (November, 1957), 7; Julius Kahn, "Why Most American Jews Do Not Favor Zionism," *New York Times*, February 16, 1919, Sec. 7, p. 7. Taft later hedged on this. "Mr. Taft Says He Is Not A Zionist," *The American Hebrew*, 105 (June 20, 1919), 137

[64] But he also believed that Wilson was practically committed to Zionism. Adler, *Jewish Social Studies*, X, 309; Esco Foundation, I, 233, 249; Stephen Wise to Louis Brandeis, February 26, 1920 and April 9, 1920, LDB, Voss, p. 98; Howard, *The Partition of Turkey*, p. 226; Military Attache at London (Slocum) to the Chief of Staff of the War Department (March), 763.72119/28741/2, November 27, 1918, *USFR:PPC*: I, 408; Simcha Berkowitz, p. 88.

President's will, he had remained "cold to Zionism." A flow of reports from Hampson Gary, America's Consul in Cairo, to the effect that "Jewish ambitions exceed whatever is implied by the phrase 'Jewish National Home,' " merely confirmed his attitude. He did not respond well to a proposed British plan to jettison the Balfour Declaration and assign the Palestine mandate to the United States: first of all, he reasoned, trusting the British was, at best naive; secondly, he did not want the United States drawn into the European peace. In correspondence with President Wilson, Lansing criticized the Zionist formula because "Jews themselves are divided" on its worth. He recommended that the President reject the Balfour Declaration because Christian sects in the Holy Land would never yield to domination by "the race credited with the death of Christ." [65] Lansing's convictions found favor with Morgenthau, Samuel Edelman and Abram I. Elkus, the anti-Zionist Jews associated with the State Department.

In July, 1919, while King and Crane traveled in the Near East, Morgenthau served on the President's Commission to Poland, investigating the nature of anti-Semitism in that country. He reported Polish-Jewish Zionism to be a disruptive, hurtful element, intruding itself like a sore upon the body politic. Even more alarming, he found that Polish Zionists thought themselves to be Polish separatists fighting for Jewish nationality within Poland without the faintest desire to go to Palestine.[66] By mid-August, when both the Morgenthau and King-Crane Commissions had been heard from, the death of political Zionism seemed all but assured.[67] There was to be no Jewish State in Palestine.[68]

The wave on which anti-Zionism crested in the summer of 1919

---

[65] Lansing was later to deny ever having authored these sentiments. They are distinctly the missionary point of view. *USFR: The Lansing Papers, 1914-1920*, 2 vols. (Washington, 1940), II, 71; Manuel, p. 172; Adler, *Jewish Social Studies*, X, 308-309; "Ex-Secretary Lansing and the Jews," *The New Jewish Chronicle*, III (March 1920), 35; Joseph Jasin, "A Flagrant Fraud," *The New Jewish Chronicle*, III (March, 1920), 44.

[66] Morgenthau, *All in a Lifetime*, pp. 363-364, 383-384.

[67] Naomi Cohen, *The Jewish Experience in America*, pp. 176, 180, 182; "The Week in Review" (editorial), *The American Hebrew*, 105 (July 18, 1919), 221-222; "Letters to the Editor," *The American Hebrew*, 105 (August 29, 1919), 362; Goldblatt, *American Jewish Historical Quarterly*, LVII, 496.

[68] Isaac Landman to Israel Friedlaender, July 19, 1919, IF.

was dissipated shortly thereafter. The missions of Morgenthau and King-Crane did not attract wide attention.   Besides, national liberation movements were popular and Zionism was often regarded as one of them. Liberal Jews were always quick to point out that any similarity between Jewish and non-Jewish state movements was purely incidental. The Irish, Greeks and Armenians, for example, were continuous residents in the lands where they agitated. Jews were eternal exiles, an urban rather than an agricultural people who had no historic claim to the Holy Land because they had been absent from there for eighteen centuries.

In 1920, Rabbi Leo M. Franklin, President of the C.C.A.R. reaffirmed the willingness of that organization to aid in rehabilitating Palestine but rejected as the instrument of that rehabilitation, the Balfour Declaration.[69] The San Remo decision, conferring the Palestine Mandate upon Britain, was acceptable to the C.C.A.R. because it was interpreted as a death blow to Zionism.[70] The Jews, it appeared, would be no more at home in Palestine under a British mandate than they were anywhere else in the world. Settlements of Jews in the Holy Land were presumed to be non-national and the religious principle of "Geulah," Jewish redemption or ingathering was negated. However, provision was made in the San Remo agreement for Zionist participation with the British in the administration of the Mandate.[71]   Thus, the Jewish position in Palestine was distinct from that of Jews in other parts of the world.

[69] Philipson, *AJYB*, XLII, 200; Philipson, *Reform Movement in Judaism*, p. 363; "Rabbis Ask World Field," *The New York Times*, July 16, 1920, p. 10; Samuel Schulman, *The Non-Zionist and the New Palestine* (New York, 1925), p. 8. This was the position of many eminent Jews who rejected nationalism. See, for example, Werner, pp. 97, 173.

[70] The C.C.A.R. refused to participate in a Zionist celebration for the San Remo Conference because they did not acknowledge the presentation of the Mandate to England as a Zionist victory. Philipson, *AJYB*, XLII, 200-201; Philipson, *Reform Movement in American Judaism*, p. 363. The verdict at San Remo was much the same among anti-Zionist organizations, publicists and writers. The Mandate meant that there would be no state. Naomi Cohen, *The Jewish Experience in America*, p. 170; "Next Year in Jerusalem" (editorial), *The Scribe*, II (April 2, 1920), 5; "The Status of Palestine" (editorial), *The Modern View*, 40 (May 7, 1920), 2; "Britain to be Mandatory in Palestine" (editorial), *The American Hebrew*, 106 (April 30, 1920), 769; "Dr. Philipson on the British Mandate," *Denver Jewish News*, VI (May 5, 1920), 1; "Israel Not A Nation" (editorial), *The New York Times*, July 7, 1920, p. 10.

The Zionists were jubilant and the liberals dismayed. At least, said one Reform rabbi, Zionist separatists were not coming to the United States to cause the same exclusiveness and clannishness within the American Jewish community which was then extant in Palestine.[72]

Although not yet apparent, there was soon to be a shift in attitude toward Zionism on the part of "liberal" Jews. The change was dictated by two events: the separation of the Brandeis-Mack Zionists from Weizmann and the challenge presented to the Reform community in America after the Congressional quota laws were enacted in 1921 and 1924. The adoption of "softer" lines on Zionism by the C.C.A.R. and U.A.H.C. indicated that organized Reform Judaism, despite inner pressures to maintain the status quo, was prepared to alter its attitude on Palestine.

The first organized attack of Arabs upon Jews in Palestine occurred in Jerusalem between April 4 and April 6, 1920. Arab extremists, encouraged by British officials, fomented a riot. In three days, six Arabs and six Jews had been killed in the unequal battle in which Jewish volunteer forces were "prevented by the British army from entering the Old City to come to the defense of their unarmed brethren." In the aftermath twenty Jews were arrested and given sentences of fifteen years for arms possession.[73] An equal number of Arabs were arrested, including Haj Amin el Husseini.

Guilt for the disturbances was assigned by "liberals" to Bolshevized, Zionist Jews.[74] Orthodox Jewry, whose dream was messianic return to Palestine through divine intervention and the reestablishment of a theocracy, skilfully employed the identical argument against the Zionists[75] as did the State Department, which was still receiving reports from Jerusalem consul Otis Glazebrook.[76] Under British rule, the thought of Palestine for refugees had become tolerable to anti-nationalists but the thought of Zionist

---

[71] Through the Jewish Agency which, in 1920, was synonymous with the W.Z.O. Israel Cohen, pp. 82, 110. At this time, the Jewish Agency was established under the authority of the Mandate and was an official agency of the Government.

[72] Naomi W. Cohen, *The Jewish Experience in America*, p. 157.

[73] Ronald Storrs, *Orientations* (London, 1937), p. 388; William L. Hull, *The Fall and the Rise of Israel* (Grand Rapids, 1954), pp. 140-142; Antonius, p. 313; Israel Cohen, *A Short History of Zionism*, p. 81.

[74] "Pogroms in Palestine" (editorial), *The Modern View*, 30 (April 9, 1920), 2; "Moslem-Christian Opposition to Zionism" *Literary Digest, 65 (May 15, 1920)*, 48.

inspired "Red radicalism"[77] was still an obstacle to a satisfactory conciliation between American Jews and American Jewish Zionists.[78] Closing out this eventful year, the Balfour Declaration was incorporated into the Treaty of Sevres with Turkey in August, 1920 and may have been a cause for a renewed concentration by Reform on the evils of race nationalism and political Zionism.[79]

Quota laws presented a new problem to American Jewish liberals. They came to realize that they were supporting two antithetical positions: immigration curbs in Palestine and immigration curbs in America. With the doors to Western Europe closing, Jews would have no outlet. The leaders of Reform were compelled to be concerned or lose their constituents who were. No suitable alternative, however, was immediately apparent. As a matter of fact, other concerns were still central to Reform thought. In

[75] Ephraim Deinard, *Aruchas Bas Ami* (in Hebrew, St. Louis, 1920), pp. 12-14, 55-64, 86-96, 100. Orthodoxy also had as little use for European Zionism because, in their estimation, both were exclusively political and atheistic. From the time of the issuance of the Balfour Declaration, Orthodoxy feared an irreligious, secular takeover in Palestine by the Zionists, especially in the schools. Ephraim Deinard, *Pachdu B'Tzion Chatoim* (in Hebrew, Arlington, N.J., 1917), 4-5, 10-11, 25-28, 43-49; Ephraim Deinard, *Tzion B'Ad Mi?* (in Hebrew, Arlington, N.J., 1918) pp. 71-77, 94-115, 188-190.

[76] Manuel, pp. 291-292.

[77] "Rabbi Harrison Presents the Jewish Question," *The Jewish Review and Observer*, XLVI (November 12, 1920), 1, 4; Joseph Leisler, "Emil G. Hirsch: An Appreciation," *The Union Bulletin*, XI (May 1921), 26.

[78] As late as November, 1920, the C.C.A.R. refused to participate in a Zionist convention, although they did subscribe to the beliefs of individual Zionists, for example, Julian Mack. "Are the Political Zionists Sincere" (editorial) *The American Hebrew*, III (June 2, 1922), 84, 96; Edward J. Cohn, "The Zionist Convention," *The American Hebrew*, 108 (December 3, 1920), 84, 102-103.

[79] Marcus Aron, "What a Layman Can Do For Judaism," *The Union Bulletin*, XI (May 1921), 10, 27. Rabbi Philipson approved heartily of a highly provocative article written by a Yale professor and Assyriologist who declaimed against racial Judaism in Palestine. "Rabbi Wise Rebukes Rabbi Philipson for Approving Anti-Semitic Article," *The Jewish Tribune*, 37 (February 11, 1921), 14. Reform Jews were also fearful of anti-Semitism, which in the early 1920's was enjoying a revival sponsored by Henry Ford's *Dearborn Independent* and several Anglo-Saxon newssheets. This, also, contributed to new assaults on Jewish nationalism by liberal Jews. See, for example, Voss, p. 101; *The Dearborn Independent*, 4 vols. (n.p. 1920-1922), I, 88-95, 98-99, 131, 144, 159, 167-168, 193, 206, 224, 228-231, II, 25, 57, 67-68, III, 100-101, 111, 115, 118-127, 135-140, IV, 62-66, 117-118, 153-154, 180, 185, 190-191, 195; *Gentile Tribune*, February 9 and 23, 1922.

deference to one of these, "Americanism,"[80] it had even been suggested that the terms "Jew" and "synagogue" be abandoned as too foreign and too closely associated with the "oriental Palestinian homeland." Instead, American "Hebrews" would assume the national name of "The Reformed Church of American Israelites." Saturday services, regarded as incompatible with the American milieu, were to be changed to Sunday.[81] Organized Reform offered no opinion on these revolutionary theological proposals, although individual viewpoints ranged from high praise to derogation.[82]

The split in Zionism between Brandeis and Weizmann in 1921 began a reordering of Reform priorities that did not end until liberal Judaism had become a partner to the Jewish Agency for Palestine and had converted its prewar philosophy into one which could exist amicably with the national home idea of the Balfour Declaration. Divided Zionism, according to Reform rabbis, was less of a threat to Jewish stability in America and seemed to offer a choice as well. Seen without Weizmann, the Brandeis position was less political and more oriented toward economic investment and free enterprise. American minority Zionists seemed more concerned with stabilizing the present Jewish population in Palestine rather than shoveling in more. It was also attractive that Brandeis deemphasized Jewish cultural nationalism, which was basic to the European philosophy.[83]

[80] "Jews Aim to Halt Drift from Faith," *The New York Times,* May 25, 1921), p. 17; "Rebukes Dr. Weizmann," *The Modern View,* 42 (June 3, 1921), 16.

[81] *CCARY,* XXVIII, 141-142;; Naomi Cohen, *The Jewish Experience in America,* p. 172; Isaac W. Bernheim, *The Reform Church of American Israelites* (n.p., 1921), pp. 4-7, 10.

[82] Naomi Cohen, *The Jewish Experience in America,* p. 173; "Bernheim Article Provokes Much Discussion," *The Jewish Review and Observer,* XLVII (October, 21, 1922), 1; Isaac W. Bernheim, *An Open Letter to Rabbi Stephen S. Wise* (Louisville, 1922), pp. 1, 6-10.

[83] "The Zionists Split," *Literary Digest,* 70 (July 9, 1921), 28; Simcha Berkowitz, p. 296; "The Zionist Situation" (editorial) *The Scribe* IV, (May 13, 1921), 3; "The America Palestine Company" (editorial), *The American Hebrew,* 108 (March 25, 1921), 521-522. It must be remembered, however, that there remained important Jewish liberals who detested Brandeis as much as Weizmann. The events of 1921-1922 simply indicate a "softening" trend. It was years before the Reform movement as a whole felt at ease with Brandeis. "A Serious Schism" (editorial), *The Modern View,* 42, (May 6, 1921), 2; "Dr. Weitzmann Parts from the American Zionists" (editorial), *Emanu-El,* LII (May 6, 1921), 2-3; Harold Berman, "Zionism at the Crossroads," *Reform Advocate,* 61 (June 11, 1921), 584-585; Goldblatt, *American Jewish Historical* Quarterly, LVII, 488; "The Zionist Break at Cleveland," *The Modern View,* 42 (June 10, 1922), 2.

But, Brandeis was dethroned: the Cleveland Convention of 1921 had ousted him and the majority of American Zionists were now affiliated with the World Zionist Organization (W.Z.O.) more closely than they had ever been.[84] Reform Jews saw an opportunity to change the direction of Zionism, but who would be their ally: the group in power, with whom they had little in common, or the schismatic Brandeisians who had initiated an independent program of their own in Palestine to which liberal Judaism could subscribe?[85]

Feelers were extended to Weizmann upon his visit to America in April, 1921, but the European leader promised nothing.[86] Smarting at the rebuff, Reform journals derided Zionism as "un-American." New riots in Palestine on May Day, 1921, triggered vehement denunciations of Jewish nationalism. Zionists were censured for instigating unrest and rebellion in the Near East; their presence could be maintained only with the force of British Arms.[87] *The American Hebrew* compared the shaky foundation of the Zionist "state" to that of the Spanish republics of Latin America.[88] Certain developments, however, caused the *Hebrew* and several other journals to withhold judgment on the Brandeis wing, namely the establishment by the minority Zionists of Palestine Development Leagues (P.D.L.) and the American Palestine Company, both of which were apolitical and economic.[89]

---

[84] The history of Brandeis Zionism will be discussed in a separate chapter.

[85] "How Palestine Will be Rebuilt" (editorial), *The American Hebrew*, 108 (May 6, 1921) 735-736.

[86] "Dr. Weizmann and the Non-Zionist," *The American Hebrew*, 108 (April 15, 1921), 588-589; "Scrap Zionism, Build Palestine" (editorial) *The American Hebrew*, 108 (April 29, 1921), 209-210; Elmer Berger, *Judaism or Jewish Nationalism: The Alternative to Zionism* (New York, 1957), p. 182.

[87] "May Riots in Palestine," *The American Hebrew*, 110 (December 23, 1921), 174, 183, 191; "Jaffa Riots Last May Due to Jewish Communists," *Denver Jewish News*, VII (November 16, 1921), 1; "The Conflict in Palestine" (editorial), *The Modern View*, 42 (May 13, 1921), 3; The new American consul in Jerusalem, Addison Southard, also held the Jews responsible. His reports stated that Palestine needed cooperation between Arab and Jew, not political Zionism. "United States Consul Reports on Zionist Bank," *Denver Jewish News*, VII (November 16, 1921), 1; Manuel, pp. 292-294.

[88] Naomi Cohen, *The Jewish Experience in America, p. 175.*

[89] "The Palestine Development League" (editorial), *The American Hebrew*, 109 (July 8, 1921), 192.

Ratification of the mandate by the League Council did not occur until July 24, 1922. The text of the mandate was the result of three years' discussion between the English Government and the Zionist Organization. The conception of a Jewish national home was supported by articles one and two of the Mandate, but any political connotation, that is to say any Jewish advance beyond "the development of self-governing institutions" to commonwealth was avoided.[90] Great Britain was anxious to gain United States approval for the Mandate.[91] Since America was not a League member, a separate treaty between the United States and England would be necessary.[92] For the present, however, an informal gesture would suffice.

The Zionists were equally determined in their efforts to elicit the good wishes of the United States because it had been President Wilson's reply to the Balfour Declaration which had been most encouraging. As Robert Lansing had noted, Balfourism had by 1919, become the de facto policy of America with regard to Palestine.[93] Two years later Britain and the Zionists strove for *de jure* recognition.

State Department officials opposed the political complications for America inherent in the Balfour Declaration.[94] They were gratified to read that a former Jewish colleague, Henry Morgenthau, regarded Zionism as the "most stupendous fallacy in Jewish history," a betrayal of the Jewish past, offering the Jews promises it could not

[90] The complete text of the mandate is given in Israel Cohen, *The Zionist Movement* (New York, 1946). Excerpts may be found in Israel Cohen, *A Short History of Zionism,* pp. 102, 250-253.

[91] America was anxious to protect its rights in the former Ottoman Empire in exchange for renunciation of former treaty and capitulatory rights. The United States signed almost identical agreements covering Syria, Lebanon and Iraq. The idea for separate Conventions outside the Mandate originated in America.

[92] The formal convention between the United States and Britain was concluded on December 3, 1924 and ratified exactly one year later. Among other things, it said that changes in the Mandate could not be undertaken without American consent. Fannie Fern Andrews, *The Holy Land Under Mandate,* 2 vols. (Boston, 1931), II, 393-394.

[93] Esco Foundation, I, 246.

[94] Including Allen Dulles, the brother of President Eisenhower's Secretary of State who, in 1922, was Chief of the Near East Division of the State Department. Manuel, pp. 277-281.

keep. He said that the Balfour Declaration had caused irreligious, unspiritual and unscrupulous Zionists to mislead their followers. For a Jew, concluded Morgenthau, Zionism was an economically impossible solution. Claiming to speak for the American Jewish majority, he ardently proclaimed America to be his Jerusalem.[95]

As Secretary of State, Charles Evans Hughes divorced himself from Zionism, pursuing a policy of maintaining economic and commercial parity with the European powers in Palestine.[96] He was approached by American and European Zionists who, by November, 1921, were attempting to secure the support of congressmen and senators for a proposed declaration of sympathy for British assumption of the Mandate.[97] If approved, the declaration would not only consent to a British Mandate but to the operation of that Mandate through the Balfour Declaration. Hughes, who was apparently influenced by Warren Robbins of the Near East Division of the State Department, offered a legal argument to Senator Charles Curtis of Kansas who, at this time, was contemplating the introduction of a pro-homeland resolution into Congress. Trying to dissuade Curtis, Hughes wrote that he saw no reason for the passage of such a resolution. The matter of Palestine could be clarified only by a definitive peace treaty with Turkey. In the meantime, no action from the American Government should be expected.[98]

Despite the intransigence of the State Department and Hughes, a

[95] Morgenthau, *All in a Lifetime*, pp. 385-404; "Zionism as a Stupendous Fallacy," *Literary Digest*, 70 (July 30, 1921), 30-31; "America Our Zion Says Morgenthau Assailing Zionism," *The World*, June 27, 1921, p. 22; "A Jewish Opponent of Zionism" (editorial), *The New York Evening Post*, July 9, 1921, p. 5. The Morgenthau article was considered a "trenchant" summary of the anti-national argument and was favorabley publicized. "Zionism as the Most Stupendous Fallacy in Jewish History," *Current Opinion*, LXXI (August 1921), 200-203; "Mr. Morgenthau and Zionism" (editorial), *The American Hebrew*, 109 (July 8, 1921), 192, 204; "Morgenthau's Peace With the Turks," *The Jewish Tribune*, 37 (September 16, 1921), 6; 'Morgenthau on Zionism," *The Union Bulletin*, XI (June-July 1921), 10.

[96] *USFR: 1922*, 2 vols. (Washington, 1938), I, 130, II, 270, 275-277; *USFR: 1921*, 2 vols. (Washington, 1936), I, 923-924, II, 95, 97, 99-105.

[97] Hughes shunted all the Zionists off to underlings, including Weizmann's representative, Nahum Sokolow. Charles Evans Hughes to George B. Christian, Jr., 867N.01/171, October 11, 1921 and Warren Robbins to Henry P. Fletcher, 867N.01/188, November 22, 1921, *GRDS: RG 59*; Richard P. Stevens, *American Zionism and U.S. Foreign Policy 1942-1947* (New York, 1962) p. 63; "Harding on Zionism," *The Jewish Tribune*, 38 (December 2, 1921), 2.

bill was introduced into the House of Representatives on April 4, 1922 by the freshman congressman from New York, Hamilton Fish. Eight days later, a kindred resolution was read before the Senate by Henry Cabot Lodge. The Fish resolution was turned over to the House Foreign Affairs Committee. Interested parties were encouraged to testify either for or against it.[99]

The debate in the Foreign Affairs Committee spurred a national Jewish interest. Louis Lipsky, President of the Zionist Organization of America (Z.O.A.) arrived in Washington to aid the cause. Ohio representative James Begg pressed Lipsky on the nature of a United States commitment in the event of the resolution's passage. When questioned by Tom Connally of Texas on the issue of American Jews returning to Palestine, Congressman Albert B. Rossdale answered that the Holy Land was a refugee haven for those fleeing Eastern Europe.[100]

The Congressional hearings lasted five days, three of which were devoted to an elaboration of the anti-Zionist argument by Jews, non-Jews and Arabs. Reform Judaism had yet to reconcile itself to the Balfour Declaration and would not stay silent if given the opportunity to revive its case before the public. On April 20, Rabbi

[98] Hughes to Charles Curtis, 867N.01/162A, October 11, 1921 and Robbins to Hughes, F.W. 867N.01/172A, October 11, 1921, *GRDS:RG59;* Manuel pp. 275-276.

[99] For a history of this resolution, see U.S. Congress, Congressional Record, *Sixty-Seventh Congress, Second Session on H. Con, Res. 52, S.J.R. 191, H.J.R. 307, H.J.R. 308 and H.J.R. 322, a Bill Expressing the Satisfaction of the Congress of the United States in the Rebuilding of Palestine by the Jews* (Washington, 1922). Part 5, pp. 5035, 5376, 5693, 5759-5760, 5894, 6240, part 6, p. 6289, part 8, pp. 7937, 8080, part 9, p. 9134, part 10, pp. 9799-9801, 9809, 9813-9815, 9818.

[100] *Hearings...Committee on Foreign Affairs...on H. Con. Res. 52*, pp. 2-15.

[101] *Hearings...Committee on Foreign Affairs...on H. Con. Res. 52*, pp. 65-67, 92-116; Friedman, *Israel of Tomorrow*, II, 490; "Dr. Landman Upheld in Stand on Zionism," *The New York Times*, May 1, 1922, p. 8; "Pure Treason" (editorial), *The Hebrew Standard*, LXXIX (May 12, 1922), 8. By 1922, the *Standard* evinced a pro-Zionist attitude, having altered its anti-Zionist stance of 1917-1921. With the exception of Agudas Yisroel and some Christian elements, Orthodox Jews had become enthusiastic supporters of Zionism and remained so. Reuben Fink, *America and Palestine* (New York, 1944), p. 41; "The Lodge-Fish Resolution of 1922," *Palestine*, I (February, 1944), 7; "The Zionist Disease and Its Cure" (editorial), *The American Hebrew*, 110 (April 28, 1922), 665, 688; Morris Lazaron, "Jewish State Opposed," *Palestine: Jewish Homeland?* ed. Julia E. Johnson (New York, 1946), pp. 174-179; Philipson, *My Life*, pp. 303-304.

Isaac Landman appeared before the House Foreign Relations Committee to oppose the establishment of a Palestinian Jewish State and to revile the Fish resolution. On the following day, Rabbi Morris Lazaron, a Southerner and defender of the King-Crane Report, said that he did not want to go to Palestine but would cooperate with Jews who did because he countenanced the United States immigration ban. David Philipson of Cincinnati affirmed that Zionism was the product of an East European invasion and that those espousing it were aliens in the countries where they lived. Stephen G. Porter of New York, Chairman of the House Foreign Affairs Committee asked Zionists and anti-Zionists a number of barbed questions. He admitted regret at "getting involved" with the Near East and concurred with the doctrine of Jewish responsibility for Palestine unrest.   After he testified before the Committee,[101] Philipson proudly acknowledged that Porter had conceded his distaste for Zionism: "Mr. Porter... told me that, in his opinion, I had performed one of the greatest services for the Jews of the United States that had ever been performed by anyone."   The Rabbi remarked that the United States should refrain from making any statement on Palestine because it was a matter of purely Jewish concern.[102] The C.C.A.R. disavowed Philipson as a spokesman for the group but nevertheless formally condemned the Lodge-Fish Resolution.[103]

Congress became convinced that the Resolution was a harmless statement of sympathy for dispossessed Jews. The Foreign Affairs Committee was deeply affected by the anti-national protestations but was unable to discern any danger for the United States if the bill was passed.[104]   Hamilton Fish, an isolationist, had admitted the document's apolitical nature and Zionists had stressed the upbuilding of Palestine as a refugee homeland.[105] No reference had ever been made to American action in case of trouble or disquiet in the Holy Land; there were no binding commitments for the United

[102] *Hearings...Committee on Foreign Affairs...on H. Con. Res. 52*, pp. 82, 96, 98; Philipson, *My Life*, p. 303.

[103] "Rabbi Landman Called 'Traitor,' " *The Jewish Tribune*, 39 (April 28, 1922), 6; Max Rhoade, "The American Balfour Declaration," *The Jewish Tribune*, 93 (October 19, 1928), 1, 6; "Rosenwald Denies, Calisch Admits Anti-Zionist Protest," *Denver Jewish News*, VIII (May 17, 1922), 5.

[104] *Congressional Record, Sixty-Seventh Congress, Second Session*, part 10, pp. 9813-9815.

States to enforce Jewish will. It was a moral document and carried the weight of American morality, but nothing else. The State Department and Secretary Hughes eventually arrived at the same view and said, while they did not propose such a resolution, there was "no objection to its adoption."[106]

Although "liberal" Judaism did not assume a passive attitude, it could not agree upon the declaration's significance. Some editorials said the whole debate was meaningless and should be dropped.[107] By dragging Jewish interests before the American people, said others, Judaism risked an anti-Semitic upsurge. Some credibility for this asseveration was provided by the popularity of Henry Ford's *Dearborn Independent*. Others like *The New York Times*, the *Israelite*, the *American Hebrew*, the *B'nai B'rith Messenger* and *The Scribe* declared that Zionism had run its course and the formal assumption of the Mandate by Great Britain was the coup de grace for political Zionism.[108] A more personal approach was taken by some individual Jews who tended to equate anti-Zionism with American patriotism. It was feared that Zionism would revive all the

[105] Arthur T. Weil, "The 77th Congress," *The American Hebrew*, 148 (December 6, 1940), 8, 13; U.S. Congress, *Congressional Record, Seventy-Second Congress, First Session* (Washington, 1932), part 13, 13912-13914.

[106] Lodge to Hughes, 867N.01/199, April 10, 1922, *GRDS:RG59*. Later, in September, when the British invited the United States to an innocuous international commission to oversee the Holy Places, Hughes, prompted by Dulles, refused. The American retreat from Wilsonism with regard to Palestine was complete. H.G.D. to Allen Dulles, 867N.01/199, September 19, 1922 and Dulles to Hughes, 867N.01/199, October 24, 1922, *GRDS:RG59*; Evans, p. 265; The resolution was signed by Harding on September 21, 1922. Subsequent endorsements were given by Presidents Coolidge, Hoover and Roosevelt, though it is doubtful that they really understood or cared about the resolution and its importance to the Jews. Hull, p. 148.

[107] Gerson B. Levi, "Editorial," *Reform Advocate*, LXII (July 29, 1922), 689-690.

[108] "The *Day* Sees the Light" (editorial), *The American Hebrew*, 111 (June 30, 1922), 169; "A Policy, Not A Provocation" (editorial), *The American Hebrew*, 110 (May 5, 1922), 693; "The Lodge Resolution" (editorial, *The Scribe*, VI (May 12, 1922), 3; A. Rosenthal, "A Useless Resolution," *The Modern View*, 44 (May 5, 1933), 3; "Zionism's Misfortune" (editorial), *B'nai Brith Messenger*, XXVI (June 9, 1922), 6; "Save it from its Friends" (editorial), *B'nai Brith Messenger*, XXVI (June 16, 1922), 6; "Confusion Worse Confounded" (editorial), *The New York Times*, May 7, 1922, Sec. 2, p. 6; "A Dangerous Movement" (editorial) *The New York Times*, May 28, 1922, Sec. 2, p. 4.

old prejudices and create some new ones. Before it could damage Christian sensibilities, Jewish nationalism was harangued by American Jewish liberals. They averred that Zionism aroused Jewish disloyalty, promoted dual allegiance, disregarded Jewish mission, harbored fanatics and encouraged Jewish particularism as evidenced by the talk of a "Jewish vote."[109]

The Churchill Memorandum of July 3, 1922, stating that British policy did not contemplate the subordination of the Arab people to the Jews but did intend to limit Jewish immigration into Palestine in accordance with the principle of "economic absorptive capacity," undercut the tenuous obligations incurred by Great Britain under the Balfour Declaration and rendered the United States declaration of sympathy pointless. Adoph Ochs, editor of *The New York Times*, believed that a modification of the Balfour Declaration would have a salutary influence upon Arab-Jewish relations and,[110] in concert with the American Jewish press, congratulated England for her acumen.[111] Generally, liberals looked upon the depressed state of Zionism with anticipation. It was an opportune time to enter the Zionist movement and possibly redirect it. In July, 1922, the Palestine Development League of Brandeis merged with the C.C.A.R. on the matter of Palestinian rehabilitation.[112]

Reform, then, had subtly changed its tactics since 1917. The

[109] "Opinions on Zionist Resolution," *The American Hebrew*, 110 (May 5, 1922), 924; Samuel Bowman, "Are the Jewish People a Nation, A Race or a Religious Entity," *The Modern View*, 44 (April 28, 1922), 9, 12; "Letters on Zionism," *The American Hebrew*, 111, (May 26, 1922), 66; "A Dangerous Movement" (editorial), *The New York Times*, May 28, 1922, Sec. 2, p. 4; Goldblatt, *American Jewish Historical Quarterly*, p. 488.

[110] The assumption of the Mandate by the British and the Churchill White Paper meant that no Jewish political entity could be established in Palestine. "Editorial" (editorial), *The Hebrew Standard*, LXXX (August 18, 1922), 8; Gerson B. Levi, "Another Chapter of Revelation," *Reform Advocate* LXI (March 5, 1921) 101-102; "A New Era For Palestine" (editorial), *The American Hebrew*, 111 (July 28, 1922), 257; "Zion's Day of Rejoicing," *Literary Digest*, 74 (August 10, 1922), 35; "Dr. Weitzmann's attitude" (editorial), *Emanu-El*, LVI (August 18, 1922), 2; Naomi Cohen, *The Jewish Experience in America*, p. 182.

[111] Judd L. Teller, *Strangers and Natives: The Evolution of the American Jew from 1921 to the Present* (New York, 1968), p. 176; Gerald W. Johnson, *An Honorable Titan: A Biographical Study of Adolph S. Ochs* (New York, 1946) pp. 260-261, 263; Louis Rich, "Adolph S. Ochs" *AJYB*, XXXVII (Philadelphia, 1935), pp 36, 50-51; Adolph S. Ochs, "The Truth About Palestine," *The Israelite*, April 27, 1922 (reprint, n.p., n.d.), pp. 5-6, 8. Ochs' father-in-law was Isaac Mayer Wise.

death of Zionism was no longer contemplated because the British had destroyed its political incitement.[113] Proof of this was offered by Israel Zangwill, at this time a territorialist but also an early follower of Herzl, who informed a gathering of the American Jewish Congress that he had become disillusioned with British pledges and Zionists' abilities to lift themselves above the mire of "cheap... diaspora nationalism." Britain, he declared was sustaining a Jewish puppet state to act as a buffer for the interests of the Empire along the Suez Canal. Consequently, Palestine was not then nor would it ever be "Jewish nor national nor a home; it is simply another outpost in the diaspora."[114]

Zangwill's speech was regarded as a triumph for the anti-nationalists.[115] But it also had less immediate, more far-reaching, effects: it

[112] The conversations, however, took many months to conclude. Jacob De Haas to Louis Brandeis, May 5, 1922, LDB; "Zionists and Non-Zionists United to Build Palestine," *The American Hebrew*, 111 (June 23, 1922), 152; "Central Conference of American Rabbis Convenes at Cape May," *The American Hebrew*, 111 (June 30, 1922), 257; "Harmony for Jewish Homeland in Palestine," (editorial), *Denver Jewish News*, VIII (October 25, 1922), 4; Gerson B. Levi, "Editorial," *Reform Advocate*, LXIII (July 29, 1922), 689-690.

[113] In 1917, Zionism and Palestine were not discussed at the U.A.H.C. Convention. In 1923, economic rehabilitation of the Holy Land was discussed but all the pertinent resolutions were tabled by the "old men" like Morgenthau who were still the leaders of liberal Judaism. De Haas to Brandeis, February 7, 1923, LDB; Alexander Lyons, "What I would have Said," *Denver Jewish News*, IX (February 21, 1923), 1; Louis Lipsky, *Thirty Years of American Zionism* (n.p., 1927), pp. 225-229; "Jews' Stand on Vital Questions," *The New York Times*, January 27, 1923, p. 4; "Rabbi Foster Denies Attack on Zionism at Williamstown," *The Jewish Tribune*, 44 (August 28, 1925), 7.

[114] "Zangwill Calls Political Zionism a Vanished Hope," *The New York Times*, October 15, 1923, p. 1. Diaspora nationalism is simply the presence of Jewish separatist movements in countries outside Palestine. Liberal Judaism declaimed against it. Territorialism refers to the settlement of oppressed Jews in all parts of the world rather than concentrating them in Palestine. Territorialists suggested Birobijan, Africa, South America and British Guiana as areas for Jewish settlement. Usually, they ignored Palestine.

[115] Especially since Zangwill was a disillusioned Zionist. Zangwill's speech, it was hoped, would foster a new commitment by all Jews to an apolitical cultural and economic program for Palestine. "Trifling With the Truth" (editorial, *The American Hebrew*, 113 (November 9, 1923), 691; "A Problem Larger than Palestine," *The American Hebrew*, 113 (November 9, 1923), 688; "Zangwill's Zip at Zionism" (editorial), *Brooklyn Jewish Chronicle*, I (October 26, 1923), 3; "Zanwillian View of the Problems," (editorial, *Emanu-El*, LVII (November 16, 1923), 2; "The Zangwill Controversy," *The Scribe*, IX (November 16, 1923), 3;

enabled warring sectors of American Jewry to proceed in easy stages toward Palestinian cooperation by prompting a closer tie between "liberal" Judaism and Zionism. The bond between them, however, never functioned to inhibit the anti-Zionist fulminations of the assimilationists. The time and money subscribed to the economic rehabilitation of Palestine by the one hand of liberal Judaism was taken away by the other. During their six year understanding prior to their entry into the Jewish Agency, liberals participated in several Palestinian projects, among them the harnassing of electric power from the Jordan River and the completion of the Hebrew University.[116] Despite their lack of trust in the Balfour Declaration, the leaders of Reform had been reluctantly converted to it through the simple expedient of day-to-day cooperation with the Brandeis minority.[117] Shared obligation, however, could and would never still their tongues on the incongruity of Zionism and American Jewish patriotism.[118] The American Jewish Congress, said Simon

"Zangwillian View of the Problems" (editorial) *Emanu-El,* LVII (November 16, 1923), 2; "Zangwill Was Right" (editorial), *The Scribe,* IX (November 16, 1923), 3; "The Zangwill Controversy," *The Scribe,* IX (November 16, 1923), 4; Gerson B. Levi, "Editorial," *Reform Advocate,* LXVI (November 3, 1923), 395-396.

[116] *CCARY,* XXXIII (Richmond, Va. 1923), p.24; Samuel Schulman, *The University in Jerusalem: A Symbol of Secular Palestine* (New York, 1925), pp. 1-12; "The Hebrew University" (editorial) *B'nai Brith Messenger,* 28 (April 24, 1925); "Zion's First University," *Literary Digest,* 85 (April 25, 1925), 32-33.

[117] Judge Julian Mack had certain reservations concerning the ability of anti-Balfourites to forsake their old position on Judaism. Talks between Zionists and anti-Zionists, begun with the best intentions usually degenerated into meaningless, inconclusive affairs. Often, the common bond between them, a dislike for Weizmannism and majority American Zionism, was not an adequate basis for an understanding. On the other hand, Reform Judaism still had doubts about the economic feasibility of the various Palestinian projects envisioned by Brandeis and were known to speak in favor of an all-Zionist-Non-Zionist conference uniting the factions in both movements. Jacob De Haas, January 19, 1924, De Haas to Barondess, January 18, 1924, Barondess to De Haas, January 19, 1924, De Haas to Barondess, January 7, 1924, Edwin Lewisohn to Barondess, January 11, 1924 and Barondess to Lewisohn, January 14, 1924, JB, Box 5; Mack to De Haas, February 14, 1923, LDB; "Nathan J. Miller on Palestine," *The American Hebrew,* 113 (May 18, 1923) 2, 17; "Winning Palestine Without Losing America," *The American Hebrew,* 113 (June 22, 1923), 113; "Editorial Comment" *The American Hebrew,* 113 (May 18, 1923), 3-4, 14; "Rabbi Landman Calls on Jews to Meet Emergency," *Denver Jewish News, X (February 7, 1924), 2.*

[118] "Non-Zionists and Palestine Reconstruction," *The American Hebrew,* 113 (July 20, 1923), 198.

Rosendale, was detrimental to Judaism in the United States. The Congress, it may be recalled, was populated with Brandeis Zionists. A strange state of affairs indeed: liberals worked with the Brandeisians one day and attacked them the next.[119] The role they played so often was that of devil's advocate, detractor of political Zionism and defender of havenism. Often, within the same address, Zionism was evil and virtuous, an economic paradise, a charitable venture for the downtrodden but also arachaic and a spur to the world-wide anti-Semitism.[120] The revulsion against Zionism was often great enough to recall territorialism with nostalgia and trot it out as a better solution to ravaged Judaism than Zionism ever was.[121] The resettlement of Jews in Russia, an undertaking initiated and financed by the Jewish Joint Distribution Committee, was also a suitable alternative for Reform when it periodically concluded that Zionism was not the answer.[122]

In 1924, the C.C.A.R. reaffirmed its 1920 stand on nationalism but recommended the cooperation of Reform with Zionism in the

---

[119] The paradox may be obviated if one realizes that the objective of Reform Jews was to enter the Zionist movement and modify it. Whether they allied with Brandeis or Weizmann was, at least initially, immaterial. They did realize that Weizmann held the balance of power. Louis Lipsky, President of the American majority loyal to Weizmann, had shown some interest in an alliance with the anti-nationalists and the reaction of Reform leadership to these overtures was not cold. Only, a year before, Rabbi Isaac Landman, an important anti-Balfourite had labeled the Zionist split "ludicrous and ridiculous," showing no preference whatever for Brandeis over Weizmann. Aside from this, although Reform leaders liked Brandeis and Mack they could not abide the more flamboyant Stephen Wise, a key figure in the minority. Along with the Orthodox, they considered Wise's interfaith appeal of the 1920s a heresy. "Zionist Propose Truce to Factions," *The New York Times*, June 18, 1923, p. 4; "The Merry Zionist War" (editorial), *The American Hebrew*, 109 (May 20, 1921), 3-4; "Judge Mack and Rabbi Landman Discuss Zionism," *The American Hebrew*, 118 (April 23, 1926), 811, 823; Ephraim Deinard, *Tzelem B'Haichal* (in Hebrew, New Orleans, 1926), p. 138; Samuel Schulman, *Judaism and Jesus and the Decadence in the Reform Jewish Pulpit* (New York, 1926) pp. 13-17.

[120] "The Arabian Demand for a Constitution" (editorial), *Emanu-El*, LVI (September 14, 1923), 2; "Says Jews Were Not Intended for One Isolated Spot," *Brooklyn Jewish Chronicle*, II (December 14, 1923), 1; "The Outpost of Judaism is the Home" (editorial), *B'nai Brith Mesenger*, 28 (November 27, 1925), 595-596; "Morgenthau's Report on Poland Stirs Up a New Controversy," *The American Hebrew*, 116 (December 12, 1924), 167, 177; "The Bomb in the Zionist Camp," *Literary Digest*, 91 (December 18, 1926), 30-31; Statement of Henry Morgenthau in *New York Tribune*, November 30, 1926, LDB; Simcha Berkowitz, p. 324; "Calls Zionism Aid to Anti-Semitism," *The Jewish Independent*, I (July 10, 1930), 1-2.

projected enlarged Jewish Agency.[123]   The C.C.A.R. remained within the purview of Zionism through its friendship with the Brandeis-Mack group but stood apart from Weizmann because it identified the European wing of Zionism with diaspora nationalism. But, there was some difficulty in apprehending the precise meaning of an enlarged Jewish Agency.[124]   Brandeisians would be represented but the influence of Weizmann would be paramount, just as it presently was in the all-Zionist Agency. Another consideration was that, friendship aside, Brandeis' first loyalty was to Zionism; neither he nor his followers had left the W.Z.O.   Under such circumstances, it seemed pointless to join the Agency, regardless of its vaunted absence of politicism, if anti-nationalist delegates were outnumbered and stood to be outvoted on every major decision. Worse still, Reform could be led where it did not want to go if it assented to abide by the majority verdict. In 1928, the U.A.H.C. failed to pass a pro-Jewish Agency resolution and there was still talk of a secular state as a Jewish tragedy, "a doubtful refuge" and an atheistic cauldron.[125]   The suspicion that Jewish nationalism was neither waning nor extinct plagued Reform until the time it joined the Agency.[126]

[121] Henry L. Frank, "Zionism on Exhibition," *Reform Advocate*, LVIII (October 25, 1919) 271; "Is Mexico a New Zion" (editorial), *The Jewish Criterion*, 56 (July 15, 1921), 10; "Jewish Colonization Projects" (editorial), *The Jewish Review and Observer*, XLVII (August 19, 1921), 14; Leon Wexelstein, "Louis Wiley Discusses Jewish Problems," *The Jewish Tribune*, 42, (November 9, 1923), 3; "Says Brazil is Vital in Future of Jewry," *The New York Times*, June 30, 1930, p. 40.

[122] "Sees Jews' Destiny Among Non-Jews," *The New York Times*, September 29, 1925, p. 10. For a complete discussion of Joint Distribution Committee Activities in Russia from 1914 to 1933 see Boris Sapir and Leon Shapiro, "The Joint Distribution Committee in Jewish Life," *Israel of Tomorrow*, ed. Leo Jung, 2 vols. (New York, 1949), I, 102-111.

[123] Samuel Goldenson, *The Present Status and Outlook of Reform Judaism* (reprint, *CCARY*, XXXIV), p. 1-20; Philipson, *Reform Movement in Judaism, p.* 365; Philipson, *AJYB*, XLII, 202; Rudolph I. Coffee, "This Year's Rabbinical Conference," *The Sentinel*, LV (July 4, 1924), 9; *CCARY*, XXXIV (Richmond, 1925), pp. 105-106.

[124] A. Leo Weil to Harry Schneiderman, February 26, 1930, AJC.

Leadership within the Reform Jewish movement was, by 1929, encountering indefatigable resistance from its nationalist-oriented youth. Pulpits and lay presidencies had come to be occupied by a new generation whose emotions were not stirred by a rereading of the 1885 Pittsburgh Platform. Some of the younger men, like Rabbis Barnett Brickner, James Heller and Abba Hillel Silver were challenging the C.C.A.R. Rabbi David Philipson was horrified when the Hatikvah, the Jewish national anthem, was sung at a C.C.A.R. meeting. Altering the content of the Union Prayer Book to include a daily hope for the redemption of Jerusalem was unacceptable to Philipson and to several other rabbis but they did not prevail.[127] The record of Reform Judaism from 1930 to 1941 was characterized by a tension between the old guard and the new and the denouement was the release of this tension, not through union but by dissolution.

The pressure for change within liberal Judaism overcame the skepticism of Reform leaders.[128] Dr. H.G. Enelow, President of the C.C.A.R. outlined the position of Reform Judaism on Palestine in late June, 1929. He declared that "Reform... cannot accept the separate nation status of Palestine," nor could it approve the idea of

[125] Although in 1927, they held a four day debate on the various aspects of Zionism. Charles Reznikoff, ed., *Louis Marshall: Champion of Liberty Selected Papers and Addresses,* 2 vols. (Philadelphia, 1957), II, 780; Union of American Hebrew Congregations, Thirtieth Council, *Conference on the Perpetuation of Judaism* (Cleveland, 1927), pp. 7-14, 30-41, 82-91.

[126] "Calls Israel A People of and for Religion," *The New York Times,* April 16, 1928, p. 26; "A Momentous Meeting" (editorial), *The Modern View,* 57 (October 26, 1928), 4; Gerson B. Levi, "Editorial" *Reform Advocate,* LXXVI (November 24, 1928), 551-552; A. Rosenthal, "Zionism as a Jewish Panacea," *The Modern View,* 57 (September 28, 1928), 5; "The Insecurity of Palestine" (editorial), *The Modern View,* 57 (October 14, 1928), 5.

[127] Zionist flags were also hung for the first time at a B'nai B'rith meeting, much to the dismay of Rabbi Samuel Koch, who was one of the few rabbis in the Northwest who was not an ardent nationalist. 'Rabbi Koch Greets U.S. Zionist President," *The Jewish Transcript,* XIV (July 30, 1937), 1, 7; "The Jewish Emblem" (editorial), VI (February 28, 1930), 4; Louis I. Newman, "Telling it in Gath," *The Scribe,* XXIII (November 7, 1930) 4, 12; Morris M. Feuerlicht, "Hatikvah and Reform," *The Reform Advocate,* LXXX (November 8, 1930), 364-365; "Rabbi Lefkowitz Heads Conference," *The Jewish Review and Observer,* LVI (July 4, 1930), 4; Philipson, *My Life,* pp. 424-428.

[128] For example, see "Scores Zealous Zionists," *The New York Times,* January 7, 1929, p. 29; A. Rosenthal, "Zionism with Non-Zionists" (editorial), *The Modern View,* 58 (August 9, 1929), 4.

Palestine as the "only" spiritual center for the Jews and the sole place where a wholesome Jewish life could be led. The recommendation was for support of a Jewish Agency and the latter's disentanglement from all political connections.[129] On August 12, 1929, Rabbi Samuel Schulman, an eminent Reform theologian, became a member of the enlarged Jewish Agency Council and lauded the accord that had knit anti-Zionism, non-Zionism and Zionism together.[130]

Membership in the Jewish Agency did not halt the inveighing by the old guard Reform against Jewish nationalism. The Agency was not permitted the luxury of resting on its laurels. Back-slapping and self-praise evaporated in the midst of one of the most severe Jewish crises of the interwar period, the Wailing Wall riots of 1929. Recorded incidents of violence between Arabs and Jews occurred in Jerusalem on August 15 and the Palestinian countryside was not pacified until September 8. Spreading outward from the Holy City, murder and looting descended upon Haifa, Hebron and Safed. By the time the British quieted the populace, one hundred thirty three Jews and one hundred sixteen Arabs had been killed; at least two hundred more on each side were injured. The Mandatory was as much responsible for the slaughter as was the instigator Haj Amin el Husseini, Grand Mufti of Jerusalem, who after August 23, enflamed the Arab mobs with his anti-Jewish oratory. Lacking the personnel and the desire to stop the Grand Mufti, the British acted sluggishly, and the police proved to be ineffective. The Arabs were initially repulsed from rural settlements by an illegal Jewish self-defense group called the *Haganah*. A descendent of the *Shomrim*, or Watchmen of the pre-World War I period, these units proved their worth by aiding poorly armed communities to withstand and escape

---

[129] A further indication of the Reform movement's willingness to join the Zionists in the Agency was the symbolic conferring of an honorary Doctor of Laws Degree upon Chaim Weizmann by Hebrew Union College at Commencement, 1929. "Reform Rabbis Approve Agency with Understanding that it be Free from Political Ties," *Detroit Jewish Chronicle,* XXVIII (June 28, 1929), 1, 3; "Weizmann Honored by Hebrew Union College," *The Jewish Transcript,* VI, (June 14, 1929), 1.

[130] "Schulman Praises Accord at Zurich," *The New York Times,* August 18, 1929, Sec. 2, p. 4. Schulman spoke for such a union since 1925. Samuel Schulman, *The Non-Zionist and the New Palestine* (New York, 1925), pp. 6-9. Anti-Balfourites enjoyed calling themselves "Non-Zionists," but as will be explained subsequently in the discussion of actual non-Zionists and their beliefs, the name when applied to anti-nationalists is a misnomer.

nearly unharmed from Arab violence.[131]

The outcry from the American Jewish community, capped by a rally at Madison Square Garden, left older liberals cold.[132] In the main, these Reform Jews assumed a pro-British bearing and a wait-and-see attitude.They felt that the Mandatory had handled a touchy situation with the utmost discretion. It remained for her to restore order, a task she was undertaking hastily and efficiently.[133] For the Zionists, there was a poignant object lesson. The *Israelite* and the *Reform Advocate* defined the task of the Jewish Agency as the "liquidation of Zionism" and the immediate cessation of immigration and colonization in Palestine.[134] Zionist leaders, so recently acclaimed, were blamed for the riots. Several Reform journals ordered the Balfour Declaration scrapped so that the real work of economic rehabilitation of the Holy Land could proceed unhindered.[135] Aligning with these anti-Zionists were the ultra-Orthodox Agudas Yisroel in America, the pro-Magnesites and the territorialists.[136] The *Brooklyn Eagle* and Rabbi Nathan Krass

---

[131]Arthur Koestler, *Promise and Fulfillment: Palestine 1917-1949 (New York,* 1949), pp. 66-71; Hull, pp. 159, 186; Israel Cohen, *A Short History of Zionism,* p. 129; Walter Laqueur, *A History of Zionism* (New York, 1972), pp. 222, 284, 329.

[132] Werner, pp. 261-262.

[133] "Lazaron Sees Arabs Checked," *The Baltimore News,* August 27, 1929, p. 4.

[134] Louis Berg, "American Public Opinion on Palestine," *Menorah Journal,* XVII (October 1929), 77.

[135] "Jottings," *Chicago Jewish Chronicle,* XVII (September 13, 1929), 1, 16; Gerson B. Levi, "Editorial," *Reform Advocate,* LXXVIII (September 7, 1929), 123-124; Gerson B. Levi, "Editorial," *Reform Advocate,* LXXVIII (September 14, 1929), 147-148; "The Plight of Palestine" (editorial), *The Modern View,* 59 (September 6, 1929), 4, 8; "Dividing the Blame for Palestine Bloodshed," *Literary Digest,* 103 (October 5, 1929), 30-31; Max Schachtman, "Palestine — Pogrom or Revolution," *The Militant* (October 1, 1929), p. 5; Berg, *Menora Journal,* XVII, 76; "The Palestine Riots" (editorial), *The American Hebrew,* 125 (August 30, 1929), 401; "Zionist Partly Blamed for Riots by Jewish Press," *Brooklyn Daily Eagle,* August 28, 1929, p. 2; Abraham Goodman, "The Peace of Death," *Every Friday,* V (December 20, 1929), 6.

[136] Judah Magnes was a native of Oakland, California, a graduate of Hebrew Union College and later President of Hebrew University. He advocated bi-nationalism as a solution of the Palestine problem which entailed renunciation of political Zionism by Jews, creation of Jewish cultural centers, proportional participation of Jews in a Palestinian government, and Arab-Jewish cooperation. B'rith Shalom was the

called for tri-religious freedom and the internationalization of the Holy Land.[137]   Drawing a fine line, Rabbi Samuel Schulman implied that one could be indifferent to Zionism without being so to Palestine Judaism.[138] Isaac W. Bernheim, founder of the Reform Church of American Israelites, hoped that liberal Jews were properly chastened by the 1929 disturbances and would in the future "steer clear of this indecent dream (Zionism) and maintain untarnished the integrity of their citizenship in the country where they dwell."[139] Anti-nationalist Jews, buttressed by Mid-West and Far West Congressmen decried the carnage but implored the American Government to refrain from interceding either physically or morally.[140]

Reform theologians were still reluctant to commit themselves fully to the Balfour Declaration. Palestine, they said, could be a Jewish "center" but not a national home.[141] By making unreason-

organization he founded at Hebrew University to spread his ideas. InAmerica, he received a measure of support from the older Reform elements. "Backs Magnes Plan to Aid Accord," *The New York Times,* November 26, 1929, p. 8; Raymond Dannenbaum, "Prof. Popper Finds Life Work in Editing History of Egypt Under Moslem Rule," *The Jewish Journal,* III (February 19, 1930), 3. Popper was the brother-in-law of Magnes. Jacob Heller, "A Solution for Palestine," *The American Hebrew*, 139 (October 9, 1936), 414; "Urges New Homeland for Jews," *New York Telegram,* September 4, 1929, p. 8; Philip Solinsky to Louis Brandeis, October 31, 1932, LDB.

[137] "The War of the 'Wailing Wall,'" *Literary Digest,* 102 (September 7, 1929), 5; "Dr. Krass's Brazenness" (editorial), *The Jewish Guardian,* December 26, 1929, p. 4.

[138] "Jewish Unity Urged in Emanu-El Pulpit," *The New York Times,* October 6, 1929, p. 30.

[139] Isaac W. Bernheim, *The Closing Chapters of a Busy Life,* (Denver, 1929), p. 101.

[140] Berg, *Menorah Journal,* XVII, 72-73.

[141] The outlook of people like Landman and Schulman (but not all original anti-Balfourites) was approaching the true non-Zionist philosophy, that is acceptance of the Balfour Declaration but rejection of Jewish nationalism in the diaspora. "Looks on Palestine as Spiritual Centre," *The New York Times,* January 6, 1930, p. 56; "Zionism a Minor Issue, J.B. Wise Declares," *The New York Times,* September 28, 1930, Sec. 2, p. 6. Jonah Bondi Wise was the son of Isaac Mayer Wise. For later developments on this theme, see "Dr. Weizmann Would Sit with the Arabs" (editorial), *The American Hebrew,* 140 (December 18, 1936), 673; "Arabs Before the High Commission in Palestine," (editorial), *The American Hebrew,* 140 (January 15, 1937), 769; "A Step Forward" (editorial), *The American Hebrew,* 140 (April 2, 1937), 1065; Aaron Gorelik to Louis D. Brandeis, January 24, 1937, LDB.

able demands, declared Henry Morgenthau, the Balfour Declaration had spoiled the Holy Land for both Arabs and Jews. The desideratum for Palestine was Arab-Jewish cooperation.[142] Moreover, the Jewish Agency (J.A.P.) had disappointed the old liberals. One reason they had joined the J.A.P. was to change the course of Zionism by mitigating its nationalistic aspect. However, the Agency had frustrated them by failing to absorb even a fraction of the Reform ideology. Although Brandeis's return to American Zionist leadership in 1930 was greeted with enthusiasm by hard-liners like Julius Rosenwald, the Justice had lost the confidence of a number of anti-Balfourites who had expected sweeping changes to follow in his wake. Gerson B. Levi, editor of Chicago's *Reform Advocate* and successor to Rabbi Emil G. Hirsch indicated that his journal would resist the new administration and its notion that exclusive settlement in Palestine would resolve the Jewish problem. Charles Joseph, one-time editor of the Pittsburgh *Jewish Criterion*, was not terribly overjoyed at the second coming of Brandeis, whom he believed was devoted to politics rather than economics both at home and abroad.[143]

Stripping the Jewish Agency of its advisory role was the course taken by Britain, a nation which was in the process of reevaluating its Near Eastern policy objectives. The Passfield White Paper of October 22, 1930, published in conjunction with the Hope-Simpson Report, proposed restrictions on Jewish entry quotas and on land sales to Jews. It was immediately protested by the Zionists and Weizmann resigned as President of the Zionist Organization. Britain was no longer collaborating with the Zionists and the anti-nationalists were exuberant.[144] *The New York Times* editorialized that the

---

[142] "Morgenthau Says Zionism Must Fail," *The New York Times,* February 10, 1930, p. 27; Humphrey Clinker (pseud.), "Louis Wiley Scoffs at Intermarriage," *Jewish Journal,* III (May 7, 1930), 4; Charles Joseph, "Random Thoughts," *The Jewish Independent,* I (June 19, 1930), 4; "Rabbi Schulman Calls Zionist Movement a 'Spiritual Escape' " *The Jewish Review and Observer,* LVI (August 29, 1930), 1, 4; "Good Will Between Arabs and Jews", (editorial), *The American Hebrew,* 127 (August 22, 1930), 377.

[143] Julian Mack to Brandeis, July 29, 1930, LDB; Gerson B. Levi, "Editorial," *Reform Advocate,* LXXX (August 30, 1930), 99-100; Charles Joseph, "Random Thoughts," *Jewish Independent,* I (July 24, 1930), 4.

[144] Despite the fact that at the same time they were supposed to be cooperating with Zionists in the Agency. Alexander Lyons, "England and Palestine," *The Jewish Press,* II (December 1930), 1; Joseph Frey, "The British Declaration of Policy," *The Modern View,* 60 (October 24, 1930), 4.

work of Zionism had moved too swiftly. Britain's revised policy was justified by events and a temporary ban on Jewish immigration would prove invigorating to Jews, Arabs and the Palestinian economy.[145] The *American Hebrew* urged American Jews to keep faith with Britain; the work of economic rehabilitation must continue through the Agency despite the resignations of Weizmann, Felix Warburg and Lord Melchett, the three highest officeholders in that organization. The editor of *Emanu-El*, a San Francisco weekly, said that the White Paper thankfully put an end to the "phantasmagoria of Jewish nationalism" which had always been incapable of solving the Jewish problem.[146] Similar sentiments were vouchsafed by Leo Franklin, past President of the C.C.A.R. and Rabbi Gerson B. Levi. A St. Louis rabbi observed that Jewish imperialism had turned a historically oppressed people into oppressors, a motif which would hopefully be reversed by the Passfield statement. An ex-State Department official, Samuel Edelman, revealed that he had predicted the present turn in British policy in 1917, when "the unthinking Jewish masses...sponsored by a few irresponsible leaders flocked to the standard of Zionism, drained the cup of Hebrew charity on this whimsical gesture of a national home in Palestine."[147]

By 1936, liberal Judaism had passed through its transitional phase. The rabbis and journals which had happily witnessed the

---

[145] Between 1925 and 1928 an economic depression occurred in Palestine caused in part, liberals thought, by the sudden and plentiful implantation of Jews in Palestine who could not find jobs or who displaced Arab labor. "The Palestine Report" (editorial), *The New York Times*, October 22, 1930, p. 14; "Palestine Gates Closed to Jews," *Literary Digest,* 107 (November 1, 1930), 12.

[146] "Great Britain's Ultimatum on Palestine" (editorial), *The American Hebrew*, 127 (October 24, 1930), 602. A.W. Voorsanger, "A Death Blow to Jewish Nationalism," *Emanu-El*, LXX (October 24, 1930), 2. Just as liberal Jews did, much of the non-Jewish press looked forward to immigration curbs in Palestine and viewed a British White Paper on this matter as an essentailly sound policy. "Peopling the Holy Land" (editorial) *The Washington Post,* May 29, 1930, LDB. Fuad I. Shatara, "Defining the New British Policy in Palestine," *The Syrian World,* V, (November 1930), 8-9; "Britain's Position in Palestine" (editorial), *New York Evening Post,* October 22, 1930, p. 10; "A Blow to the Zionist Dream" (editorial) *The New York Herald Tribune,* October 22, 1930, p. 24; "The Principle Issues," *Outlook,* 156 (November 5, 1930), 366.

[147] Sermon by Rabbi Ferdinand Isserman, November 14, 1930, LDB; "Britain's Statement Scored by Leaders," *The Detroit Jewish Chronicle,* XXX (October 25, 1930), 315-316; "Urges Jews to Drop Palestine Ideal," *The Detroit Jewish Chronicle,* XXX (November 28, 1930), 2.

unseating of Weizmann from both the Agency and the W.Z.O.[148] had either outlived their own dogma, retired or died.[149] There were younger men who thought in an assimilationist vein[150] but they were not going to guide the destinies of revitalized Reform Judaism. Serving to weaken the hold of old line liberal Jews upon the movement was the fact that Zionism had succeeded in cutting across religious lines among Jews and Christians. Orthodox and Conservative Judaism were overwhelmingly pro-Zionist and Reform was split. The depredations of Hitler and the dread of Fascism had also resulted in the formation of the Christian American Palestine Committee, whose inspiration was drawn from the timely nationalism of American Zionists.[151]

A better bridge was constructed between Zionism and liberalism between 1933 and 1935. Jacob Rader Marcus, then Associate Professor of Jewish History at Hebrew Union College was the first to articulate the bases on which a fresh understanding was to be found. While defending spiritual Hebraism and the mission of Judaism as valid extensions of an historic trend, he thought that the philosophy was being misused by men who were protecting their own unique

---

[148] "Zionists Change Pilots to Save the Ship," *Literary Digest,* 110 (August 8, 1931), 20-21; "Schulman Sees End of Zionism at Hand," *The New York Times,* August 30, 1931, p. 17.

[149] By 1936, the change in Reform leadership was nearly total as was the editorial policy among those liberal Jewish journals that survived the Depression. Samuel Schulman and David Philipson still maintained a roseate faith in Jewish emancipation which, by 1939, had become irrelevant to the immediate Jewish problem. In terms of age, these men were no longer leaders; Schulman was seventy-seven and Philipson seventy-nine. Isaac W. Bernheim, Rabbi Henry Berkowitz, Rabbi Isaac Landman, Professor Morris Raphael Cohen, Henry Morgenthau, Morris Jastrow, Jr., and Rabbi Emil G. Hirsch were all either retired or dead. By the mid-1940s, many liberals were no longer convinced that their previous course had been the right one. In publishing, Gerson B. Levi was the sole survivor of the journalistic housecleaning until he, too, was replaced as an editor in 1937. *The Modern View* became noticeably pro-Brandeis and then pro-Zionist after the departure of its editor, A. Rosenthal. *B'nai B'rith Messenger, The Scribe, The Reform Advocate* and that anti-Zionist bulwark, *The American Hebrew* all shifted to Zionist advocacy. Journals like *Jewish Comment* simply faded.

[150] Bernard Brown, *From Pharoh to Hitler* (Chicago, 1933), pp. 132-167, 192-193, 202-203; Lion Feuchtwanger, *Nationalism and Judaism* (New York, 1933), pp. 4-6, 13-15, 18-20.

[151] Fink, p. 59; Goldblatt, *American Jewish Historical Quarterly,* LVII, 512.

status in American society. Conversely, he alleged that Zionism was misunderstood. The movement's strength had become more economic, social and cultural and less political. He felt that Zionism would not encourage anti-Semitism but would function as a bulwark against it. The national home in Palestine would lend dignity to the Jews and become a source of pride to them, even if they never left the lands of their birth. Assimilation, the undesirable path toward obliterating the Jewish identity would be checked by the presence of a homeland. In addition, Zionism had suffered many setbacks: The British were only lukewarm to it and there had been riots which confirmed the hostility of the majority population. Zionism had need of the liberals, "this sturdy, clear-sighted and responsible group in American life, a group...in its own way...devoted to Jewish ideals." Reform needed the vibrancy and vitality offered by Zionism before it became fully engrossed within the surrounding society. He advocated a mutual surrender of extreme positions, enabling Reform Jews to join the Zionist movement with no qualms, while permitting Zionists to accept them with no reservations.[152]

A C.C.A.R. resolution of 1935 announced that Zionism was to be entirely "a matter of personal conscience." No official stand, for or against Zionism, was adopted. The Conference simply agreed to continue its economic alliance with the Agency for the rebuilding of Palestine and was amenable to labor Zionism. The debate on refugees assumed a greater importance. All liberal Jews realized that immigrant havens must be found.[153] However, older Reform rabbis looked to the West,[154] while younger ones opted for the Holy Land.

The acceptance of Palestine as more than a refuge was decided

[152] Jacob Rader Marcus, "Zionism and the American Jew," *The American Scholar*, II (May 1933), 282-283, 285-291.

[153] These pronouncements reversed the 1885 platform, thereby isolating the old Reform group who fell back on a rationalization to justify what had happened. The plank on labor Zionism is particularly important, as it represents ane extension of the Progressive Social Justice philosophy of liberal Judaism from America to labor groups abroad. Louis Wolsey, "Rabbis and Zionsim," *Christian Century*, LII (March 20, 1935) 370; Philipson, *AJYB*, XLII, 203; Philipson, *My Life*, pp 463-465; Halpern, p. 197; Louis Minsky, "Is Zionism Going Fascist," *Christian Century*, LII (February 20, 1935), 237-239; "Rabbis End Fight on Aims of Zionism," *The New York Times*, June 29, 1935, p. 8.

[154] "Dr. Franklin Urges Opening of Doors of U.S. and England for Jewish Refugees from the Reich," *Detroit Jewish Chronicle*, XXXVII (January 10, 1935), 2.

upon by the C.C.A.R. in May, 1937. In accordance with the Balfour Declaration, the Columbus Platform affirmed the obligation of all Jewry to aid in the rebuilding of the Jewish homeland by endeavoring to make it more than a haven for the oppressed. Palestine was also to be a center for Jewish culture and spiritual life.[155]   A minority, headed by Samuel Schulman and Jonah B. Wise, opposed the resolution, which was ultimately carried.[156] In essence, the structure of liberal theology — spiritual, messianic Judaism — was repudiated as was the fifty year old Pittsburgh Platform.

The findings of the Peel Commission, which in July 1937 recommended the partition of Palestine into two sovereign, independent Jewish and Arab states, while reserving to Great Britain the administration of the Holy Places, hastened the split of liberal Judaism into a pair of irreconcilable factions. The moderates were against partition for the same reasons as were the Zionists. The boundaries of the Jewish State were unrealistically small and would be unable to cope with the huge migrations from Europe. By July, 1937, Reform Judaism regarded a Jewish State as a distinct possibility and was willing to wait, along with American Zionists, for future discussions with Britain to yield a more advantageous settlement. Meanwhile, the present Mandate arrangement was quite satisfactory, since Jews were entering Palestine at an accelerated pace. Palestine was the key to Jewish survival because the nations of the world had locked them out. The entire country had to remain open. Under the partition plan, the proposed Jewish State would have been approximately one-fifth the size of Palestine.

The remaining anti-Zionist Reformers were composed of the doctrinal descendents of traditional Reform, as handed down through the Pittsburgh Platform. As leaders of Reform Jewry, they

---

[155] Laqueur, *Journal of Contemporary History,* VI, 180; "Rabbis in Conference Back Labor's Rights," *The New York Times,* May 28, 1937, p. 13. For a complete statement and summary of the Columbus Platform, see Glazer, pp. 103-104. The program of 1937 was called a "natural outgrowth" of spiritual, universal Reform but this was not the case. The C.C.A.R. had simply converted to Balfourism and, by 1940, was reading Zionist Organization bulletins at its gatherings. Stanley G. Brav, "Zion: False Messiah," *Reform Advocate,* XCII (June 11, 1937), 16-19; *CCARY,* L (Philadelphia, 1940), p. 24. In 1937, the C.C.A.R. protested against the limits placed upon Jewish immigration into Palestine by the British "as an effort to curb the development of Jewish life in the country." "Rabbis Denounce Fascists in Spain," *The New York Times,* May 31, 1937, p. 10.

[156] Samuel Cauman, *Jonah Bondi Wise* (New York, 1966), pp. 174-175; "Rabbis in Conference Back Labor's Rights," *The New York Times,* May 28, 1937, p. 13.

had been obliged to collaborate with the Zionists after 1921, but they always demurred on whole-hearted cooperation. A portion of their psychology was founded on their inability to submit to the idea of a "national home" as projected by the Balfour Declaration. Thus, they were not only anti-nationalists but anti-Balfourites as well. The former trait was held in common with non-Zionists but the latter was not and serves to distinguish between American critics of Zionism. For reasons of convenience and necessity the old guard tolerated Zionism, even to the extent of partnership within the Jewish Agency. These contingencies notwithstanding, they vocally repudiated the Balfour Declaration and Jewish nationalism at every opportunity. Whatever was tendered by them to Zionists and non-Zionists was given grudgingly; for a short time, they were converted but never committed to Zionism. After they departed, unreserved support for Balfourism followed and Reform Judaism entered the pro-national phase of its existence.

The bitter-end anti-Zionists opposed partition because they decried all Jewish statism, whether then or in the future.[157] As alternatives, they proposed an Arab-Jewish understanding, under permanent British tutelage, the bi-national scheme of Judah Magnes, President of Hebrew University[158] and settlement of Jews anywhere in the world except Palestine.[159] The State Department was less

[157] American Jewish leaders of all Zionist persuasions found out the content of the Peel Report six weeks before it was officially published. The information was given them by the Second Lord Melchett, son of the late English Zionist, for the probable purpose of preparing the public for the ominous tidings. As anticipated, Old Guard Reform Jews opposed partition because, in their opinion, the establishment of a Jewish State meant the end of Reform Judaism in America. The C.C.A.R., having adopted a more nationalist viewpoint, rejected partition as inadequate to suit Jewish needs. There were some who favored partition because they feared that Britain would withdraw its "half a loaf" and deal with the Arabs instead. See Lord Melchett to Arthur Hays Sulzberger, May 22, 1937, James G. McDonald Papers, School of International Relations, Columbia University and the following periodicals: *Reform Advocate*, July 9, 1937, *The New York Times*, July 8, 1937 and January 7, 1938, *The American Hebrew*, March 11 and 15, 1938, *Opinion*, April 1938, *The Jewish Transcript*, October 8, 1937 and the *Jewish Examiner*, April 8, 1938.

[158] Alfred Segal, "Plain Talk," *The Jewish Transcript*, XIV (July 30, 1937), 1, 7; Alfred Segal, "Plain Talk," *B'nai Brith Messenger*, 40 (July 16, 1937), 3, 11; "'Don't Fix Eye on Palestine,' States Rabbi," *The Jewish Transcript*, XIV (August 6, 1937), 6; "Danger Seen in Jewish Nationalism," *The New York Times*, July 27, 1937, p. 20; "The Will to Unity Spells a Happier Year," (editorial), *The American Hebrew*, 141 (September 3, 1937), 5; "Partition to the Fore" (editorial), *The American Hebrew*, 142 (March 11, 1938), 3.

intimidated by Rabbi Stephen Wise than it might have otherwise been because it was known that prominent Jews opposed his efforts "to emphasize racial rather than...religious differences between them and American citizens...."[160] A helpful ally was the Agudas Yisroel, an extremist group on the right of traditional orthodoxy to whom Zionists were atheistic and power-hungry. Jacob Heller, an Agudah spokesman, told Reform Jews that the Zionists persecuted the orthodox in Palestine and, within the Jewish Agency, non-Zionism had become the pawn of nationalism.[161]

Until 1939, no secessionist movement was initiated within Reform. Although divided on Palestine, liberal Jews were unanimous in their disapprobation of the World Jewish Congress, sponsored by Stephen Wise. The Congress was to unite Judaism in a confederation against anti-Semitism; it was also sympathetic to the national home movement in Palestine. The charge leveled by liberal Judaism was that a world-wide Jewish union, or the mere contemplation of one, would precipitate a deluge of hate and perhaps total annihilation of the Jews by anti-Semites. Even in the temperate climate of America, there was no desire to reawaken the dormant charge of diaspora nationalism.[162]

Due to a zealous Arab-Jewish resistance, the partition plan was squelched in November 1938 and in its stead was placed the White Paper of 1939, which severely limited Jewish immigration to Pales-

---

[159] Territorialism was the special project of Bernard Baruch, who was attempting to obtain either Africa or the Belgian Congo for Jewish settlement. Birobijan was not overlooked either. Melech Epstein, *The Jew and Communism: 1919-1941* (New York, 1959), pp. 312-315; Henry L. Feingold, "The Politics of Rescue: A Study of American Diplomacy and Politics Related to the Rescue of Refugees, 1938-1944" (Doctoral Dissertation, New York University, 1966), pp. 51, 160, 167-174, 201-204; Margaret L. Coit, *Mr. Baruch* (Boston, 1957), pp. 171, 671-672; Mason, p. 635; Harold L. Mack, *The Problem of the Jews* (Del Monte, Calif., 193), pp. 1-10; Joseph Otmar Hefter, *Nai Judea* (New York, 1938). Even former President Hoover, who had once spoken in favor of the Balfour Declaration, agreed that the African solution was best. Earl Browder, *The Jewish People and the War* (New York, 1940), p. 12.

[160] Wallace Murray to Judge Moore, 867N.01/469, May 28, 1937, *GRDS:RG59*.

[161] He told this to Jewish Socialists and Gentiles as well. Samuel Halperin, *The Political World of American Zionism* (Detroit, 1961), pp. 68-69; "Not All Jews are Zionists," *Christian Century*, LIV (January 20, 1937), 84-85; "Jews are the Victims of Zionist Injustice," *Commonweal*, XXV (March 12, 1937), 558; Jacob Heller to Baruch C. Vladeck, January 3, 1937, Baruch Charney Vladeck Papers, Part I, Box 113, Tamiment Institute, New York City.

tine. Since the Evian Conference closed the doors of Europe and the Western Hemisphere to Jewish refugees the Jews became a people without a country. Immigration quotas in America were strictly enforced. *The New York Times* favored resettlement but could only suggest the forbidding African Continent. [163]

Morris Lazaron was the only Reform Rabbi to call upon American Jews to confirm Britain in its White Paper policy. Rabbi Lazaron had always been pro-British and was a crusader for anti-Balfour, American Judaism. He concurred with the *New York Herald Tribune* that England had no choice but "to impose her imperial will through the White Paper." As a form of "manifest destiny," Zionism was defunct. Lazaron urged the Jewish Agency to dissolve into a purely economic enterprise and disparaged its illegal immigration work. [164] He was in contact with the State Department in an abortive effort to prevent Chaim Weizmann from visiting the United States. [165] Lazaron distributed pamphlets to the Joint Distribution Committee, the American Jewish Committee, the U.A.H.C. and the C.C.A.R.

[162] The World Jewish Congress caused some controversy among liberal Jews before 1938. Morris D. Waldman to Cyrus Adler, September 24, 1935, AJC; Morris S. Lazaron, "Judaism's Message to the World," *The American Jewish Times,* II (April 1937), 9, 15; "The Basis of Jewish Unity" (editorial), *The American Hebrew,* 142 (December 17, 1937), 3; Morris Lazaron, *Common Ground: A Plea for Intelligent Americanism* (New York, 1936), pp. 65-129; Fanny R. Adlerstein, "The Congress Referendum — Pro and Con," *The American Hebrew,* 143 (June 10, 1938), 6, 14; "Congress Pyrotechnics Dazzle but do not Illumine" (editorial), *The American Hebrew,* 143 (June 3, 1938), 12; "The Current American Scene," *The American Hebrew,* 143 (June 3, 1938), 12; "The Congress Plebiscite" (editorial), *The American Hebrew,* 143 (May 20, 1938), 3.

[163] "No Partition of Palestine" (editorial) *The New York Times,* November 10, 1938, p. 25; Feingold, p. 176. By this time, even the *American Hebrew,* seeing the desperate plight of the Jews, was willing to countenance Palestine immigration and, generally, had taken a softer attitude toward the Holy Land. "Five Years of Terror" (editorial), *The American Hebrew,* 142 (January 21, 1938), 3.

[164] Morris Lazaron was born in Savannah, Georgia in 1880. He was a graduate of Hebrew Union College and a rabbi of the congregations in Wheeling, West Virginia and Baltimore. He was Secretary of the C.C.A.R. in 1924 and a member of the League of Nations Association. For many years, he was associated with the National Conference of Christians and Jews, an organization promoting better understanding between the two faiths. He was also on the board of directors of the Jewish relief organization, the Joint Distribution Committee. "Rabbi Lazaron's Letter" (editorial), *Jewish Ledger,* LXXXIX (June 23, 1939), 4; Morris Waldman to Sidney Landsburgh, March 8, 1940, AJC; Morris D. Waldman, *Nor By Power* (New York, 1953), 207-208.

detailing his position on Jewish nationalism. His "Five Point Plan" was printed in the *Baltimore Sun* for March 7, 1940. It called for Jewish minority rights in Palestine, unconditional assent to the White Paper and Arab-Jewish cooperation. For Jews outside Palestine, he sought cultural autonomy and full rights of citizenship in the countries where they lived.[166]

Lazaron's concern with dual citizenship, a Jewish vote and good Americanism had become extreme.[167] He launched a one-man campaign against the America Palestine Committee in February, 1941, and captured the interest of Wallace Murray, Chief of the Near East Division of the State Department and Adolph A. Berle, Jr., Undersecretary of State.[168] The Zionist Emergency Committee was corresponding with well-known Christian leaders, requesting their help in a combined Jewish-Christian effort to re-open Palestine. Lazaron informed his non-Jewish friends, among them Samuel McCrea Cavert, General Secretary of the Federation of Churches of Christ in America and Paul Hutchinson, editor of the *Christian Century*, that if they volunteered their names to Zionism it would be "tantamount to underwriting not only a secular nationalist philosophy...but (they) will be involved innocently in a controversy on a question about which Jews themselves were divided."[169]

[165] The State Department was quite concerned with the Weizmann visit and was anxious to gather opposition opinion. The Assistant Secretary of State, G.S. Messersmith, had personally interviewed Lazaron. Memorandum by G.S. Messersmith, 867N.01/1675, November 29, 1939, *USFR: 1939*, 5 vols. (Washington, 1955), IV, 810; Waldman, p. 206.

[166] Morris Waldman to Sidney Lansburgh, march 8, 1940, Morris Waldman to Edward S. Greenbaum, March 7, 1940, Lazaron to Greenbaum, March 1, 1940 and Morris D. Waldman to Sol M. Stroock, May 9, 1940, AJC.

[167] Morris Lazaron, *Homeland or State: The Real Issue* (New York, 1941), pp. 4, 7, 8-9, 13-15.

[168] Memorandum by Adolph A. Berle, Jr., 867N.01/1729 1/2, April 14, 1941; Memorandum by Wallace Murray, 867N.01/1740, April 10, 1941, *USFR:1941*, 7 vols. (Washington, 1959), III, 596-598.

[169] Lazaron to Samuel McCrea Cavert, February 21, 1941, Lazaron to Paul Hutchinson, February 21, 1941, Lazaron to Richard Rothschild, February 21, 1941, AJC; In correspondence with British Foreign Secretary Anthony Eden, Lazaron suggested that the Churchill White Paper be used as a basis for determining the number of Jews permitted to enter Palestine in a given year. He also desired that the fate of the Palestinian Jewish community be determined in consultation with the Arabs and the Mandatory administration. Memorandum of Remarks to Mr. Anthony Eden by Morris S. Lazaron, October 2, 1941, AJC.

Lazaron failed to secure a following among any but a small, assimilated group. Zionists and non-Zionists reproved him.[170] His theories were seconded by old-line liberals like Professor Morris Raphael Cohen and Samuel Edelman,[171] to whom a Zionist-liberal union on Palestine was inconceivable.[172] In late 1941, the threat of a Jewish army being raised in Britain and America to defend Palestine may well have driven Lazaron out of the mainstream of Reform.[173] Along with America Firster Lessing Rosenwald,[174] Mrs. J. Walter Freiberg and Rabbis William Fineshriber, Louis Wolsey, Irving Reichert and Edward N. Calisch, he founded the American Council for Judaism in April, 1942.[175]

Thus, the conversion of Reform Judaism in America, first to a limited countenancing of the Balfour Declaration, then to open support for Palestine as a refugee haven and finally to recognition of Palestine as *the* Jewish homeland, was nearly complete. A set of complex circumstances had been presented to the old Reform movement and its ability to cope with them was questioned by Zionists, non-Zionists and young Reform Jewish nationalists. By 1942, the old leadership was forced to retreat, simply acting defensively at times when it felt its preferred status was seriously threatened. For the time being, the old philosophy and its adherents were forced

[170] Cyrus Adler, head of the American Jewish Committee, condemned Lazaron's stand on Palestine as a hindrance to the saving of Jewish lives. Lazaron to Adler, march 9, 1939; Adler to Lazaron, March 10, 1939, *Ibid.*

[171] Morris R. Cohen to Joseph Willen, October 31, 1941, Morris R. Cohen to Sidney Wallach, November5, 1941, and Samuel Edelman to H. Louis Levinthal, November 23, 1941, *Ibid.* It is significant to note that Edelman had not budged an inch from his 1917 position.

[172] unless it was on anti-Zionist terms. Incidentally, such a union was consummated in 1942. Halperin, p. 125.

[173] U.S. Congress, *Congressional Record, Seventy-Seventh Congress, First Session,* part 9, p. 9576. In 1917, there was an equal fear of raising an all-Jewish regiment to fight in Palestine. "Jewish Regiments in Palestine" (editorial), *Jewish Criterion,* 49 (August 24, 1917), 10.

[174] He was the son of Julius Rosenwald and was President of Sears Roebuck when General Robert E. Wood was Chairman of the Board. Teller, p. 190; Wayne S. Cole, *America First: The Battle Against Intervention 1940-1941* (Madison, Wisconsin, 1953), p. 132.

to yield to American Jews who realized the times demanded of them that they be both visible and vigorous.

---

[175] Sol Bloom received letters from Alfred M. Cohen and Rabbi Edward N. Calisch during the Second World War. Apparently, they had not mellowed. Edward N. Calisch to Sol Bloom, May 31, 1944; Alfred M. Cohen to Sol Bloom, May 25, 1943, Sol Bloom Papers, Box 45, New York Public Library.

IV

Jewish Non-Zionism:
The Committed Wing

Julius Haber, an American Zionist, noted a very important conversion in Jewish life: Jacob Schiff had been won over to Zionism by 1920.[1] But Mr. Schiff wrote of his interest in Zionism in less exuberant terms: "'... these correspondents are entirely mistaken for I want Zionism without the 'ism.' '"[2] Indeed, Jacob Schiff had modified his ideas on Jewish nationalism between 1914 and 1920 but he never formally joined the Zionist Organization.[3] In 1901, Schiff's friend Louis Marshall believed political Zionism to be a thing of the past, a "poet's dream," an irreverent protrusion of religious Judaism. After having read a book by a Russian Zionist in 1908, he claimed to have been inspired with a better understanding and a greater sympathy for Zionism. By 1914, pogroms and privation compelled Eastern European Jews to leave their ghettos. Unfortunately, they could not settle en masse in England or America because those countries had become interested in quota legislation. Not by design, Marshall realized, but by necessity, the Holy Land would have to be developed to support a new rural and urban

---

[1] Haber, pp. 174-175.

[2] "Schiff Favors Home for Jewish Culture," *The New York Times*, April 23, 1917, p. 8; Cyrus Adler, *Jacob H. Schiff: His Life and Letters*, 2 vols. (Garden City, N.Y., 1929), II, 307-308.

[3] Adler, *Jacob H. Schiff*, II, 167.

population. It would be a home for those who had no home.[4] In this respect, he thought, Zionism had matured from imaginative prophecy to a workable imperative.

But this was not Zionism in the political sense. If it were, Schiff would not have split hairs on "isms" nor would he have proclaimed Jewish nationalism to be a harmful element in Jewish life, compromising the convictions of those who wished to keep America as their first land of citizenship.[5]   Similarly, Louis Marshall, Herbert Lehman, Felix Warburg and Cyrus Adler would have exerted themselves less strenuously on behalf of the European Jews who intended to stay where they were. Through the American Jewish Committee (A.J.C.), founded in 1906, and the Joint Distribution Committee (J.D.C.), established in 1914, the will of non-Zionism was made manifest. The former organization vigorously defended the civil, cultural and communal rights of Jews living in Europe and the Ottoman Empire. The latter organization was called into existence to meet the needs of Jewish war sufferers by providing them with the means of survival.[6] It relied on the philanthropy of wealthy American Jews. David A. Brown, a member of the A.J.C. and a principal fund raiser for the J.D.C. stated that the vast sums of money allocated for relief originated from non- and anti-Zionists, inferring that the Zionists were little concerned with the fate of Jews outside Palestine.[7] This firmly held conviction caused a great deal of friction between American Jews in future years when certain priorities in foreign aid had to be established.

In 1917, the A.J.C. favored Palestine strictly as a home for Jewish

[4] Halpern, p. 199; Charles Reznikoff, ed., *Louis Marshall: Champion of Liberty Selected Papers and Addresses*, 2 vols. (Philadelphia, 1957), II, 703-704. 706, 709-710. Louis Marshall was born in Syracuse, New York, in 1856. He was a Republican, a liberal lawyer and a civil rights advocate. From 1912-1929, he was President of the American Jewish Committee.

[5] Adler, *Jacob Schiff*, II, 296-305.

[6] Lehman helped organize the J.D.C. During World War I, Marshall was its Chairman and Warburg its treasurer. Morton Rosenstock, *Louis Marshall: Defender of Jewish Rights* (Detroit, 1956), p. 44; Sapir and Shapiro, *Israel of Tomorrow*, I, 104-105; Sachar, *The Course of Modern Jewish History*, p. 527; American Jewish Committee, *In Vigilant Brotherhood: The American Jewish Committee's Relationship to Palestine and Israel* (New York, 1965), pp. 6-9.

[7] Zosa Szajkowski, "Concord and Discord in American Jewish Overseas Relief, 1914-1924," *Yivo Annual of Jewish Social Science* (hereafter abbreviated *YAJSS*), XIV (New York, 1969), 130; *AJYB*, XXVIII, 89.

refugees. The country's resources were to be utilized in such a way as to make settlement desirable, even attractive, but without "fanfare or flags," with Jews "enjoying the traditional tolerance of the Muslim Government."[8] Zionist slogans did not engage the Committee's Chairman, Louis Marshall, who for the sake of Jewish unity had attempted, abortively, to bring Reform Jews into the American Jewish Congress movement. Interestingly, Marshall was no friend of the Congress, having opposed its formation in 1915 and again in 1917 when, along with Schiff, he felt constrained to withdraw from its Executive Committee because of the intense national feelings it had stirred among Jews in the United States.[9]

The vision of Marshall and Schiff was a more spiritual one than the Zionists' and more traditionally religious than the anti-Zionists'. Jacob Schiff had viewed the Russian Revolution with trepidation. On April 24, 1917, he addressed the League of Jewish Youth, to whom he revealed what was subsequently termed his "change of heart." He had arrived at the conclusion that one of the results of the war would be the disintegration of the old Jewish centers, religious and cultural, of Eastern Europe and that some other reservoir of Jewish learning and religion should be created in their stead. He was not a believer in a "Jewish nation" but declared the "mission" of the Jews to be one of dispersing religious idealism, a task which could be successfully undertaken in Palestine.[10] That same day, Schiff wrote to Israel Maltin that the fall of the Czar was a mixed blessing: "With the emancipation of Russian Jewry, Jewish cultural emanations may cease from there." In consequence, "it might become ... desirable to turn Palestine into a Jewish homeland" where Jews would be able to develop spiritually and culturally, "unhampered by the materialism of the world."[11] To young Zionist Elisha M. Friedman, Schiff confided that he would embrace Zionism had not it and nationalism become synonymous. He told Rabbi

[8] Naomi Wiener Cohen, *Not Free to Desist: A History of the American Jewish Committee 1906-1966* (Philadelphia, 1972), p. 105.

[9] Janowsky, p. 271; Reznikoff, II, 513; Jacob De Haas to Louis D. Brandeis, March 23, 1917, LDB.

[10] Adler, *Jacob Schiff,* II, 307, 314; "Jacob Schiff Joins the Zionist Movement," *The Jewish Tribune,* XXIX (April 27, 1917), 1; "Mr. Schiff is not a Zionist" (editorial), *The Jewish Review and Observer,* XLIII (May 11, 1917), 4.

[11] Jacob Schiff to Israel Maltin, April 24, 1917, LDB.

David Philipson that his modified views on Palestine bore no resemblance to nationalism. In advocating the settlement of large numbers of Jews in the Holy Land, he contemplated neither a racial nor a political entity. The "seed for a large, if not exclusive Jewish population" would be cultural.[12]

With the exception of Weizmann Zionism, Schiff, Marshall and Adler had the most to say in defense of culturalism, Hebraism and the restoration of the historic Jewish spirit. Yet, the mood was ill-defined. It was heralded and defended but never quite explained by American non-Zionists.[13] It is incorrect to rule out Orthodox Judaism as an interpreter of the non-nationalist mind. Schiff and Marshall were reared in the traditional manner and maintained some emotional attachment for it but as adults became affiliated with Reform. Cyrus Adler, too, was the son of devout parents and until July, 1917, was President of the United Synagogues of America representing Conservative Judaism in the United States. [14] He resigned his post as a result of his opposition to the American Jewish Congress and in protest to a United Synagogues' decision to send a delegate to the Congress proceedings scheduled for September 2. The Congress, said Adler, was "unrepresentative of Judaism" and "untimely in its purpose." Personally, he thought it unwise to discuss Palestine as long as it remained under the sway of the Turks and cautioned the United Synagogues of America lest its hastiness to be represented at such a meeting give the impression that the Jews of the United States were solidifying into a nationalistic group.[15]

Practical objections notwithstanding, Cyrus Adler believed in divine intervention. He could not accept the Herzlian view of Jewish redemption as contingent upon anti-Semitism rather than messianism. He was repelled by Herzl's concept of Zionism as a theory of

[12] Adler, *Jacob Schiff*, II, 307-308; "Mr. Schiff not for Zionism," *The New York Times*, May 21, 1917, p. 11.

[13] "Symposium on Zionism," *The New York Times*, May 14, 1917, p. 9; "Symposium on Zionism," *The American Hebrew*, 101 (May 18, 1917), 43.

[14] Cyrus Adler (1863-1940) was a Conservative Jew. He was President of Dropsie College and succeeded Solomon Schechter to the Presidency of Jewish Theological Seminary in 1915. From 1929 until his death, he was President of the A.J.C.

[15] "United Synagogues Clash Over Zionism," *The New York Times*, July 3, 1917, p. 7; "United Synagogue Convention Holds Turbulent Session," *The Jewish Tribune*, XXX (July 13, 1917), 1.

race and nation; he also divorced himself from anti-Zionist Reform theology, arraigning it as a "heresy." In short, Adler held a romantic love for Zion but not for Zionism: throughout his life Zionism represented an unsolved spiritual dilemma. It was too politically radical to gain his sympathy but the miraculous return of the Jews to their ancient home was never far from his thoughts.[16]

Non-Zionism was not an American creation, although some of its very famous theorists, notably Rev. Dr. Henry Pereira Mendes of New York's Portuguese Synagogue and Judah Magnes, Chancellor and later President of Hebrew University, were born in the United States.[17] The source of non-Zionism was, in fact, European and the doctrine, itself, may be designated, quite accurately, as "cultural Zionism" or Achad Ha-Amism. The Achad Ha-Am cultural philosophy accommodated a wide range of non-Zionist thought, from the territorialism of Jacob Schiff to Marshall's refugeeism and Adler's hope of divine return.

Achad Ha-Am preferred cultural preparation prior to Aliyah. "The primary problem was not saving Jews by ameliorating their physical existence but the preservation and development of the Jewish spirit." In his opinion, the spiritual disintegration of the Jew could be healed only in Palestine, although the Holy Land offered no solution to alleviating political disabilities of Jews in other parts of the world. Convinced that the Jews would remain in the diaspora for generations to come, Achad Ha-Am urged the Zionists to concentrate their energies on "evolving in Israel's historic land a community which would be a true miniature of the Jewish people." There, a cultural and spiritual center would be created from which "the currents of influence should radiate throughout the diaspora and thus all Jews would be invigorated and unified." Achad Ha-Am recognized that even a spiritual center must have an economic base but he attached minimal significance to materialism.[18] Among Americans, economics and refugeeism acceded to primary positions but the fundamental tenets of the philosophy continued unchanged.

[16] Abraham Neuman, *Cyrus Adler: A Biographical Sketch* (Philadelphia, 1942), pp. 198-200, 207-208.

[17] H. Pereira Mendes, "The Jewish Nation," *The American Hebrew*, 105 (September 26, 1919), 496, 515; Arthur A. Goren, *New York Jews and the Quest for Community: The Kehillah Experiment 1908-1922* (New York, 1970), p. 24; Judah L. Magnes, *War-Time Addresses 1917-1921* (New York, 1923), pp. 91-95, 101.

[18] Sachar, *Course of Modern Jewish History*, pp. 275-276; Israel Cohen, *A Short History of Zionism*, pp. 35-37.

It was not the A.J.C. but individuals who first tried to make peace with Zionism.   In the two months preceding and immediately following the Jewish homeland announcement by Great Britain, Jacob Schiff wanted to join the American Zionist movement. He was in contact with Elisha Friedman, who faithfully relayed the gist of the talks to Brandeis and Julian Mack. Schiff felt that the whole purpose of Zionism was jeopardized by the quest for an independent state and averred his willingness to identify himself with the movement if the Zionists would relinquish this idea and promote instead a proposal for an autonomous protectorate under some great power, for instance England.[19] Friedman continued: "Further, I repeated to them (Eugene Meyer, Jr. and Brandeis) that you thought the Transvaal a typical example of realized Zionism politically...." Schiff would have liked millions of Jews sent to the South African province, rather than mere thousands to Palestine, and established there on firm foundations and colonization principles to farm the rich coastal plain under British tutelage.[20] Friedman assured the non-Zionist banker that "your own concept of a locally autonomous regime under the aegis of a Great Power is in complete accord with sober Zionists and is totally in harmony with the Basel Program." In a matter of days, Schiff explained his predilections in greater detail. Since he still adhered to the dual loyalty argument, he was prepared to accept a large Jewish settlement but not a Jewish nation in Palestine. If any solution along these lines was practicable, he would "be most willing to cooperate." Three days afterward, on September 28, 1917, Schiff received a reply: with regard to Palestine, bubbled Friedman, his ideas "coincided precisely" with those of the Zionists.[21]

Thus, Schiff saw his way clear to enter the Zionist movement with no reservations. Events, however, made him wary of the Zionists' true motives. The American Jewish Congress had been finally postponed in October through the arduous endeavors of Henry Morgenthau, Samuel Schulman and Louis Marshsall, all of whom were convinced that such a proceeding would engender a rash display of Jewish nationalism.[22] As a negotiator at the preliminary

[19] Schiff to Friedman, September 25, 1917, LDB; Adler, *Jacob H. Schiff,* II, 308-310.

[20] Friedman to Schiff, September 21, 1917, LDB.

[21] Friedman to Schiff, September 28, 1917, *Ibid.*

[22] Jacob De Haas to Brandeis, October 14, 1917. *Ibid.*

Congress sessions, Marshall represented only himself: the A.J.C., under pressure from its anti-national members, remained aloof.[23] Despite the frequency of his meeting with the Congress organizers Marshall was displeased, having rejected the body peremptorily as a forum of Russian immigrants rather than third generation American citizens. The tenacity with which the Zionists grasped the Congress idea indicated to Schiff that they had yet to display "good faith." His conditions, restated to Friedman, were that he was willing to become a Zionist and sit at an international conference if all the assurances made to him in private would be made public. As a concession, he would agree to the autonomy situation outlined by Friedman: if the Jews became a majority in Palestine, some sort of self-governing policy would be installed.[24] Schiff was closer to Zionism than he realized, for this was the extent of Zionist demands in 1917.

The Zionists showed their displeasure that an arrangement with Schiff should have to end in their renunciation of nationalist ideology. American Zionists, with whom Schiff was dickering, offered him no satisfaction. Friedman did not lead the banker astray; Schiff simply assumed too much with regard to American Zionism. If he was nervous about a Jewish "state" the man he should have approached was Chaim Weizmann, an East European by birth who tempered his nationalism with a good measure of Achad Ha-Am culturalism.[25] On the other hand, Brandeis, Julian Mack, Jacob De Haas and Stephen Wise were all inured to the Herzl strain, distinctly Western and lacking in religious sentimentalism or cultural romance. On December 3, 1917, Jacob Schiff wrote directly to Judge Mack and reiterated his intention to officially join the Zionist Organization. He said, in part: "Though long considered an opponent of Zionism, my opposition has not been to Zionism itself but to the proposition to reestablish an independent political and sovereign Jewish nation." Recalling his own religious upbringing, he employed a Biblical tone, in which nationalism was subordinated to "the principle of Judaism" as a pivotal factor in Jewish resettlement. Zionism was a "restorer of Jewish self-consciousness, returning many to the fold who would have been lost to the Jewish

---

[23] "Reconvening of the American Jewish Congress" (editorial). *Emanu-El*. XLVII (May 14, 1920), 2.

[24] Adler, *Jacob H. Schiff*, II, 310-311.

[25] Schiff to Friedman, October 26, 1917, LDB.

people.'' The political philosophy of Zionism, as Schiff had earlier told Friedman, was unimportant.[26] What he had inferred to Mack was communicated to Israel Zangwill in no uncertain terms: he wanted religion to be explicitly a cornerstone of Palestinian revival under British suzerainty.[27]

Mack's reply was curt. If Schiff desired to state his frank, personal views, they should not be confused with those of Zionism in general, lest a misunderstanding divide the movement at a crucial time. Neither critical nor laudatory remarks were volunteered on Schiff's contemplated Zionist membership.[28] Having requested the fulfillment of certain conditions prior to his joining the University Zionist Society, Schiff was compelled to withdraw his membership when such assurances were not forthcoming.[29]

Schiff's independent actions anticipated a more significant debate by the A.J.C. The cultural apotheosis of Zionism challenged it.[30] Both the Balfour Declaration and the British capture of Palestine in December, 1917, were deserving of comment and such comment should properly come from an organization whose raison d'etre was the preservation of Jewish liberty in all countries. What hampered the A.J.C. in the drafting of an announcement was that the organization was obliged to accommodate a welter of disparate notions. It will be recalled that the Committee was apolitical in the first years of its life and attempted a pose of neutrality even after its statement on the Balfour Declaration. As such, Jews of all Zionist leanings were represented: Morgenthau, Rosenwald, Bernheim, Mack, Friedenwald, Frankfurter, Schiff and Magnes.[31] Louis Marshall was its President and, as far as Jewish nationalism was concerned, he was convinced of the rightness of both Brandeis and Mack on Palestinian development.[32] Adler was his close friend but his opponent on

[26] Schiff to Julian Mack, December 3, 1917, IF; Schiff to Mack, December 3, 1917, LDB; Adler, *Jacob H. Schiff*, II, 316.

[27] Adler, *Jacob H. Schiff*, II, 316.

[28] Mack to Schiff, December 6, 1917, LDB

[29] Adler, *Jacob H. Schiff*, II, 316.

[30] ''Jerusalem for Idealists,'' *The New York Times*, December 23, 1917, p. 7.

[31] For example, see Cyrus Adler to Harry Schneiderman, February 11, 1918, AJC and Rabinowitz, p. 9.

Zionist matters, having rejected Weizmann and Brandeis for Samuel Edelman's "internationalization" theory and Orthodox messianism.[33]

There was a determined anti-Zionist resistance in the A.J.C. as a result of the Balfour Declaration and a division loomed imminent. The Committee's stand was hotly contested in the first two months of 1918.[34]   Jacob Schiff, who was still upset at the indifference of Zionist leaders to the religious issue, declared that the Balfour promise would result in "the breakup of this Committee."[35]   Marshall threaded his way among the combatants' conjectures, at once an Achad Ha-Am culturalist, a believer in Solomon Schechter's Zionism, but also fundamentally concerned with homeless refugees and most interested in the investment theories of Brandeis.[36]

Because of Zionist differences, Frankfurter and Friedenwald had quit the American Jewish Committee in 1916.[37] Mack was soon to follow. In early April, 1918, the A.J.C. had prepared a statement sympathizing with the Balfour Declaration. The document represented the prevailing opinion of the Committee's leaders. It was thoughtful and conciliatory, perhaps too much so for the Zionists in the A.J.C., and mindful of world and domestic events since the previous November. It seemed pointless for Jews to resist the national home idea, reasoned Marshall. For one thing, the English promise had received the approval of various European and Asian powers, among them Serbia, France, Italy, Greece, Siam, Holland, China and Japan.[38] For another, it would seem ungracious, even vaguely disloyal, to the Allied cause for Americans to back away from a British pledge. American Jews of German descent felt it incumbent upon them to demonstrate a loyalty to the Allies that the

---

[32] Reznikoff, II, 710-714.

[33] Cyrus Adler to Louis Marshall, March 1, 1915, AJC. Internationalization means that a city or a country should be regarded as the property of all peoples rather than just one.

[34] Rabinowitz, pp. 8-10; Rosenstock, p. 43; Rischin, *Herzl Year Book*, V, 73-74.

[35] Schiff to Friedlaender, January 7, 1918, IF; Rabinowitz, p. 9.

[36] Marshall to Friedlaender, March 5, 1918, IF.

[37] Frankfurter to Marshall, June 23, 1916, AJC.

[38] *Hearings... Committee on Foreign Affairs,... on H. Con. Res. 52*, pp. 152-153.

pacifist German-American coalition was disparaging.[39]

In any event, Adler, Marshall and Judge Mack worked on the text of the statement. Mack fought for the insertion of the words "a national home for the Jewish people." Adler and Marshall preferred a more innocuous phrasing wherein Palestine would be simply a "centre for Judaism." The Marshall-Adler version won out by April 10 and Mack resigned from the A.J.C. in protest.[40] In the two weeks prior to its publication, the document's contents were submitted to Secretary of State Lansing, who approved them.[41] The short but precise statement became the official stand of the A.J.C. for the next two decades. While receiving the English declaration "with profound appreciation," the Committee stated as "axiomatic" that "the Jews of the United States have here established a permanent home ... and recognize their unqualified allegiance to this country...." The A.J.C. added that in other democratic lands as well, most Jews will continue "to live ... where they enjoy full civil religious liberty." But, continued the statement, the Committee was not unmindful that there were Jews everywhere who, moved by traditional sentiment, yearned for a home in the Holy Land for the Jewish people. To this home, they subscribed "our wholehearted sympathy" and pledged cooperation with those who "shall seek to establish in Palestine a centre for Judaism, for the stimulation of our faith, for the pursuit of literature, science and art in a Jewish environment and for the rehabilitation of the land."[42]

A dedication to cultural Zionism was thus present among some American Jews who, by April 1918, were energetically distinguishing their philosophy from that of Rabbinic Reform.[43] During the

---

[39] Marshall to Lionel De Rothschild, July 12, 1918, AJC; Rabinowitz. p. 11.

[40] Harry Schneiderman to Schiff, April 8, 1918, AJC; Rischin, *Herzl Year Book*, V, 74.

[41] Reznikoff, II, 714-716; Rabinowitz, p. 11.

[42] Marshall to De Rothschild, July 12, 1918, AJC; Neuman, pp. 204-205; Esco Foundation, I, 109; *AJYB*, XXI (Philadelphia, 1919), 660; *AJYB*, XXXII (Philadelphia, 1930), 324; "Jews Favor British Offer," *The New York Times*, April 29, 1928, p. 8; Laqueur, *Journal of Contemporary History*, VI, 179; American Jewish Committee, *Jewish Post-War Problems; A Study Course* (New York, 1943), p. 66; Rischin, *Herzl Year Book*, V, 75. The full text of the statement may be found in A.J.C., *In Vigilant Brotherhood*, p. 62.

[43] Reznikoff, II, 716-718.

interwar years, non-Zionists did not retract or modify what Zionists were wont to suppose was a literal, rather narrow, interpretation of the Balfour Declaration.   Furthermore, non-Zionists were never disabused as to the correctness of their own beliefs but, nevertheless, exercised admirable restraint in their dealings with Jewish nationalists. [44]   It was an unusual instance if non-Zionists criticized the Palestinian politics of the Zionists in the press, from the pulpit or in debate.   Not that they were always pleased with Zionism, but they discovered more areas of accord than discord and, with a number of notable exceptions, succeeded in submerging mutual tensions.   Nor were they indifferent to Palestine.   From the outset, non-Zionists were committed to the Balfour Declaration and its non-national ramifications.

Jacob Schiff and Louis Marshall refused to join either David Philipson's anti-Zionist league or Julius Kahn's Paris claque.[45]   As President of the A.J.C., Marshall brought the organization into a pragmatic association with the American Jewish Congress in December, 1918, and mollified the resistance of the undecided in his own group by trying to impress the primacy of the cultural philosophy upon American Zionists.[46]   On this score, however, his triumph was more illusory than actual.

Marshall went to Paris in February, 1919, and, after Julian Mack stepped down in March, headed the Committee of Jewish Delegations which, though involved in securing minority rights for Jews in Europe, supported the Zionist program vis-a-vis Palestine.[47]   The Committee's theme was Jewish unity and, as Mack had done, Marshall played down nationalism.   The non-Zionist press cemented the budding relationship by displaying an indomitable faith in the peacemakers to solve the Jewish problem in Europe through agreements with the states of Central and Eastern Europe and in Palestine via British assumption of a mandate. [48]   Broadly speaking,

[44] *AJYB*, XXXII, 108.

[45] Schneiderman to Schiff, March 16, 1919, AJC; "Jacob Schiff Opposes Anti-Zionist Conference," *The American Jewish World*, VII (September 20, 1918), 51; Reznikoff, II, 719-724.

[46] "Jews Plan Unity at First Congress," *The New York Times*, December 16, 1918, p. 24; "Louis Marshall Explains," *The New York Times*, December 17, 1918, p 11; Reznikoff, II, 351-353.

[47] Janowsky, pp. 290, 303-308; Kessler, *YAJSS*, II, 232-235.

this was the Zionist program as well.

The problem, however, was one of emphasis. As a representative of the non-Zionists at Versailles, Marshall was more interested in revitalizing European Jewish communities than championing an extensive Palestinian Jewish immigration. Having been educated on Jewish minority rights in Palestine by a pair of American Jewish Socialists, he resolved to obtain the identical legal guarantees he had suggested for European Jews, physical safety, national language and government subsidized communal institutions, for his co-religionists in the Holy Land. The Palestine memorandum he drew up at Paris said as much and reflected what Marshall assumed were the limits of Zionist aspirations. 49 On March 5, 1919, he appealed to Adolph Ochs to reconsider printing a memorial which was submitted to President Wilson on behalf of the oppressed Jews of Russia, Poland and Rumania, who were being encouraged to emigrate to Palestine. Marshall assured *The New York Times* editor, to no avail, that "the idea of Jewish statehood is dead. The statement issued by the American Jewish Committee in April, 1918, has been practically adopted by the Zionist Organization."[50]

In the United States, Marshall's efforts were complemented by those of Jacob Schiff, who continued to abjure political Zionism but did pledge twenty-five thousand dollars to Zionist educational projects and made special appeals to Jews for the upbuilding of Palestine.[51] The United Drive for Zion was an early Zionist-non-Zionist plan, whose objective was the union of the J.D.C. with the leaders of the Zionist Organization in a ten million dollar relief fund for the world's Jews, one-third of the funds to be applied exclusively to Palestine and administered directly by the Zionist Organization. Despite the fact that Schiff was acting as mediator and Justice Brandeis was present to add his influence, the plan was vetoed by Julius Rosenwald, who wanted no money allocated for Zionist

[48] "Where is Our Sense of Proportion" (editorial), *New Jewish Chronicle,* II (February 1919), 76-77; "The Day is Dawning" (editorial),*The New Jewish Chronicle,* II (June 1919), 148.

[49] Yaakov Shalom Hertz, *The Jewish Socialist Movement in America* (in Yiddish, New York, 1954), p. 186; Jacob A. Rubin, *Partners in State Building: American Jewry and Israel* (New York, 1969), p. 59; Kessler, *YAJSS,* II, 232; Janowsky, p. 290.

[50] Reznikoff. II, 724-725.

[51] Adler, *Jacob H. Schiff,* II, 318, 320.

purposes.[52]

Nevertheless, Schiff's work was indicative of the non-Zionist ethic. Like Adler and Marshall, he would do nothing to oppose Zionism. The possibility of eventual Jewish hegemony in Palestine was a consideration but the pressing need was for a refugee haven and, at that moment, only the latter circumstance appeared relevant. Great Britain was the necessary overseer of what Schiff probably hoped would become a rebirth of traditional Judaism in the land where it was born.[53]

But it was the World Zionist Organization under Weizmann and not the non-Zionists who entered into partnership with Britain on the administration of the mandate. The Jewish Agency, however, was not ungrateful to either the A.J.C. or individual non-Zionist endeavors to consummate the social and cultural dream of Palestine; nor was it unmindful of the financial resources which would become available to Zionism through a union with the Marshall forces. Until the Brandeis-Weizmann split, the Zionist Organization in London had kept its lines of communication open to non-Zionists through Louis Brandeis but were unable to do so subsequently. It was only then that Weizmann and Marshall began a series of personal discussions and eventually arrived at an understanding.

Before 1925, it seemed that Marshall would be unable to choose between an association with Brandeis, whom he respected, or Weizmann, whose feelings on the importance of Jewish culture were akin to his own. For a while, he tried to obviate the necessity of a choice by acting as an arbitrator during the Zionist imbroglio of 1921.[54] Unable to resolve the quarrel between Brandeis and Weizmann, he momentarily shifted to the American leader. The American Palestine Company impressed Marshall as a practical investment in Palestinian rehabilitation and he praised its founding

[52] "Special Weekly Letter From New York," The Jewish Criterion, 53 (December 26, 1919), 3.

[53] Schiff to Schneiderman, March 17, 1919, AJC; De Haas to Brandeis, October 27, 1919, LDB; O.J. Campbell, A Report on Zionism, WYP, EMHC, Drawer 52, Folder 143, p. 2605; "Jews Will Honor Dr. Wise's Memory," The New York Times, March 11, 1919, p. 5; Adler, Jacob H. Schiff, II, 317.

[54] Reznikoff, II, 731-732. The 1921 imbroglio was a power struggle between Brandeis and Weizmann. Allocation of funds and diaspora nationalism were the key issues. See Chapter 5.

with the assistance of Judge Irving Lehman. [55] Whether he was on the verge of conversion to Brandeis Zionism was doubtful, although Joseph Barondess may have assumed so when he expressed the hope, in June 1921, that Marshall would join the Zionist movement formally and represent the Brandeis faction at the World Zionist Congress.[56] Nevertheless, in concert with all Zionists and a majority of non-Zionists, he approved of assigning the mandate to Britain in 1920 at San Remo and its confirmation by the League of Nations two years later.[57] He was an eloquent defender of the Lodge-Fish Resolution, although the A.J.C., like the W.Z.O., did not object to the Churchill Memorandum.[58]

Marshall's dedication to some sort of cooperation with the Zionists was extraordinary, especially since he encountered some testiness from his colleagues in the A.J.C. Cyrus Adler's spiritual turn of mind was repelled by American dollars and suspect of the secular European associates of Weizmann.[59] The President of Dropsie College and Jewish Theological Seminary of America was rather pleased that the Churchill White Paper had clarified the limits of the Balfour Declaration.[60] And what of the "new" men who had replaced the recently deceased Schiff as non-Zionist leaders? Marshall was hard put to convince Felix Warburg and Herbert Lehman of Zionism's beneficence. Both were jealous of the fund-raising prerogatives of the J.D.C. and the key role played by the A.J.C. in securing the rights of Jews in the countries where they lived.[61] They desired that neither function be appropriated by

[55] "To Develop Palestine by American Methods," *The American Hebrew,* 108 (March 25, 1921), 523; Reznikoff, II, 725-726.

[56] Joseph Barondess to Marshall, June 28, 1921, Joseph Barondess Letterbooks (hereafter abbreviated JBL), no. 51, pp. 871-872, New York Public Library.

[57] Naomi Wiener Cohen, *A Dual Heritage*, p. 293.

[58] Reznikoff, II, 729-730; Rosenstock, p. 44; Rischin, *Herzl Year Book,* V, 81; A.J.C., *In Vigilant Brotherhood,* p. 13.

[59] Mack to Brandeis, January 29, 1921, LDB.

[60] Cyrus Adler to George W. Ochs-Oakes, undated, AJC.

[61] Herbert Lehman's secretary, Carolin Flexner, was more impressed with Brandeis Zionism than her employer. Carolin Flexner to Herbert Lehman, May 28, 1923, Lehman to Alfred Mond, November 13, 1923 and Lehman to James Becker, April 28, 1926, Herbert Lehman Papers (hereafter abbreviated HL), School of International Affairs, Columbia University; Szajkowski, *YAJSS* XIV, 134-135

Zionism, with its inordinate concentration on fund-raising for Palestine and its apparent lack of concern for the welfare of Jewish communities outside the Holy Land. Presaging future difficulties, in 1921 Julian Mack failed to interest Colonel Lehman on a meeting of the minds regarding Palestine.[62]

The moment of decision arrived in 1924 when two pressing problems demanded resolution. In the first place, Weizmann had been assiduously petitioning "all Jews" to support a World Jewish Congress which was "soon to meet" for the purpose of enlarging the Jewish Agency to include all shades of non-and anti-nationalism.[63] There is no question that his appeal was directed at those Jews whose financial resources were the greatest. Marshall thought that Weizmann needed some knowledgeable assistance because, in his estimation, the Zionists were not qualified "to deal with industrial enterprises... and cannot run them on a business basis."[64] Secondly, the passage of the National Origins Act in 1924 made Marshall firmer in his idea of Jewish economic and cultural revival in Palestine for the benefit of Jewish refugees. He was keenly aware of rising indifference to Jews on the part of the Gentile community, whose insecurities had bred a Ku Klux Klan revival and encouraged the conspiratorial mind of Henry Ford. Equally disquieting was the fact that Jews no longer resisted but welcomed assimilation. It seemed to Marshall that his American co-religionists had lost interest in their heritage and in each other.[65]

Louis Marshall discovered that he could no longer work with American Zionists. Over a two year period, Stephen Wise had challenged the J.D.C. on the importance of Russia as opposed to Palestine as the theater of Jewish philanthropy.[66] In the words of David Brown and Herbert Lehman, it was "Russia before Palestine;" the Jews still had to solve their problems where they lived.[67]

---

[62] Mack to Lehman, October 7, 1921, Mack to Brandeis, November 4 and 5, 1921, LDB.

[63] "The Jewish Agency for Palestine" (editorial), *The American Hebrew*, 111 (September 8, 1922), 385, 404.

[64] Reznikoff, II, 732-734.

[65] A.J.C., *Jewish Post-War Problems*, p. 68.

[66] Louis Lipsky, *Thirty Years of American Zionism* (n.p., 1927), pp. 194-201; Reznikoff, II, 750-760; "Sees Destiny of Jews Among Non-Jews," *The New York Times*, September 29, 1925, p. 10.

Rival fund-raising bodies were organized and in late 1925, a massive Keren Hayesod (Jewish National Fund) — Hadassah drive buried the Crimea issue and earned for Wise and the Brandeis group the opprobrium of the non-Zionists. [68] Thus encouraged to sever his ties with Brandeis and Mack, Marshall turned his attention to Weizmann.

As he contemplated cooperation within the proposed enlarged Jewish Agency, Marshall probably reasoned that the presence of anti-Zionists could only enhance American Jewish strength when it came to bargaining with Weizmann. So, between 1924 and 1928 Marshall, with the assistance of Felix Warburg, explored areas of non- and anti-Zionist accord with regard to Palestine at the Non-Partisan Conference, held in New York City. Anticipating the success of these talks, Marshall concluded a working agreement with Weizmann on March 1, 1925. [69]

As stated by the A.J.C. in 1926, the aim of the enlarged Jewish Agency for Palestine (J.A.P.) was to establish that country as a "Jewish center of literature, science, art, religion and culture." [70] The 1924 conditions of membership were adopted: The Council of the J.A.P. was to consist of fifty per cent membership selected from the W.Z.O. and an equal number of non-Zionist (including anti-nationalist) organizations. All affiliates were bound to cooperate with the Mandatory. In addition, forty per cent of the non-Zionists would be American Jews and fifty per cent of the Agency's Executive Committee would be drawn from Zionist bodies while a like number would be chosen by non-Zionists. [71] In a symbolic union of purpose, Marshall signed a pact of friendship (also known as the

[67] Lehman to Hon James B.M. Hertzog, March 8, 1929, and Carolin Flexner to Herbert Lehman, July 23, 1926, HL; Voss, p. 131.

[68] Lipsky, pp. 194-201; "Zionists and the J.D.C. to Carry on Separate Campaigns," *The American Hebrew*, 118 (December 4, 1925), 146; James H. Becker to Julian Mack, April 28, 1926, HL; "The Baltimore Conference and the United Palestine Appeal" (editorial), *Emanu-El*, LXI (December 18. 1925), 2.

[69] *AJYB*, XXXI (Philadelphia, 1929), 76-77; A.J.C., *Jewish Post-War Problems*, p. 66; *AJYB*, XXVIII, 88, 512-513; Reznikoff, II, 742-743; Isaac Landman. "American Jews for Palestine," *The American Hebrew*, 116 (March 6, 1925), 496. 540; Herbert Bernstein, "The Fourteenth Zionist Congress," *The Jewish Tribune*. 44 (September 4, 1925), 1, 17.

[70] *AJYB*, XXVIII, 512-513.

"Pact of Glory") with Weizmann and combined with him on a United Palestine Campaign wherein Marshall, attempting to display a solidarity among all non-nationalist Jews, even solicited a contribution from Julius Rosenwald.[72]

A Joint Survey Commission to investigate the diverse aspects of Palestinian politics, immigration, industry and agriculture was appointed, in March, 1927, by distinguished Zionists and non-Zionists. The non-Zionists who served were Dr. Oscar Wasserman of Germany and the Americans Lee K. Frankel and Felix Warburg. The report was submitted to the non-Zionists and the W.Z.O. Executive in June, 1928. The peace between Zionists and non-Zionists, blessed at many places in the past few years, including the Zionist Congress of 1927 at Basel, had finally been propelled beyond the discussion stage.[73] Whatever reservations Marshall and Lehman harbored in 1928 and 1929 as to the "unbusinesslike methods of the Zionists were not publicly revealed, although they shared many residual doubts."[74] The Zionist-non-Zionist wings of Judaism were no longer verging on unity: they had been dramatically and finally joined. American non-Zionists ratified the previous actions between Marshall and Weizmann in October, 1928. At this time, Marshall appointed seven men, Warburg, Adler, Frankel, Herbert Lehman, David Brown, James Becker and Julian Morgenstern to select the non-Zionist delegates to the Jewish Agency.[75] Climaxing nine months of speculation and fanfare, the Zionists ratified the agreements in August, 1929.[76] On the fifteenth of that month, three days

[71] Since most of the non-Zionists were from the United States, it is not surprising that half of their Agency delegates were supposed to be Americans. Marshall to Felix Warburg, July 1, 1929, AJC; *AJYB*, XXVIII, 88-89.

[72] "Zionists at Peace with Non-Zionists," *The New York Times*, January 23, 1927, Sec. 2, p. 7; "Issues Palestine Appeal," *The New York Times*, January 25, 1927, p. 10; "Palestine Peace Hailed by Leaders," *The New York Times*, February 7, 1927, p. 3; Reznikoff, II, 750-764.

[73] "Accord on Zionism Hailed at Dinner," *The New York Times*, March 23, 1927, p. 15; *AJYB*, XXX (Philadelphia, 1928), 109-123; "To Extend Jewish Agency," *The New York Times*, September 10, 1927, p. 3; *AJYB*, XXXI, 76-80.

[74] Marshall to Schneiderman, July 24, 1928, Marshall to Morris Rothenberg, June 21, 1929. Marshall to Warburg, June 21, 1929, Zionburo to Marshall, July 25, 1929 and Marshall to Weizmann, June 6, 1929, AJC; Waldman, p. 203; Samuel Schulman to Herbert Lehman, May 7, 1929 and Lehman to Schulman, May 10, 1929, HL.

after the enlarged Agency met for the first time, the Agency Council unanimously adopted a "constitution of harmony."[77] Exactly one month after his great triumph, Louis Marshall died in Zurich.

With Marshall's death, the non-Zionist leadership shifted to Felix Warburg, Chairman of the J.A.P. Administrative Committee and Cyrus Adler, an Agency representative and the new President of the A.J.C.[78] They were to dominate American non-Zionism in the 1930's without straying from the fundamental principles of Marshall: forbearance for Britain's difficulties as Mandatory, at least until 1939, commitment to the Balfour Declaration and, with the single exception of partition, cooperation with Weizmann's leadership. No sooner had Warburg and Adler assumed their duties when the first of many crises threatened to overwhelm them.

Speaking temperately at Madison Square Garden on August 29, 1929, in the midst of the Palestine outbreaks, Herbert Lehman asked that the Mandatory live up to her promises.[79] However, no formula

[75] "Sees Big Possibilities in Non-Zionist Parley," *The New York Times,* October 18, 1928, p. 22; "Non-Zionists Meet on Palestine Unity," *The New York Times,* October 21, 1928, Sec. 2, p. 2; "Appoint 7 Non-Zionists," *The New York Times,* November 3, 1928, p. 4; Halpern, p. 197; *Non-Zionist Conference Concerning Palestine: Verbatim Report of Proceedings, October 20-21, 1928* (New York, 1928), pp. 41-66, 93-94.

[76] "Non-Zionists to Meet Today," *The New York Times,* January 13, 1929, p. 31; "Lauds Jewish Agency," *The New York Times,* August 18, 1929, Sec. 2, p. 4; "Warburg Reports Zionist Agreement," *The New York Times,* April 28, 1929, Sec. 2 p. 1; "Jewish Seminary Creates 10 Rabbis," *The New York Times,* June 10, 1929, p. 16; "Hails Harmony on Zionism," *The New York Times,* April 29, 1929, p. 23; "Zionist Congress in Deadlock over Composition of its New Executive," *The Jewish Review and Observer,* LV (August 9, 1929), 1, 4; Lionel Hill, "America Dominant at Zionist Congress." *The American Hebrew,* 125 (August 2, 1929), 328.

[77] "Baron De Rothschild Heads Jewish Council," *Christian Science Monitor* August 15, 1929, p. 3; "Zionist Congress in Deadlock over Composition of its New Executive," *The Jewish Review and Observer,* LV (August 9, 1929), 1, 4.

[78] Neuman, pp. 207-208.

[79] Lehman to Morris D. Waldman, August 29, 1929, HL; "The Wailing Wall" (editorial), *The Jewish Review and Observer,* LV (December 28, 21928), p. 4. At least one non-Jewish American daily, *The Springfield Daily Republican,* embraced the non-Zionist viewpoint. See "The Riots in Jerusalem" (editorial), *The Springfield Daily Republican,* August 26, 1929, p. 6.

for action was devised. *The Jewish Review and Observer*, for example, deplored the tragedy, called upon all Jews to support the non-partisan Palestine Emergency Fund, but was silent on controversial issues.[80]   Cyrus Adler had faith that Great Britain would restore order in the Holy Land but nevertheless petitioned the American Government, through the State Department, to communicate with Near Eastern nations on measures to prevent the unrest from spreading.[81]   G. Howland Shaw, Chief of the Near East Division of the State Department, answered the A.J.C. telegram evasively, his reply suggesting that the United States had communicated and would communicate with no one. [82]

Among the non-Zionists, Warburg was the only one to evince disenchantment with England. He was seconded in his criticism by Brandeis and Judah Magnes, two men with whom he shared more than a passing acquaintance. In America, Magnes had a small but determined following which had arisen after he founded the B'rith Shalom Society at Hebrew University in 1926.[83] Magnes's ideas on an Arab-Jewish federation were well-known, as was his determination to cement a permanent understanding between the two peoples.[84] Warburg was in the Holy Land in 1927 and was touring the country in August, 1929, when his visit was abbreviated by the onset of the disorders. By all indications. Warburg had been moved by the candor and sincerity of Magnes, Hebrew University's Chancellor. From the time of his return to the United States in 1929 to the partition controversy, Warburg stressed the importance of Arab-Jewish cooperation. He called the events at the Wailing Wall "an

[80] Luis Berg, "American Public Opinion on Palestine," *Menorah Journal,* XVII (October 1929), 78.

[81] Adler to A.M. Greenfield, September 3, 1929, AJC. The AJC was well aware of the fact that the State Department was receiving communiques from Vincent Sheean and Pierre Crabites, both anti-Zionists. George Ochs-Oakes to Cyrus Adler, November 21, 1929, AJC.

[82] G. Howland Shaw to Morris D. Waldman, September 5, 1929, *Ibid.*

[83] Herbert Parzen, "The Magnes-Weizmann-Einstein Controversy," *Jewish Social Studies,* XXXII (July 1970), 190; "Zionists Aroused" (editorial), *The Jewish Review and Observer,* LVI (December 20, 1929), 1, 4; A.H. Fromenson, "Cyrus Sulzberger is Seventy," *The American Hebrew* 123 (July 13, 1928), 286.

[84] "Dr. Magnes Scored in Jewish Press," *The New York Times,* November 22, 1929, p. 6; "Magnes Explains Palestine Stand," *The New York Times,* November 24, 1929, p. 12.

incredible mistake on the part of the British authorities." He was quite sure that the "better part of the Arab population regretted the uprising," a "result of misunderstandings" which could have been prevented.[85]

Warburg learned about Brandeis investments as an eyewitness and his respect for the American minority Zionists increased. A meeting between the two men at Brandeis's Washington apartment in September, 1929, was cordial. Brandeis told Warburg of his negative feelings on the present Zionist Organization. The Zionist Executive in Palestine, Brandeis maintained, did not have British confidence and was incompetent to deal with critical matters like riots. "To all this, Mr. Warburg assented." As to the inquiry into the riots, Brandeis believed that it was the duty of the American Government and not the American Jews to make representations to the English. Warburg agreed to this and to the Brandeis idea that "the call for Palestine in America should be for investment purposes and business rather than for relief which is a government function."[86] In ten weeks time, another discussion between the two men, held at Warburg's insistence, in the presence of eminent members of the American Jewish community, yielded a unanimous decision to create an American business corporation for the investment of funds, with a view toward furthering the economic development of Palestine.[87]

The Brandeis-Warburg detente was not directed against Weizmann but against the man who had replaced Brandeis as the leader of the Zionist Organization of America (Z.O.A.), Louis Lipsky. After Marshall's death in September, 1929, Warburg campaigned for the restoration of Brandeis to a preeminent position in American Jewish affairs.[88] When the support of the W.Z.O. was withdrawn from him through the exertion of much pressure upon Weizmann, Lipsky succumbed and the Brandeis group returned that June.

[85] "Jews at Wall an Error, Says Felix Warburg," *New York Herald Tribune*, September 5, 1929, p. 14.

[86] *Minutes of Conference at the Apartment of Justice Brandeis, Washington, D.C., September 19, 1929*, LDB.

[87] "Justice Brandeis Resumes Work for Palestine," *The Jewish Transcript*, VI (December 6, 1929), 1, 8.

[88] Jacob De Haas, "How Brandeis Again Heads Zionism," *Chicago Jewish Chronicle*, XIX (September 19, 1930), part 2, pp. 5-7.

Regarding the Passfield White Paper of October, 1930, as a violation of the Balfour Declaration, most non-Zionists were firm in its denunciation.[90] Cyrus Adler, however, consistently held to the A.J.C.'s fundamental position: opposition to any privileged status for Palestine's Jews at the expense of the majority Arab population. He further commented that, by relying on the Jewish Agency, America's Jews could make the best of a bad situation.[91] On October 24, he issued a stern warning against harmful anti-British agitation by American Zionists.[92] Adler's optimism was not echoed by Melchett, Weizmann or Warburg. They led a movement of mass resignations within J.A.P.[93] Confronted by united resistance, the British hard line receded. Prime Minister Ramsay MacDonald reassured the three on British intentions to uphold the Balfour Declaration. In the interim Melchett died but Warburg and Weizmann returned to their high positions in the Jewish Agency.[94] The episode had effecively demonstrated Warburg's intentions to keep faith with Weizmann.

Until 1936, the activities of the Jewish Agency were temporarily eclipsed by the crisis of Europe's Jews. From non-Zionists there emanated refreshing, even hopeful, reports on the growth of Jewish education in Palestine, not as political indoctrination but as a form of cultural freedom.[95] With the exception of Warburg, however, American non-Zionists were not caught up in the excitement. Many were still A.J.C. members and felt more bound to that organization and its commitment to worldwide Jewry than they did to Palestine's Jewish population.

[89] De Haas to Mack, April 24, 1930, LDB.

[90] *AJYB*, XXXIII (Philadelphia, 1931), 51.

[91] "Leaders Express Distress," *The New York Times*, October 22, 1930, p. 14; *AJYB*, XXXIII, 50-53; Neuman, pp. 207-208.

[92] "Zionists Here Plan Huge Protest November 2," *The New York Times*, October 24, 1929, p. 11.

[93] "Felix M. Warburg and Melchett Quit their Zionist Posts," *The New York Times*, October 22, 1930, p. 1; "Great Britain's Ultimatum on Palestine" (editorial), *The American Hebrew*, 127 (October 24, 1930), 577.

[94] "Jewish Opinion Divided on British White Paper Explanation," *The American Jewish World*, XIX (February 20, 1931), 1.

[95] Isaac B. Berkson, "Jewish Education in Palestine," *Annals of the American Academy of Political and Social Science*, 164 (November 1932), 139-154.

Since the formation of the Agency, the American Jewish Committee had taken no unilateral action on Palestine. Time and again, the A.J.C. had declared the Agency to be the limit of its involvement.[96] In the mid 1930s, the A.J.C. did not attack Nazism while Zionists did.[97] In 1933, the Committee still clung to the belief that Palestine, though absorbing many Jews, was not the sole haven for them. "Cyrus Adler commented ... that Hitler would be pleased no end if all the Jews in Germany left for Palestine."[98] Such rhetoric masked the hard-dying non-Zionist fear of diaspora nationalism. From 1932 to 1936, the A.J.C. resisted what it felt was a careless drift toward a monolithic Jewish concern for Palestine. On at least four distinct occasions, its Executive Board rejected proposals to discuss a World Jewish Congress in the Agency or separately, with Zionists.[99] In the midst of the 1936 uprisings in the Holy Land, the A.J.C. thought it wise not to protest against the curbing of Jewish immigration by the Mandatory Power, although the Zionists appealed for them to do so.[100]

Rumors of partition in April, 1937, augured the return of Felix Warburg to the public eye. Knowing something of the contents of the Peel Report before its publication, Warburg feared the worst, a split in the Agency.[101] His fears were justified. Non-Zionists within and without the Agency were grimly opposed to participation which would, at once, deny the Balfour Declaration, the growth of Judaism under British guardianship, menace the world's Jews with a powerless state and obscure the major crisis for Jews, the disposition of refugees.[102] A more spiritual objection occurred to Cyrus Adler, who may have been influenced by the Hebraic sentiment of Henry

[96] *AJYB*, XXXVIII (Philadelphia, 1936), 45.

[97] Teller, pp. 176-177.

[98] Naomi Cohen, *Not Free to Desist*, pp. 188-189.

[99] Waldman to Adler, September 24, 1935, and *Stenotyped Remarks at Union of American Hebrew Congregations*, April 30, 1941, Morris Waldman Speeches, AJC; Voss, p. 173; "Shame Dr. Adler! Remember History" (editorial), *The Jewish Transcript*, XIII (June 20, 1936), 6.

[100] *AJYB*, XXXIX (Philadelphia, 1937), 56-57, 819.

[101] J.C. Hyman to Paul Baerwald, October 11, 1937 and *Verbatim Minutes of Meeting Called by Mr. Henry Ittelson*, April 29, 1937, HL; Lord Melchett to Arthur Hays Sulzberger, May 22, 1937, JGMcD.

Pereira Mendes, a lifelong exponent of Bible Zionism. "On his deathbed, with the threat of ... partition menacing the land of Israel ... (Mendes) whispered: 'Palestine without Jerusalem is unthinkable.''[103]

The W.Z.O. was opposed too, but it was prepared to launch into negotiations with the British for more territory, using the Peel proposals as an opening wedge. The non-Zionists, unable to accept the premise of the talks, sought a solution short of partition but in doing so, they consorted with individuals and groups whose motives were certainly not in conformity with either the survival of cultural Judaism or the Balfour Declaration. An American non-Zionist and member of the Jewish Agency Executive, Maurice Hexter, supplied the anti-Zionist American consul in Jerusalem, George Wadsworth, with anti-national propaganda. Hexter informed Wadsworth of the trepidation with which Western Jewry regarded the establishment of a Jewish State under the leadership of ''persecuted and less culturally advanced East European Jewry.'' Wadsworth absolutely concurred and relayed the substance of his informant's remarks to Secretary of State Cordell Hull. [104]

Meanwhile, Felix Warburg contended that the British could not negotiate with the W.Z.O. because the Jewish Agency, a non-partisan organization, had been charged with this task in 1929. He warned that no solution to the Palestine problem could legitimately ignore the non-Zionists and any attempt to exclude them would

---

[102] Carolin Flexner to Lehman, June 28, 1937, HL; "Partition," *Jewish Examiner*, XIX (April 8, 1938), 6; Herbert Parzen, "A Chapter in Arab-Jewish Relations During the Mandate Era," *Jewish Social Studies*, XXIX (October 1967), 204, 207, 222; "The Nays Have it," (editorial). *The Jewish Transcript*, XIV (March 4, 1938), 2; "Palestine Conference," *Jewish Community Press*, IV (January 28, 1938), 7; Frederick Landau, "Jewish Unity Declared Impractical," *The American Hebrew*, 141 (November 5, 1937), 4; "American Opinion on Palestine Partition," *The American Hebrew*, 142 (April 15, 1938), 6, 19; "Proskauer Leaves in Midst of Debate," *The New York Times*, December 3, 1937, p. 8; William Zuckerman, "For and Against a Jewish State," *Menorah Journal*, XXVI (Spring 1938), 139-151.

[103] Cyrus Adler, *Observations on the Report of the Palestine Royal Commission* (n.p., 1938), pp. 9-12; *AJYB*, XL (Philadelphia, 1938), 87; David De Sola Pool, "Henry Pereira Mendes," *AJYB*, XL 46.

[104] Parzen, *Jewish Social Studies*, XXIX, 222; George Wadsworth to Cordell Hull, 867N.01036, February 19, 1938, *USFR:1938*, 5 vols. (Washington, D.C., 1955), II, 900-901.

culminate in disaster. The Zionist Congress, he intoned, did not speak for the Agency.[105] He declared that non-Zionists would be satisfied by the implementation of the Magnes-Warburg proposal, actually a revival of bi-nationalism with an emphasis on the co-operation of the minority Jewish population in the realization of an Arab federation.[106]

Non-Zionists in the United States and the A.J.C. were determined to aid Warburg. In July, three of the financier's friends and fellow A.J.C. members met with American Arabs at the New York law offices of Lewis Strauss. The discussions were inconclusive, but Weizmann was obviously impressed with Warburg's influence and resolve.[107] By the end of September, the European Zionist leader had been dissuaded from partition and, for a very short time, the bi-national plan gained within the Agency.[108]

Bi-nationalism was, essentially, the solution of Warburg but not of the non-Zionists as a whole. The Warburg-Magnes proposal was a political formula and was popular with the A.J.C. and the non-Zionist American public as long as Warburg was there to promote it. When Warburg died suddenly in October, 1937, non-Zionists, now led by Cyrus Adler, Morris Waldman, Herbert Lehman and Sol

---

[105] Memorandum by Wallace Murray, 867N.01/753 1/2, September 17, 1937, *USFR:1937*, 5 vols. (Washington, D.C., 1954), II, 908; " 'Zionist Congress Doesn't Talk for All' — Warburg," *The Jewish Transcript*, XIV (August 13, 1937), 1; "Non-Zionist Council Delegates Leave," *B'nai Brith Messenger*, XL (August 13, 1937), 1.

[106] "Dr. Magnes and Palestine Neutrality," (editorial), *Intermountain Jewish News*, XXII (January 10, 1936), 2; "Bi-Nationalism Gains Within the Agency," *The American Hebrew*, 141 (August 27, 1937), 2, 22; "The Will to Unity Spells a Happier Year" (editorial), *The American Hebrew*, 141 (September 3, 1937), 5; " 'Zionist Congress Doesn't Talk for All' — Warburg," *The Jewish Transcript*, XIV (August 13, 1937), 1.

[107] Stephen Wise to Brandeis, July 16, 1937, and Cable to Weizmann, July 16, 1937, LDB; *Confidential Report on Exchange of Views Between Arab Leaders and a Group of Jewish Gentlemen, July 14, 1937*, AJC; Susan Lee Hattis, *The Bi-National Idea in Palestine During Mandatory Times* (Haifa, 1970), p. 185; Naomi Cohen, *Not Free to Desist*, pp. 190-191.

[108] Warburg to Waldman, September 22, 1937, AJC; "Bi-Nationalism Gains With the Agency," *The American Hebrew*, 141 (August 22, 1937), 2, 22. There were also secret negotiations between Magnes and such Arab leaders as Nuri al-Said in 1937 and 1938 that represented a major, though covert, diplomatic effort to bring an end to the conflict in the Holy Land.

Stroock, assumed a less doctrinaire stance. It was true that they opposed partition and favored Arab-Jewish cooperation but they did not propose bi-nationalism as a remedy. The position of the non-nationalists was still that of the American Jewish Committee: strict adherence to the Balfour Declaration and a retention of the mandate for as long as necessary. In so far at the immigration ban on refugees violated the Balfour Declaration, it was universally condemned.[109]

In sum, the non-Zionists desired that the British refrain from altering their policy in any way. Accordingly, Adler and Lehman rejected all sorts of militant Jewish nationalisms, including Revisionism and the World Jewish Congress movement, as inimical to the primary task of saving Jewish lives.[110] The Warburg group was present at the World Zionist Congress in June, 1938, for the purpose of impressing upon Weizmann the need for an Arab-Jewish understanding in Palestine and the danger of nationalist agitation.[111] In America, B'nai Brith and the A.J.C. were "astounded at the plan of plebiscite" brought forth by Stephen Wise. Carolin Flexner, Governor Lehman's secretary, was told confidentially by the A.J.C.'s Executive Secretary Morris Waldman that "Judge Rosenman is going to see President Roosevelt and try to get him to influence Dr. Wise to stop the whole thing."[112]

The World Jewish Congress was organized and did convene in the autumn of 1938, much to the consternation of the A.J.C. Blaming Rabbi Wise for the presence of such a tangible expression of unwelcome nationalism, Cyrus Adler declined A.J.C. participation in the American Zionist Emergency Committee for Palestine.[113] In November, after the Woodhead Commission recommended the termination of partition, Dr. Adler found himself in agreement with

---

[109] Lehman to Franklin D. Roosevelt, October 10, 1938, HL; Unsigned Memorandum, March 1, 1940, AJC; *AJYB*, XLI (Philadelphia, 1939), 31-32; "Address of Sol M. Stroock Introducing a Resolution on the Partition of Palestine," *AJYB*, XL, 102-107; "Partition Plan Hit by Committee," *B'nai Brith Messenger*, XLI (January 21, 1938), 1.

[110] Adler to Waldman, October 28, 1937, AJC; Lehman to Franklin Roosevelt, October 10, 1938, HL.

[111] Wadsworth to Murray, 867N.01/1113, June 9, 1938, *USFR: 1938*, II, 921-923.

[112] Carolin Flexner to Lehman, May 12, 1938, HL.

[113] Cyrus Adler to Solomon Goldman, October 27, 1938, AJC.

American Zionists, including Wise, on the impracticality of the entire Peel venture. In its place, he noted happily, Britain had announced its sponsorship of an Arab-Jewish conference. [114]

In March, 1939, England adjourned the sessions in disgust and two months later issued its White Paper. Immediately, the A.J.C. proposed that the "status quo ante" be restored by a new international trusteeship embodying the substance of the mandate. The Committee mobilized with Zionists to prevent an overthrow of the mandate and the Balfour Declaration. [115] The United Jewish Appeal (U.J.A.) was formed by an unprecedented merger of Zionist and non-Zionist fund-raising organizations. Even the confirmed non-Zionist Herbert Lehman accepted a post on the Jewish National Fund's Board of Directors; a year later, he agreed to serve as Honorary Chairman of the United Palestine Appeal. [116] There is little exaggeration in the assertion that the White Paper of 1939 served as a point of union between Zionists and non-Zionists from whence there would be no retreat. [117]

Territorialism was not as vital an issue with non-Zionists as with anti-Zionists. There was desultory talk of resettling Jews in South America or British Guiana but the comments were few and well spaced. [118] Non-Zionists were not reluctant to consider Palestine but they felt that a new understanding between themselves and Weizmann would have to be reached on their status and responsibilities within the Agency.

It soon became apparent to Weizmann that the non-Zionists would settle for no less than the reconstitution of the J.A.P. The American non-Zionist members of the Administrative Committee of the Jewish Agency, Adler, Irving Lehman, James Becker, Sol Stroock, Horace Stein and Henry Wineman addressed a series of complaints to the European Zionist leader. They displayed a grave dissatisfaction with

[114] "Leaders to Hail Palestine," *The New York Times*, November 10, 1938, p. 5.

[115] Unsigned Memorandum, March 1, 1940, AJC; Halpern, p. 207; Morris Fine, "Events of the Year 5699," *AJYB*, XLI, 200.

[116] Carolin Flexner to Lehman, December 12, 1939 and Lehman to Abba Hillel Silver, January 21, 1941, HL.

[117] Naomi Cohen, *Not Free to Desist*, p. 192.

[118] Lewis Strauss to James G. MacDonald, August 21, 1939, JGMcD; Voss, p. 239; Feingold, 162.

the way the Jewish Agency had been run since its inception and insisted that the non-Zionists had never had sufficient power. If they had, "many of the present difficulties facing Palestine might have been avoided." Surprisingly, they were opposed to having the Jews kept as a permanent minority in Palestine and, predictably, they scored Weizmann for his yielding to the type of British intransigence which had rendered the Agency helpless. Like the Zionists, the non-Zionists protested the crystallization of the Jewish position in Palestine on the basis of the White Paper and deplored the Jewish Agency's activities on behalf of illegal immigration. The wrongs could be righted only with increased non-Zionist control in the Agency and the erection of a Palestinian state wherein Arab and Jew were equal citizens with an equal say. [119]

"When the World Jewish Congress called for joint efforts for a peace program in 1940, the anti-Zionists of the A.J.C. were strong enough to reject the suggestion out of hand." Judge Joseph Proskauer said: "Let the chips fall where they may and let those Zionists who don't like it, get out." Most of the A.J.C. though, including Waldman and Stroock did not think that the position was justified. After all, "the A.J.C. had approved the Balfour Declaration and the position of the American Jewish Committee had never precluded cooperation with the Zionists." [120]

In the spring of 1941, the A.J.C., minus Adler who had died, entered into unofficial discussions with Dr. Weizmann to consider the reconstitution of the Jewish Agency and to revive its non-partisan character "which had disappeared with the appointment of outspoken Zionists to some of the European 'non-Zionist' seats within the Agency." [121] According to A.J.C. memoranda, Weizmann asked that organization's Secretary, Morris Waldman, to secure the cooperation of the non-Zionist leaders in a combined effort to

[119] American Non-Zionist Members of the Administrative Committee of the Jewish Agency for Palestine to C. Weizmann and the Members of the Executive of the Jewish Agency for Palestine, July 17, 1939, AJC.

[120] Naomi Cohen, *Not Free to Desist*, p. 250; Joseph Loeb to Sidney Hollander, February 26, 1940, Morris Waldman to the Members of the Executive Committee March 27, 1940 and Waldman to Sol M. Stroock, May 9, 1940, AJC. Within three years, though, Morris Waldman's efforts were channeled into distinctly anti-Zionist causes. See Herbert Druks, *The Failure to Rescue* (New York, 1977), pp. 86-88.

[121] A.J.C., *In Vigilant Brotherhood*, p. 18.

persuade the Powers to deal justly with Jewish claims in Palestine. In the course of their meeting, Waldman laid down the ground rules for future discussions. He expressed the conviction to Weizmann that no modus vivendi would be arrived at "unless and until the Zionists eradicate the universal nationalist conception from the Zionist movement and repudiate the World Jewish Congress movement." Despite the admonition, negotiations were started with a non-Zionist team of eleven men. [122]

Basic questions were raised at the meeting of Zionists and non-Zionists held at the Commodore Hotel on October 21, 1941. In twenty-four years, none had deigned to clear the air on fundamental philosophy: What was the meaning of Jewish nationalism? Might it exist outside Palestine? What will be its fate after the possible erection of a Jewish State? Will diaspora nationalism continue to plague the world Jewish community or will it, thankfully, pass away after the destiny of the Palestinian Jew is finally settled? Does one have to be a nationalist in order to be a Zionist? The consequences of the meeting were not immediately apparent, but one thing was clear: diaspora nationalism and not Palestine nationalism was the major problem. By evening's end, Zionist ideology had been thoroughly probed. Suspicions concerning a Jewish state, theocracy and dual citizenship were laid to rest. The Zionists had convinced their opposite numbers among non-Zionists that if a state were to come into being, it would "be in accord with the modern principles of statehood: Church-State separation and civil equality of all its inhabitants." [123]

The meetings did not end inconclusively, as Morris Waldman had supposed. They were temporarily derailed by the death of the chief non-Zionist negotiator, Sol Stroock, in September, 1941. Maurice Wertheim, President of the A.J.C., then assumed control of the

---

[122] They were Stroock, Waldman, George Backer, Jacob Blaustein, Maurice Hexter, Morris R. Cohen, Solomon Lowenstein, George Z. Medalie, Edward M.M. Warburg, Joseph Willen and Morris Wolf. The Zionist negotiators were Stephen Wise, Abba Hillel Silver, Morris Rothenberg, Nahum Goldmann, Carl Sherman and Louis Lipsky. Unsigned Memorandum, April 7, 1944 and Sidney Wallach to Stephen Wise, August 12, 1941, AJC; Waldman, *Nor by Power*, p. 210; Paul Baerwald to Edward M.M. Warburg, March 26, 1941, HL.

[123] *Statement of M.D. Waldman to be Presented at the Weizmann-Stroock Conference on October 21, 1941, Notes on Meeting of October 21, 1941 at the Commodore Hotel,* and *Speech of Morris D. Waldman Prior to the Meeting of October 21, 1941,* p. 17, AJC.

stalled talks. [124]   At last, in 1942, the A.J.C. agreed with Zionists to support a Jewish State program if they would renounce diaspora nationalism. When the news of the agreement leaked out, there was immediate opposition from such anti-nationalists in the A.J.C. as Lessing Rosenwald, Joseph Proskauer, Lewis Strauss, James Rosenberg and Joseph Willen. [125]   Some malcontents, like Rosenwald decamped to the American Council for Judaism but most hesitated to employ such extreme measures. Maurice Wertheim carefully distinguished between anti- and non-Zionism for those who continued to confuse the two: "We are not anti-Zionists because ... anti-Zionists are those Jews who are opposed to a Jewish national home now or in the future." Non-Zionism to the writer meant "non-opposition to a future Jewish State." As a matter of fact, non-Zionists would be fully prepared to welcome such a state if they were assured that diaspora nationalism would cease. [126]   Characteristically, A.J.C. leaders eschewed perverse or malicious critiques of Jewish nationalism. They would not defeat the idealism of the Balfour Declaration nor speak against the proprieties of a Jewish life in Palestine. Although some, like Morris Waldman, would remain unconvinced as to the ultimate wisdom of Jewish nationalism, [127] a spirit of evolutionary change unquestionably stirred the A.J.C. In February, 1942, one member in particular adopted the new mood: "If there are American Jews who wish to fight Zionism, let them organize for this purpose outside the American Jewish Committee. [128]

[124] Waldman, *Nor By Power,* p. 211-222.

[125] Halpern, p. 125; Naomi Cohen, *Not Free to Desist,* p. 250.

[126] Maurice Wertheim to Sidney Wallach, February 5, 1942, AJC.

[127] Druks, pp. 86-87.

[128] Fred M. Butzel to Maurice Wertheim, February 10, 1942, AJC.

V

House Divided: Brandeis Zionism Versus Weizmann Zionism

When, in June, 1930, the followers of Louis D. Brandeis wrested control of the American Zionist Organization from Louis Lipsky, Jacob de Haas was jubilant: "We are going to strengthen political Zionism as understood by Herzl," he declared. [1] De Haas was fond of saying that "Weizmann never in the vaguest way understood the man (i.e. Herzl) and the ideas for which he was struggling"; save Brandeis, "there is no Jew in America who understood or understands Herzl." [2]

If one is to apprehend de Haas correctly, two Zionisms existed at the time of his writing, Brandeis's and Weizmann's. That portion of American Zionism led by Brandeis stressed rational economic development of Palestine and a controlled pattern of in-migration as against the Weizmann dominated World Zionist Organization which emphasized hurried, unplanned in-migration and the cultural aspects of Judaism. The long, heated power struggle did not begin immediately upon Brandeis's assumption of American Zionist leadership in 1914. At the outset, American Zionists had no formal economic plan for Palestinian development. Politically, it was easy to cooperate with Weizmann because all Zionism was united on

---

[1] Joseph Brainin, "The Program of the Brandeis Group," *The American Jewish World,* XVIII (July 18, 1930). 1

[2] Jacob de Haas to Louis D. Brandeis, May 17, 1926, LDB.

winning Palestine. Only in the aftermath of World War I did crucial differences emerge which were grounded on the major protagonists' clashing world views.

On August 31, 1914, the Provisional Executive Committee for General Zionist Affairs (P.E.C.G.Z.A.) was organized, with Louis Brandeis at its head. In the same year, Woodrow Wilson had assured the American Zionist leader of his support. By 1916, the President's chief adviser, Colonel Edward M. House, was both optimistic and encouraging.[3] There were two reasons for the American Government's initial friendliness. The first had to do with the public assurances of Rabbi Stephen Wise, a close associate of Brandeis, that the Zionists had no "statist motivations" in Palestine; the second dealt with the importance of Zionism to Jews in the United States and the effect of Jewish interest groups on American political life.[4] In 1917, there were, perhaps, three and one-quarter million Jews in the United States and ten per cent of these belonged to the Zionist Organization of America (Z.O.A.). Furthermore, there were a proliferation of subsocieties: one hundred seventy attached to the older Federation of American Zionists which had been superseded by the Z.O.A., forty-one to Hadassah, ninety-five to Zionist labor and one hundred ninety to Mizrachi.[5] It was in the best interests of the White House not to alienate them.

At this time, the major problem confronting Brandeis was organizational unity. The various branches of American Zionism appeared to be moving in different directions, only some of which were satisfactory to the leader and his lieutenants, among whom were Wise, the silver-tongued orator and firebrand, Jacob de Haas, who first met Brandeis in 1910 and introduced him to the Herzl vision, Chicago judge Julian Mack, Professors Felix Frankfurter and Horace Kallen and Washington attorney Robert Szold. The Socialist ideology of the Poale Zion found no defender in Brandeis, whose concern in 1917 was to keep American Zionism above reproach by eliminating any taint of radical dogma. Mizrachi, the Orthodox segment of Zionism, agitated for the establishment of a religious commonwealth in Palestine. Brandeis grew impatient with their theocratic temporizing and open rebellion, realizing that until Pales-

[3] Adler, *Jewish Social Studies*, X, 303-304; Mason, p. 452.

[4] "Zionists Want U.S. Rule," *The Jewish Tribune*, XXVIII (February 2, 1917), 1.

[5] O.J. Campbell, *A Report on Zionism*, WYP, EMHC, p. 1206.

tine was acquired, such academic controversy would serve to defeat rather than advance the cause. Occasionally, men of an independent nature, for instance Joseph Barondess, President of the Order of the Sons of Zion and Commissioner of Education for New York City, ventured to attack the sometimes high-handed tactics of Brandeis subordinates de Haas and Louis Lipsky, whose efforts were directed at achieving unity regardless of hurt feelings and bruised sensitivities.[6]

Complementing the internal difficulties were external dilemmas. Tact was never a vice of Rabbi Wise. In dealing with important counter-movements to Zionism in the United States, especially the non-Zionist alternative, Stephen Wise spoke with the utmost candor. Wise never liked the idea of non-Zionists in the Zionist Organization and he, more vehemently than others, objected to Jacob Schiff's proposed membership in November, 1917.[7] Another, even more pressing matter, was that of the Balfour Declaration. In April, Balfour and Wilson discussed at the White House what American newspapers carelessly referred to as "a Jewish Republic." The inference of a "state" and the fact that the P.E.C.G.Z.A. issued a favorable statement on Zionism as a result of the talks, sent the Europeans scurrying for confirmation. Weizmann wired Brandeis, the gist of his communication being that he hoped all rumors in the American press were unfounded. A state, said Weizmann, was not even considered in London; "existing conditions were against it" and the very thought would "raise new antagonisms and complicate the international position in general."[8]

The state idea hampered American Zionists as it temporarily overturned the advantage they enjoyed with the President. As was their wont, American Zionists kept in close contact with all influential Presidential aides and cabinet members. Brandeis sent Secretary Lansing a copy of English Zionist aims and Stephen Wise conferred with Wilson on the advisability of convening an American Jewish Congress.[9] Then the tide turned. Though indicating his

---

[6] Joseph Barondess to Meyer Berlin, July 5, 1917, JB, Box 4; Joseph Barondess to Jacob de Haas, January 15, 1918, JBL, no. 50, pp. 346-347.

[7] Stephen Wise to Julian Mack, November 19, 1917, and Wise to Brandeis, December 12, 1917, LDB.

[8] Weizmann, James de Rothschild and Joseph Cowen to the P.E.C.G.Z.A., May 3, 1917, LDB.

[9] Adler, *Jewish Social Studies,* X, 305.

sympathy for the Congress, Wilson advised its temporary postponement and, shortly after Wise's departure, commissioned Henry Morgenthau to go to Turkey. Wilson and Brandeis remained affable but the totality of events left an unfavorable impression upon Colonel House.[10]

House's ambiguity toward Jews and Zionism is well-known but mysterious. After Wilson received a draft of the Balfour Declaration from Lord Robert Cecil, House conferred pleasantly with Brandeis.[11] The next month, he prevented Wise from committing Wilson to the English statement until after the British had made a formal pronouncement. Wise, however, was informed that following the Declaration's issuance, the President would be prepared to make its sentiment part of administrative policy. Once told this, Wise readily agreed to keep silent.[12] But, Colonel House also told Wilson on September 4 that he was "chary" on voicing approval of the Balfour Declaration and the Zionist movement, because of his distrust for Britain's motives and his dislike for those Jews who would break into Palestine "with a jimmy" if they could not do it any other way.[13] Apparently, though, Colonel House was fond of Louis Brandeis, perhaps because the latter's intellect reminded him of Wilson's. Sometimes, House was known to assist Brandeis, via personal intervention, in sending Weizmann reassuring messages.[14]

American Zionists received the news of the Balfour Declaration with great joy. Wilson believed that a millenial age for all humanity would accompany a Jewish national revival in the Holy Land.[15] Although the Fourteen Points fell short of an absolute Palestinian promise, Zionists saw more in them than there actually was, doubtlessly because they trusted the President's avowed sincerity.[16]

[10] Tenzer, *The Immigrants' Influence*, p. 302; Manuel, pp. 155-157.

[11] Manuel, p. 168; Tenzer, *The Immigrants' Influence*, p. 302; Adler, *Jewish Social Studies*, X, 306-307.

[12] Wise to Brandeis, October 17, 1917, LDB.

[13] Carl J. Friedrich, *American Policy Toward Palestine* (Washington, 1944), pp. 6-7; Esco Foundation, I, 242; Adler, *Jewish Social Studies*, X, 305-306.

[14] Stein, p. 510.

[15] Adler, *Jewish Social Studies*, X, 311.

[16] Tenzer, *The Immigrants' Influence*, p. 306.

Brandeis, however, did not savor the victory as Europeans did and, indeed, often appeared troubled. In January, 1918, Cecil Spring-Rice, British Ambassador to the United States, extracted from Brandeis the reasons for his annoyance: Weizmann's misconceptions concerning American Jewish nationalism and the opposition to both Weizmann and Brandeis within the Zionist Organization itself.

What irked Brandeis was Weizmann's patent unwillingness to understand American Zionism. The movement was not yet strong, the masses of Jews and the Socialists were "bitterly opposed" to Zionist leaders[17] and the wealthy Jews were divided into anti- and non-Zionists, many of whom voiced their nationalist apprehensions through the influential American Jewish Committee. The Orthodox press jeered both Zionist leaders' spiritual deficiences and Mizrachi, at first cajoled, had to be forcibly threatened with expulsion and loss of all Zionist accreditation before that organization would yield.[18] Additionally, a different and less comfortable situation reigned in America vis-a-vis the belligerents which precluded any suspicious surges of Jewish nationalism. As long as Turkey was in the war, Brandeis was compelled to tread cautiously. The United States had not declared war on that country and, therefore, Palestine, an Ottoman possession, did not fall within the purview of "American idealism." As a matter of fact, Brandeis's allusions to the Jewish homeland in early 1918 were made with deference to the present owners.[19]

Obviously, American Zionists found themselves in an anomalous position. As United States citizens, they supported the Allies but as Jews were ready to concede the point that Turkey might conceivably win the war and thus be the power with which Zionists would have to deal. American Jews of German descent were regarded as particularly susceptible to a Turco-German plot involving a grant of Palestine in exchange for Jewish fealty to the Central Powers.

Brandeis was cognizant of all this. His every attempt was directed

---

[17] Stein, pp. 583-584.

[18] Louis Lipsky to Israel Friedlaender, February 27, 1919, Israel Friedlaender Papers (hereafter abbreviated IF); de Haas to Brandeis, January 8, 1918, de Haas to E.W. Lewin-Epstein, April 8, 1918, Lipsky to Brandeis, February 27, 1919, and Lipsky to K. Whiteman, February 27, 1919, LDB; "Orthodox Rabbis of U.S. and Canada Convene," *Denver Jewish News,* V (May 14, 1919), 1; Goldblatt, *American Jewish Historical Quarterly,* LVII, 490-492.

[19] Campbell, *A Report on Zionism,* WYP,EMHC, p. 2609.

at legitimizing American Jewish nationalism before its detractors while placing it above the "dual loyalty" charge. In October, 1917, Brandeis altered the wording of the Balfour Declaration. Instead of Jewish "race," he inserted the phrase "Jewish people." He also added a clause guaranteeing the rights of all Jews to citizenship and "their existing nationality" in the countries where they lived.[20] His later actions involving Professor Israel Friedlaender, though understandable, were most disturbing and tend to justify the assertion that American Zionists in 1918 were as concerned with "one hundred per cent" American conformity as were Jewish anti- and non-nationalists, and Gentile patriots.

An American Zionist born in Poland but educated in Germany, Professor Israel Friedlaender of New York's Jewish Theological Seminary, was obliged to decline a Red Cross assignment in Palestine as a result of merciless verbal and printed bombardments from Stephen Wise and Columbia University's Professor Richard Gottheil. Ostensibly, their conviction mirrored that of American Zionism as a whole: that in a superheated patriotic climate, the media and the citizenry at large would simply regard Friedlaender as a Jewish nationalist with a German background and pro-German sympathies. The incident not only abashed its victim but also hampered the efforts of the Hadassah Medical unit in Palestine in the achievement of cooperative understanding with Red Cross representative John Huston Finley, whose opinion of the Zionists had never been very high.[21]

At home, American Zionism waited intently for the armistice while assuming a more stable, distinctly American, form. For the first time, Brandeis issued a public statement that was in no way related to European Zionism or its objectives. The Pittsburgh Platform of June, 1918 (not to be confused with the C.C.A.R. Pittsbugh Platform of 1885), defined an American approach to Zionism which was to become the Brandeis trademark: it opposed land speculation in Palestine, proposed safeguards against the ex-

[20] Adler, *Jewish Social Studies*, X, 307.

[21] Marshall to Friedlaender, March 5, 1918, IF; *Minutes of a Special Meeting of the Joint Distribution Committee*, March 11, 1918: Richard Gottheil to Friedlaender, January 8, 1919, and N.I. Stone to Friedlaender, March 10, 1918, and *Minutes of a Special Meeting of the Joint Distribution Committee*, March 11, 1918 and Brandeis to Friedlaender, January 19, 1919, IF; Wise to Finley, April 17, 1918 and September 1, 1918, John Huston finley Papers, box 74; Campbell, *A Report on Zionism, WYP,EMHC, p. 1905.*

ploitation of natural resources and embodied a neo-Jeffersonian faith for establishing a community of "social justice and human co-operation."[22]

In one document, Brandeis had drawn the broad distinctions between himself and Weizmann on the issue of Palestinian development and on the meaning of Jewish nationalism to Europeans and Americans. According to Brandeis, securing the Holy Land would complete the work Herzl had begun in 1897: this objective was in sight and would be realized as soon as Turkey capitulated. Afterwards, Brandeis envisioned years of economic experimentation in accordance with the American Progressive philosophy with a view to turning Palestine into a self-sufficient country of independent farmers and businessmen.[23] Weizmann had never thought in terms of these priorities. As a European, he was most concerned with the sort of Jewish suffering Brandeis had rarely seen. While Brandeis could afford to approach matters from the vantage of American freedom, diversity and experimentation, Weizmann could not. Saving people could not wait for the economic projects to materialize. Refugees would continue to stream into Palestine in great numbers and Weizmann would sustain them, not on independent private investment, but on worldwide donations, a form of charity which Jews had used for centuries to support their brethren in the Holy Land.[24]

What prompted Brandeis to show his independence at this early date, even before war's end? Generally speaking, it was probably Weizmann's failure to look upon American Zionists as anything but his principle fund-raisers, admiring their fiscal potential but scorning

---

[22] Zionist Organization of America, *Summary of the Position of the Zionist Organization of America in Conference with Dr. Weizmann and his Associates* (n.p., 1921), pp. 7, 10.

[23] Melvin Urofsky contends, with much justification, that American Zionism, as formulated by Brandeis, can be understood only within the context of American social, economic, intellectual and political history. By this he means that Progressivism, cultural pluralism and New Freedom — New Deal reform explained the American response to Zionism far better than do European exigencies and the diplomacy of Weizmann. See both Urofsky's books on Brandeis, *A Mind of One Piece: Brandeis and American Reform* and *American Zionism from Herzl to the Holocause* for lucid elaborations on this thesis.

[24] George L. Berlin, "The Brandeis-Weizmann Dispute," *American Jewish Historical Quarterly*, LX (September 1970); Sachar, *The Course of Modern Jewish History*, pp. 271-272, 276-277, 282-283; Mason, p. 463.

their grasp of Zionist ideology and their ability to make constructive suggestions.   Particularly disconcerting to Brandeis was Weizmann's snub of Americans when selections were being made for membership on the Zionist Commission, which traveled through Palestine in February and March, 1918. No American was appointed by Weizmann but one accompanied the Commission as an observer.[25]

In the opening months of 1919, European and American Zionists coordinated their activities to achieve a Jewish homeland in Palestine.   Some friction between Americans and Europeans, however, was already apparent, as were the different approaches employed by the two Zionist wings in their appeals to government officials.

Weizmann erred when he petitioned America through the State Department, especially since Wilson was so much more accessible. In June, 1919, when the King-Crane Commission was investigating Zionism, Weizmann submitted "confidential" reports to Leon Dominian of the American delegation in an effort to gain official sympathy. Members of the delegation passed them around and sent them to the State Department in Washington as indications of the Zionist plan to "establish a Jewish State in Palestine."[26]

American Zionists, however, knew better; they realized that American peacemakers wanted nothing more than to abandon the "whole disgusting scramble" of the Near East.[27] In early March, Wilson received Julian Mack at the White House to reaffirm his August, 1918 pledge to Stephen Wise, but William Westermann would not have known of it had he not read American newspapers and cables which were sent to Paris.[28] Using a more direct path to the actual decision makers than did Weizmann, the Americans (Felix Frankfurter and Jacob de Haas) at Versailles did not tell him, preferring to approach Colonel House instead.[29] The two Zionists were circumspect in their dealings with the Near East experts from the United States.   Frankfurter, a Zionist since 1913, addressed

[25] Doreen Ingrams, *Palestine Papers 1917-1922: Seeds of Conflict* (New York, 1973), pp. 21, 30; Hull, p. 133; Israel Cohen, *A Short History of Zionism*, p.77; Marvin Lowenthal, *Henrietta Szold: Life and Letters* (New York, 1942), p. 116, maintains that this attitude was continued into 1919.

[26] Manuel, p. 246.

[27] *Ibid.*, p. 255.

[28] "President to See Zionist Leaders," *The Washington Post*, March 1, 1919, p. 5; Adler, *Jewish Social Studies*, X, 322; Manuel, pp. 233-234.

himself mainly to House who, at the time, was engaged in the selection of two commission leaders for their Ottoman assignment.[30] Preoccupied and rather cold, House disregarded Frankfurter's mandate proposal. In a matter of days, the Frankfurter draft had been completely disfigured by William Yale.[31]

The imminent departure of the Inter-Allied Commission on Turkish Mandates spurred Frankfurter to seek, through House, the renewed assurances of the President that any agreement involving the boundaries of the Jewish national home would require American approval in addition to French and English. Thus, Frankfurter attempted to insure a Jewish survival in Palestine through the good offices of Wilson, the one man who could prevent the French from pushing the Syrian boundary further south to include the watershed of the Hermon, the Litany River and the plains of Jaulon and Hauran. Had the French plan succeeded, Palestine would have been left a barren wilderness.[32] The message was transmitted to Wilson and, as was hoped, the President respected the Americans' boundary requests. Wilson's preferences had some bearing on shaping the character of the San Remo agreement, although, by April 1920, the enfeebled President had lost contact with the Zionists, as their fate became entwined with the State Department and the Republicans.[33]

Frankfurter also was able to stall the incipient clash of wills between de Haas and Weizmann. Although he was to change his opinion in 1921, at Versailles Frankfurter believed it necessary to have an accord with Weizmann. He wrote Brandeis that his views were diametrically opposed to those of de Haas, whose disdain for the European Zionist leader was both well-known and irritating.[34]

[29] Paris Peace Conference, 184.00101/49, Minutes of Meetings of the American Commissioners Plenipotentiary, April 13, 1919 and Paris Peace Conference, 184.00101/52, Minutes of Meetings of the American Commissioners Plenipotentiary, April 18, 1919, *USFR:PPC*, XI, 150, 155.

[30] Robert Katz, "Prof. Felix Frankfurter," *The Jewish Review and Observer*, XLIII (August 10, 1917), 5; Howard, *The American Inquiry*, p. 37; Rabinowitz, p. 97

[31] See Chapter 2, Footnote 60.

[32] Howard, *The American Inquiry*, p. 37; Rabinowitz, p. 97.

[33] Tenzer, *The Immigrants' Influence*, p. 315; Manuel, p. 257; Adler, *Jewish Social Studies*, X, 333.

[34] Frankfurter to Brandeis, March 3, 1919, LDB.

Normally, Frankfurter, Mack and Brandeis defended de Haas, whose penchant for biting sarcasm and personal vendettas estranged him from many American Zionists, including the equally volatile Stephen Wise.[35] Significantly, even when Mack and Frankfurter deserted de Haas in the 1930s, Brandeis did not. In April, 1919, de Haas, Brandeis's Zionist mentor, became convinced that the economic solution for Palestine was best and may have predisposed the Justice to find fault with Weizmann.[36]

An American-European impasse was reached in September. American Zionism, which had been in the "process of becoming" during the war and at Versailles had finally "arrived" after Brandeis returned from his summer journey to Palestine in 1919.[37] At the American Zionist Convention in Chicago, Brandeis imparted a shocking revelation to his listeners: he believed Zionism had performed its full political purpose and that, in obtaining Palestine, the Basel program of 1897 had been realized. In measured tones, he demanded the cessation of all political propaganda. The duty of Zionists was to enter a new epoch: for the time being, the immigration flood must be stopped while a program of societal development, consonant with economic buildup, was initiated. Until the program was definitively charted, stated Brandeis, Zionists were expected to stand firmly by the Pittsburgh Platform.[38]

The San Remo verdict hastened the inevitable confrontation. By April, 1920, it was apparent that the American leadership and Weizmann were moving further apart on philosophy and methodology. The Z.O.A., prompted by spokesman Julian Mack, denied the concept of diaspora nationalism. Jewish nationalism was made irrelevant to the actual development of Palestine; it had only been necessary to attain it.[39]

At the London Conference of July, 1920, the superficial amenities between Brandeis and Weizmann were observed, but neither man

[35] Barondess to Lipsky, December 14, 1920, JBL, No. 51, pp. 349-354; Mason, p. 463; Berkowitz, p. 302.

[36] De Haas to Brandeis, June 3, 1924, LDB.

[37] Zionist Organization of America, *Summary*, p. 8; Manuel, p. 262.

[38] *Minutes, National Executive Committee of the Zionist Organization of America*, April 13, 1919, IF; *Report of Justice Brandeis to the National Executive Committee of the Zionist Organization*, September 9, 1919, LDB; Berkowitz, p. 138; Berlin, *American Jewish Historical Quarterly, LX, 42; Reznikoff, II, 725-726.*

was particularly cordial to the other. The two leaders had apparently fallen out on the single issue of Keren Hayesod (the Palestine Foundation fund or P.F.F.). In Weizmann's opinion, all donations, dues, collections and profits flowing into the Zionist organization would be channeled into the Fund, whose major function would be the support of various educational, agricultural, urban and welfare agencies in Palestine. Brandeis was appalled at the cavalier attitude of Weizmann and the Europeans, who drew no distinctions between legitimate investments and charity for those with no visible means of support.[40] Accusations were hurled from one camp to another but one thing had become clear: money merely masked the actual source of tension, which was diaspora nationalism.

Remaining a national unit in the countries where they lived was not a vital issue for American Jews. It was a personal choice rather than an imperative because all citizens held their civil and religious liberties in common. If an American migrated to Palestine, he did so of his own free will; he was not constrained to leave. For Weizmann, diaspora nationalism was the proper method for Jews to employ in their own defense. The environment from which East European Jews fled was chronically anti-Semitic and those who left could only rely on other Jews for succor. Group consciousness was the essence of Weizmann's beliefs just as cultural pluralism was to Brandeis.

Brandeis was disappointed with the outcome of the London Conference and, at his behest, Americans refused to serve on a Weizmann-dominated Executive Board and declined to endorse the Keren Hayesod.[41] In August, 1920, Brandeis framed the Zeeland Memorandum, which was henceforward the "Bible" for his group. American Zionists, he wrote, intended to populate Palestine with a "self-supporting Jewish population who woud eventually become "self-supporting Jewish population who would eventually become he continued, "can be affected now because Jews in Europe are

---

[39] "Zionists Deny Charge that Movement is Political," *The Jewish Review and Observer*, XLVI (April 2, 1920), 1, 4; Zionist Organization of America, *Summary*, pp. 15, 28; "The Fundamental Difference," *The American Jewish World*, X (September 9, 1921), 8; "Judge Mack and Rabbi Landman Discuss Zionism," *The American Hebrew*, 118 (April 23, 1926), 811, 823.

[40] *Jewish Press Abstracts* (hereafter abbreviated *JPA*) no. 1, pp. 2-4; "Zionist International Conference Meets," *The American Hebrew*, 106 (July 16, 1920) 230-231; Berlin, *American Jewish Historical Quarterly*, LX, 42; Berkowitz, pp. 179-182; Lipsky, pp. 71-72.

[41] Berlin, *American Jewish Historical Quarterly*, LX, 55; Manuel, p. 266.

miserable" and "can be revived in Palestine." This objective, however, must be met practically by buying land and developing resources. Fund-raising efforts must be conscientiously pursued, with the obligation that the money be used "wisely and efficiently;" investments would be made "with great economy." Credit facilities should be developed, he emphasized, for the installation of public utilities. Brandeis concluded with the affirmation that nothing would be accomplished along these lines if the Z.O.A. was not quickly reorganized.[42]

At succeeding conferences, the Americans, even Brandeis and Mack, voted for resolutions of cooperation with the W.Z.O. as long as their conditions concerning separation of funds into identifiable investments and charities were met.[43] The idea of decentralizing the Z.O.A. into "small, manageable units" and regional federations was popular with Brandeis planners but the bulk of Americans were loyal to Weizmann. The leaders of the pro-Weizmann Americans was the Secretary of the Z.O.A., Louis Lipsky, an American of great literary power and little faith in Brandeis. But in the autumn of 1920, Lipsky had yet to play his hand, simply because he was unsure of Brandeis's position in the W.Z.O.[44] Weizmann seemed anxious to avoid trouble and momentarily pacified the Brandeis group by dispatching a "Reorganization Committee" to Palestine in the hope that it would finally vindicate the P.F.F. Upon the Committee's return, it offered pro-Brandeis recommendations which were peremptorily rejected by the World Zionist Executive.[45]

The arrival of Weizmann in the United States in April, 1921, to campaign for Keren Hayesod resulted in the rending of American

[42] Louis D. Brandeis, *Memorandum of My Views As To Future Activities*, August 24, 1920, LDB.

[43] *Minutes of the Executive Committee of the Zionist Organization of America,* September 29 and 30, 1920 and *Address Delivered by Stephen Wise,* November 27, 1920, LDB; Edward J. Cohn. "The Zionist Convention," *The American Hebrew,* 108 (December 3, 1920), 84, 102-103; "Zionist Reorganization," (editorial), *The American Jewish World,* IX (November 26, 1920), 8.

[44] Barondess to Lipsky, December 11, 1920, JBL, no. 51, pp. 347-349; *Administrative Committee Minutes of the National Executive Committee of the Zionist Organization of America, August 5 to October 19, 1920,* LDB; Abba Hillel Silver, *Memorandum of a Conversation with Justice Brandeis at Washington,* October 12, 1920, LDB.

[45] Robert Szold to Benjamin V. Cohen, January 30, (n.y.), LDB; *JPA,* no. 1, p. 3.

Zionism. Ostensibly, the sole purpose of Weizmann's visit was to raise funds for the P.F.F. It appears, however, that Weizmann's expedition was elaborately arranged to prove a point. What the European leader did, and most effectively, was to take his case to the people. It had been mentioned in the past year that Brandeis was not a man of the people, that his economics were as cold as his relationship with the Jewish masses.[46] Weizmann, urbane, fascinating, of Russian decent, articulated the dreams of the folk whence he came.

But Brandeis fought back. Weizmann may have declared a "Holy War" but de Haas said he was ready to lead a "grand secession." Nevertheless, Yiddish dailies, with a circulation of four hundred thousand, continued carrying stories of the hour-by-hour humiliation of Brandeis.[47]

One such paper, *The Day*, staffed by many Poale Zionists, tore at the American leadership with gusto.[48] The pro-Weizmann inclination from this sector was partially offset by the American Jewish weeklies, organs of Reform Judaism, which displayed a preference for Brandeis if, indeed, they preferred any Zionist.[49] American Zionists endeavored to bring their case to the people by taking out ads in the Jewish press.[50] It was futile. Slowly but surely, the New York districts of the Z.O.A. deserted Brandeis, and districts from other parts of the United States followed.[51]

Talks between the warring factions were begun in April and

---

[46] "American Zionists Will Ask For Vote of Confidence," *The Jewish Review and Observer*, XLVII (May 13, 1921), 1, 4; *JPA*, no. 16, p. 3 and no. 12, p. 4.

[47] Sachs to Mack, March 14, 1921, Jacob de Haas, *Policy Toward the European Delegation*, March 9, 1921, and Mack to Brandeis, February 21, 1921, LDB; "New Yiddish Orthodox Paper Announced; Shuns Unionism Burden," *American Examiner — Jewish Week*, January 6, 1972, p. 2

[48] *JPA*, no. 7, p.3, no. 18, p. 2, no. 31, p. 4. Another anti-Brandeis Yiddish daily was *Die Zeit*. See *JPA* no. 1, pp. 4-5, no. 2, pp. 3-4, no. 14, pp. 3-4, no. 18, pp. 2-3, no. 26, pp. 3-4, no. 73, p.4

[49] Simon Glazer, *The Palestine Resolution: A Record of its Origin* (Kansas City, Mo., 1922), p. 52.

[50] *JPA*, no. 45, pp. 1-2, no. 47, pp. 1-3, no. 51, pp. 3-5.

[51] Although some districts, for example Buffalo and Philadelphia, stayed loyal to Brandeis. Jacob Sobel, "The Zionist Opposition," *The Jewish Tribune*, XXXVII (April 29, 1921), 11, 16; *JPA*, no. 4, p. 5, no. 9, p. 2, no. 14. p. 1, no. 16, p. 1, no. 26, p. 3, no 59, p. 2, no. 67, p. 1.

broken off; they were resumed in May and terminated as each attested to the other's responsibility for the break.[52] Lipsky, now sufficiently confident to quit the Z.O.A., tendered his resignation from the office of Secretary and authored a stinging rebuke to Mack.[53] The Judge responded by justifying his own lack of faith in Keren Hayesod and announcing that a rival fund-raising organization, loyal to the Brandeis philosophy, would be established.[54] The next day, April 20, Weizmann countered by opening Keren Hayesod offices in downtown New York City.[55] Mack demanded a vote of confidence for the American leaders in June, and the Cleveland convention of the Z.O.A.[56]   As President, he was repudiated (Brandeis was honorary President) and, along with Brandeis and fifty Brandeis Zionist officials, resigned from the Zionist Organization.[57] The Brandeis program was not surrendered. At a separate convention held at Pittsburgh in July, 1921, the dethroned leaders agreed that a protest would be carried out most tellingly if the "Minority," as Brandeisians were now called, remained within the movement.They simply would hold no responsible position in either the Z.O.A. or W.Z.O. nor would they subscribe to the Keren Hayesod.[58] Palestine Development Leagues

---

[52] "Weizmann Appeals for Funds for Zion," *The New York Times,* April 18, 1921, p. 6; "Zionists to Agree," *The New York Times,* June 5, 1921, p. 7; *JPA,* no. 12, p. 3, no. 19, p. 1, no. 22, addendum, no. 54, p. 3, no. 57, pp. 2-3, no. 67, p. 1, no 71, p. 3. It was during this time that Marshall was asked by Weizmann to intercede. Reznikoff, II, 750-860.

[53] Lipsky, pp. 70-79; *JPA,* no. 23, p. 2, no. 29, addendum.

[54] "World Zionists Ask Judge Mack to Quit," *The New York Times,* April 23, 1921, p. 15; *JPA,* no. 24, p. 1, no. 30, pp. 1-2.

[55] "Zionists at Odds on American Funds," *The New York Times,* April 19, 1921, p. 6; *JPA,* no. 24. p. 3.

[56] "Demands Vote of Confidence," *The New York Times,* May 25, 1921, p. 17; *JPA,* no. 37, pp. 1-2, no 42, pp. 1-2.

[57] "Zionist Factions Fail to Harmonize," *The New York Times,* June 6, 1921, p. 13; "Zionists are Split on Palestine Funds," *The New York Times,* June 7, 1921, p. 17; "News Summary," *Christian Science Monitor,* June 8, 1921, p. 4; "Zionist Minority Organize to Fight," *The New York Times,* June 8, 1921, p. 17; "Zionists Adopt Commission Rule," *The New York Times,* June 9, 1921, p. 15; *JPA,* no. 71, pp. 1-3, no. 72, pp. 1-3; "After the Storm," *The Jewish Advocate,* 34 (June 9, 1921), 4.

(P.D.L.), the small, managable units beloved of Brandeis and the "New Freedom" philosophy, were founded on July 4, 1921, "as a constructive step in the direction of restoring Palestine." Non- and anti-Zionists were asked to support either the leagues or the American Palestine Company, both superficially non-national, economic ventures.[59] Together with Felix Frankfurter, Brandeis drafted an apologia which was read at the World Zionist Congress at Carlsbad in September, a gathering at which the Minority refused to participate.[60] In December, Brandeis received a Weizmann lieutenant, Nahum Sokolow, at the Capitol but, short of another upheaval, there was to be no reconciling the American and European titans. In short, there would be "no bridge between Washington and Pinsk."[61]

The four-month quarrel had debilitated the Zionist movement in America. Suddenly, the vitality of American Zionism was drained; the movement stagnated. Keren Hayesod was permanently established in America but the Europeans paid dearly for their victory. Brandeis as Weizmann would later concede, was American Zionism: a separatist perhaps, but one on which he would have to rely.[62] Without Brandeis as a skilful fiscal partner the inefficiency of Weizmann's Palestine policy was to become more evident than it was in 1921.[63] Zionist unity was gone by the end of the year; during

[58] *Report of Program and Organization Committee,* July 4, 1921, LDB; "Defeated Zionists Formulate A Policy," *The New York Times,* June 11, 1921, p. 14; "Minority Zionists to Meet July 3," *The New York Times,* June 18, 1921, p. 10; *JPA,* no. 73, p. 4.

[59] "The Palestine Development Leagues" (editorial), *The American Hebrew,* 109 (July 8, 1921), 192; "Minority Zionists to Develop Palestine," *The American Hebrew,* 109 (July 8, 1921), 198, 204.

[60] By September, 1921, Frankfurter believed that "there was no working with Weizmann," quite a change since 1919. Frankfurter to Brandeis, September 9, 1921, LDB; Berkowitz, pp. 298-300; "Twelfth Zionist Congress Opens on September 4," *The American Hebrew,* 109 (August 26, 1921), 358; "Minority Zionist Group Issues Statement," *The Jewish Review and Observer,* XLVII (September 2, 1921), 1.

[61] "Harding on Zionism," *The Jewish Tribune,* 38 (December 2, 1921), 2; Berlin, *American Jewish Historical Quarterly,* LX, 40.

[62] Berkowitz, p. 233.

[63] For example, see "Mrs. Fels Criticizes World Zionist Organization," *The American Hebrew,* 109 (July 22, 1921), 243.

the battle, Z.O.A. membership suffered a precipitous decline.[64] It was approximated that one hundred thirty thousand members had dwindled to seventeen thousand. In February, 1923, the paltry sum had ebbed by another two thousand.[65]

The middle years of the 1920s were highlighted by a gnawing apathy emanating from the regular American Zionist under Lipsky and a further development of fundamental Minority arguments against Weizmann who, according to Stephen Wise and Jacob de Haas, had lost face not only in Palestine but with the British Government as well. By 1929, the Brandeis group was ripe for return.

With regard to the American Government, Brandeisians employed the technique of "watchful waiting." American Zionism had lost a great friend in Wilson and sustained an incalculable setback with Harding. Following the Jaffa outbreaks of 1921, Harding issued one of his many favorable, innocuous statements on Palestine restoration. This particular one was read at a Zionist luncheon given for Chaim Weizmann. At the time of the greatest dispute among Zionist leaders, Harding recognized no split, endorsed Weizmann and displayed a startling insensitivity toward and incomprehension of the Minority. In July, 1921, when Brandeis's organization began its important work on a planned basis, Harding ignored him and received Louis Lipsky at the White House. Further confusion and lack of commitment to anything save a "Jewish vote" was apparent during the height of the Brandeis-Weizmann feud when the President welcomed a C.C.A.R. delegation and complimented its work, which was often the opposite of Zionism's.[66]

Unlike Lipsky, the Minority had little confidence in the supposed American Declaration of Sympathy for Palestine. Senator Lodge was a knowledgeable, eloquent defender of the resolution but Julian Mack cited Hamilton Fish for his "abysmal ignorance."[67] Harding and his successors, also well-meaning, had not the slightest insight into Zionism. The intimacy which Zionists had once enjoyed with

---

[64] James de Rothschild to Brandeis, November 4, 1921, LDB.

[65] *JPA*, no. 43, p. 7; *Memorandum of Meeting*, February 7, 1923, LDB.

[66] "Zionism Endorsed by Harding and Coolidge," *The Jewish Tribune*, 37 (June 10 1921), 1; "President Receives Zionists," *The Jewish Tribune*, 37 (July 22, 1921), 3; "Calisch Elected Head of Rabbis' Conference," *The Jewish Review and Observer*, XLVIII (April 22, 1921), 1.

Wilson was no longer possible and activist Americans were constrained to depend on the State Department. The Department, however, lacking any distinct policy objectives in Palestine and the Near East, was more than happy to interpret the 1924 Anglo-American Convention in the most restricted sense. The Treaty governed Anglo-American relations during the Mandatory era. American business and missionary interests were explicitly protected. The only reference to Zionism was in the preamble to the Treaty, where the text of the Balfour Declaration was reproduced.[68] Originally, the State Department balked at the Balfour inclusion but was finally satisfied as to the Convention's harmlessness.[69] Articles seven and twenty-seven of the agreement asserted that there were to be no changes in the Mandate without American consent but the State Department never harbored a thought of exercising its option.

The capitulation of the W.Z.O. to the Churchill Memorandum clarified the politics of Weizmann to Brandeis's followers. In 1926, Secretary of State Kellogg defined the 1924 Convention to Weizmann in a way that would later make Stephen Wise wince. America, intoned Kellog, would protect its nationals in Palestine; they would be allowed the same rights as nationals of countries who belonged to the League of Nations.[70] This definition, satisfactory to the W.Z.O. head, negated the efficacy of articles seven and twenty-seven, as Americans were subsequently to point out. Stephen Wise declared that Weizmann's conciliatory air had failed with England and would fail with the United States.[71] Determination with a hint of bellicosity was to be the American response.

A Weizmann-Brandeis union was still mentioned, even by the

[67] Mack to Brandeis, April 4, 1922, LDB; Herbert Parzen, "The Lodge-Fish Resolution," *American Jewish Historical Quarterly,* IX (September 1970), 74; *Hearings... Committee on Foreign Affairs... on H. Con. Res. 52,* pp. 132-135.

[68] Richard H. Nolte, "United States Policy and the Middle East," *The United States and the Middle East,* ed. Georgiana G. Stevens (Englewood Cliffs, N.J., 1964), p. 152; Manuel, p. 4. For excellent summaries of the Treaty, see Fanny Fern Andrews, *The Holy Land Under Mandate,* 2 vols. (Boston, 1931), II, 393-394 or Esco Foundation, I, 253.

[69] Department of State to British Embassy, 867N.01/260 ca. July 10, 1922, *USFR: 1922,* 2 vols. (Washington, 1938), II, 290, 306.

[70] Wallace Murray to R. Walton Moore, 867N.01/727 1/2, November 18, 1936, *USFR:1936,* 5 vols. (Washington, 1953), III, 457.

Yiddish press in America, but only slight hope was held out for its consummation. There were too many outstanding grievances and harmful personality conflicts.[72]   In his search for an adequate replacement for the Brandeis minority, Weizmann turned to Louis Marshall and the non-Zionists. He spent five years in complicated negotiations which culminated in the establishment of the enlarged Jewish Agency for Palestine (J.A.P.).   But, he wasted valuable time. In the interim, the Brandeis forces regrouped. Keren Hayesod proved inadequate to halt the depression which overtook Palestine between 1925 and 1927. The asseveration that this organization was financially mismanaged was lent additional credibility.[73] More than any single event, the depression shattered the Weizmann myth of invincibility and it soon was manifest that Zionism could not endure without some drastic reorganization measures.[74]

And Brandeis was prepared, for he had cautiously made inroads into non-Zionism and Palestinian improvement. One project he was particulary interested in involved harnassing the waters of the Jordan River and its upper tributary, the Yarmuk, as a source of hydro-electric power, an idea strikingly similar in outline to the Tennessee Valley Authority of the New Deal. Brandeis agreed with the engineer who designed the project, Pinhas Rutenberg, to finance a portion of it through the Palestine Development Council (P.D.C.), the Minority's investment organization. As much as Brandeis would have liked to finance the plan entirely, he couldn't because he lacked sufficient funds.[75]

At this juncture, Brandeis chose to conclude an arrangement with non-Zionists like Louis Marshall and Felix Warburg. To do this, he

[71] "Stephen Wise Leaves Suddenly to Attend Zionist Sessions in Berlin," *The Jewish Review and Observer,* LV (December 21, 1928), 1; "Dr. Stephen Wise Leaves Zionist Congress in Anger," *The Jewish Transcript,* IV (September 16, 1927), 1; *The New York Times,* March 30, 1928, p. 25, April 2, 1928, p. 15 and January 4, 1929, p. 52.

[72] De Haas to Brandeis, February 7, 1923, LDB; "Reconciliation proposed at Zionists' Convention," *The Jewish Advocate,* 39 (June 29, 1922), 1, 8.

[73] Joseph Barondess to Emanuel Neumann, July 9, 1923, Barondess to de Haas, October 23 and December 22, 1923, JBL, no. 54, pp. 236-237, 670; de Haas to Brandeis, December 13, 1923 and Brandeis to R.D. Kesselman, November 27, 1927, LDB; C. Wortman, "Is the Keren Hayesod Mismanaged?" *The American Hebrew,* 133 (May 18, 1923), 3-4.

[74] Rosensohn to Brandeis, October 12, 1927, LDB.

created the Palestine Economic Corporation (P.E.C.) in 1926, which united the assets of the Palestine Cooperative Company, a four-year old Brandeis investment company, with the Reconstruction Finance Committee (R.F.C.) of the non-Zionist J.D.C. The two organizations were separate entities and remained so,[76] with Marshall making it plain that Palestine investment was only one area of non-Zionist interest, the others being the status of Jews throughout the world and possible resettlement of Jews in Russia.

Chaim Weizmann did not object to non-Zionist actions with regard to Brandeis, despite the fact that Marshall had signed many agreements with the W.Z.O. Above all, Weizmann was a realist: he knew that hindering Palestinian development would, in the long run, be hurtful to Zionism. Even if he wished to make his peace with Brandeis, the hostility of his associates, particularly Menahem Ussischkin, precluded a parley. Ussischkin had even threatened to "break" Weizmann if he exhibited any flexibility toward Brandeis.[77] It was apparent that the European leader could do little to convince his colleagues that Brandeis might be necessary for the overall success of the Zionist endeavor. If Weizmann believed this, he would have to wait patiently and hope for the return of the Minority to positions of power within the Z.O.A.

For the Brandeis group, the hour of their redemption was close at hand. In 1925, Harry Friedenwald, Julian Mack and Stephen Wise filtered back into the Z.O.A. and began agitating for their leader's return. By 1927, the Minority bitterly assailed Z.O.A. President Louis Lipsky for his supposed European genuflecting; at the Washington Conference it discussed the "Jewish Agency plot" and how to oust Weizmann.[78] Brandeis, however, was not carried away by the moment. Three of his associates favored the introduction of the Justice's name at the forthcoming Zionist convention. Work in

[75] Brandeis to Rutenberg, April 25, 1922, *Rutenberg Hydroelectric Project* and Committee on the Rutenberg Project to Rutenberg, February 28, 1923, LDB; "Rutenberg Authorizes Zionists and Brandeis Group to Finance His Scheme," *Denver Jewish News*, VIII (June 14, 1922), 1.

[76] Bernard Flexner to Edward M.M. Warburg, July 8, 1941, HL.

[77] *Why Did Weizmann Break With the Zionist Organization of America?* (unsigned, undated), de Haas to Frankfurter, August 14, 1923 and de Haas to Brandeis, August 15, 1923, LDB.

[78] De Haas to Brandeis, December 31, 1926, LDB; *Conference at Washington*, November 5 and 6, 1927, LDB.

Palestine, said Samuel J. Rosensohn was at a standstill; the return of Brandeis could stave off disaster. Brandeis was buoyed but not swayed. He suggested that the Minority became more militant; that it challenge the Lipsky administration until it buckled and that they find a younger man to lead: Brandeis felt he could no longer bear the entire decision-making burden.[79]

Minority Zionists rallied to an anti-Lipsky, anti-Weizmann banner. Though most were disillusioned with Weizmann, the Brandeis-Mack group did not divide on the issue of the Agency. Professor Leo Wollman, Julius Simon, Dr. Horace Kallen and Ben V. Cohen, one-time secretary to Judge Mack, believed that the J.A.P. proposal was in actuality the culmination of the Brandeis program of 1920. They said that the Agency "will bring strength where theoretical discussion will bring only dissension."[80] Brandeis, though, was still susceptible to the de Haas rhetoric. In 1923, de Haas had used much the same critique of the non-Zionists as he did in 1928. Any organization, he claimed, that would link Zionists and non-Zionists in a position of equal power would be turned into a charity fund. Like Wise, de Haas believed that "neither Warburg, nor Lehman nor Marshall will take a first-class interest in Palestine ... the leopard will noth change its spots." The safe investment, no originality method of Marshall and Warburg would be terribly damaging for the future of Palestine and, averred de Haas, would have to be avoided at all costs.[81]

Heeding the Brandeis admonition, the Minority stepped up its attack in 1928, right in the midst of a huge Zionist fund-raising campaign for Palestine.[82] In March, two Minority Zionists resigned from the Administrative Committee of the Z.O.A.[83] Barondess, on

---

[79] Rosensohn to Brandeis, June 24, 1927, Charles A. Cowen to Brandeis, June 24, 1927, Abraham Tulin to Brandeis, June 24, 1927, Brandeis to de Haas, June 5, 1927, *Ibid.*

[80] "Jewish Agency Plan," *The Jewish Review and Observer*, LV (February 1, 1929), 1, 4.

[81] De Haas to Brandeis, December 22, 1923, LDB; "Correspondence," *Intermountain Jewish News*, XIV (March 29, 1928), 6.

[82] "Head of Hadassah Joins Zionist Split," *The New York Times*, March 31, 1928, p. 7; "Insists Hadassah Has No Part in Row," *The New York Times*, April 1, 1928, sec. 2, p. 5.

[83] Samuel J. Rosensohn and Lawrence Berenson to the Administrative Committee of the Z.O.A., March 19, 1928, LDB.

the publication committee of *Hadoar*, the only Hebrew language weekly in the United States, reviled the Z.O.A. for engaging in "one thousand and one useless schemes."[84] Brandeis, however, provided the most stimulating battle cry. Writing to Judge Mack and Robert Szold, he commanded the Minority to push for unconditional surrender:

> I think the situation is quite difference (sic) from what it was in 1921 ... We had our convictions then of the wrongness of the W-L (Weizmann-Lipsky) alliance and of their allies. Now we have abundant proof. To my mind, it is clear now that it were better that no money should go (to Palestine) than it should go through this dishonest, wicked and corrupt administration. [85]

The "proof" of Brandeis was soon revealed. Certain irregularities had been discovered in the Z.O.A. financial records which upheld the opposition charges of "Zionist mismanagement" of United Palestine Appeal proceeds and accumulation of a "relatively enormous" deficit in the Palestine Securities Corporation.[86] Lipsky claimed that he was under fire from the "Nordic element of Zionism" and was still buttressed by the formidable Yiddish dailies.[87] But Weizmann listened. The charge was a black mark on his own fiscal policy and required investigation, if only to dissipate the cloud of suspicion that descended upon all Zionism.

A Committee of Inquiry, whose members bore no affiliations with Zionism was duly appointed. At the beginning of May, the six commissioners reported back to Weizmann. They stated that there was no reason to lose confidence in the Z.O.A. because there was no proof that any individual "acted for his own personal, financial gain." Lipsky, however, was found to have indeed "mismanaged funds." The Z.O.A. President granted personal loans out of the

---

[84] Barondess to de Haas, March 12, 1928, JB, Box 7.

[85] Brandeis to Mack and Szold, March 27, 1928, LDB.

[86] "The Enquiry into American Zionist Affairs" (editorial), *The American Hebrew*, 123 (June 22, 1928), 189; "Zionist Leader is Called Unfit," *The New York Times*, May 4, 1928, p. 27; "Zionism at Odds as Meeting Nears," *The New York Times*, June 23, 1928, p. 18.

[87] De Haas to Brandeis, May 3, 1928 and June 22, 1928, LDB; I. Landman, "Nordics and Semites in American Zionism," *The American Hebrew*, 123 (July 27, 1928), 326, 334.

organization's treasury and placed the American Zion Common-wealth in debt to several Palestinian banks for one hundred eighty thousand dollars. The Committee further discovered that trust funds have been "improperly transferred from regular channels to the general funds of the Z.O.A." The verdict: that the credit of the Z.O.A. should under no circumstances be allowed to extend to private organizations; immediate steps should be taken to prevent future "irregularities" from occurring; no additional liabilities should be incurred by the Z.O.A. without the consent of a majority of the Executive Committee, Z.O.A. officers should not be paid and the present leaders should not hold office.[88]

Despite heavy opposition, the Lipsky regime was confirmed in July, 1928, although a compromise resolution was pushed through by Stephen Wise, wherein the Z.O.A. President would share his "burdensome" duties with an administrative committee, an execu-tive committee, three vice-presidents, two treasurers and a secre-tary.[89] Meeting at Pittsburgh, the Minority drew up a list of proposals, which included abolishing the Presidential office and replacing it with a governing council. The Brandeis Zionists declared themselves "permanently opposed" to the current regime and dedicated themselves to the "restoration of morale within the American movement." The fact that Lipsky was returned to office by a slim margin convinced Wise that the Z.O.A. leader would do anything to stay in power, even throw the responsibility of Palestine upon non-nationals like Marshall and Warburg, who would turn the Holy Land into a "Near East counterpart of the Crimean provinces ... of the J.D.C."[90] The organized opposition to Lipsky

[88] "Zionist Administration Proposes an Inquiry on Opposition Charges," *Jewish Daily Bulletin*, V (May 18, 1928), 1; "American Jews and Palestine Regeneration" (editorial), *The American Hebrew*, 123 (July 13, 1928), 285; "Investigating Committee of Judges Appointed by Dr. Weizmann Renders Report," *The Jewish Tribune*, 93, (May 11, 1928), 5.

[89] "Zionists Uphold Lipsky Administration and Adopt Program for Palestine Work," *The American Hebrew*, 123 (July 6, 1928), 241; "Louis Lipsky Re-Elected President of Zionist Organization of America," *The Jewish Review and Observer*, LIV (July 6, 1928), 1, 4.

[90] "Zionist Opposition Declares Itself a Permanent Organization for Recon-struction Work," *The Jewish Tribune*, 93 (July 29, 1928), 10; "The Reorganization of the Z.O.A." (editorial), *The Jewish Tribune*, 93 (September 28, 1928), 6; Voss, p. 156.

met in October, 1928, and April, 1929, to draft anti-Z.O.A. resolutions.[91] Hadassah, loyal to Brandeis since the Cleveland convention of 1921, voiced its disapproval of Lipsky's "collection agency." The decline of American Zionist influence in the World Organization was as disconcerting as the aforementioned numerical loss: between 1921 and 1929, American representation at the World Zionist Congress had been slashed from thirty-five to seventeen.[92]

In 1929, Brandeis seized the initiative from Weizmann in America and in Palestine. Those with the least faith in government, the Brandeisians, attempted the Herzl method of direct intervention in foreign affairs after the Wailing Wall outbreaks of 1929. Some well-known Gentile Americans blasted the British policy which had led to the riots, but did not encourage United States action on the basis of the 1924 convention. One of these was Senator William Borah, who spoke grandly at the Madison Square Garden Zionist rally.[93] Stephen Wise doubtlessly recognized the Idaho Senator as a British foe but thought he possessed less desirable qualities, a non-interventionist, and an unreliable opportunist.[94] Therefore, Wise placed but a minimum of confidence in Zionism's public champions and turned to Secretary of State Henry Stimson. Apparently he was too late. Paul Knabenshue, United States Consul General in Jerusalem, had accepted the stories of two non-Jewish Americans in Palestine, foreign correspondent Vincent Sheean and Judge Pierre Crabites, that the Jews' "provocative acts" initiated the disturbances, and wired the same to Washington. In turn, Knabenshue was told to concern himself only with American nationals.[95] Zionist delegations presented themselves to G. Howard Shaw, Chief of the Near East Division and Stimson, who felt obliged to defend his Consul.[96]

[91] "Call for Changes in Zionist Policy," *The New York Times*, October 15, 1928, p. 29.

[92] "The Z.O.A. Convention" (editorial), *Chicago Jewish Chronicle*, XVII (June 28, 1929), 6.

[93] "Hoover Foresees Safe 'Homeland' for Jews in Rebuilt Palestine," *Christian Science Monitor*, August 30, 1929, p. 1; U.S. Congress, *Congressional Record, Seventy-First Congress, First Session* (Washington, 1929), part 4, pp. 4533-4535; "Borah to Speak at Garden Rally of Jews Tonight," *New York Herald Tribune*, August 20, 1929, p. 12; Fink, p. 45.

[94] Vivian Pierce to Frank P. Walsh, 1927, Frank P. Walsh Papers, Box 112, New York Public Library; Henry S. Prichett to Nicholas Murray Butler, September 18, 1929, Nicholas Murray Butler Papers.

After the Jews and Arabs were suppressed, Stephen Wise requested that Stimson aid the case of the Zionists before the Shaw Commission by appointing an American lawyer for their defense; he may have also suggested that Jewish consular officials to Palestine be appointed to offset the anti-Zionist predilection of the Consul General.[97]   The State Department demurred to both proposals, claimed to favor "self-determination," and excused itself from any further responsibility.[98]

The Wailing Wall crisis had placed Weizmann Zionism on the defensive. Perhaps Wise had accomplished little, but he was vocal; Weizmann seemed to be anesthetized. Wise clamored that Weizmann had destroyed Zionism with the Agency and was a silent, albeit guilty, bystander to England's "pacification" of the Palestinian countryside.[99]   The riots, the Agency and Lipsky's inability to restrain the opposition converged to topple the latter's administration in June, 1930.

[95] Paul Knabenshue to Henry Stimson, 867N.404 Wailing Wall/264, October 12, 1929, GRDS:RG 59; Acting Secretary of State Carr to Knabenshue 867N.404 Wailing Wall/24 telegram, August 24, 1929 and Knabenshue to Stimson, 867N. 404 Wailing Wall/5 telegram, August 24, 1929, USFR:1929, 3 vols. (Washington, 1944), III, 47-48; Another important State Department anti-Zionist source at this time was the Foreign Policy Association, an organization from which government officials gathered information concerning Near Eastern "self-determination." See de Haas to Brandeis, February 16, 1930 and magazine article by Elizabeth MacCallum entitled "An Arab Voice," LDB; Elizabeth MacCallum, "Why the Arab Massacres," News Bulletin of the Foreign Policy Association, VIII (August 30, 1929), 1-2.

[96] Memorandum by Shaw, 867N.404 Wailing Wall/228, August 27, 1929, USFR:1929, III, 51; "Zionists See Stimson," New York Herald Tribune, August 27, 1929, p. 9; "Stimson Defends Jerusalem Counsul," The New York Times, September 8, 1929, p. 22.

[97] Memorandum by Shaw, 867N.404 Wailing Wall/255, September 23, 1929, G. Howland Shaw to Stimson, 867N.404 Wailing Wall/257, October 21, 1929 and Stimson to Hoover 867N.404 Wailing Wall/258, GRDS:RG, 59; Manuel, pp. 302-303.

[98] De Haas to Brandeis, February 6, 1929, LDB.

[99] "Stephen Wise Calls Z.O.A. 'Sounding Board' for the Voice of London," The Jewish Review and Observer, LVI (February 14, 1930), 1, 4; Voss, pp. 167-168. The Orthodox viewpoint was, at this time congenial with Wise's. See Ephraim Deinard, Cherpas Brittania (The Shame of Britain, in Hebrew, New York, 1929), pp. 74, 94-95, 135-138, 140-148.

Even the Yiddish press, perpetually pro-Lipsky, had begun to forsake him in February, 1930. [100] In their determination to exploit this change in attitude, the Minority arranged with *The Day* to have a Zionist page under its exclusive control. With the Yiddish press, though, it was largely by choice of the lesser of two evils: having disavowed Lipsky, they sought a stronger though undesirable alternative. [101] Felix Warburg exercised his influence on Weizmann to jettison Lipsky and the European leader, apparently aware of Warburg's new feelings of friendship toward Brandeis, complied. [102] By May 7, Weizmann had withdrawn his support from the Z.O.A. President and Lipsky was "ready to quit." [103] A groundswell of popular support from the Anglo-Jewish press, from journalists and from the local organizations which had disowned him in 1921, returned Brandeis to leadership on July 1, 1930 at Cleveland, the city of his undoing nine years before. [104]

Brandeis had promised and delivered a Zionist reorganization. Robert Szold became Executive Director of the Z.O.A. and no President was elected until the end of the year. An Executive Committee of forty was chosen, in which Brandeis Zionists totaled half, or twenty; Brandeisians were also assured representation in the

[100] De Haas to Brandeis, February 17, 1930 and February 24, 1930, LDB.

[101] De Haas to Brandeis, June 2, 1930 and June 26, 1930, LDB; Marion Rubenstein, "How Peace Came to the American Zionists," *The American Hebrew,* 127 (July 11, 1930), 258, 260; Samuel Margoshes, "When Jacob de Haas Shook Hands with Louis Lipsky," *The Jewish Transcript,* VII (July 11, 1930), 1, 8; "Leaders Voice Optimism Over Peace Effected in American Zionism," *The Jewish Independent,* I (July 17, 1930), 1, 3; "Zionist Leaders, Yiddish Press Voice Optimism," *Buffalo Jewish Review,* XXII (July 11, 1930), 1.

[102] De Haas to Mack, April 24, 1930, LDB.

[103] De Haas to Brandeis, May 7, 1930, *Ibid.*

[104] He still met with some minor opposition. De Haas to Brandeis, June 18, 1930 and de Haas to Julius Meyer, June 19, 1930, LDB; "Zionist Districts throughout America Take Action on Brandeis-Mack Proposal," *The Jewish Review and Observer,* LVI (June 20, 1930), 1, 4; "Zionists Favor Brandeis Proposal," *The American Jewish World,* XVIII (June 20, 1930), 13; "Adopt Brandeis Plan" (editorial), *The Chicago Jewish Chronicle,* XIX (June 6, 1930), 8; "Brandeis and Zionist Leadership" (editorial), *Detroit Jewish Chronicle,* XXX (June 20, 1930), 4; "Is it Brandeis or Will Zionism Perish" (editorial), *The Jewish Advocate,* 56 (June 20, 1930), 4; "Brandeis Makes a Proposal to Zionists" (editorial), *The Scribe,* XX (June 6, 1930), 4; "Dr. Wise Excoriates Zionist Leadership and is Called 'Traitor' " *The American Hebrew,* 127 (July 4, 1930), 236.

J.A.P. Leadership in the American movement was vested in a Committee of Eighteen, twelve of which were to be from the Brandeis-Mack group; the remaining six were Lipskyites. A National Advisory Committee of one hundred fifty was established, fifty of whom were selected directly by Brandeis and his followers. The remaining one hundred were chosen by the Z.O.A. convention. Interestingly, at the time of Lipsky's defeat, the Z.O.A. was running at a deficit of one hundred thirty-five thousand dollars. In a matter of days, pledges eradicated nearly eighty per cent of the shortage. [105]

Vitality was the byword of the American Zionist approach to government in the last full decade before World War II. As will be recalled, Brandeis and his associates attempted to avoid State Department subalterns in Washington and Paris. A preference was shown in 1919 for dealing with undisputed authority, as embodied by the Chief Executive. After the League's assignment of the mandate to England, the Minority publicized its dissatisfaction with that country's hesitant, halting Palestine policy. The WZO and the Lipsky-led ZOA, on the other hand, receded from the precincts of power, fell back upon British assurances and maintained a low profile with regard to the Churchill Memorandum and the generally unsatisfactory conduct of the Mandatory. After 1929, the Brandeis methods in the foreign sphere were no longer ignored by Weizmann , slowly they were to absorb him. Even though it would never influence another president as profoundly as it did Woodrow Wilson, American Zionism did adapt itself to the fascist emergency and became a persistent, if not always effective presence to the State Department and the White House. It taught Weizmann to do the same and by example coaxed the European Zionist away from his passive dependence on the altruism of those who in the 1930s could no longer be relied upon. Nevertheless, an appreciation of Brandeis's role must not gainsay the reality of the Americans' position: they were the only protesters available for, by 1941, theirs was the

[105] "The Brandeis Ultimatum and the Zionists" (editorial), *The American Hebrew*, 127 (May 30, 1930), 82; "Acts on Brandeis Offer," *The New York Times*, May 29, 1930, p. 28; "Coalition Brings Peace to Zionists," *The New York Times*, July 2, 1920, p. 4; "Reorganization of American Zionists Unanimously Agreed Upon By Delegates," *The Jewish Review and Observer*, LVI (July 4, 1930), 1, 4.

only viable Jewish community extant. In short, with the possible exception of the Yishuv and Revisionism, the absence of all competition facilitated the ultimate triumph of the Brandeis group.

Dismayed at Weizmann's submission to the Shaw findings, Felix Frankfurter nearly sailed to England himself to obtain guarantees that Sir John Hope-Simpson, presently in Palestine, would sympathize with the Zionists.[106] In America, Wallace Murray, then chief of the Near East Division of the State Department, was inspired by America's Consul General in Palestine, Paul Knabenshue, to spread anti-Zionist propaganda among his State Department colleagues. Knabenshue had become an outspoken anti-Zionist, probably because he planned to leave his post to go into business in Beirut, as manager of a bank which was to operate under the Federal Reserve Act. The Zionists, therefore, were concerned with his successor. Stephen Wise spent the better part of four years petitioning the State Department to install at Jerusalem a man of less pronounced anti-Zionist tendencies. American Zionists were also lobbying to have Murray replaced by Addison Southard, a former Consul General in Palestine who was believed to be only mildly antagonistic toward Jewish nationalism.[107] In both these endeavors, the Zionists were frustrated.

After the publication of the Passfield White Paper, the American Zionist leadership was absolutely disgusted with Weizmann.[108]

Brandeis Zionists appealed to the American Government on the basis of the 1924 Protocol. Their reasoning, as it was to be during the course of the 1930s, was that the White Paper (and all successive decrees) changed the character of the Mandate and, therefore, could not go into effect until United States assent, necessitated by articles seven and twenty-seven of the Anglo-American Treaty, was received by Britain. The non-committal State Department reply was that the United States was bound to protest a change only if American nationals were affected; Jews who claimed Palestinian citizenship but were still American nationals should expect to take the consequences of their actions, along with other Palestinian Jews.[109]

---

[106] Mark de Wolfe, ed., *Holmes-Laski Letters*, 2 vols. (Cambridge Mass, 1953) II, 1261.

[107] Mack to Brandeis, June 20, 1930, J.C. Hyman to Mack, July 18, 1930, Mack to Brandeis, July 19, 1930, Emanuel Neumann to Robert Szold, August 16, 1932 and Max Rhoade to Morris Rothenberg, April 7, 1933, LDB.

[108] De Haas to Szold, November 6, 1930, *Ibid.*

After American Zionists interceded directly with Weizmann, the protested the White Paper later but eventually reconciled himself to it. In February, 1931, he accepted a Ramsay MacDonald pledge that the Balfour Declaration would be respected. Six months later, under a Stephen Wise bombardment, Weizmann was confirmed in his pro-British policy by a scant ten votes.[110]

Event tumbled on event. Upon the rise of Hitler, Brandeis favored a voluntary boycott of German goods. "The World Zionist Congress fought down" this proposal and, instead, invoked "the aid of the world in colonizing German Jews in Palestine." However, a boycott was declared by the Second World Jewish Conference, which heeded the appeals of Stephen Wise, the American Jewish Congress and the Assembly of Orthodox Rabbis of Canada and New York.[111]   Wise and Robert Szold complained to Brandeis of Weizmann's "pandering" to the British.[112]   In November, 1933, Lipsky, who had returned as a "figurehead" President of the Z.O.A. in 1930, was upset that, upon the nomination of James G. McDonald as League of Nations High Commissioner for German Refugees, no specific reference to Palestine as a haven was made, probably in deference to Britain.[113] American Zionists surmised the Weizmann would offer no objection.

Revisionism, as a reply to Weizmann's futility, was becoming popular with Brandeisians, including Robert Szold, Samuel Rosensohn, Abraham Tulin and Jacob de Haas.[114]   Since their American

[109] "Zionists Here to Plan Huge Protest November 2," *The New York Times*, October 24, 1930, p. 11. The clearest illustrations of this type of State Department response occur in later years, for example, Cordell Hull to George Wadsworth, 340. 1115A/1700 telegram, January 25, 1941, *USFR:1940*, 5 vols (Washington, 1958), III, 888.

[110] Albert Howe Lybyer, "Zionist Dispute Over Palestine," *Current History*, XXXIV (August 1931), 790-792; "Zionists Change Pilots to Save the Ship," *Literary Digest, 110 (August 8, 1931), 20-21.*

[111] "The Zionist Congress and the German Boycott," *Literary Digest*, 116 (September 23, 1933), 16; Robert L. Baker, "The Zionist Congress," *Current History*, XXXIV (October 1933), 122-123; Mason, pp. 595-596.

[112] Wise to Mack, June 7, 1933 and Robert Szold to Joseph S. Shubow, June 16, 1933, LDB.

[113] Lipsky to McDonald, November 28, 1922, James G. McDonald Papers (hereafter abbreviated JGMcD); "Zionists Elect Lipsky," *The New York Times*, December 29, 1930, p. 21.

emergence in 1926, Revisionists had claimed a basic political kinship with Herzl and an economic one with Brandeis. The extreme variation on Herzl's philosophy, however, made Revisionism distasteful to most American Zionists, particularly Frankfurter, Mack and Wise. [115]   Revision advocated an armed Jewish uprising to overthrow the Mandatory and the annexation of Transjordan to a Jewish State. [116] Irredentism and war were not the natural avenues of the Zionist and were consequently abjured by those Americans whose visions of grandeur merely encompassed a Jewish sovereignty founded on peaceful cooperation with Arab neighbors. Nevertheless, Revisionism grew rapidly in the United States. De Haas, who had become friendly with the American Revisionist President Mordecai Danzis during the Lipsky affray of 1930, wrote to Brandeis of his "admiration" for those people who dealt courageously, single-mindedly, even "fanatically;" with the pressing issues of the day. [117]

British attempts to qualify the Balfour Declaration out of existence merely provided a fertile field for Revisionism which, in America, had begun to interest Jewish youth. [118]   De Haas surprised and infuriated Stephen Wise by heading an American delegation to the first session of the rump congress called by the New Zionist Organization (N.Z.O.) which had recently seceded from the W.Z.O. In 1936, de Haas became President of the Palestine Mandate Defense League, an arm of the parent N.Z.O. [119] At that time, he revealed to

[114] *Peronsal, Unofficial Report,* November 22, 1933, LDB.

[115] L. Altman to Szold, March 4, 1931, LDB; Johan J. Smertenko, "The Present Conflict in Zionist Policy: The Case for Revisionism," *The Menorah Journal,* XII (1926), 473; "Zionists Oppose Strife in Palestine," *The New York Times,* June 29, 1926, p. 12.

[116] Harry Schneiderman and Melvin M. Fagen, "Review of the Year 5695," *AJYB,* XXXVII (Philadelphia, 1935), 149.

[117] Mordecai Danzis to de Haas, April 7, 1930, and de Haas to Brandeis, June 19, 1934, LDB.

[118] "Gives View on Palestine," *The New York Times,* January 2, 1935, p. 23; "Jabotinsky Calls Revisionism 'New Deal' in Zionism," *Detroit Jewish Chronicle,* XXXVII (September 13, 1935), 10.

[119] "Jabotinsky Calls Revisionism 'New Deal' in Zionism," *Detroit Jewish Chronicle,* XXXVII (September 13, 1935), 1; Louis I. Newman, "Telling it in Gath," *Intermountain Jewish News,* XXII (November 6, 1936), 1.

Brandeis his nearly obsessive hatred of Weizmann's concilation. There should be "no truckling under to Britain," he said; if one stood firm, like Hitler, Mussolini and the Arabs, England would back down; she had always yielded to pressure and the lesson ought to be learned by the Jews.[120] Frankfurter and Wise believed de Haas' hatreds to be "too strong" and they, rather than his rational intellect, were guiding. Before de Haas and his Revisionist activities became objects of real concern to American Zionists, he died in 1937.

By comparison, the militancy of Wise paled. The State Department allowed its position under the 1924 Convention to be defined by Britain on the basis of articles two through six.[121] From 1936 to 1941, the Department was aware of but tried to ignore him. State Department records are replete with references to Wise, surveys of his activities and acknowledgements of his ubiquity. Yet, his overall impact on Washington was minimal. Wise's greatest success appears to have been in converting Weizmann to an activist stance by example rather than by accomplishment.

Despite the injunctions of Wise, George Wadsworth, an ardent anti-Zionist, became American Consul General in Palestine, following the departure of Leland Morris, the American official who had blamed "the Jews of Jaffa" for raising "the blood pressure" of the Arabs, thereby provoking new outbreaks in April, 1936.[122] In an effort to mobilize as many Zionists as he could behind an American interventionist policy, Wise ran for and was elected to the Presidency of the Z.O.A. He was displeased by non-Zionist dallying within the Agency and was anxious to avoid working through it.[123]

In July, 1936, Senators Royal S. Copeland of New York, Warren Austin of Vermont and Daniel Hastings of Delaware left to investigate the situation in Palestine. Because of Zionist interest, the State Department regarded the tour as "propagandistic," designed to cater

---

[120] De Haas to Brandeis, October 15, 1936, LDB.

[121] Cordell Hull to U.S. Ambassador in England, Bingham, 867N.00/474 telegram, July 3, 1937, *USFR:1937*, 5 vols. (Washington, 1954) II, 887.

[122] Franklin Roosevelt to Wise, February 21, 1936, Wise to Brandeis, February 27, 1936, and Frankfurter to Wise, February 27, 1936, LDB; Leland B. Morris to Hull, 867N.00/283, April 25, 1936, *USFR:1936*, III, 440.

[123] Voss, pp. 212-213; Daniel L. Schorr, "The American Zionists Go to Their Annual Convention," *The Chicago Jewish Chronicle*, XXXI (July 3, 1936), 3.

to the Jewish vote in the coming elections. Perhaps this was true, but equally devious were the methods of the Acting Secretary of State, who called Wadsworth to tell the the Senators to cancel their trip and return home because Palestine was "unsafe." Officially, Secretary of State Cordell Hull expressed "neither approval nor disapproval" for the "unofficial mission" but his choice of words implied that he had already taken a stand. When he returned, Copeland called upon Murray and informed him that he was favorably impressed by the Jews of Palestine; the Arabs had benefited by their presence. The British, he said, were overturning the Mandate. Murray's answer was that he would recommend no American action, not even a reprimand. If this country decided to interfere, warned Murray, "we might be reminded of the fact that, at one time, this government was asked to assume the Palestine Mandate." [124]

Shortly afterward, Rabbi Wise was told by the State Department that it would transmit no American Jewish protest to England. [125] Privately, Murray informed R. Walton Moore that the Zionist memorandum was "an outright deception" since it made no mention of the Treaty of Lausanne, the definitive Turkish agreement, which, in turn, was silent on the Balfour Declaration and the erection of a Jewish National Home. Wise had insisted on emphasizing the defunct Treaty of Sevres which did refer to the establishment of a Jewish homeland. In addition, the letter ignored the findings of the King-Crane Commission and assumed that the 1922 Congressional Declaration of Sympathy bound America to aid the Jews, "which it most assuredly did not." [126]

The Peel Commission returned to England on January 24, 1937; both Wise and the State Department knew of its findings in May. [127]

---

[124] Wadsworth to Hull, 867N.00/358, August 22, 1936, Acting Secretary of States Phillips to Wadsworth, 867N.00/364 and Memorandum by Wallace Murray, 867N. 00/393, September 22, 1936, *USFR:1936*, III, 446-451; Arthur T. Weil, "Hints of Senate Action on Palestine," *The American Hebrew*, 139 (September 25, 1936), 369.

[125] Memorandum by R. Walton Moore, 867N. 00/420, December 2, 1936, *USFR: 1936*, III, 458-459.

[126] Murray to Moore, 867N. 01/420, December 2, 1936, *GRDS:RG 59*.

[127] Lord Melchett to Arthur Hays Sulzberger, May 22, 1937, JGMcD; Murray to Moore, 867N. 01/749 1/2, May 10, 1937, Memorandum of Paul H. Alling, 867N. 01748a, June 1, 1937, Bingham to Hull, 867N. 01/768 telegram, June 7, 1937, *USFR: 1937*, II, 883-886, 891.

The State Department would not appeal to Great Britain, although the proposed partition clearly altered the Mandate. On the other hand, Stephen Wise would appeal and convinced Weizmann that he should appeal. As a result, the outmoded, faltering Weizmann approach to Britain was soon abandoned.

The "Judgment of Solomon," as one optimistic newspaper called the Peel Report, divided American Zionism unequally.[128] The majority, including Brandeis, Mack, Wise, Robert and Henrietta Szold, Tulin, Abba Hillel Silver and Hadassah were opposed. Orthodox and Reformed Jewish Zionists were opposed. Jewish columnists and the secular, non-Jewish press, including *The New York Times,* the *Herald Tribune* and the *World Telegram* were opposed. At least a score of Jewish periodicals across the United States added to the opposition clamor. House Concurrent Resolution Twenty-Two protested against partition; Secretary of the Interior Harold Ickes and Senator Copeland demanded that Britain fulfill her obligations to the Jews under the Balfour Declaration.[129]

Initially Chaim Weizmann favored the Peel findings as an instrument to pry more concessions out of Britain at the bargaining table. He sought to win Felix Frankfurter over to partition but Frankfurter's reply was to draft an anti-partition communication which was hurriedly sent to Roosevelt.[130] There was, however, a pro-parti-

---

[128] "Palestine Plan's Reception Proves Satisfying to London," *Christian Science Monitor,* July 9, 1937, p. 2.

[129] Szold to Brandeis, July 6, 1937, Mack to Brandeis, July 19, 1937, Tulin to Brandeis, August 4, 1937, LDB; "Brandeis is Firm Against Partition," *The Jewish Transcript,* XIV (July 30, 1937), 1; Stephen Wise, *The Partition of Palestine* n.p., n.d.); "Hadassah Rejects Palestine Partition," *The American Hebrew,* 141 (November 5, 1937), 7, 18; "American Opinion on Palestine Partition," *The American Hebrew,* 142 (April 15, 1938), 6, 19; Joseph Brainin, "The Balfour Declaration is Dead!" *Emanu-El,* LXXXIII (July 9, 1937), 4; Joseph Salmark, "Review of the Jewish Week," *Texas Jewish Herald,* XXXIII (July 29, 1937), 4; "Solomon's Plan Without Solomon's Wit," *New York Evening Post,* July 9, 1937), p. 6; "The Palestine Partition," *Brooklyn Daily Eagle,* July 9, 1937, p. 10; U.S. Congress, *Congressional Record, Seventy-Fifth Congress, First Session* (Washington 1937), part 7, p. 7712, part 8, p. 8674; U.S. Congress, *Congressional Record, Seventy-Fifth Congress, Third Session* (Washington 1937), part 9, pp. 366-368; Robert Szold, *The Proposed Partition of Palestine* (New York, 1937). Any of the following periodicals can be consulted on anti-partition feeling for the dates of July and August, 1937: *B'nai Brith Messenger, Chicago Jewish Chronicle, Jewish Community Press, The Jewish Ledger, The Jewish Spectator, The Jewish Standard, The Scribe, The Modern View, Westchester Jewish Weekly, Hadoar* (in Hebrew), the *American Jewish Times* and the American Jewish World.

tionist sentiment in the United States disseminated by Louis Lipsky, who was at first against but then returned to Weizmann, the Yiddish press, but not the Orthodox *Jewish Morning Journal*, a Brandeisian, Ben Rosenblatt, Bernard G. Richards, David De Sola Pool, Ludwig Lewisohn, Reuben Fink and the President of the Z.O.A., Rabbi Solomon Goldman. A portion of the Anglo-Jewish press saw partition as the "redemption of the Jews," a decision which would give them the power to decide their own fate and remove that power from Western Europe and America. [131] One Zionist even suggested a "Back to Uganda" movement. In the margin of that correspondence, Brandeis penciled "inadvisable." [132]

The League concurred in Palestine Partition on September 17, 1937 but in another month the plan was "pretty well abandoned," largely owing to its international unpopularity with both Jews and Arabs. [133] Zionist pressure groups in the United States could not stir Hull to express disapproval of partition; neither he nor the White House were prepared to make a statement. [134] State Department records, however, betray Hull's anxiety. He was apprehensive lest the British consider partition a change in the Mandate requiring American approval in accordance with the 1924 Treaty. Present at the World Zionist Congress was the American Consul General at Zurich, from whom Hull received "discreet reports" on the American Zionists. For a few days, it appeared as if Stephen Wise and the anti-partitionists were going to be defeated. The existence of a Lipskyite, pro-partition faction and a Warburg, non-Zionist, anti-

[130] Berkowitz, pp. 455-457.

[131] Rosenblatt to James G. McDonald, September 14, 1937, JGMcD; Rosenblatt to Brandeis, July 6, 1937, LDB; "Zionist Head is for Partition," *Westchester Jewish Weekly*, VII (September 16, 1938), 1; S. Margoshes, "News and Views," *The Day* (in Yiddish), July 25, 1937, p. 1; Ludwig Lewisohn, "This is the Hour of Destiny," *The Jewish Transcript*, XIV (Rosh Hashana, 1937), 18-19; "Death Threat Received by Noted Zionists," *Westchester Jewish Weekly*, V (September 17, 1937), 2; Meyer Abrams, "The Opportunity of Israel: A Jewish State," *Chicago Jewish Chronicle*, XXXIII (August 13, 1937) 3-4, 12; "Palestine Division is Protested Here," *The New York Times*, July 9, 1937, p. 10; "Palestine Division Arouses World-Wide Interest — Arab Leaders Protest and Jews Seen Divided," *Philadelphia Jewish World*, XXIV (July 10, 1937), 8; See *Southwest Jewish Chronicle* XI (July 1937), and *Youngstown Jewish Times*, IV (July 16, 1937), 2.

[132] Alexander Sachs to Brandeis, August 6, 1937, LDB.

[133] Lambert to Morris D. Waldman, October 6, 1937, AJC.

partition faction demonstrated the disunity of American Jews to Wallace Murray.   Although Secretary Hull was aware that the principle of "economic absorptive capacity," as formulated by the 1922 Churchill Memorandum was about to be exchanged for a Palestinian immigration quota on Jews, he felt no obligation to act. After all, he reasoned, Rabbi Wise, the activist Jewish spokesman for maintaining the British Mandate, had been repudiated. The Felix Warburg group, desirous of realizing the Magnes plan, seemed to be in command.   Wise, wrote Murray, "must produce some proof that he speaks on behalf of all American Jewry before we comply to any ... request he may make."[135]

Soon Wise compelled the State Department to issue an explicit policy statement by stimulating a new Jewish agitation.   In June, 1938, the cause celebre for American Jewry was the Congress referendum, which was a shrewd construction by Wise to keep the Jewish question in the public eye: it did not matter to him whether the World Jewish Congress was voted up or down as long as the controversy was news-making.[136]   Before it met, Wise predicted the failure of the Evian Conference and gave the lie to Roosevelt's previous pro-homeland gestures.   The President, alive to British misgivings, struck Palestine off the Evian agenda and instructed American delegates not to mention it.   Personally, Roosevelt seemed to favor Jewish resettlement in Africa or Angola.[137]   Wise's fair weather political friends offered him no respite.   He was told bluntly by William Borah, that, since 1929, the Jewish situation had become

[134] "Hull Promises Statement on Situation," *The Buffalo Jewish Review*, XXIX (July 16, 1937), 6; "For and Against the Palestine Report" (editorial), *Christian Century*, LIV (July 28, 1937), 940-941.

[135] Mack to Brandeis, August 4, 1937, LDB; "Jewish State Partition is Given O.K. of Congress," *The Jewish Transcript*, XIV (August 13, 1937), 1; "Impressions of the Zionist Congress," *The American Hebrew*, 141 (August 27, 1937), 12, 17; Hull to Consul in Geneva Everett, 867N.01/836a telegram, August 3, 1937, Everett to Hull, 867N.01/837, August 5, 1937, Hull to Consul General at Zurich, Frost, 867N.01/845a, August 11, 1937 and Frost to Hull, 867N.01/848, August 13, 1937, *USFR: 1937*, II, 900-904, 908-910.

[136] Adlerstein, *The American Hebrew*, 143, 6, 14; "The Congress Plebiscite" (editorial) *The American Hebrew*, 143 (May 20, 1938, 3.

[137] Murray to Wadsworth, 867N.01/1106, July 2, 1938, *USFR: 1938*, 5 vols (Washington, 1955), I, 752; Richard P. Stevens, *American Zionism and United States Foreign Policy 1942-1947* (New York, 1962), pp. 64-66; Hull, pp. 196-197; Teller, p. 199; Feingold, pp. 51-71, 152-204.

more explosive, and he would no longer intercede on behalf of the national home. He would not attend a Zionist rally and said that "we should not criticize Britain unless we are willing to shoulder its burdens."[138]

Though personally unsuccessful in gaining government support, Wise kept the air crackling with Jewish issues. The publicity and attention he received had at last taken its toll on those in the State Department who felt constrained to justify their indifference. They held no single viewpoint on Jewish nationalism save a common dislike. Knabenshue, as Consul General in Iraq, regarded the Jews as the main block to a Near Eastern settlement. Murray and Wadsworth were both partial to the Magnes solution because it provided a convenient out for America. Wadsworth also proved to be a very avid defender of missionaries and the Christian religion in Palestine. Hull didn't care either way. "So far as the Balfour Declaration is concerned," mused one State Daprtment official, "we have never been committed to its fulfillment."[139] But the time had come to take a stand: no one was committed to the Balfour Declaration, or the Congressional Declaration of Sympathy or to the Anglo-American Convention of 1924, or to partition. When the Woodhead or "Re-Peel Commission," as Ann O'Hare McCormick of *The New York Times* cleverly dubbed it, returned in November, 1938, the State Department was "informed" but uncommitted.[140] The activities of foreign and domestic Revisionists corroborated the Department's most dire anti-Zionist prejudices.[141] Nevertheless,

[138] "Borah Fears Involvement," *The New York Times*, October 27, 1938, p. 1.

[139] Memorandum by J. Rives Childs, 867N.01/1482, March 8, 1939, *USFR: 1939*, 5 vols. (Washington, 1955), IV, 727-729; Knabenshue to Murray 867N. 01/1055, March 3, 1938 and 867N.0./1079, March 31, 1938, Knabenshue to Hull 867N.01/1208, October 25, 1938, Memorandum by Murray 867N.01/1330, November 29, 1938, *USFR:1938*, II, 908, 916-917, 968-969, 989-990; Herbert Parzen, "A Chapter in Arab-Jewish Relations During the Mandate Era," *Jewish Social Studies*, XXIX (October 1967), 222, 224, 227, 230; Hattis, pp. 211, 285.

[140] Ann O'Hare McCormick, "Europe," *The New York Times*, July 9, 1938, p. 12; "British Abandon Palestine Split," *New York Post*, November 9, 1938, pp. 1-2; George Wadsworth liked the Woodhead Report. Wadsworth to Hull, 867N. 01/1279, November 12, 1938, *USFR:1938*, II, 985.

[141] "An Unholy Land" (editorial), *The Jewish Ledger*, LXXXVIII (November 18, 1938), 4; Wadsworth to Hull 867N.01/1114, July 10, 1938 and U.S. Ambassador in Poland, A.J. Drexel Biddle to Hull 867N.01/1372, December 28, 1938, *USFR: 1938*, II, 933, 1002.

Stephen Wise had forced the issue. An official position paper was issued in October, 1938, in response to memoranda issued by diverse Jewish organizations who were fearful that Britain would renege on the Balfour Declaration and the Mandate. The document cogently stated the American position: no obligation.[142]

Britain's efforts to mediate Arab and Jewish differences via the round table discussions failed. The result of Whitehall's frustrations was the White Paper of May, 1939 which, though damaging to Jewish interests, may have been necessitated by the situation in Europe and the need to gird for the oncoming conflict with Hitler. Congress was united in its censure, the State Department wasn't interested and President Roosevelt seemed amenable to Britain's lead because he wished to subordinate all other interests to maintain solidarity between the two powers.[143]

Meanwhile, Weizmann had been converted to the militant American diplomatic style. Stephen Wise had become American Jewry's chief activist and had urged Weizmann to see State Department officials in Washington. The interviews, though inconclusive, left the Zionists confident because, somehow, Jewish nationalism in America had been aroused. The charismatic Wise, who became American Zionism's official leader after the death of Brandeis in November, 1940, attracted huge crowds at Carnegie Hall, incurred the wrath of the isolationist, anti-Semitic Christian front and badgered Hull. Combined with Palestine pavilion at the World's Fair, Wise's dynamism sparked nascent American Jewish pride.[144] Cementing these events before they faded was the horror of Germany. Unaware that a corner had been turned, the State Department, with the possible exception of Undersecretary of State Sumner Welles, disregarded Wise and the Zionists.[145] In mid-1941, the

---

[142] Press release issued by the State Department, 867N.01/1178, October 14, 1938, *USFR:1938*, II, 954-955: Memorandom of Conversation by J. Rives Childs with Peter George, Jamil Beyhum, Amil Ghory, Murray and Alling, 867N. 01/1402, January 20, 1939, *USFR:1939*, IV, 701-703; Evan M. Wilson, "The American Interest in the Palestine Question and the Establishment of Israel," *Annals of the American Academy of Political and Social Seience*, 401 (May 1972), 65; Raymond Hare, "The Great Divide: World War II," *Annals of the American Academy of Political and Social Science*, 401 (May 1972), 24.

[143] *Congressional Record, Seventy-Sixth Congress, First Session* (Washington, 1939), part 6, pp. 5901-5902, 5930, 5936, 5972, 5997, 6042, 6115, 6167 and part 13, pp. 2231-2232; *USFR:1939*, IV, 736-737, 756; *USFR:1940*, 5 vols. (Washington, 1958), III, 836, IV, 757; Morris Fine, "Review of the Year 5600," *AJYB*, XLI (Philadelphia, 1939), 201.

Department had its hands full anyway, denying "a report from Baghdad ... that President Roosevelt had promised to obtain from Britain a cancellation of the Balfour Declaration.... The Declaration has been a sore point with the Arabs." [146]

Undeniably, Wise's flamboyance, his influence on Weizmann and Brandeis's planning succeeded in reviving the American Jewish conscience. For those who were cognizant of it or sympathetic to it, the rumblings of Jewish national awakening was an exciting event. Byt the end of 1941, the economic future of Palestine was assured, largely through the efforts of the P.E.C. which, after fifteen years, was still functioning. [147]   In the United States, the Z.O.A. had enrolled two hundred fifty thousand members, most of whom had joined after the Minority insurgency of the 1930s. [148]

[144] "Zionist Parley Re-elects Goldman for Second Term," *Intermountain Jewish News*, XXV (June 30, 1939), 1-2; Voss, pp. 233, 239; *USFR:1939*, IV, 760-761, 797-799; Joseph B. Schechtman, *The United States and the Jewish State Movement* (New York, 1966), p. 53; Memorandum of Conversation between Murray and Weizmann, 867N.01/1689, February 6, 1940, *USFR:1940*, III, 838-839; Memorandum by Berle 867N.01/1729 1/2, April 14, 1941, Memorandum of Conversation between Berle, Weizmann and Emanuel Neumann, 867N.01/1739, April 15, 1941, Memorandum by Sumner Welles, 867N.01/1741, April 21, 1941 and Murray to Welles, 867N.01/1829 1/2, April 16, 1941, *USFR:1941*, 7 vols. (Washington, 1959), III, 598-600; "Fair Palestine Pavilion Opens as Note of Protest Against Britain," *New York Herald Tribune*, May 29, 1939, p. 9.

[145] American Consul in Jerusalem, Christian R. Steger to Hull 367N.1115/218 telegram, May 1, 1941, Steger to Hull, 367N.1115/219 telegram, May 10, 1941, Steger to Hull, 867N.55/239, May 22, 1941, Welles to Lord Halifax, 867N.01/1743,May 8 1934,Murray to Hull, 740.0011 European War 1939/11258, May 27, 1941, Welles to Kirk, 740.0011 European War 1939/12842 telegram, July 15, 1941, Welles to Wise and Welles to Murray, 867N.01/1780, October 4, 1941, *USFR:1941*, III, 601-602- 605, 611-612, 615-616, 618, 622-623.

[146] "Hull Parries Point of Iraq Recognition," *The New York Times*, May 13, 1941, p. 2.

[147]Bernard Flexner to Edward M.M. Warburg, July 8, 1941, HL.

[148] Edwin M. Wright to William L. Westermann, December 9, 1941, WLW, Box 4.

VI

Socialists And Communists: The Radical Response To Zionism

As an American Socialist, Meyer London was not attracted to Zionist concerns. During the First World War, he alluded to the removal of spiritual and civil disabilities from European Jews occurring as a natural result of the international proletarian revolution, but "did not consider the question of Palestine of practical importance." He regarded Jewish nationalism as a "separatist movement" detracting from the united struggle of all workers, regardless of ethnicity, against capitalism. [1] Judge Jacob Panken and Morris Hillquit were likewise anti-Zionists. Hillquit was an outspoken defender of Americanization in its most extreme form, assimilation, and opposed the presence of any Jewish tendencies in the Socialist Party. He remained unaffiliated with the Jewish Federation of the American Socialist Party, the Verband, founded in 1912, whose interests, if not nationalist, were always profoundly "Jewish." [2]

This dichotomy in thought produced an initial tension between

---

[1] Harry Rogoff, *An East Side Epic: The Life and Work of Meyer London* (New York, 1930), pp. 116, 118-119.

[2] Interview with Yaakov Shalom Hertz, September 11, 1972, New York City. Y.S. Hertz, born 1893, was a Russian Bundist who arrived in America during the Second World War. He became a writer for the Jewish Labor Bund and Jewish Socialist movement in the United States. He co-edits the Bundist paper *Unser Tsait* and is editor of a four volume study entitled *The History of the Bund.*

American Socialist leaders and recently arrived Europeans, who read the *Forward, Die Naye Zeit* and the *Arbeiter Zeitung*. Those who bought the De Leonist *Arbeiter Zeitung* were doctrinaire Marxists in comparison to the *Forward* faithful, who were apt to advocate an unideological, pragmatic approach for the workingman, reminiscent of the German Socialist Eduard Bernstein.[3] But, they held a common heritage which bound them together on the question of Zionism. This heritage included a common language, Yiddish, a common exposure to the harsh realities of anti-Semitism and a common concern for the preservation of Judaism. As the Europeans entered the ranks of American Socialism, they became a force to be reckoned with, eventually superseding in importance the native American Jewish Socialists.

The Palestine formula evolved by Jewish Socialists in the United States owed an immeasurable debt to the Bund, the European Jewish labor organization founded at Vilna in 1897. Bundists were proponents of European Revisionist Socialism and sought, as did Zionists, a revival of the Jewish national consciousness.[4] The means to be employed in achieving the desired end was the point of departure for the two philosophies. A Jewish Palestine was the climax for the political and cultural Zionists; it would have been an anticlimax for the Bund. Its leaders were dissatisfied with Zionism because it was predominantly bourgeois. Several other complaints complemented this central one. Herzl had maintained that Palestine was "a country without people for a people without a country." The presence of a large Arab population, said Bundists, rendered Herzl's hyperbole dangerously inaccurate. Jewish Socialists generally regarded the establishment of a Jewish national home as utopian; it would never become a state with a majority of Jews and the effort to transform it was likely to entail a perennial Arab-Jewish conflict. To Bundists, the crux of the Jewish problem lay in the "common struggle" with democratic non-Jews for a democratic Socialist order. It was believed that Zionism diverted many Jews from the world-wide struggle. Bundist rhetoric did not countenance assimilation and rebelled against ghettoization. Wherever the Jews were, went the argument, the accoutrements of their past attended. But, what sustained the Bundist was often his "Socialist Jewish past" rather than "the Jewish past." Hebraic culture and language

[3] Sachar, *The Course of Modern Jewish History*, p. 327.

[4] *Ibid.*, p. 328.

were not nearly as significant to him as the Yiddish as an exemplar of Jewish life and the future paths it would take.[5] Anti-Semitism, "one of the... foundations of Zionist ideology," was combated by Jewish Socialists and exhorted against but the nationalist panacea was discarded.[6] As a matter of fact, Jewish Socialists, whether native American or European born, never distinguished between Brandeis and Weizmann. Zionism in any form was simply not their way of life. Both the Workmen's Circle (*Arbeiter Ring*) and the Yiddish speaking section of the American Socialist Party, the Verband, adopted their nationalist predilections from the Bund, although some Socialists were more receptive than others to the idea of a Palestinian Jewish homeland.[7]

During World War I, Jewish worker groups in America were as interested as their non- and anti-nationalist counterparts in relieving the distress of European Jews. The daily *Forward*, however, warned against contributing to Zionist collections for overseas relief because part of the funds would doubtlessly be used for political purposes. Moissy Olgin, then a Socialist but after 1922 editor of the Communist *Freiheit*, was skeptical that Zionists would send a fixed percentage of the money they had collected to Palestine. In 1915, Jewish Socialists, both pro- and anti-Zionist, organized their own People's Relief Committee for Jewish War Sufferers (P.R.C.) and shortly thereafter allied with the J.D.C. Anti-Zionist labor activists opposed Zionist relief work in Palestine as did the Socialist Poale Zion which, at that time, was not on good terms with American Zionists.[8]

The P.R.C. was one of many ways in which the National Workmen's Committee (N.W.C.) disseminated anti-national propa-

---

[5] Interview with Emanuel Scherer, September 14, 1972, New York City. Dr. Scherer is the Executive Head of the Jewish Labor Bund, co-author of the *Struggle for Tomorrow* and a member of the Executive of the World Coordinating Committee of the Bund. See also B. Meyers, "The Bund and Zionism," *Perspectives* I (Winter 1964), 14-15; Gabe Ross, "Zionism and the Jewish Radical," *The Other Way* 1 (Spring 1971), 6.

[6] Abraham I. Golomb, "Jewish Self-Hatred," *YAJSS*, I (New York, 1946), 253; Emanuel Scherer, "On Anti-Semitism," *The Other Way* (Spring 1971), 4-5.

[7] Interview with Y.S. Hertz, September 11, 1972.

[8] Szajkowski, *YAJSS*, XIV (New York, 1969), 122-123, 138-140. The Poale Zion was mainly displeased with American Zionists' neglect of the workers' groups when doling out Palestinian relief.

ganda. The N.W.C. was founded in April, 1915, in response to Brandeis's unification of American Zionism seven months before. The first members were the United Hebrew Trades, the Jewish Socialist Federation of America, the *Arbeiter Ring* and the Forward Association. Later entries were the Socialist Territorialists, the Jewish National Workers Alliance and the Poale Zion.[9] Within a few months some members of the N.W.C., notably the Poale Zion and smaller labor groups, seemed to have fallen into line with the idea of an American Jewish Congress and the anti-nationalist Workmen's Committee was forced to make some concessions to Zionism. In September, 1915, the Convention of Labor Organizations declared that the "more comprehensive definition of the demand for national rights and national autonomy is left to the Jews of their respective lands, such as Russia, Galicia, Rumania and Palestine." But, it expressed its preference for the protection of Jewish national autonomy by international guarantee.[10] Hence, the compromise was in the direction of non-Zionism, although individual Jewish trade unions in the United States were loath to subscribe to it. The *Arbeiter Ring*, the Socialist Verband and the daily *Forward* regarded Zionism as "nationalist pipedreaming." Bundists and anarchists declaimed against the Zionist "illusion"; people in the garment trades spread the message of Socialist anti-Zionism.[11]

On May 27, 1917, the N.W.C. withdrew from the American Jewish Congress, as did its representative on the Congress Executive Committee, Morris Hillquit.[12] The vote was one hundred seventeen to five and was ratified by the local labor bodies.[13] In the Congress, the labor group, representing different labor organizations, was

[9] Kessler, *YAJSS*, II, 222; Janowsky, pp. 163-164.

[10] Janowsky, p. 171.

[11] Isaac M. Fein, *The Making of an American Jewish Community: A History of Baltimore Jewry from 1773 to 1920* (Philadelphia, 1971), p. 196; Arthur A. Goren, *New York Jews and the Quest for Community: The Kehillah Experiment 1908-1922* (New York, 1970), p. 19; Tenzer, *The Immigrants' Influence*, p. 289.

[12] Hillquit to Bernard G. Richards, June 13, 1917 and Jacob de Haas to Brandeis, May 11, 1917, LDB; Franklin Jonas, "The Early Life and Career of B. Charney Vladeck" (unpublished doctoral dissertation, New York University, 1972), p. 147; Janowsky, p. 246n; Zosa Szajkowski, "The Jews and New York City's Mayoralty Election of 1917," *Jewish Social Studies*, XXXII (October 1970), 292.

[13] "Refuse to Oppose Draft," *The New York Times*, May 31, 1917, p. 2.

comprised of thirteen men: Sholem Asch, Ab. Bisno, Dr. Max Goldfarb, Morris Hillquit, Hon. Meyer London, Moissy Olgin, Jacob Panken, Max Pine, Dr. Frank P. Rosenblatt, Jacob B. Salutzky, B. Schlessinger, Joseph Schlossberg and Baruch Charney Vladeck. Salutzky, a Bundist from Vilna and Secretary of the Jewish Verband, explained the vote to Nathan Strauss, Chairman of the Executive Committee of the American Jewish Congress, in terms of recent events in Russia. He said that labor had joined the Congress at a time when only international interference could aid the Russian Jews, but the Revolution "had removed any and all causes for international action." From now on, "we should refrain from any such steps that might cause harm and avoid results as deplorable as those which another Jewish agitation (i.e. Zionism) brought upon the Jewish settlement in Palestine." The N.W.C. further objected to the "undemocratic" election methods employed by the Congress. [14] "The important question on the Congress agenda must now certainly be Palestine," noted Die Naye Welt, "and Jews who are not Zionists have no interest in attending such a Congress." [15] The New York Times reported another Socialist argument, a forerunner of the communist and Trotskyite position of the 1930s:

> This action (withdrawal from the Congress) was taken ... as the direct result of President Wilson's peace proclamation concerning the 'rights of small nations.' One-seventh of the population of Palestine are Jews and the Socialists contend that to give this land exclusively to the Jews would be taking the state away from others of the population who have a greater right to it because of greater numbers and nationality. However, Socialists will not oppose a Jewish colony there.... [16]

Jewish Socialists and labor leaders protested against the American Jewish Congress until it was canceled in October, 1917. [17]

The opening round of the Balfour controversy witnessed some

---

[14] J.B. Salutzky to Nathan Strauss, June 8, 1917, LDB; Yaakov Shalom Hertz, *The Jewish Labor Bund 1897-1957* (New York, 1958), p. 64.

[15] Jonas, pp. 146-147.

[16] "Refuse to Oppose Draft," *The New York Times*, May 31, 1917, p. 2.

[17] "Zionists Uphold Peace Agreement," *The New York Times*, June 27, 1917, p. 6; R. Litwak, "The Jewish Conference (Yiddish)," *Die Naye Welt*, October 19, 1917, p. 6.

sparring between American Bundists and American Zionists. Significantly, Hillquit and Meyer London, the New York Socialist member of the House of Representatives, preferred to remain uninvolved, not because of any overriding principle but, less nobly, because the Palestine problem, on which they had no opinion, interested them neither as Americans nor Socialists. Dr. Ben-Zion Hoffman, a contributor to the *Forward* and editor of the *Gerechtikeit*, organ of the I.L.G.W.U. defended the Arab case against Zionism's "impractical dreaming." *Die Naye Welt* was ardently anti-Balfour and welcomed the lucid expositions of Hoffman, which were carried over into 1918. [18]

The *Forward* made no mention of the Balfour Declaration until November 24, when an article by A. Litvin stated that the pledge was made "in the interest of Great Britain, with the support of the Rothschilds and Jacob Schiff." To the writer, this was sufficient evidence that Jewish capital "was interested in the venture for its own reason, namely profit and exploitation." Another *Forward* writer, Samuel Hertz Burgin, said that "Zionist work was not the work of the laboring class," that Socialism was the only aim of the working class and that "the class struggle was the only path to it." [19]

Most Bundists, however, were aware that Palestine could not be so easily dismissed and took steps to develop a program which would rival that of the American Jewish Congress. In May, 1918, a Jewish Socialist conference grappled with the issue of Zionism. On the Balfour Declaration, there was a division of opinion and a majority resolution, pushed through by Louis Budin, declared against altering the position on Palestine which had been decided upon three years before. [20] Independently of the conference, the Workmen's Circle, under the direction of two Bundists, Philip Geliebter and Joseph Baskin, admitted to the press that Palestine "belonged to the conquerors," meaning the Arabs and that "America is good enough for us." [21] A colleague of Geliebter and Baskin, Jacob Salutzky, Secretary of the Jewish Socialist Federation of America and director

---

[18] Zivion B. Hoffman, "Is it Much to Ask (Yiddish)?" *Die Naye Welt,* December 7, 1917, p. 3; Zivion B. Hoffman, "Arvin and Princip Against a Jewish State (Yiddish)," *Die Naye Welt,* November 3, 1917, p. 3; Zivion B. Hoffman, "What's the Difference (Yiddish)?" *Die Naye Welt,* January 11, 1918, p. 13; Interview with Y.S. Hertz, September 11, 1972; Hertz, *Jewish Labor Bund,* p. 64.

[19] Goldblatt, *American Jewish Historical ?Quarterly,* LVII, 481-482.

[20] Hertz, *Jewish Socialist Movement,* p. 170.

of the Amalgamated Clothing Workers, averred that the Poale Zion was incorrect in its assumption that Palestine would become a Socialist country: in fact, the Jewish bourgeois would set Jew against Arab, pawns in a capitalist intrigue of worker exploitation.[22]

In November, a larger conference assembled to decide whether to send delegates to the Paris Peace Conference. Two paths were open: either dispatching an independent group or joining the American Jewish Congress and operating through it. The majority of Bundists looked upon the Jewish nation as a cultural-social entity which could be achieved anywhere, not necessarily Palestine. Dr. Chaim Zhitlowsky, an important European Socialist, who had recently emigrated to the United States, introduced a trenchant analogy. Zionism, he commented, was akin to assimilation; as many Zionists had proved, it was possible to be both an assimilationist and a Jewish nationalist. A Jewish State, continued Zhitlowsky, would be neither Jewish nor Christian and certainly not Socialist. The destiny of the Jews, he emphasized, was their union with the peoples of the world in a proletarian struggle.[23]   The failure of Meyer London to acknowledge the existence of a Palestine issue was disturbing to some Bundists but, on the whole, excusable. The Verband supported London in the 1918 Congressional elections but he lost his seat to a joint Republican-Democratic candidate by a mere seven hundred votes. The margin of defeat had been supplied by a so-called "united Jewish front" composed of the Socialist Poale Zion, displeased with London's evasiveness on the Balfour Declaration, acting in concert with wealthy American Jews of German descent who were dubious of the incumbent's war record and the anti-American image of the Jew he projected as a member of the Socialist Party.[24]

As the Peace conference neared, American Socialists, especially those of the younger generation, reevaluated the Party's previous

[21] "The squaring of the Circle" (editorial), The American Jewish World, VI, (May 25, 1918), 640; Hertz, Jewish Labor Bund, p. 65; Interview with Y.S. Hertz, September 11, 1972.

[22] Interview with Y.S. Hertz, September 11, 1972; J.B. Salutzky "The Old Zionist Utopia (Yiddish)," Die Naye Welt. May 3, 1918, pp. 3-4.

[23] Hertz, Jewish Socialist Movement, pp. 183-185; Janowsky, pp. 171-172.

[24] Interview with Y.S. Hertz, September 11, 1972; Hertiz, Jewish Socialist Movement, p. 169; Rogoff, pp. 121-123, 160-161.

neutrality on the Palestine question. Norman Thomas was one of these. Harry Fleischman, a biographer of Thomas, wrote that the minister-pacifist shared the guilt of the Christian world for anti-Semitism. A number of his close friends, for example Judah Magnes, were Zionist sympathizers. Yet, Thomas had reservations as early as 1919. "We must remember that ... in this ancient land of his fathers, the Jew today and for centuries past is in a minority among the inhabitants." The most the Zionists could request, he concluded, was that Jews should eventually share in a free Palestinian government on a proportional basis, with Arab nationalist and Zionist movements complementing each other.[25] The first Jewish Labor Congress was in substantial agreement. At the conclave of January 20, 1919, Baruch C. Vladeck, a Bundist all his life, business manager of the *Forward* and later a member of the New York City Board of Aldermen, advocated the homeland idea as long as its realization would not endanger the rights of other resident nationalities. The resolution was nevertheless displaced by a second one which stated that no national group should receive precedence in Palestine: every citizen must be assured equal rights. Vladeck, never doctrinaire, then supported the second proposal of Salutzky, Olgin and Panken, which was subsequently carried.[26]

The Bundists did not fare well at Versailles. They had decided that they did not want the American Jewish Congress to represent them, but through Louis Marshall, their Palestinian viewpoint received ample publicity.[27] On their own they accomplished little. The Jewish Socialist Committee sent a statement to the Peace Conference demanding cultural autonomy for the Jews in Europe; an N.W.C. contingent arrived in Paris but registered no gains upon the achievements of Louis Marshall.[28] It was probably just as well.

---

[25] Harry Fleischman, *Norman Thomas: A Biography 1884-1968* (New York, 1969), p. 281.

[26] Interview with May Bromberg, September 13, 1972, New York City. Mrs. Bromberg is the daughter of Baruch Charney Vladeck. Israel Friedlaender to Judah Magnes, January 22, 1919, IF; "Oppose a Jewish Republic," *The New York Times*, January 20, 1919, p. 8; Hertz, *Jewish Socialist Movement*, p. 186; Interview with Y.S. Hertz, September 11, 1972; Hertz, *Jewish Labor Bund*, p. 64; Jonas, pp. 175-176. For an elementary, thumbnail sketch of Vladeck's early life and career, see Harry Gersh, *These Are My People* (New York, 1959), pp. 341-349.

[27] Hertz, *Jewish Socialist Movement*, p. 186.

[28] Kessler, *YAJSS*, II, 222; Hertz, *Jewish Socialist Movement*, p. 186.

The Jewish Socialists could not have found a more reliable associate than Marshall, "American" rather than foreign and, therefore, not subject to the accusations leveled against the Bund. Through the carelessness of Abraham Cahan, that organization had recently become linked to Bolshevism. Cahan, a sometimes opportunist and pro-Bolshevik, knew Lenin personally, a fact that clouded the *Forward's* claim as an "Americanizer" of immigrants. In April, 1919, during the Red-White unrest in Russia, Cahan reported that the Poale Zionists "in Kiev and other cities were Bolsheviki."[29] He thus armed anti-Semites and anti-Zionists in the United States with powerful ammunition to blast a considerable sector of the American Jewish population: Zionists, Socialists and all Jews who read the "radical" and "alien" Yiddish press.

No wonder American Socialists were wary of Palestine and the general question of Jewish nationalism. American Socialism was "respectable" and aimed to stay that way. In 1921, Hillquit refused to sign a petition favoring the allocation of tools to Palestine workers. He feared being used as a "pawn on the checker board of politics between contending organizations on the East Side," where feeling against a restored Jewish homeland in Palestine ran especially high among Socialists and trade union leaders.[30]

When the Socialist Party in America split over revolutionary tactics between 1919 and 1921, Jewish Socialists followed suit. Remaining in the gradualist camp were Vladeck and Cahan, both of whom accepted the leadership of Victor Berger and Hillquit. Interestingly, the remainder of the *Forward* staff, Morris Winchevsky, Moissy Olgin, Ben-Zion Hoffman and Harry Rogoff seceded. In 1921, a rump left wing that had stayed within the Socialist Party of America followed the *Forward* columnists into the Communist Party.

The Jews who remained within the Socialist Party were hardly distinguishable from the non-Zionists or the A.F.L. in their attitudes toward the Holy Land.[31] They saw nothing corrupt in the Jews' resettling Palestine. In general, American Jewish labor had become

[29] Charles A. Cowen to Brandeis, April 2, 1919, LDB; Interview with Y.S. Hertz, September 11, 1972.

[30] Morris Hillquit to Judah Magnes, March 17, 1921, Morris Hillquit Papers (hereafter abbreviated MH), Tamiment Institute, New York City; Teller, p. 11.

[31] Jewish National Fund of America, *Acts and Pronouncements of the American Federation of labor on Palestine and the Jewish Race from 1917-1938 (n.p. 1938),* pp. 1-24.

less suspicious of Zionism.   Before 1923, it had looked upon Zionism as primarily a religious middle class movement which obscured the basic social issues of the time. To turn one's attention to it meant supporting capital against labor. That year, however, appears to have heralded a change. The legitimacy of the Palestine labor movement was assured and American Jewish labor responded sympathetically. In August, 1923, the United Hebrew Trades considered sending representatives to Palestine to assist Jewish labor organizations there.[32] In December, 1925, Abe Cahan, after having returned from a tour of the Near East, enjoined the uncommitted to "give Zionism a chance" by not defeating it with cynicism.[33]

Modification, however, must not be mistaken for retraction. Cahan still wrote many compassionate pieces in defense of the Arabs. He didn't think that Palestine was capable of nurturing a self-sufficient Jewish community "for at least another twenty-five years." He stated, rather prophetically, that solid industry, not agriculture or speculation, would finally solve the dilemma of Palestine. As for language, he saw the happy inevitability of Yiddish "swamping Hebrew" because of the large numbers of East European immigrants.[34] Cahan contracted with Morris Hillquit in 1926 to do a feature story for the *Forward* on anti-Zionism. In April, after its appearance, Hillquit received this accolade from the editor's desk: "...I am delighted with your statement and ... am sure that it will go far in sobering up a number of our nationalist nuts."[35]

As did non-Zionists, Jewish Socialists protested against the "primacy of Palestine" in Jewish life. In December, 1925, during the Marshall-Wise confrontation on the relative importance of Russia as opposed to Palestine as foci of Jewish philanthropy, Vladeck clarified the Jewish Socialist position: "The Zionists have over-estimated their strength as leaders of American Jewry.... Many Jews do not put Palestine in the forefront of Jewish philanthropy.... The Zionists would have done a lot better for... their cause if they could display... a little more self-effacement and... consideration for

[32] Morris Seremsky, "The Jewish Laborers and Zionism," *Denver Jewish News*, IX (August 30, 1923), 4.

[33] Lipsky, pp. 213-216; Maximilian Hurwitz, "Spying out the Holy Land," *The Jewish Tribune*, 44 (December 11, 1925), 1.

[34] Hurwitz, *The Jewish Tribune*, 44, 1, 18-19.

[35] William M. Feigenbaum to Hillquit, April 15, 1926, MH.

the opinions of non-Zionists."[36]   The Jewish Socialist Verband seconded Vladeck's statement which was, in 1926, the American Socialist Party's position on Palestine. Furthermore, in 1928, there were ominous signs signaling the end, or at least the disturbance, of the five-year honeymoon between American Bundists and Jewish labor organizations in Palestine. Nathan Chanin, the secretary of the Verband and director of the Workmen's Circle, evinced his displeasure with labor Zionists for ignoring the Arabs while concentrating only on Jewish workers in Palestine.[37]

This theme received wider coverage during the Wailing Wall riots. Socialist newspapers like *Die Wecker* and the *Forward* termed Arab attacks on Jews as "pogroms."[38] They believed the Arab revolt was not a true national uprising led by workers but a massacre instigated by Arab feudalists.   In their estimate, however, the Zionists were no better than their attackers; both held back the workers' revolution at the expense of hundreds of lives. Baruch C. Vladeck opposed the violence of the outbreaks and probably agreed with Cahan on the culpability of both sides.[39]   The *Forward* editor thought that Zionism should not even be a Socialist concern.[40]   The *Verband*, unsympathetic to Zionism while advocating a Palestinian union of Arab and Jewish workers, attributed the violence to "the activities of political Zionists" who were attempting to force a Jewish national home upon a hostile Arab majority.   A resolution stating that Jewish labor in the Holy Land should be aided only in proportion to Jewish labor throughout the world was introduced at several Verband meetings but failed to pass, owing to the fervent defense of Palestinian Jewish workers by a number of Federation members.[41]

---

[36] "Let There Be Peace!" *The Jewish Tribune*, 44 (December 11, 1925), 6, 14-15.

[37] Interview with Y.S. Hertz, September 11, 1972; Hertz, *Jewish Labor Bund*, p. 65; Hertz, *Jewish Socialist Movement* pp. 267, 285.

[38] David Shub, *On the Revolving Stage of History: Memoirs*, 2 vols. (Yiddish, New York, 1970), II, 760-762; Max Schachtman, "Palestine — Pogrom or Revolution," *The Militant*, October 1, 1929, p. 5.

[39] Interview with May Bromberg, September 13, 1972.

[40] Hertz, *Jewish Socialist Movement*, p. 285.

[41] "Jewish Socialist Attacks Zionism," *The New York Times*, November 29, 1929, p. 16; Hertz, *Jewish Socialist Movement*, p. 285.

American Socialists held a somewhat different point of view and were beginning to gain greater influence in the Jewish ranks of the Party. Eugene Debs, Meyer London and Victor Berger were dead. Morris Hillquit survived unti 1933. The Old Guard Socialists were being replaced by the Norman Thomas faction or Progressive group which, by 1934, had acceded to a primary position in American Socialism. Thomas came down more forcefully on Zionists in 1929 than he had ten years before. In the *New Leader*, Thomas doubted the ability and the justness of "idealistic Zionists," who were driving the Arabs into a frenzy with the assistance of "British standing armies." A Jewish homeland "can only be established in Palestine by winning the acquiescence of the Arabs."[42] Editorially, the *New Leader*, a "sympathetic observer of the Zionist experiment," hoped for "a minimization of friction" but was not surprised with the incidents of August which were more or less expected, an inevitable result of planting Jews "in the heart of a region inhabitated by a large majority of Arabs."[43] After an audience with the Grand Mufti, Haj Amin el Husseini, Kirby Page, a Socialist associate of Thomas, rose to the defense of the Arabs. They were, he said, provoked by Jewish nationalists who were placed in a privileged position by the Mandatory.[44]

In December 1931, the Socialist Party refused an application for membership submitted by the Socialist Zionist Poale Zion. A committee consisting of James Oneal, editor of *The World Tomorrow*, Algernon Lee and Norman Thomas indicted Socialist Zionist hypocrisy and indifference to the international proletarian struggle. The Verband stated that the Poale Zionists would be permitted to enter the Socialist Party as individuals but not as a federation. Among the reasons offered were that Zionists relied on the untrustworthy, colonial British Government, the "eternal Jewish problem" found no solution in Palestine, the Poale Zionists, just by being Zionists, collaborated with "bourgeois capitalists and orthodox clericals against the worker and their brand of "socialism" was spurious. The Poale Zion made the Socialist struggle dependent on a Jewish

---

[42] Norman Thomas, "Tragic Days in Palestine," *The New Leader*, August 31, 1929, p. 1.

[43] "The Arab Rising" (editorial) *The New Leader,* August 31, 1929.

[44] Kirby Page, "Zionism Clashes with Islam," *The World Tomorrow*, XIII (January 1930), 29-32; Sherwood Eddy, "The Grand Mufti on Palestine's Problem" *The Christian Century*, XLVI (December 18, 1929), 1574.

homeland, meaning that an authentic Jewish proletariat outside Palestine could never exist, that the workers' struggle in Europe and America was a "chaotic... fantasy." This was all untrue, wrote the Verband, and provided real Jewish Socialists with no alternative but to refuse the Zionist petition.[45]

The arrival in Germany of Hitler arrested the Socialist criticism of Palestine. Under the sponsorship of Vladeck, the Jewish Labor Committee (J.L.C.), representing the Amalgamated Clothing Workers, the United Hat, Cap and Millinery Workers, the Workmens' Circle and the I.L.G.W.U., was formed in 1934 as a united front to combat Jewish problems. Led by Bundists, it stayed aloof from Zionism, even the labor variety.[46] Its position, like that of its founder, Vladeck, was that Jewish refugees must be provided for and Jewish workers must be helped. Palestine, however, was only one of many available avenues for these beleaguered groups. The Committee's sentiments were echoed by the Verband at Cleveland in 1935.[47]

It was obviously going to take some time before Socialists became accustomed to even this limited concept of the Holy Land's serviceability. Thomas Socialists were still prone to labeling Palestine "an economic failure" and a "political mistake." Upon his return from Palestine, Vladeck claimed that there were "well-organized bodies for propaganda, fund-raising and politics" but there were none to build the Yishuv "according to plan and with a purpose." The economy was dragging, seemingly dependent on the low wages of the workingman; prices were high.[48] Vladeck did not hold the Yishuv responsible. Consequently, whose fault was it? Socialist writers and Trotskyites, who had recently joined the Party, blamed the Histadrut, the organization of Palestine Jewish labor, headed by David Ben-Gurion. The Socialist allegation was that the Histadrut, by its practice of Arab Labor exclusion, had deliberately estranged

[45] *Memorandum on the Jewish Socialist Verband Concerning the Application of the Poale Zion*, MH; Hertz, *Jewish Socialist Movement*, pp. 302-303.

[46] Halperin, pp. 162-164; Interview with May Bromberg, September 13, 1972.

[47] Interview with Y.S. Hertz, September 11, 1972; Hertz, *Jewish Socialist Movement*, pp. 336-340.

[48] B.C. Vladeck, "A Non-Zionist Looks at Palestine," *The Jewish Ledger*, LXXXXV (January 1, 1937), 12; "Editor Calls Zionism a Political Mistake," *The New York Times*, September 22, 1936, p. 17.

the majority population and contributed to the high unemployment rate. Socialists favored Jewish immigration, as long as it was not selectively directed against the Yiddish-speaking European Jew who had no use for Zionism or the Hebraic culture and sought the cooperation of the Arab worker. Trotskyites, who joined the Socialist Party were more inflexible. As far as they were concerned, the pro-Jewish policy of the Mandatory had to be overturned. The Arabs had been betrayed by the British who used the Jews as objects of imperialism. The Zionists had capitulated to England through the Jewish Agency: the only salvation for the oppressed Jewish masses was to seek an Arab rather than a Western rapproachement. [49]

All Socialist affiliates, whether Thomas followers or Trotskyites, followed a consistent line. Like Socialists, Trotskyites did not attack the Yishuv, believing it to be a true indication of the triumph of Jewish labor over capitalism. But, they were highly suspect of all Jewish immigrants who were not the "right" sort: Yiddish-speaking, Marxist proletarians who would not be indifferent to their Arab fellows. [50] Until the late 1930s, Communists were wont to acclaim the Mufti as the organizer of the national workers' revolt in Palestine. Members of the Socialist Party, with the exception of Page and the Trotskyites, thought Haj Amin el Husseini to be no better than a nationalist Zionist, that is, a fascist, a brigand, a feudal lord and an exploiter of the masses he supposedly was freeing.

After July, 1937, the month of the Peel Report's publication, all similarity between Socialists and Trotskyites ended, with the former displaying an interest in the fate of Palestinian and European Jews and the latter concerned with winning converts to their own philosophy. The *Forward* and Norman Thomas suggested Birobijan as an alternative to Palestine for refugee Jews. As a Socialist, Thomas was

---

[49] Felix Morrow, "For a Socialist Policy in Palestine," *American Socialist Monthly,* V (October 1936), 48-54; Samuel Weiss, "Statement on the Present Situation in Palestine," *American Socialist Monthly* V (August 1936), 18-19; Herbert Solow, "The Sixteenth Zionist Congress," *The Menorah Journal,* XVII (November 1929), 111-125; Herbert Solow, "The Realities of Zionism," *The Menorah Journal* XIX (November-December 1930), 99-102, 104, 111-115, 117, 123; Herbert Solow, "Camouflaging Zionist Realities," *The Menorah Journal,* XIX (March 1931), 223-226, 234-241; Samuel J, Rosensohn, "The Prospects of Zionism," *The Menorah Journal* XIX (June 1931) 388, 395, 399.

[50] L. Rock, "British Policy in Palestine," *The New International,* IV (October 1938), 311-312; L. Rock, "The Jewish-Arab Conflict," *The New International,* IV (November 1938), 335-337; L. Rock, "Class Politics in Palestine," *The New International,* V (June 1939), 169-173.

disillusioned with Stalin but not by many of the social and economic innovations in Russia; hence, his advocacy of Birobijan.[51] Trotsky-ites would never have mentioned the Siberian experiment because they believed all of Stalin's changes to be misguided and evil, especially a settlement which separated Jewish workers from their natural non-Jewish compeers when revolutionary unity should have been paramount. Trotskyites were also ardent in their condemnation of partition as the culmination of Revisionist Jewish fascism, in league with Great Britain and Italy.[52]

Opposition to Jewish nationalism did not prevent the Socialists from making a more deliberate, constructive assessment.[53] After the United States Labor and Socialist Zionists voted for partition at the Zionist Congress in August, 1937, the Bundists in America were shaken.[54] The Bund had always held that a Jewish State would entail perennial Arab-Jewish conflict.[55] If Bundists were wary of Norman Thomas's recent support of the Warburg-Magnes proposal, they were doubtlessly affronted by the outright defection of Vladeck.[56] As leader of the Jewish Labor Committee and as a man who felt a deep responsibility toward all Jews, he fought to keep the gates open everywhere, including the Holy Land.[57] Although a non-Zionist, he was offended by Stephen Wise's failure to invite the J.L.C. to participate in a visit to Cordell Hull, to discuss the plight of Jewish refugees.[58] Vladeck voted "yes" on a resolution introduced by

[51] Melech Epstein, *The Jew and Communism 1919-1941* (New York, 1959), p. 312; Halperin, p. 160; John Dewey was similarly impressed with Birobijan. See Louis I. Newman, "Telling it in Gath," *Intermountain Jewish News*, XXII (January 24, 1936), 312.

[52] Herbert Solow, "Zionism in Extremis," *The Nation*, CXLV (July 31, 1937), 125-126; Jack Weber, "The Jewish Question," *The New International*, IV (April 1938), 110-112; Ben Herman, "Zionism and the Lion," *The New International*, IV (August 1938), 236-238.

[53] Adlerstein, *The American Hebrew* 143, 6; "The Current Scene," *The American Hebrew*, 143 (May 27, 1938), 8.

[54] American Consul General at Zurich, Frost, to Cordell Hull, 867N.01/848 telegram, August 13, 1937, *USFR:1937*, II, 904.

[55] Interview with Emanuel Scherer, September 14, 1972.

[56] Fleischman, p. 282.

[57] Interview with May Bromberg, September 13, 1972.

Councilmen Sharkey and Schanzer at the New York City Council meeting on October 14, 1938, requesting President Roosevelt and Secretary Hull to ask the British Government to establish a Jewish homeland.[59] Ironically, Vladeck did not favor such a homeland, nor a homeland for Jews anywhere in the world, but by the late 1930s, he probably would have been willing to consider a territorial solution.[60]

His defection from the Socialist attitude on Palestine stemmed from his pro-partition preference. He wrote to Felix Warburg on August 3, 1937: "It is my opinion that the partition plan is the best way out, not because it is the best solution... but because, under the circumstances, no other solution is possible. As long as the Zionists will dictate Palestine policy, there will be no peace between Jews and Arabs." Since he believed the Jewish Agency to be too weak to shoulder the burden of the Holy Land, at least partition would throw the responsibility on the Palestinian Jews themselves and "clear up the possibilities of Palestine as a solution to the Jewish problem in Eastern Europe." Anything done to jeopardize the plan, he said, would be injurious to the world's Jews.[61]

The White Paper of 1939 inundated the Trotskyite extremists.[62] Most of the comment in the American Socialist Party opposed Jewish nationalism as a "catspaw of British imperialism" but stressed the Jewish emergency above all.[63] Zionists were said to have brought the trouble upon themselves by collaborating with Great Britain against the Arabs but Jewish immigration went

---

[58] Vladeck to Stephen Wise, September 20, 1937, Baruch C. Vladeck Papers (hereafter abbreviated BCV) Tamiment Institute, New York City.

[59] *Remarks of Councilman B. Charney Vladeck in Explaining His Vote on a Resolution Introduced by Councilmen Sharkey and Schanzer at the Meeting of the City Council Held on October 14, 1938, Requesting the President of the United States and the Secretary of State To Make Representations to the British Government for the Establishment of a Jewish National Homeland in Palestine, Ibid.*

[60] Interview with May Bromberg, September 13, 1972.

[61] Vladeck to Felix Warburg, August 3, 1937, BCV.

[62] Revolutionary Workers' League, *Where Shall the Jewish Masses Turn?* (Chicago, 1939), pp. 4-6, 8-12; Charles Crompton, "Notes on the Jewish Question," *The New International, V (April 1939), 123-124.*

[63] Abraham Ziegler, "The Zionist Answer," *The Industrial Unionist,* VII (January -February 1939), pp. 4-6, 8-12; Charles Cromptom, "Notes on the Jewish Question," *The New International,* V (April 1939), 123-124.

unopposed.[64] In June, the British, more than the Zionists, became Socialist targets. The J.L.C. praised Jewish labor in Palestine and censured the White Paper. Norman Thomas did the same and, in 1939, spoke of "unrestricted Jewish immigration" not only to Palestine but to America as well.[65]

After 1921, it will be remembered that the most radical Jewish and non-Jewish Socialists were drawn into the Communist Party. It is a relatively simple exercise to trace the Communist position on Zionism in the interwar years. All one must be aware of is the presence of conformity and the concomitant absence of variety among the theorizers on all subjects, including Zionism and Palestine. It is also helpful to know that Jewish Communists were rarely at odds with their non-Jewish leaders; if differences arose, they were forcibly eradicated and, as an object lesson, the transgressor was publicly humiliated. With regard to Palestine, as with all other Communist issues, the Party line altered to accomodate the current thought from Moscow. Abrupt and sweeping changes on Zionism emanating from Russia often embarrassed the American Communist Party, whose duty was largely to juggle the worn polemic to fit new situations.

According to Earl Browder, the Jewish Bureau of the Communist Party contained approximately two thousand five hundred members, or about two and a half per cent of the total party membership in the United States.[66] Some Jews were there at the start, having left Socialism in 1919 when the Communist Party formed. Others followed in 1921 as part of the Socialist Workers Party.[67] American Socialists, the old guard particularly, did not immediately ap-

---

[64] "Britain Placates Arabs to Maintain Lifeline," *The Weekly People*, XLIX (June 3, 1939), 1, 5; John Newton Thurber, "George and Elizabeth: Salesmen of Empire," *The Socialist Call*, May 27, 1939, p. 4; "The Jew: Catspaw of British Imperialism" (editorial) *The Socialist Call*, June 10, 1939, p. 4; Charles Edward Russell, "It's Simple When You Know How," *The New Leader*, May 20, 1939, p. 3; "No Talk of Immigration Quotas Now While Millions Suffer," *The New Leader*, November 26, 1938, p. 1.

[65] Fleischman, p. 282; Halperin, pp. 162-164.

[66] Halperin, p. 170-173.

[67] Members of this Party included J. Louis Engdahl, editor of *The Workers' Council* and Alexander Trachtenberg. For a sample of their philosophy on Zionism, see Alexander Trachtenberg, "International Notes," *The Workers' Council*, I (June 15, 1921), 92.

prehend the importance of educating the European Jewish Socialists to the American point of view. This cannot be said of American Communists. The Jewish Bureau was a respected subsection of the Communist Party. As soon as Jews were present in sufficient strength, the daily *Freiheit*, a Yiddish language newspaper was published under the editorship of the *Forward* rebel, Moissy Olgin. Between 1921 and 1928, the American Communist Party was silent on Zionism. Whatever comment the Party had was left to the *Freiheit*. Generally, Olgin did not arraign the Yishuv.[68] After the confirmation of the Mandate upon Great Britain in July 1922, Olgin cited Jewish capitalists and the Mandatory as partners in imperialism: "The Jewish workers... can be free only if they link hands... with workers of all other lands in their fight for freedom...."[69]

Increasing stabilization of the Party as a consequence of the expulsion of the Trotskyites, and the initiation of the Five Year Plan gave the Communists more confidence. The theme of Communist "inevitably" presaged a harder line with the capitalist powers and the Zionists, who were seen as puppets of England, bloodily engaged in arresting the Arab revolution. The Arab national liberation movement was viewed as uniformly good; the presence of Jews, unless they were Communists, uniformly bad. Every Arab, from the Mufti to the impoverished storekeeper and landless tenant were hailed as freedom fighters. By the same token, nearly all Jews were Zionists, having bartered Palestine for the pottage of imperial preferment.

Freiheit did not quite see the "black and white" of it and was shortly compelled into a degrading reversal. On August 24, 1929, at the inception of the Holy Land uprisings, the newspaper talked of "imperialism built on hate." Wherein England manipulated both Arabs and Jews, whose destinies were inextricably bound.[70] On August 30, Olgin deviated from the official line of the *Daily Worker*, the central organ of the Communist Party in America, rebuking Arab rioters as "pogromists," just as the *Forward* had done.[71] The following day, *Freiheit* did penance to Moscow. The Arab "pogromists" became proletarian revolutionaries, the "hooligans"

---

[68] Epstein, p. 222.

[69] "The Beginning of Jewish Redemption" (editorial, Yiddish), *Freiheit*, July 27, 1922, p. 4.

[70] "England Supports the Workers in Palestine" (editorial, Yiddish) *Freiheit*, August 24, 1929, p. 4.

were renamed heroes and Zionist youth was scorned as "cowardly attackers." In brief, *Freiheit* was coerced into compliance with the *Daily Worker*.[72]   To insure the continued fealty of *Freiheit*, the paper and the Communist Party became "joint" sponsors of a Communist picnic in Cleveland, at which Melech Epstein, editor of the *Jewish Communist Daily*, regaled his audience with the "glorious struggle" of the Arabian masses against Zionism.[73]   In two weeks, Moissy Olgin was to "convict" the *Forward* of betraying the Arab masses at a mock public trial. The judge at the trial was Paul Yuditch of the *Freiheit*.[74]   As a direct result, there was a Jewish Communist split. Four of the *Freiheit's* most prominent writers resigned; they claimed not to be Zionists but nevertheless regarded Jewish colonists "who were being murdered by Arab pogromists" with the greatest respect. As a final touch, they labeled the Arab "revolutionaries" cowards, committing "mayhem on hapless women and children."[75]

There was a noticeable increase in the activities of the Jewish Bureau, whose supremacy had been brought into dispute by the *Freiheit* episode. Help was on the way from the *Daily Worker*. On September 3, the *Worker* asked for all Communists to aid in the "correction" of *Freiheit's* error while holding firm to the Communist stand: that Palestine was an Arab country, Zionism had deceived the Jewish masses, British imperialism masked its aggression with the "Zionist fig-leaf," so-called leftist or Socialist Zionists were the "shock troops" of British imperialism in Palestine and the present Arab rising was neither a religious nor a political war, as the Britons and Americans had postulated, but a class conflict.[76]   Jewish

---

[71] Schachtman, *The Militant,* October 1, 1929, p. 5; Berg, *The Menorah Journal,* XVII, 75; "Zionists Partly Blamed for Riots by Jewish Press," *Brooklyn Daily Eagle,* August 28, 1929, p. 2; Epstein, p. 226.

[72] Berg, *Menorah Journal,* XVII, 75; "Britain Incites Palestine Feud; Over' 50 Killed," *The Daily Worker,* VI (August 26, 1929), 1, 5; "U.S. Demands More Troops in Palestine War," *The Daily Worker,* VI (August 27, 1929), 1, 5; "The Fruits of Zionism" (editorial) *The Daily Worker,* VI (August 29, 1929), 6.

[73] "Cleveland Workers Support Party," *The Daily Worker,* VI (September 7, 1929), p. 3.

[74] "Zionist Tools Found Guilty," *The Daily Worker,* VI (September 24, 1929), 2; Epstein, pp. 232-233.

[75] Berg, *The Menorah Journal,* XVII, 75.

Communists in the United States were called upon to "greet" the Arabian masses and join them as brothers in the struggle against the Jewish bourgeoisie who had driven the Arab peasants from their lands, "which is transferred to the Zionists." Banners were displayed by Jewish Communists at their gatherings which read "Zionists slaughter Arab men, women and children." There was a precipitate rise in the meetings of Jewish Communists, spurred by the Jewish Bureau, in close cooperation with the American Communist Party, to check embryonic Jewish protest.[77] Rivaling the aid given Jewish sufferers by Zionists, non-Zionists and anti-Zionists in America, Communists established an organization called Workers' International Relief and issued an appeal on behalf of both Arab and Jewish workers in Palestine.[78] The Communist Anti-Imperialist League circulated a statement denouncing "Zionist-imperialist" activities in Palestine and noting "the truly pan-Arabian sentiment in the revolt, as illustrated by the fact that Arabs in Transjordania, Syria and Egypt in conjunction with the masses of Indian people supported the revolt.[79] On September 6, the *Daily Worker* congratulated "the valiant" Communist Party of Palestine, including Jewish, Arabian and other workers "who will continue to fight against imperialism and its Zionist flunkeys."[80]

Until 1936, American Communists embellished upon but did not alter their prior attitudes. They opposed anti-Semitism because ethnic background had no part in the workers' struggle; Birobijan, the Stalinist answer to the Jewish question, was highly praised.[81] The Hope-Simpson Report, the Passfield White Paper, the resigna-

"The Revolutionary Uprising in Palestine and Tasks of the Party," *The Daily Worker*, VI (September 3, 1929), 6.

[77] "Jewish Workers Support Arabs Against British," *The Daily Worker*, VI (August 29, 1929), 1, 5; "Zionists Plan to Attack Meet," *The Daily Worker*, VI (September 2, 1929), 1; "Zionist Drive Against C.P.," *The Daily Worker*, VI (September 4, 1929), 1, 2; "Lynch Threat by Zionists," *The Daily Worker*, VI (September 10, 1929), 1; "Zionists Attack YCL Speakers," *The Daily Worker*, VI (September 13, 1929), 1; "Zionists Attack Bronx Meeting," *The Daily Worker*, VI (September 28, 1929), 2; Epstein, pp. 226-227.

[78] "Aid Workers in Palestine," *The Daily Worker*, VI (September 13, 1929), 1.

[79] "League Defends Arabian Revolt," *The Daily Worker* (September 16, 1929), 1.

[80] "Programs (sic) Under the Slogan, 'Down with Programs (sic),' " *The Daily Worker*, VI (September 6, 1929), 4; Epstein, pp. 230-233; Berg, *The Menorah Journal*, XVII, 71.

tion of Weizmann from the J.A.P. and the return of Brandeis were stoically regarded as indications of the rising importance of the United States in the Zionist-capitalist framework. The Zionists had apparently abandoned Britain to pursue "American dollars."[82]

In the early and mid-1930s, many American Communists were convinced that the United States and Britain were going to become fascist before they toppled. The thought that Weizmann might be reuniting with British imperialists was not nearly as important as the arrival of Jabotinsky, a genuine "Jewish fascist." Zionists were now not only imperialist pawns but fascist deceivers. American Zionists, notably Stephen Wise, "the tool of Wall Street," were apparently eyeing a Revisionist alliance.[83]

In a sensational series of nine articles, published in late 1934, John L. Spivak, editor of the *New Masses*, called on American Jews to combat anti-Semitism by adopting communism. This had been done in Russia and persecution had ceased due to the evolution of a classless society. He dismissed Zionism as a "reactionary... nationalist" movement seeking hegemony over the Jewish masses."[84] But Spivak did not reach the vitriolic level of Robert Gessner who, in February 1935, likened Jabotinsky to a "Jewish Hitler."[85] The bankruptcy of Palestinian Jewish labor organizations was described by Paul Novick in August, and formed the basis for a revised Jewish Bureau platform drawn up by Olgin four months later.[86] It asked all

---

[81] "No Jewish Central Committee," *Revolutionary Age*, II (September 26, 1931), 3; "Biro-Bidjan" (editorial), *Workers Age*, III (June 15, 1934), 8. Actually, both these periodicals represented what was known as a "right opposition" (Trotskyites were the so-called "left opposition") to Stalinism, but on the issue of Zionism, Stalinists and Lovestonites were in agreement.

[82] "The New Zionist Adventure Arrives Today at Central Opera House" (editorial Yiddish), *Freiheit*, October 29, 1930, p. 4; "Britain Makes Anti-Zionist Turn," *The Revolutionary Age*, I (November 22, 1930), 3; "Fascists Gain in Palestine," *The Revolutionary Age*, II (December 20, 1930), 3; "World Zion Meet is Postponed," *The Revolutionary Age*, II (February 14, 1931), 1; "U.S. Forces Win at Zion Meet," *The Revolutionary Age*, II (July 18, 1931), 2; "Between Hammer and Anvil," *The Revolutionary Age*, II (July 18, 1931), 4.

[83] "Attack Britain at Zion Meet," *The Revolutionary Age*, II (July 11, 1931), 1.

[84] "Anti-Semitism:, What to do About it" (editorial) *The New Masses*, XIII (December 4, 1934), 8-9; Halperin, p. 171; Martin, I, 368-369.

[85] Robert Gessner, "Brown Shirts in Zion," *The New Masses*, XIV (February 19, 1935), 11-13.

"responsible Jewish leaders" of mass organizations in Palestine "to declare that the Jews were not out to capture the land but to live in peace with the Arabs." The same leaders were to denounce British imperialism and support instead a democratically elected parliament with minority rights for Jews. Jewish unions must immediately desist from their discriminatory anti-Arab practices and admit non-Jews to membership with full equality. Henceforth, Jews would purchase their land only with the consent of those living upon it. Finally, "Jewish immigration to Palestine shall be freed of Zionist domination." It was hoped that the Histadrut, once it had relinquished its nationalist ties, would act as an organizer of Arab and Jewish laborers into a Palestinian Workers Alliance.[87]

The Presidential candidacy of Earl Browder was one of two events which highlighted a shift in the American Communist stand on Zionism and Palestine. The other was the new Moscow line which brought the Communists into a Popular Front alliance with the Western Powers. From 1936 to 1939, American Communists mounted an offensive upon Jewish nationalism, the Yishuv and the Histadrut but not against Jewish Communists either in Palestine or those emigrating there.[88] The Popular Front precluded the undisciplined use of anti-British invective since the "capitalist" West was now a "democratic ally" against fascism. Hence, the Jewish settlement in Palestine was destined to absorb the bilious verbal overflow that, for years, had been directed at England.

The Arab general strike, following the renewal of unrest in April, 1936, persisted until October. *The Daily Worker, Workers Age* and the *Freiheit* approved, the latter fulminating against Ben-Gurion for fostering the bitterness among Arab workers.[89] Writing in *The New Masses*, Alter Brody underlined the recent change in Communist thought and related it to Palestine: "What type of united front against fascism shall there be: a state with a mere four hundred thousand Jews or an Arabia with a population of twelve million when

86 Paul Novick, *Zionism Today* (New York, 1936), pp. 3, 5, 12-13, 15-20, 24-31, 34-40, 52-58.

87 I. Brill, "Communists and Palestine," *Workers Age*, V (June 13, 1936), 2; Paul Novick, *Palestine: The Communist Position* (New York, 1936), pp. 11-14, 24-27.

88 Epstein, p. 328; Novick, *Palestine,* pp. 11-14.

89 "Arabs Call General Strike: Palestine Death Toll at 18," *The Daily Worker*, XIII (April 23, 1936), 1; Epstein, p. 298; I. Brill, "Communists and Palestine," *The Workers Age*, V (June 13, 1936), 2.

Mussolini has suddenly invaded Ethiopia and Hitler has remilitarized the Rhineland?"[90]

Communists repeated that the struggle against Zionism was not directed against Jews; neither the Party nor the Arabs were anti-Jewish.[91] Isaac Brill declaimed against "the Jewish nationalistic press, which was endeavoring "to make the world believe that what is happening in Palestine is an old-fashioned pogrom." Far from it, he said. The Zionists were segregating Jewish from Arab labor, thereby polarizing the country. Conversely, Arab leaders "have an attitude that befits a progressive movement."[92] The slogan of the Jewish Bureau, "Arab-Jewish Brotherhood," defined the position of Earl Browder, who spoke as a Presidential candidate at the Hippodrome on June 8, 1936. Browder did what no Communist to date had done: he drew a sharp distinction between the Jewish masses and their leaders. All labor in Palestine, he insisted, desired union and the Palestine Communist Party was to span the gulf dividing the Jewish and Arab peoples. As for immigration, a pressing issue, Browder ordered its domination by Zionists to cease and its rapid replacement by a system utilizing some means of popular control.[93]

Partition was an alarming presence for those Communists who were sure that Jewish assimilation had gone far enough. The exacerbation of the "Jewish problem" was a result, they said, of the "assimilationist... (and)... Zionist myths" arising from bourgeois reaction; anti-Semitism would cease only "in a non-competitive social order which would uproot its cause." Fortunately for the Jew, they emphasized, such a society was a triumphant reality in Soviet Russia.[94] It appeared as if the myth was again to be perpetrated by the ghettoization of Jews in an imperialist pseudo-state. *Freiheit* and

[90] Alter Brody, "Palestine Under Britain's Heel," *The New Masses,* XIX (May 12, 1926), 13-14.

[91] "The Struggle of the Palestine Peoples," *The Western Worker*, June 1, 1936, p. 5.

[92] I Brill, "Palestine — A Power Keg," *The Workers Age,* V (May 30, 1936), 2.

[93] Earl Browder, *Zionism: Address at the Hippodrome Meeting July 8, 1936* (New York, 1936), pp. 5-17, 21-24; Epstein, p. 299.

[94] Benjamin Stolberg, "The Jew and the World," *The Nation*, CXLII (June 17, 1936), 766-770; Martha Gruening, "Prejudice Unlimited," *New Republic*, XC (March 24, 1937), 217; Martin, II, 691-692.

the *Western Worker* challenged the Peel findings while suggesting an Arab-Jewish union against Britain and the attainment of minority rights as the Jews' last, best hope.[95]

Under the auspices of the Jewish Bureau of the Communist Party, *Jewish Life*, a monthly under the editorship of John Arnold, appeared at the height of the partition debate.[96] Weizmann's choice to treat with the British on the basis of the Peel findings, Arnold stated, flaunted Zionism's "submission to imperialism,"[97] Anti-partitionist articles were contributed by the editor himself and by Earl Browder.[98] By the autumn of 1937, the Communist Party of Palestine, predominantly Arab, broke with American and European Communism by its open advocacy of a Jewish immigration ban. Even if the Americans did not precisely support this position, they did nothing to amend it. Labor Zionism was energetically decried as a "cloak for imperialism," a dagger at the heart of Arab liberty.[99] But the dagger cut two ways: soon, it was to be acknowledged by the Communists that the Grand Mufti, leader of the "national revolution" sought an alliance with the Reich.[100]

In 1938, the American Communists stuck to the anti-homeland, anti-World Jewish Congress position of the Comintern, but the task of winning Jewish "unity" forbade reverting to the militant pro-

[95] "The Real Problem in Palestine" (editorial, Yiddish), *Freiheit*, July 10, 1937, p. 4; "Partition of Palestine is Opposed," *The Daily Worker*, XIV (July 11, 1937), 12; "Jewish-Arab Unity Against Britain is Needed," *The Daily Worker*, XIV (July 10, 1937), 6; "British Divide Palestine to Cement Rule," *The Western Worker*, July 12, 1937, p. 3; "Arabs Uniting to Oppose Partition," *The Western Worker*, July 15, 1937, p. 2.

[96] Epstein, p. 320.

[97] "Notes of the Month" (editorial), *Jewish Life*, I (September 1937), 3-4; John Arnold, "Zionism, Bundism, Socialism," *Jewish Life*, I (September 1937), 25-30.

[98] John Arnold, "British Scissors Over Palestine," *Jewish Life*, I (August 1937), 13; Earl Browder, "About the Crisis in Zionism," *Jewish Life*, I (September 1937), 8-9.

[99] "Notes of the Month," *Jewish Life*, I (November 1937), 3-5; Epstein, p. 329.

[100] Of course, the change in attitude toward the Mufti was gradual. The first ot the following articles illustrates a favorable attitude. the last two, written a year and two years later are clear reversals. "Plot Revealed in Palestine," *The Western Worker*, October 21, 1937, p. 1; "New Strife in Palestine," *The Workers Age*, VII (July 16, 1938), 1; Paul Novick, *Solution for Palestine: The Chamberlain White Paper* (New York, 1939), 17.

Arab stand of 1929. [101] At this time, Zionist leadership was taken to task for its link to Britain, but the Yishuv was showered with tenderness. Thus, the Party adhered to the 1936 Browder design of Arab-Jewish worker solidarity overcoming all imperialist obstacles. [102]   Communists averred that the cultivation in Palestine of "genuine Jewish Socialists" seemed to have had a salubrious effect on Arab-Jewish relationships, which were constantly being undermined by Zionist "statism." [103]   Communist interest in Palestine, however, should not be overestimated: the real fight of the Jews was in Spain, said *Jewish Life*, as part of the Lincoln Brigade, where Jews would not be isolated from "the vital...currents of our time." Placing Palestine before Spain would constitute a "cynical (Jewish) denial of fascist realities," a denial of which only Zionists were capable. [104]

The Nazi-Soviet Pact dramatically ended the reign of the Popular Front. The Communists did not recede from their more benevolent attitude toward the Jews, but the White Paper, by dint of its propinquity to the Russo-German agreement, occasioned a storm of anti-British protest which had not been equaled since the early 1930s. The Jews were urged to counter the "anti-Semitic White Paper" by joining with the Arabs against the British oppressors. [105]

The White Paper, it was contemplated, would have a lasting psychological effect on Jews. American Communists were then in the process of redirecting Jewish enmity away from Germany and toward England. The idea of one periodical, *Workers Age*, was to demonstrate that the "democratic imperialism" of London was no more beneficial to the Jews than the climate in Berlin, perhaps even

---

[101] Adlerstein, *The American Hebrew*, 143, 6; Epstein, p. 328.

[102] Paul Novick, "Nationalism and the Class Struggle," *Jewish Life*, II (February 1938), 18-22.

[103] "Problem in Palestine," *The Workers Age*, VII (August 27, 1938), 4; Bertram D. Wolfe, "Curse of Anti-Semitism," *The Workers Age*, VII (November 26, 1938), 4-5; Fenner Brockway, "Crisis in Palestine," *The Workers Age*, VII (November 19, 1938), 3.

[104] "Zionists and the Lincoln Brigade," *Jewish Life*, II (February 1938), 6.

[105] "The White Paper and the Need for Jewish-Arab Unity," *The Daily Worker*, XVI (May 20, 1939), 6; Paul Novick, "No Comfort in Zion," *The New Masses*, XXXI (May 30, 1939), 14-15; "United Socialist Party Urged for Palestine," *The Workers Age*, VIII (June 24, 1939), 4.

less so. The article was confident that the White Paper would curb those Jews whose enthusiasms were infecting some sectors of American society with a "pro-British war spirit." [106]

Between 1939 and 1941, the American Communists were anti-Britain, pacifist, and opposed to any Jewish action favoring the Allies. "The Jewish masses," said Browder, "want no part of this war. Their place is in the ranks of a mighty peace front that will put a stop to all plans to drag America into the war." Incessantly, he reminded the Jews of "Chamberlain's betrayal" and its violent Palestinian aftermath of censorship, execution, and repressions. [107] The daily *Freiheit*, which by 1940 was the only Jewish newspaper in the United States that was not clamoring for American support of the Allies, approved the Browder summation. [108] The brilliant solution of the Soviet Union was touted by John Noble; but by this time, American Communsts had lost out to Franklin Roosevelt and had been compromised by the German juggernaut which had turned its heavy artillery on Russia. [109]

Without changing its political philosophy, the Jewish Bureau of the Communist Party responded to a unity call against Hitler issued by American Jews. Zionist ideology was still rejected but Palestine worker Jewry was highly regarded. [110] In January, 1942, the official line was handed down from the Kremlin to international Communism: division among Jews must cease and the Axis must be crushed. [111] Thus chastened, the American Communists went to war.

[106] "Jews Curbed in Palestine," *The Workers Age*, VIII (May 24, 1939), 1.

[107] Earl Browder, *Jewish People and the War*, (New York, 1940), pp. 3-8, 12-19; "Earl Browder and the Jewish People," *The Jewish Voice*, I (May 1941), 12-13.

[108] Browder, *Jewish People*, p. 8.

[109] John Noble, "Illusions of the Jewish Middle Class," *The Jewish Voice*, I (March-April 1941), 22; John Noble, "American Imperialism Turns to Zionism," *The Jewish Voice*, I (May 1941), 14-16, 24.

[110] Halperin, pp. 171-172; Max Steinberg, "An Answer to Dr. S. Margoshes," *The Jewish Voice*, I (September-October 1941), 5-6, 9.

[111] "The Road to Victory" (editorial), *The Jewish Voice*, II (January 1942), 3-4.

VII

American Missionaries
And Zionism

American missionary influence was well-established in the Near East by 1917. Southern Baptists, Mormons, Christian Scientists, Pentecostalists, Congregationalists, Presbyterians and Quakers proselytized among Moslems and Jews. From 1894 on, the Christian Missionary Alliance conducted its work in Jerusalem along Fundamentalist lines. While being moderately successful with Arabs, its work was futile among Jews.[1]

The Protestant religion claimed the greatest number of converts in Syria, twenty-two thousand by 1918.[2] Its missionaries had built American Universities which had become "civilizing" agencies in the Near East. Some major American Protestant missionaries were antagonistic toward Zionism, a philosophy in competition with their own cultural concepts and objectives in Palestine.[3] One American

---

[1] Esco Foundation, I 540; Eldin Ricks, "Zionism and the Mormon Church," *Herzl Year Book*, V, (1963), 147-174. The anti-Zionist Quaker mind is revealed through the writings of Elihu Grant, a missionary-turned archaeologist. He was sent to the Near East by the Quakers in 1901 and taught at the Friends School at Ramallah for several years.

[2] Lewis Bayles Patton, *Report on the Geography, History, Ethnology, Religion, Economics, Domestic Life and Government of the Land of Palestine*, April 15, 1918, Inquiry Document no. 459, WYPLC, Box 40, p. 26.

[3] Manuel. p. 3

clergyman elucidated these objectives: "(we) sympathized with the Arabs because we (the clerics) work amongst them... and... feel that if Jewish ambitions (Zionism) are accomplished, it will be at the expense of Christian missionaries and Christian influence in the Holy Land." Sympathetic understanding, however was not to go as far as condoning Arab self-determination: "From the Christian standpoint," the above mentioned minister continued, "Arab ambitions for independence are just as menacing" as Zionism.[4] Dean of the most influential missionary family in the Near East, Daniel Bliss became the first President of the Syrian Protestant College in Beirut. In 1902, he retired and was succeeded by his son, Howard.[5] Another missionary phenomenon was the American Colony in Jerusalem, a Protestant organization which had been consistently hostile to Zionism since its 1887 founding by a Chicago merchant named William Spafford.   After World War I, the Colony catered to tourists, performed charitable functions and disseminated an anti-Zionist point of view.[6]

The war and the Balfour Declaration spurred the missionaries in their anti-Zionist efforts. They became informally allied with the Arabs and the State Department after November, 1917. "American missionaries, especially in Beirut, joined forces with "The Young Arabs," a secret Arab nationalist society, in order to fight Zionism. They jointly opposed the Balfour Declaration.   Hampson Gary, American Consul-General in Cairo, was aware of the mounting anti-Zionist propaganda emanating from the Moslems and Christians in Beirut and welcomed it. Gary, himself, had always believed that the most feasible solution for Palestine was placing it within a unified Syrian State with a capital at Damascus.[7]

A number of American missionaries felt that their position in the

[4] George Wadsworth to Cordell Hull, October 26, 1938, 867N.01/1295, *USFR: 1938*, II, 969-971, 974.

[5] George Antonius, *The Arab Awakening* (New York, 1965), p. 43n; Bayard Dodge, "American Educational and Missionary Efforts in the Ninteenth and Early Twentieth Centuries," *Annals of the American Academy of Political and Social Science*, 401 (May 1972), 21.

[6] Esco Foundation, I, 546-547. One of the travelers influenced by the Colony was Henry Smith Pritchett of the Carnegie Foundation who traveled through Palestine in 1926. See, in this chapter, footnote 52, and the related text.

[7] Selig Adler, "The Palestine Question in the Wilson Era," *Jewish Social Studies*, X (October 1948), 317, 321.

Ottoman Empire ought to be protected and, perhaps improved, once Turkey was defeated. What they desired and what they were willing to offer the United States Government in return was contained in the report of the Reverend James L. Barton of Boston, an alumnus of Oberlin College and secretary of the well-known American Board of Commissioners for Foreign Missions. Barton was appointed by Colonel House to study the Ottoman Empire and submit his findings to the Inquiry. The clergyman's paper, entitled *Suggested Possible Form of Government for the Area Covered by the Ottoman Empire at the Outbreak of the War, Exclusive of Arabia but Inclusive of the Trans-Caucasus,* presented the American Government with some fascinating possibilities. Barton's "Grand Design" called for economic control of the Near East and several additional areas, a "single protector" (probably the United States) and domination of the spiritual and educational life there by American missionaries. Though never totally realized, this program, which recognized the existence of a bond between religion and American investment, served as a model for subsequent diplomacy, including the 1924 Anglo-American Convention. Barton's original plan made no provisions with regard to the Arabs or their national aspirations; the Bostonian strongly advised that the Near East be kept intact "because any subdivision... would retard development."[8]

Though not a minister, John Huston Finley was a man with a Christian mission and, in the years 1918-1920, was a friend and colleague of Barton and Howard Bliss. A Presbyterian, Finley was a well-known figure in New York State affairs. From 1903 to 1909, he was President of the City College of New York; subsequently, he held the post of Commissioner of Education for the State of New York and in the years 1921-1940 was associate editor of *The New York Times.* In 1918 and 1919, Finley served in Palestine as Commissioner for the American Red Cross.[9] He had a marked preference for Christian anti-Zionist politics.

Upon his arrival in Palestine in July, 1918, Finley was greeted by General Arthur Money and Sir Ronald Storrs, military governors of Palestine and Jerusalem respectively. Most impressive, however, was his meeting with the Grand Mufti[10] on American Independence

---

[8] Love, p. 106; Manuel, pp. 214-215, 224 It has already been mentioned that Dr. King was President of Oberlin. He probably knew Barton. See also John A. De Novo, *American Interests and Policies in the Middle East 1900-1939* (Minneapolis, 1963), p. 124.

[9] Campbell, *A Report on Zionism*, WYP, EMHC, p. 1905.

Day, July 4. On that day, Finley was to assume his official duties as an agent of the American Red Cross by presiding over the ceremonial opening of the organization's new administrative building. At the celebration, Finley spoke of restoring Jerusalem "for all religions."[11] In the following weeks, the Grand Mufti took pictures with the Red Cross commissioners, feted Finley and his entourage and enveloped them all in an embrace of pro-Americanism.[12] At one such function which he hosted, the Mufti delivered a speech which afterward was translated by Hadad Bey, the chief of police in Jerusalem, a University of Beirut graduate and an American zealot. Finley was pleased that the Arabs, even those who spoke and read no English, were as enthusiastic for the United States "and our Fourth of July celebration as any native American." By August, Finley was absolutely charmed by the Grand Mufti and the Arab deliverer Major T.E. Lawrence, to whom he offered the opportunity of meeting "...our people (i.e. Red Cross officials)... in various parts of the country."[13]

Conversely, Finley's papers indicate that he saw little or nothing of Jewish life in the Holy Land. His formidable slide and photograph collections, replete with scenes of Arabs and Americans engaged in cooperative tasks, are nearly devoid of Jews. As a subject, the latter were portrayed not as sturdy pioneer farmers or shopkeepers but as a people reduced to beggary.

Having left a subordinate in charge, Finley returned to the United States in October, 1918. Up until this time, his feelings on Zionists and Zionism were simply not publicized, but this was an oversight soon to be corrected. On his way home, Finley stopped off in England and Zionist leaders, aware that his opinions would soon be available for public consumption, tried to intercept him. Chaim Weizmann asked him to come to his office "to have a little chat...

[10] *Jerusalem: Its Redemption and Future as Described by Eyewitnesses* (New York, 1918), pp. 186-187.

[11] Address of John Huston Finley entitled "Fourth of July in Jerusalem," JHF, Box 80.

[12] "Legends Inserted in Photographs Sent to the Red Cross," November 15, 1918, picture no. 13 and "Lantern Slides," undated, *Ibid.*

[13] Address by the Grand Mufti to Finley, July 31, 1918, *Ibid.*, Box 73; "Legends Inserted in Photographs Sent to the Red Cross," November 15, 1918, picture no. 13, *Ibid.*, Box 80; undated memorandum from Finley to T.E. Lawrence, *Ibid.*, Box 75.

and to talk over a number of matters."[14] There is no evidence that a meeting between the two men took place. If it did, it was to have little bearing on succeeding events.

In *The New York Times* statement on November 17, 1918, Finley asked for the missionary and Reform Jewish solution. As Barton had desired, Finley opted for a single power protectorate in the Near East. He did not specify the United States nor did he advocate outright possession of the Turkish domain, merely its submission to a temporary Western trusteeship of protection and guidance.[15] His other idea, one he would never relinquish, was modeled on the conception of Reform Jews like David Philipson, Samuel Goldenson, Simon Rosendale and Edward Lauterbach. Finley was advised by them that internationalizing Palestine, freeing it for all religions, with no preferential treatment accorded Jews, was an ideal solution.[16] What was Finley to think after prominent American Jews rejected the Balfour Declaration because it ostensibly acknowledged "dual citizenship" and a "separate Jewish nationality?" Finley was impressed by the assertions of Reform Jews in New York City that Zionism represented an "undesirable conjunction of Church and State." Dr. Abram I. Isaacs, Professor of Semitics at New York University put the assmiliationists' argument directly to the former City College President:

> I dread a special Jewish state as being likely to develop into a narrow religious commonwealth which cannot but arouse antagonisms and lead to early extinction.... Many thoughtful Jews ...favor... internationalizing Palestine with civil and religious liberty assured to all its residents.... We (Reform Jews) believe the dispersion of the Jew to all corners of the globe is preparing the Jewish religion for its international era....[17]

The Zionists tried but could not sway Finley from his conviction, which had been reenforced by Abram I. Elkus and

[14] Weizmann to Finley, October 25, 1918, *Ibid.*, Box 80.

[15] Ameen Rihani to Finley, November 25, 1918, *Ibid.*, Box 76.

[16] Voss, p. 120; Edward Lauterbach to Finley, November 18, 1918, Finley to Lauterbach, November 19, 1918, Rosendale to Finley, June 18, 1919 and Samuel Goldenson to Finley, November 19, 1918, JHF, Box 74.

[17] Abram I. Isaacs to Finley, November 29, 1918, JHF, Box 74.

Henry Morgenthau. [18] Alexander Sachs, assistant to de Haas, who was then Executive Secretary of the Z.O.A., reminded Finley of Wilson's assent to the Balfour Declaration. Jerusalem's deliverance, a subject on which Finley was scheduled to speak in New York City might, Sachs hinted, include a thought on Zion's restoration. Finley's answer had been proffered three weeks before in an *American Hebrew* interview: internationalization of Palestine with Great Britain as mandatory. [19]

Not surprisingly, Finley called for a British rather than an American trusteeship. On this issue, the popularity of Barton's antithetical plan was waning although, at the end of 1918, its lone promoter was still pushing for United States control of vast chunks of the Turkish Empire and a missionary-government understanding to promote American investments there. Other missionaries, not so well attuned to practical finance, believed that their religious work would prosper just as well under English rule. One theologian stated that Zionism would retard his evangelical activities: "Jewish nationalism will be... the greatest obstacle to the spread of... His (Christ's) gospels... on Earth." [20] Finley, himself, spoke eloquently enough to be a man of the cloth. "America," he said, "you must send not only the Red Cross to this front. You must send... Christ... you must have a part in the redemption of the Holy Land." [21]

These small, subjective differences notwithstanding, a friendly disposition was maintained between the idealists like Finley and the pragmatists like Barton. Squabbles between Palestinian Christianizers were discouraged although individual preferences persisted. With the concluding of an armistice in November, 1918, the war work of the Red Cross ended. The organization would soon leave the field to reconstruction, rehabilitation and relief groups best qualified to deal with the appalling state in which the Holy Land, momentarily quies-

---

[18] Henry Woodrow Hurlbert to Finley, December 14, 1918, *Ibid.*

[19] *Jerusalem: Its Redemption*, p. 185; "Palestine Will Not Be Handed Over To Any Nation, Race or Creed," *The American Hebrew*, 104 (November 22, 1918), 55; Alexander Sachs to Finley, December 15, 1918, JHF, Box 74.

[20] Goldblatt, *American Jewish Historical Quarterly*, LVII, 471.

[21] John Huston Finley, *A Pilgrim in Palestine* (New York, 1919), p. 55.

cent, then found itself.

The group immediately prepared to take over from the Red Cross was Barton's American Committee for Relief in the Near East (A.C.R.N.E.). To facilitate a smooth transfer of power, the Red Cross entered into an agreement with Barton which redounded to the latter's benefit. The A.C.R.N.E. received gifts and supplies at a reduced cost. Some Red Cross officials were quite pleased to offer Barton this bounty and, in turn, discriminated against all Jewish Relief agencies, including the Zionist medical unit, as far as gifts and purchasing were concerned.[22]   Finley was not entirely responsible for this situation since it developed soon after his return to America. Once informed, though, he did nothing to stop it. Judge Julian Mack complained to the vice-president of the Red Cross that the A.C.R.N.E. was being sold supplies at their cost in Palestine while the Zionist medical unit was compelled to buy at American prices.[23] The Zionists, however, had no inkling as to the full extent of their isolation in the Red Cross-Barton intrigue. Originally, the Red Cross was supposed to leave Palestine on March 1, 1919, turning over its entire operation to the A.C.R.N.E. Instead, it left in July. During the six month interval, January through June, when both relief organizations were in the Holy Land, the A.C.R.N.E. was subsidized by the Red Cross at the rate of twenty-five thousand dollars a month; in January and February, 1919, a lump sum of five hundred thousand dollars was given to Barton.[24] No equal favors were bestowed on Zionist relief organizations.

Barton appeared at Versailles in March, after the sessions there were well under way and after Howard Bliss had made significant progress with the American State Department. President of the University of Beirut, Bliss had lived his whole life in the Near East. He was a Congregationalist, as so many of the missionaries were and, as a boy, received an exacting religious education. He was well-known to Woodrow Wilson

---

[22] Solomon Lowenstein to Major Stanley Stoner, May 8, 1919, JHF, Box 75.

[23] Walling to Mack, July 29, 1919 and Lowenstein to Walling, August 1, 1919, *Ibid.* Walling was vice-president of the Red Cross.

[24] Lowenstein to Finley, December 13, 1918, *Ibid.*, Box 75 and undated, unsigned memorandum, *Ibid.*, Box 79.

but it was not the President who invited him to Paris. On
January 5, 1919, Bliss received a telegram from the State
Department. He left for Versailles on the ninth and four days
later conferred with Lansing, White and other American Peace
commissioners. He put his views in writing to Lansing on
January 26 and to White on January 31.[25]

Bliss, the man whom T.E. Lawrence claimed was "the root
of all good in the Near East," was the only person outside of
Faisal to set the Arab case for independence formally before the
Peace Conference.[26] Addressing the Council of Ten on
February 13, Bliss requested the appointment of a mixed,
international commission to investigate the wishes of the
Syrians whose views, he charged, "were being suppressed by
censorship." Bliss predicted that such a commission would
find a "universal desire for a United Syria under an American
protectorate."[27]

Wilson was shaken by the very thought of collusion with
European colonialism. The next day, February 14, Westermann, Wilson and Lansing attended a meeting of the Arab
Higher Council at which Bliss spoke, again urging the appointment of an international commission for Syria. "The President
seemed restless during the oration of Chekri Ganem, the
French-Syrian poet, got up with Lansing and walked around
the room."[28] Wilson was not the only one to feel his nerves
tense. The American delegation as a whole did not like the drift
of Bliss' thought, feeling, perhaps, that it was becoming
dangerously involved in Anglo-French politics. In any event,
Bliss wrote to Wilson regularly in the month of February.
The Arabs, went his ardent plea, desired self-determination and
the only means to that end was to dispatch an inter-Allied

[25] Zeine, p. 69; Evans, p. 125.

[26] *PDWLW*, January 12, 1919, p. 19; Mousa, p. 225; Evans, p. 153; Manuel, pp.
227-228.

[27] Manuel, pp. 223-224. Some of the preliminaries involved in appointing this
commission, which later became the King-Crane Commission, are discussed by me
in Chapter 2. Another view may be obtained in Joseph L. Grabill, *Protestant
Diplomacy and the Near East: Missionary Influence on American Policy 1810-1927*
(Minneapolis, 1971), pp. 160-165.

[28] *PDWLW*, February 14, 1919, 37.

commission to Syria. He made it clear that he was relying on the twelfth of Wilson's Fourteen Points, the one dealing with the right of national development specifically relating to Turkish affairs. On February 26, the tireless Bliss continued his campaign before the American Peace Delegation but Lansing, who admitted his sympathy for an impartial inquiry, told him that the project was impossible without French and British consent. The peacemakers were taken aback when Bliss recommended the appointment of a purely American team if the two major European powers demurred.[29] Lansing offered him no encouragement on that score and had no really effective rejoinder: a commission, he knew would illustrate the proper function of disinterested American idealism, the lack of one, American insincerity and inability to cope with devious European politics.

The fate of the commission had not yet been decided when the redoubtable James Barton came to Paris. For the moment, he had nothing to hold him in the Near East. An agreement between John Huston Finley and himself on March 8, 1919, insured that the A.C.R.N.E. would indeed inherit the Red Cross legacy in Palestine after that organization departed.[30] At Paris, Finley had been heard from by proxy: two signers of the Kahn petition were Red Cross officials and at least one of them was Jewish.[31] Now it was Barton's turn. As chairman of the A.C.R.N.E., he acted as spokesman and liaison for its trustees and officials. The letterhead of the Committee, incorporated by an act of Congress in 1915, reveals that Barton was associated with the major anti-Zionists of his generation: Henry Morgenthau was Vice-Chairman of the A.C.R.N.E. and Cleveland Dodge its treasurer. Abram I. Elkus, Oscar Straus, Albert T. Shaw and Charles R. Crane were trustees as were

---

[29] American Commission to Negotiate the Peace, Minutes of the Daily Meetings of the Commissioners Plenipotentiary, February 26, 1919, Henry White Papers; Zeine, pp. 94n., 70n.3, 74, 219n.4; Adler, *Jewish Social Studies,* X, 324; Manuel, p. 229, Esco Foundation, I, 214-215.

[30] Memorandum of Agreement Between Dr. James L. Barton, Director of the American Commission for Relief in the Near East and Col. John Huston Finley, Commissioner of the American Red Cross for Palestine, March 8, 1919, JHF, Box 73.

[31] "Prominent Jews Protest Against Zionism," *The Jewish Review and Observer,* XLV (March 14, 1919), 1, 4.

Henry Churchill King, William Howard Taft, Charles Evans Hughes, Livingston Farrand, Chairman of the American Red Cross and John Huston Finley.[32]

In no way may Barton be construed to have been a spokesman for or defender of Arab interests, as was Dr. Bliss. In fact, Barton was not only anti-Zionist but also pro-Turkish. It was a position that, in 1919, was considered odd by those who were unaware of Barton's interest in a broad missionary enterprise whose support would be drawn from the American Government and, possibly, American business interests. The Turkish cause was not a popular one for Americans, even missionaries. The so-called "Armenian deportations" during the spring and summer months of 1915 were carried out with organized brutality: Armenian labor battallions in the Turkish army were slaughtered in cold blood.[33] In Palestine, from 1915 on, military rule existed and the Arabs and Jews lived in a relentless state of siege. Zionists and Arab nationalists were suppressed: both Jews and non-Jews were on the edge of starvation. Although the Palestinian peoples were relieved by the Red Cross, the American Jewish Committee and the Zionists, the memory of Turkish cruelty in the Holy Land and elsewhere lingered on in the Untied States. Nevertheless, the Boston clergyman wanted conquered Ottoman territory returned to Turkish suzerainty at the peace table; he was convinced that missionary activities could be best carried out in backward rather than progressive or libertarian climates. He realized that neither Arab nationalists nor Zionists would permit Near Eastern society to exist as it had in the past; they would encourage pride; nationalism, economic development and independence, not docile submission to Christianity. It had been easy for missionaries to achieve conversions in the impoverished areas ignored by the Ottoman Empire: if the same areas became free, Christian influence would surely decline. In 1918, Barton publicized his belief that America should refrain

[32] Charles Evans Hughes to Charles V. Vickrey, February 26, 1921, H.C. Jacquith to Albert Shaw, May 7, 1920 and *Report of Near East Relief to the Congress of the United States for the Year Ending December 31, 1920*, pp. 9, 16, Albert Shaw Papers. Also, see any letterhead on American Red Cross stationary ca. 1918-1920 in JHF, Box 80.

[33] Chambers, pp. 50-51. Armenia is discussed fully as a field of American missionary activity by Grabill in his *Protestant Diplomacy and the Near East*.

from declaring war on Turkey. In sum, Barton, working for an undivided Ottoman Empire, was anti-Armenian and anti-Arab as well as anti-Zionist.[34]

The Arabs were nearly as afraid of Barton's evangelism as they were of Zionism. The one hundred eighty million Moslems in the British Empire loathed him, especially after he said that the "Hejaz Kingdom is hardly worth the name" and deemed it altogether proper to keep the Ottoman Empire "as intact as possible" to ease the way of the missionaries.[35] Barton's scheme, favored by Colonel House, envisoned Henry Morgenthau as a puppet governor of a state at Constantinople, superintended and protected by American ships, American money and American religion.

Far from attacking Barton, the missionaries at Versailles closed ranks behind him. The esprit de corps among the missionaries conquered whatever anti-Barton reservations they and their champions may have had. A welcome addition to their side was the Reverend Otis Glazebrook, American Consul General in Palestine. Glazebrook inundated Washington and Paris with anti-Zionist reports from Jerusalem. He leveled every conceivable, contradictory, anti-Semitic charge available against the Jews: they were Bolshevists but also pro-German; they were religious fanatics who would curry the displeasure of the Vatican but they were atheists as well; they were not merely violating the will of the majority population but also "historic" French rights in the Holy Land.[36] In addition, Julius Kahn, Isaac Landman and Henry Morgenthau threw their combined weight behind the anti-nationalism of Barton and Glazebrook.[37] The Arabs at Paris from America and the Near East ignored Barton but not Bliss or the anti-Zionist cause. The strong feelings of anti-Zionist Reform Jews, missionaries, and Arab Americans circulated among the American officials including Colonel House, whose task it was to nominate Americans for the Inter-Allied Commission on Turkish Mandates.

Needless to say, Bliss, Barton and a third American missionary at

[34] Aaronsohn to Provisional Executive Committee of General Zionist Affairs, November 1, 1918, LDB.

[35] Unsigned memorandum to Stephen Wise, February 3, 1919, *Ibid.*

[36] Adler, *Jewish Social Studies,* X, 331; Manuel, pp. 222, 238; *Jerusalem: Its Redemption,* pp. 104-140.

[37] *PDWLW,* March 27, 1919, p. 50.

Paris, William H. Hall, were delighted with the selection of Henry King, a fervent Congregationalist with proselytizing tendencies and Charles R. Crane, a Unitarian and unofficial representative of American oil and business interests.[38] The story of the Commission, which has already been related, need not be repeated. After King and Crane was selected, their departure was delayed until France and England absolutely refused to participate. In the meantime the loose coalition between Arabs, missionaries and Jews disintegrated. Aside from the King-Crane Commission, the three groups had little in common: in many respects, missionary ideals were antagonistic to Arab nationalism and Reform Jews, wishing no tie whatever to the Middle East, crusaded for their assimilationist cause in the United States. Moreover, from the time King and Crane were chosen to the time they returned from Palestine and other parts of the defunct Ottoman Empire there elapsed six months, during which time great changes occurred in the health of President Wilson and the convictions of the United States Congress. Through no fault of its own, the King-Crane Commission had lost its momentum. Its findings were neither repudiated nor affirmed in official circles.

While in the Near East, King and Crane acquired many American friends. Possibly the greatest of these was John Huston Finley, who had achieved modest fame as a defender of both Christian and Arab interests in the Holy Land. Finley's stand had become synonymous with that of Reform Jewry: he advocated the internationalization of Palestine and the universal mission of Judaism. He claimed to oppose neither spiritual nor cultural Zionism but doubted that any but "pogrom-persecuted Jews" would settle in Palestine. Those Jews seeking a "higher experience," he said, would remain where they were.[39]

Finley was unquestionably a valuable ally to King, Crane and the missionaries. He was friendly with Sir Ronald Storrs, the Grand Mufti and the missionary editor of the *Moslem World,* Samuel Zwemer.[40] Apparently, Finley was not an easy man to forget. The Mufti, in an unusual display of cordiality, wrote to him

---

[38] Manuel, p. 329; Selig Adler, *Jewish Social Studies*, X, 325. Also, see my chapter on the King-Crane Commission.

[39] Finley to General Arthur Money, August 5, 1920, JHF, Box 75; "The Case Against Zionism," *Literary Digest*, 61 (June 14, 1919), 30-31.

[40] W.D. McCrackan to Finley, March 2, 1920 and July 3, 1920, JHF, Box 74.

expressing a strong desire to visit the United States and his Red Cross benefactor. Zwemer, of the American Reformed Church, thought of Finley first when he wished to include an article in *Moslem World* on the future of Syria and Palestine.[41] He instructed Finley to write an inspirational piece, "something that will encourage faith and lead the Christian people to a deeper realization of their obligation in the Near East."[42]

Whatever Finley said was buttressed by first-hand accounts. He had become a subscriber to the *Jerusalem News*, which regularly printed his observations and comments.[43] The paper was founded by one American, Elizabeth L. McQueen and edited by another, William D. McCrackan. McCrackan was one of a party of independent relief workers who entered the Holy Land in 1919. He lingered until July 1920, and he left after the British civil administration assumed power. In this short time, he cemented the amicable relationship existing between Finley, the Mufti and Sir Ronald Storrs while gaining for himself the confidence of all three. Besides her work for the paper, Mrs. McQueen was active in Syrian relief and through McCrackan was acquainted with the Mufti. In order to calm the Arabs when they threatened to riot in December, 1919, Mrs. McQueen addressed them, in a conciliatory manner, saying that if the Jews were wrong, "they would suffer for their faults" but "to gain the world's respect, you must act like gentlemen." On January 3, 1920, the Mufti sent her a grateful letter of thanks for alleviating the tensions.[44]

In three months time, however, the Arabs could not be checked by verbal balm or casual praise.[45] With the appointment of a Jewish civil governor for Palestine, Sir Herbert Samuel, they rioted, indicating that British pro-Zionism had, in their estimation, gone too far.

The missionary impulse lapsed after the Mandate was conferred

---

[41] McCrackan to Finley, December 17, 1919, *Ibid.*, Box 74; Finley to Samuel Zwemer, February 5, 1920, *Ibid.*, Box 77.

[42] Zwemer to Finley, February 3, 1920, *Ibid*, Box 77. For examples of the *Moslem World's* anti-Zionist style, see Alfred J. Nielson, "The International Islamic Conference at Jerusalem," *Moslem World*, XXII (October 1932), 347-353; Alfred J. Nielson ·, "Islam in Palestine," *Moslem World*, XV (October 1935), 354, 357. Finley, February 27, 1920, JHF, Box 74.

[43] Finley to McCrackan, January 28, 1920 and April 2, 1920 and McCrackan to Finley, February 27, 1920, *Ibid.*, Box 74.

[44] William D. McCrackan, *The New Palestine* (Boston, 1922), p. 37.

upon Great Britain in April, 1920. Not that the force of missionaryism abated, just the public clamor surrounding it. Missionaries,
however, were no less important. Some continued to hold the same
ideas about Jewish Bolsheviks, Jewish immigration and Jewish
history and occasionally, gave vent to their feelings.[46] For example,
W.D. McCrackan denied any semblance of the religious element in
Zionism. Christ, he said, had come to save the Jews in a spiritual
sense and it was their refusal to acknowledge Him that resulted in
Jewish national destruction. The return to Palestine predicated upon
Mosaic law was, incontestably, a "reactionary movement" destined
to fail because "the Jews are determined to live in B.C., whereas the
rest of the world lives in A.D."[47] The point to be made, though, is
that harangues of this nature were becoming increasingly uncommon
among missionaries, principally because they didn't work: diatribe
simply skirted the main issue which could no longer realistically be
skirted. The Jewish national home, to some the forerunner of a
Jewish state had been called into being. No amount of verbiage
could inhibit or erase it; to subdue it, a more subtle path would have
to be taken.

The very success of the American missionaries depended on the
consolidation of gains and the accumulation of powerful friends.
And missionaries never wanted for friends: John Whiting, himself
an ex-Vice Consul in Jerusalem, was head of the American Colony.
In this capacity, he served a dual function as missionary and State
Department informant.[48] Zionists frequently alleged that consular
officials were under the influence of the American Colony which, in
their opinion, was "distinctly hostile" to Jewish nationalism.[49]
Livingston Farrand, Chairman of the American Red Cross, never
dissociated himself from and even defended the anti-Zionism of his
subordinates.[50] Expansion of missionary work, however, would
soon entail something more: encouraging the growth of and bringing

[45] "A Peaceful Demonstration" (editorial), *The Jerusalem News*, I (March 1, 1920), 2, JHF, Box 74.

[46] Frederick Jones Bliss, "A Reply to Dr. Gottheil," *The New York Times*, April 11, 1920, Sec. 7, p. 9; Manuel, pp. 291-292.

[47] McCrackan, pp. 54, 255-260, 287-290, 298-302, 371-377, 386.

[48] Williams, *The New York Times*, July 10, 1921, Sec. 2, p. 3.

[49] Emanuel Neumann to Robert Szold, August 16, 1932, LDB.

[50] Edward Bliss Reed to Finley, January 19, 1920, JHF, Box 76; *Hearings... Committee on Foreign Affairs... on H. Con Res. 52*, p. 88.

important Christian organizations to Palestine with the objective of securing closer ties with the American Government.

One of these organizations was the Y.M.C.A. which, by 1932, had become a fixture in Jerusalem as a center for missionary activity in the Near East.[51] A very interesting anti-Zionist chapter could be written on a second organization, the Carnegie Foundation for International Peace and its association with Palestine in the first post-World War I decade. Inspired by Nicholas Murray Butler of Columbia University, the Carnegie Foundation began an independent study of Zionism in 1925. Henry Smith Pritchett, then a trustee and later the Foundation's President was advised by Butler to collect information which could best show how the Endowment could "establish contacts with the Arab world." Butler suggested that Pritchet initiate his research in Egypt and branch out to include Syria and Palestine. Pritchett departed in January, 1926, and traveled in the Near East for more than three months. He met and was impressed by Judah Magnes but, while in the Holy Land, spent much of his time at the American Colony outside Jerusalem and the Y.M.C.A. The Report he submitted was a classic anti-Zionist evaluation. Recommendations not included in the published report, but forwarded directly to the Endowment suggested that the Carnegie Foundation subsidize American missionary-oriented educational institutions in the Near East, notably the American University at Cairo, the College at Beirut, Robert College and Women's College, both at Constantinople.[52]

Still vibrant was Barton's A.C.R.N.E. On January 24, 1924,

---

[51] Robert D. Kesselman to Brandeis, August 30, 1932 and Joseph Baratz to Brandeis, August 12, 1932, LDB; " 'Y' in Jerusalem," *The Evening Mail,* September 29, 1923, p. 2; Sherwood Eddy, "Politics in Palestine," *The Christian Century,* XL (June 28, 1923), 813-816.

[52] Nicholas Murray Butler to Henry S. Pritchett, November 9, 1925 and Pritchett to Butler, November 10, 1925, Carnegie Endowment for International Peace (hereafter abbreviated CEIP), Vol 1.A.4. Trustees, no. 3192, Box 29, Butler Library, Columbia University; Pritchett to Henry Haskell (undated), no. 3209 and Butler to Pritchett, October 15, 1926, *Ibid.*; Henry S. Pritchett to the President of the Endowment, April 29, 1926, *Ibid.*, Vol I.A.2.b., Report no 459, box 6; "Pritchett Reports Zionism Will Fail," *The New York Times,* November 29, 1926, pp. 1, 3. Henry S. Pritchett, "Observations in Egypt, Palestine and Greece," *International Conciliateion,* no 225 (December 1926), 517-520; Henry S. Pritchett, *A Report to the President Concerning the Situation in the Near East,* November 18, 1926, CEIP, Vol I.A.2.b Report no. 478, Box 7. "The Zionists Enterprise" (editorial) *The New York Times,* November 30, 1926, p. 28; Henry S. Pritchett to Nicholas Murray Butler, September 18, 1929, Butler Papers.

Barton and a colleague, Dr. Caleb Gates, President of Robert College, were quoted by Secretary of State Charles Evans Hughes before a meeting of the Council on Foreign Relations to the effect that "smart leaders of American religious-philanthropic organizations in the Near East have a tendency to combine religious, educational and medical services with business investments." At the same time, petroleum groups in the United States, for example Standard Oil Company of New York, were pressuring the government to defend their financial interests in Palestine and the State Department may have looked to Christian organizations as the proper means of dealing peacefully with Arab resistance.[53] In return, the missionaries were offered security, and the United States Government became their dependable champion. The Anglo-American Convention of 1924 provided explicitly for the protection of missionary-educational enterprise and American investments. As a result of having achieved this privileged status, missionary controlled Syrian Protestant College, Robert College, Women's College and Cairo University continued to graduate Western-educated, pro-American Arabs and Moslems.[54]

Jewish determination to stay in Palestine and successive riots turned the Arabs into a desperate majority whose lukewarm attitude toward missionaries abruptly changed. Before 1930, the majority population drew a tacit distinction between educational people like Howard Bliss and business-oriented ones like Dr. Barton; no such distinction is evident afterwards. The Y.M.C.A. prospered; one of its leaders, Sherwood Eddy, justified the Arab case in American journals. The American press in Beirut was an important disseminator of anti-Zionist propaganda, much of it written by native Arabs.[55] It, too, was missionary-led and enjoyed its greatest success in the years immediately preceding World War II. Most important was that it attested to the feelings of the American Christian clergy in Palestine. In the United States, ministers with a proselytizing

[53] Paper entitled Future in Europe by Alan Gregg, March 1, 1940, WLW, Box 5; De Novo, pp. 169-176, 338, 344-345; Safran, pp. 37-38.

[54] *Carnegie Endowment for International Peace: A Report to the President Concerning the Situation in the Near East,* November 18, 1926, CEIP, Series I.A.2.b Report no. 478, Box 7.

[55] Sherwood Eddy, "The Grand Mufti on Palestine's Problems," *The Christian Century,* XLVI (December 18, 1929), 1573-1576; W.F. Boustany, *The Palestine Mandate: Invalid and Impractical* (Beirut, 1936).

tendency lent support to the *Missionary Review of the World*, an impressive looking periodical with little to say on the Arabs. Its point of view was strictly evangelical. Christians, it lamented, would accept neither Arab nor Jewish hegemony: the only hope for peace in Palestine was for both warring peoples to recognize the Saviour. Zionism, it maintained, was not only atheistic but also false, since peace in the Holy Land depended ''not (on)... the domination of one class or in the physical development of the country'' but upon the ''loyal submission to Jesus Christ.''[56]

But Jews were reluctant to submit to Christian teaching, and missionaries had ceased their activities in Palestinian Jewish communities before the Second World War. Nevertheless, Jews were not forgotten. Several clergymen, among them Bayard Dodge, the current President of the University of Beirut, continued cannonading ''extremist Jews'' and the partition formula.[57] They would not countenance Palestine as a refugee haven nor would they permit the Western powers to solve the ''Jewish problem'' by ''shoving Jews upon helpless Arabs.'' The fully developed argument was presented by an American minister, C.T. Bridgeman, in a letter to the *London Times*, written two weeks prior to the abandonment of the Peel plan. He disapproved of partition because it provided insufficient safeguards for the rights of Christian inhabitants residing in either the prospective Arab or Jewish state; missionaries preferred a continuation of the mandate. Bridgeman's comments were sent to the United States via George Wadsworth, who trusted that they would be of interest to the President and ''Christian leaders in the United States.''[58] At this stage, the Near Eastern Division of the State Department needed no prompting from the Palestinian-based consul. It knew full well the importance of ''good missionaryism.'' By 1941, it advised Cordell Hull to resolve the Zionist conflict once and for all by making certain ''effective promises to the Arabian groups'' through American Arabs and missionaries.[59]

---

[56] ''Unrest in Palestine,'' (editorial), *Missionary Review of the World*, LII (November 1929), 857-858; ''The Outlook in Palestine'' (editorial), *Missionary Review of the World*, LXIX (November 1936), 516-517.

[57] Bayard Dodge to Nicholas Murray Butler, February 16, 1937, Butler Papers.

[58] George Wadsworth to Cordell Hull, October 26, 1938, 867N.01/1295, *USFR: 1938*, II, 969-971, 974. Also see footnote 4 in text.

[59] Memorandum by Adolph A. Berle, Jr., 867N.01/1729 1/2, April 14, 1941, *USFR:1941*, III, 597-598.

For American missionaries, then, the years 1917-1941 were ones of expanded opportunity. Having recognized the advantages of performing services for the United States Government as well as to their individual faiths they acted and, by and large, were successful in maintaining State Department interest in their educational projects. They did not alter their previous convictions on Zionism and, in this respect, held a community of interest with some Reform Jews in the United States and a portion of the Arab American community.

VIII

Arab-Americans And Zionism

Jewish settlement in Palestine between the two World Wars enervated the group consciousness of Arab-Americans. Their search for a cultural identity began between 1900 and 1912, when the first of their twentieth century immigrant waves pressed into America. As a rough estimate, there were perhaps one hundred to one hundred fifty thousand Arabs in the United States between 1912 and 1929. About half of them became farm laborers and many became successful farmers in Georgia, Texas, Tennessee, Mississippi, New Mexico and Arizona. Another quarter stayed on the East Coast in New England and the Middle Atlantic states. The remaining numbers became small merchants, peddlers and unskilled workers in Illinois, Indiana, Iowa, Michigan and Ohio.[1] In order to preserve custom and heritage and to combat loneliness, many Arab immigrants congregated in either large or small groups in Houston, Galveston, Boston, Chicago, Detroit and New York City. Previously, the relatively small number of Arabs in the United States had little trouble assimilating. After 1912, though, they were to meet with the same dilemma as Jews, whose American ranks had been swelled by their recent East European migrations. For both Jews and Arabs, a new balance would have to be struck between a

---

[1] Abdo A. Elkholy, "The Arab-Americans: Nationalism and Traditional Preservations," *The Arab-Americans: Studies in Assimilation*, edd. Elaine C. Hagopian and Ann Paden (Willmette, Ill., 1969), pp. 3-5.

former national consciousness and the process of Americanization.

In the case of Arab-Americans, as with most American minorities, the building and shaping of a cohesive ethnic community involved the exploration of a common past and the discovery of common interests. But, by World War I, the burgeoning Arab population had no prior national consciousness to speak of. The Arabs who had come to America seemed to have been the most likely to assimilate. They were mainly Lebanese and about ninety per cent were Christians, the Moslems being fearful of leaving their homelands lest their offspring lose their religion "in the countries of disbelievers."[2] Furthermore, many Arab-Americans had escaped from Turkish rule to find a new life in the United States. Though proud of their heritage, they were understandably sensitive to and displeased with nearly four hundred years of Ottoman oppression. Having prospered in America, their national consciousness temporarily lapsed.

For most, the Balfour Declaration was a shock, but it was not wholly unexpected. It left a deep impression and acted as a catalyst directing the Arab world toward self-awareness. In future years, the English promise to the Jews proved to be a cataclysmic event, but only a slight tremor was felt in 1917. Initially, Arabs in the United States were taken aback. For decades past, it had been reported, not quite accurately, that Arabs and Jews in Syria lived in peace and contentment; never had the reigning brotherhood been as strong as in the first years of the twentieth century.[3] However, while in Palestine, William Yale noted that Arab-Jewish hostility was endemic before 1914, with the animus of the majority population focused on Zionist agricultural settlements.[4] Nevertheless, the tranquility myth was hard-dying.

To say that the Arabs in Syria were incapable of counteraction in the face of the Balfour pledge does them a disservice. They were momentarily bewildered but they were not paralyzed. Some must have witnessed, in an agonizing mental spectacle, the fruitless passage of four centuries. The moment of freedom, having arrived in the late afternoon of British Field-Marshal Edmund Allenby's

[2] Zeine, p. 220n. 1; Elkholy, *The Arab Americans*, p. 4.

[3] For example, see Ameen Rihani, "Palestine and the Proposed Arab Federation," *Annals of the American Academy of Political and Social Science* (hereafter abbreviated *AAAPSS*), 164 (November 1932), 67.

[4] E.H. Byrne, WYP,EMHC, pp. 29, 84.

November ride into Palestine, had turned to ashes. In a memorandum composed for the State Department, Yale told of the Arabs' initial upset; they were neither confused nor naive as to the implications of the Homeland Declaration. At the insistence of British officials, including General Clayton and Sir Mark Sykes, that homeland and state were not equivalent terms, the Arabs became more temperate and some even began to speak of cooperating with the Zionists.[5]

At this juncture, the Arab-Americans, at least those who were interested and aware, roused themselves from their lethargy. The presence of other liberation movements in foreign lands and their encouragement by avowed American patriots gave them food for thought. Nonetheless, the essential consideration came out of the Near East. T.E. Lawrence was leading his controversial "revolt in the desert." All the romance and brilliance of the Arab past appeared to be converging on a single moment in time and the Arabs of the United States were invigorated. Knowing little or nothing of the Sykes-Picot Agreement, Arab-Americans prepared, in early 1917, to consummate the promise of the Husain-McMahon correspondence against a rising tide of powerful American Jewish nationalism.

Although a division of belief on an eventual Syrian protector was present among American Arabs, it was transient. At the outset of the unity drive, two forces in the Arab populace had to be reconciled: the Christian and the Moslem. The problem was readily solved in America, where Christians outnumbered Moslems by nine to one and were therefore easily able to pursue their anti-Turk, pro-French, pro-English policy. Arab Moslems were less willing to declare against the Turks and when they eventually did, favored not the Continental powers but the United States. Arabs in America were united, as were Arabs in the Near East, in their detestation of Zionism.[6] Shortly, this factor out-weighed any and all minor differences.

In April, 1917, when Balfour arrived in Washington to confer with Wilson, the first Arab-American nationalist organization called

---

[5] William Yale to State Department, *Arab Activities and the Balfour Declaration*, Report No. 9, December 29, 1917 and William Yale to State Department, *Notes on the Zionist Question*, Report No. 10, December 31, 1917, WYPLC, Box 1; O.J. Campbell, *A Report On Zionism*, WYP,EMHC, pp. 1402-1403, 2705; Byrne, WYP,EMHC, pp. 89-90.

[6] Byrne, WYP,EMHC, pp. 50-52, 53n.

itself into session. It was a branch of an international society called the Syria-Mt. Lebanon League of Liberation (S-Mt.L.L.L.). The American group had contacts in Europe and South America. The purpose of the organization was to "secure the autonomy of Syria under the effective protection and guidance of a Western democratic power, preferably France." Further details were offered President Wilson in July when the American Arabs in the League petitioned the White House. At this early date, Arab-Americans put great stock in Wilson's statements, particularly those he had made relating to self-determination. Their first point expressed the wish that Syria come under the influence of a Western democracy after the war. This request demonstrated that Arab-Americans and other League members were realists, since the consensus viewpoint recognized the need for a trusteeship, under which a series of modernization programs would be launched in Syria. Second, Syrians "naturally look to France for such aid," because it "is realized that the United States" will not care to assume the responsibility and Great Britain's other responsibilities will prevent her from doing so." The remark concerning America's disposition was not only perspicacious in 1917 but also prophetic. Third, the deliverance of Syria from Turkish rule was "an absolute necessity." The Syrian Central Society and its affiliates put themselves on record as "opposed... to a Jewish state in Palestine" but, interestingly, four months before the Balfour Declaration was issued, were convinced that the Jews were going to receive a national home. They were prepared to accept this because they saw "no way out of it."[7]

In the United States, the organization's leaders were Lebanese Christians. The President and Secretary was Dr. E.G. Tabet, a Protestant and a graduate of the American University of Beirut; the Chairman was Ameen Rihani, an emigre and irreligious intellectual for whom Arab nationalism, itself, had become a unique faith.[8] Rihani, a poet and historian of King Ibn Saud, came to America in 1889, where he was a businessman and an actor before joining the Young Turks in the Revolution of 1908. After it was demonstrated to him that the Young Turks intended to treat the Arabs with the same ill-will as their predecessors, Rihani became an Arab nationalist, imbued with "nostalgic devotion toward his ancestral homeland."[9]

[7] De Novo, p. 113; Byrne, WYP,EMHC, pp. 48-49, 53, 107.

[8] Byrne, WYP,EMHC, pp. 21, 48; De Novo, p. 113.

[9] Esco Foundation, I, 552.

As the summer of 1917 waned, the Syria-Mt. Lebanon League of Liberation experienced a twinge of discomfiture, even disenchantment, with Great Britain. In July, the homeland idea was assented to grudgingly: in September, though, a change in attitude was heralded by Rihani. With established lives and homes in Russia, Germany, England and the United States, why, queried Rihani, "should the Jews want to be cooped up and cribbed in Palestine?" It was well-known, he stated, that they, as a commercial people, would find no prosperity in the Holy Land, an agricultural country with barely enough arable land to support its current occupants. Displaying the existing confusion among many anti-Zionists on the exact nature of Jewish nationalism, Rihani opted for religious orthodoxy. He maintained that Zionism was fundamentally a religious pehnomenon capable of reawakening dormant religious hatred. Its reactionary character stemmed from its non-national orientation; the erection of a Jewish state, he believed, would spell the return of theocracy which "only now (i.e. 1917) is losing its force in the Near East." Rihani said that he cherished the rebirth of all peoples whether Moslem, Christian or Jew under the banner of Syrian nationality. If the Jews intended to dominate, they would have to be prepared to fight, for the Arabs would permit them neither religious nor financial privilege. "In such a case," mused Rihani, "no one doubts who would succumb." Consequently, Zionism should appeal to no Jews, although its strategic benefits for Britain in Palestine were obvious. Rihani's last lines were perhaps penned to win the gratitude of Reform Jews. David Philipson and Samuel Schulman could not have put it more forcefully: Zionism would expose Jews in other lands, but principally in America, to increased anti-Semitism, hyphenism and dual allegiance. In case of a war between the United States and Palestine, he shrewdly asked, with whom would American Jews side?[10]

Soon, Arab-Americans and the League itself were given an additional reason for distrusting Britain. They were annoyed with Sir Mark Sykes, whose telegram of comfort to the Palestine Syrians, dated November 16, 1917, was sent without consulting the New York, Paris and London Arab committees. But they found that it was unprofitable to dwell on disappointments for too long. In America, the task for the ensuing months was to prepare for the armistice and present a united front at the peace table.[11]

---

[10] Ameen Rihani, "The Holy Land: Whose to Have and to Hold?" *The Bookman*, XLVI (September 1917), 8-14.

The pivotal position of Arab-Americans was acknowledged by E.H. Byrne who, in 1918, was in the process of preparing a comprehensive paper on the Syrians for the Inquiry. "The confidence of all factions among the Arabs in the United States," he wrote "may prove a determining factor in welding together" the sundry "racial and religious groups in Syria."[12] Evidently, many Arabs in the United States did feel strongly, did make their desires manifest and probably served as an inspirational force for their Near Eastern brethren. However, having an organization and program is one thing; prevailing on the uncommitted to accept them quite another. The concept of Syrian independence seemed, at once, all-encompassing and yet, uncomfortably vague. The fate of Greater Syria was no longer in doubt; it appeared unlikely that Britain would renege on the public promise to Husain. Since McMahon had not clarified the status of Palestine in a satisfactory manner and the Balfour Declaration extended the right of Jewish settlement there, it is conceivable that knowledgeable Arabs in America and elsewhere singled the Holy Land out as a potential trouble spot. This hypothesis, at any rate, would explain why Palestine, over and above the rest of the Arab domain, was honed in upon and the issue of Zionism came to the fore. Henceforth, the Arabs would weigh the measure of their success by their ability to stop the Jewish national home.

Even here, it was necessary to redirect opinion. In July, 1918, five of the eight Arab-American newspapers evidenced no hostility toward Zionism, possibly because they thought the movement to be apolitical. *Meraat-Ul-Ghaarb, Ash-Shaah, As-Siratt, Al-Hoda* and the *Eagle* felt that Arabs and Jews had a future together in the Holy Land if the two peoples would cooperate. Conversely, there were three, *As-Sayeh, Fatat* (Boston) and *Al-Fatat* (New York City), which envisioned a Jewish political entity and did not like it.[13] There was also a tendency to favor a United States rather than either a French or British trusteeship in Syria. By dint of the Fourteen Points, Wilson had rapidly become an Arab-American folk-hero. Joseph Balesh, Chairman of the Syria Division of the Fourth Liberty Loan, wrote to the President that he ardently looked to him as the

[11] Byrne, WYP,EMHC, p. 106.

[12] *Ibid.*, p. 32.

[13] "Editors of Arabian Newspapers Give Opinions on Zionism," *The Jewish Criterion*, 49 (July 5, 1918), 16.

guardian of Syrian national rights.[14]   A Unitarian minister from Boston, Abraham Mitrie Rihbany.underscoredthe trend toward pro-Americanism among Arabs in his book, published in October, 1918, entitled *America Save the Near East*. In it, he recommended an American mandate, which is something Syrian Christians would not have done and did not do a year before, appealed to moral mission-aryism, that is to say, "striking the Teuton" while heeding the call of the oppressed, asked for Palestine's internationalization, presented the Arab case and denied the efficacy of political Zionism. Rihbany also petitioned the British Government, then in occupation, to safeguard non-Jewish property and make Arabic the official lan-guage in Syria. [15]

By the end of the year, the S-Mt.L.L.L. was nearly impotent and new organizations had supplanted it. The program of free Syria was no longer as effective a rallying cry as anti-Zionism; the idea of a French protectorate was discarded and in its place there arose a demand for America's "evenhanded" justice. Most important, the distinctions separating Arab Christians and Arab Moslems receded as did nearly all the pro-Jewish commentary in the American or Anglo-Arab press. The Hamaliah Young Men's Society of New York, meeting in Brooklyn on November 8, 1918, reaffirmed the religious basis for Zionism and the fear that a Jewish state would be theocratic rather than racial. The members passed a resolution objecting to the "usurpation of Arab homes" and the "artificial flooding" of the Holy Land with Jewish refugees. The speakers at the affair, Professor Philip K. Hitti of Princeton University and Fuad I. Shatara, a surgeon living in Brooklyn, were, in later years, to add their influence to Rihani's.[16]

After the armistice, the Arab case against Zionism gained momen-tum, largely attributable to the Anglo-Jewish Reform press, the statements of Finley and the ministers, and the imminence of the international peace discussions. The fate of Arabian nationalism was as precariously suspended as that of the Jews' and both peoples

[14] De Novo, p. 113n.

[15] Abraham Mitrie Rihbany, *America Save the Near East* (Boston, 1918) intro-duction, vii, pp. 15-16, 26, 101-124, 164; "Zionism As A Menace to World Peace," *Current Opinion*, LXVI (February 1919), 110.

[16] *American Hebrew* enclosure dated November 15, 1918 in a letter from Edward Lauterbach to John Huston Finley, November 18, 1918, JHF, Box 74; "Oppose Zionist Plan," *The New York Times*, November 9, 1918, p. 4.

proved to be equally determined combatants. Syrian-Americans reacted as a typical interest group and started firing off propaganda material to Washington.[17] Fuad Shatara, who had recently founded the Syrian Educational League and the Palestine Anti-Zionism Society (P.A.Z.S.), wrote to Secretary of State Lansing that "Palestine is our home... we have been taken unawares."[18] Meanwhile, Shatara's two organizations contacted John Huston Finley, who was then in America. The correspondence intimated that a favorable word on the Arabs by the Red Cross Commissioner would offset reams of Zionist literature.[19] Hitti, then Secretary of the Syrian Educational Society, arranged for Finley to address a gathering December 27, on the topic of Turkish reconstruction; a second speaker was to be Abraham Rihbany. Alexander Sachs of the Z.O.A. requested permission, through Red Cross official Solomon Lowenstein, to write the arrangements committee about including a Zionist speaker.[20] Sachs' suggestion was not seriously considered, for he received no reply.

Ameen Rihani also sought the assistance of Finley. Within a space of ten days, he sent three separate communications to the Education Commissioner's office. "I am entirely in agreement with you," he wrote, "Palestine... certainly should be a trusteeship and not a permanent occupation or any form of colonization. Every Syrian is opposed to the idea of possession."[21] About three weeks later, December 19, 1918, Shatara sent Finley a list of P.A.Z.S. aims: to ask the peace conference to preserve Syria intact and that "Palestine not be detached therefrom," allow the Syrians to work out their problems without foreign interference, limit Zionist aspirations by the principle of the "open door" and grant no one "special privileges" which "would eventually lead to control of the land."[22] The open door, naturally, did not mean the same thing to Syrian-

[17] Manuel, p. 222.

[18] Selig Adler, *Jewish Social Studies,* X, 318.

[19] Shatara to Finley, November 27, 1918, JHF, Box 74.

[20] Alexander Sachs to Solomon Lowenstein, December 4, 1918, *Ibid.,* Box 75.

[21] Rihani to Finley, November 17, November 25 and November 27, 1918, *Ibid,* Box 76.

[22] Shatara to Finley, December 19, 1918, *Ibid.,* Box 74.

Americans in 1918 as it did in 1900 to Theodore Roosevelt. It meant Arab-Jewish cooperation within a unified Syrian state. The demands were well thought out, although Shatara implied that they had been hurriedly assembled: the American Jewish Congress was meeting at precisely the same time and the Arabs, cognizant of this event, raced to collect their information in the two weeks remaining before the peacemakers met in the Hall of Mirrors to redraw the world's maps.

The campaign of the Arab-Americans was successful in one major respect. On the eve of Versailles, national unity had been achieved. Another body, recently formed, the New Syria National League (N.S.N.L.), was instrumental in mobilizing opinion. Its motto was short but incisive: "Syria for the Syrians, independent and undivided."[23] The most accurate gauge of solidarity, and probably where the entire organizational campaign of the previous six months was directed, was the press. Winning it over meant accustoming all Arab-American newspaper readers to a single point of view. By mid-January, it was apparent that the feat had been performed. *As-Sayeh* had launched an uninhibited attack on Zionism.[24] *Al-Bayan*, a Druse sheet, and *Meraat-Ul-Ghaarb* were veering toward a Hejaz independence position; just a few months before, it will be recalled, the latter paper was hotly advocating a French protectorate and the general program of Dr. Tabet.[25] Arabs in Philadelphia had organized themselves and had cabled President Wilson and Prince Faisal of their desire to see Palestine united with the Hejaz Kingdom. The Zionists, who had been following the Arab surge closely, noticed that Arab newspapers in New York City were canvassing for new subscribers.[26] The newspaper offensive yielded unexpected dividends. Six weeks after its inception, other Arab societies were chartered to augment the N.S.N.L. and P.A.Z.S., namely the Syrian National Society and the Syrian-American Club. They were soon joined by Arab committees formed in Boston, Norfolk, New York City and Crookston, Massachusetts.[27]

---

[23] Zeine, p. 220n. 1.

[24] Alexander Sachs to Israel Friedlaender, January 23, 1919, IF.

[25] Unsigned memorandum to Stephen Wise, February 3, 1919, LDB; Habib I. Katibah, ed, *The Case Against Zionism* (New York, 1922), p. 43.

[26] Unsigned Memorandum to Wise, February 3, 1919, LDB.

[27] "America As Mandatory" (editorial), *New York Tribune*, March 1, 1919, p. 12; Selig Adler, *Jewish Social Studies*, X, 322.

Because a great number of their defenders were on hand, Arabs at Versailles were relatively inconspicuous. Still, they were surrounded by power: Reform Jews, Colonel House and the missionaries. In March and April, the loose confederation of ethnic groups and interests jelled: representing the Arab-American nationalists at Paris, and specifically the N.S.N.L. and the P.A.Z.S., was the Reverend Rihbany, who acted as Faisal's interpreter.[28] He must have had some doubts as to America's intentions because, originally, he advised the Emir to bargain for a French mandate. On April 20, 1919, however, in a dejected mood, he visited William Westermann. Possibly the King-Crane selection had altered his view on potential United States involvement. In any case, he asked Westermann to intercede with Faisal to persuade the potentate to reject French control. The Boston clergyman admitted that he was reluctant to approach Faisal, lest the King "suspect him of playing a double game." Rihbany added that, though he felt his American loyalties keenly, "I am an Arab by birth."[29] Confident that the Arabs had won much in the appointment of King and Crane, he left their advisement to the polyglot Syrian commission and returned to the United States.[30]

The backing enjoyed by the King-Crane Commission in its early stages evaporated, except for the Arabs. In the summer of 1919, the Arab-American press and the N.S.N.L. kept the faith.[31] The League slogan, "Syria for the Syrians, independent and undivided under American guardianship," topped every one of its circulars. It extolled the King-Crane Commission which was subsequently to assume a legendary quality for Arab-Americans and Palestinians alike.[32] When Zionism was not chastened at Versailles, when King and Crane returned unheralded, the Arabs stopped enumerating their victories and, to be sure, they had won more than they had lost in preceding months. No number of independent Arab nations, no reminders of Arab fulfillment and no European promises would ever

[28] Habib I. Katibah, *The New Spirit in the Arab Lands* (New York, 1940), p. 58.

[29] *PDWLW*, April 20, 1919, p. 65.

[30] *ALD*, May 28, 1919.

[31] *Executive Committee Minutes of the Zionist Organization of America,* August 11, 1919, IF.

[32] General Circular of the New Syria National League in JHF, Box 79.

cleanse the stain of colonialism which Zionism represented for them. They were continually to regard Jews as an invading Western people, having no relation to the Middle East or its problems. To them, Jews, with the exception of the old settlements in the Holy Land tracing back to antiquity, were foreigners, the vanguard of British imperialism or Russian radicalism, neither of which they had any use for in their struggle for freedom.[33] Furthermore, the Jewish faith was in conflict with Islam; more Jews would threaten Moslem spiritual supremacy and the inevitable consequence would be fanatic religious revivals and ceaseless war. Rightly or wrongly, Arab-Americans and their kinsmen were loath to admit, and this became more apparent later on, their Zionist antipathies extended beyond the borders of nationalism and politics into religion and economics. After all, some said, we are Semites and we, therefore, harbor no hatred for our cousins. But there was a significant reservation. Cousins referred only to Jews already in Palestine; the majority population claimed that Western Jews were not authentic Semites or, if they were, they were strangers whose claims, like Mark Twain's death, were "greatly exaggerated."[34]

In 1920, Lansing received eight Syrian societies in Washington.[35] The P.A.Z.S., aggrieved and depressed at the impending confirmation of the Jewish homeland and the British mandate, vented its anguish upon the Secretary of State. Writing to Washington in February, Shatara recapitulated the events of 1919 and then, pleaded with Lansing "to do justice for the Arabs." He placed worlds of confidence in the King-Crane Commission and its findings "as full proof of the Arab case." Recent developments, he said "have shown that it is impossible to grant Zionist demands without jeopardizing the rights of the Arabs." Shatara reminded him that prominent American Jews like Ochs, Morgenthau and Kahn "had openly opposed political Zionists."[36] With Wilson incapacitated and Lansing resigning, the Democrats decided to leave the Arab-Jewish cause celebre in the hands of their successors and the legacy

---

[33] Frank C. Sakran, "A Protest Against the Zionists in Palestine," *Current History*, XV (December 1921), 495-496.

[34] Shatara to Finley, December 19, 1918, JHF, box 74; "Ardent Zionists Mostly Non-Semitic Says Katibah," *The Syrian World*, VIII (June 1, 1934), 4.

[35] Zeine, p. 220n. 1.

[36] Shatara to Lansing, February 10, 1920, 867N.01/89, *GRDS:RG59*.

was passed along to Warren G. Harding.

The Republican "hot potato" was the Congressional Declaration of Sympathy for Jewish Palestine, which had been in the works since December, 1921. It was now April, 1922; Arab-Americans, Reform Jews, Zionists and former Red Cross officials, like Edward Bliss Reed, flocked to Washington. The Arabs had no hopes of renewing any of the old alliances but they were doubtless heartened by the Syrio-Palestinian anti-Zionist Congress of the previous September and the compassionate portrayal of the Arab cause in the *American Hebrew*[37]   The Palestinian unrest of the past two years, Arab-Americans alleged, had been precipitated by Zionists and vindicated the observations of King and Crane. The Palestine National League of Chicago protested the Lodge-Fish Resolution and demanded, via telegram to Charles Evans Hughes, an investigation into the circumstances surrounding the suppression of the King-Crane document; Youngstown Palestinians agitated for its immediate publication.[38] The King-Crane Report had obviously become more than a sentimental quest: for Arab-Americans it was a national symbol, in fact, a crusade.

On April 21, 1922, Arab-Americans testified before the House Foreign Affairs Committee.[39]   The combination of Arab address and Congressional interrogation consumed the greater portion of the day. A wire from the Palestine National League, read by Senator Lodge on the nineteenth, served to introduce the speakers, Shatara and New York attorney Selim Totah. It was apparent that the Arabs were no longer capable of treating with Britain or the Zionists; they had advanced beyond the 1917 position of reconciliation to a Jewish national home.   By late afternoon, a patchwork of anti-Zionism emerged from the statements: Arabs opposed the Hebrew language in Palestine, preferential treatment accorded Jews, Jewish immigration and the Balfour Declaration.[40]   On the other hand, they

[37] Harry Aaron Goodman, "Arabs and Jews in the New Palestine," *The American Hebrew*, 109 (October 29, 1921), 610, 623; Michael Lotfallah to the President of the Senate, September 24, 1921, *GRDS:RG59*.

[38] Palestine National League to Charles Evans Hughes, 867N.01/194, April 11, 1922 and K.J. Rafcedie to Senator Frank D. Willis of Ohio, 867N.01/196, April 11, 1922, *GRDS:RG59*.

[39] "The Lodge-Fish Resolution of 1922," *Palestine*, I (February 1944), 6-7.

[40] U.S. Congress, *Congressional Record, Sixty-Seventh Congess, Second Session* (Washington, 1922), part 5, p. 5760; Fink, p. 41.

acclaimed the Husain-McMahon correspondence and the idealistic Wilson spirit as embodied in the findings of King and Crane.[41] To quote Shatara, the resolution was "railroaded through" but his and Totah's vigorous prosecution of the case for King and Crane was successful.[42]   On December 2, 1922, *Editor and Publisher* reprodused the entire Report with appended anti-Zionist remarks from a representative sampling of Americans.[43]   For the discerning reader, the reason for all the secrecy was disturbingly explicit and laden with guilt: the American Government, ostensibly, did not want it known that its two commissioners had, in those exuberant times, encouraged an American mandate for Syria.   Now, the moment was gone and the area despoiled by predators.   This country, it appeared, was no less culpable because if its non-participation.   Arab-Americans were wont to charge the United States with an even greater crime: voluntary acquiescence in a conspiracy of silence.

The strain of the preceding months and the concentration of maximum effort on publicizing the King-Crane Report drained the Arab minority.   In addition, it was likely discouraged by the lack of tangible gain.   The promulgation of the King-Crane findings was positive but after that there was little in which to find solace.   The Jews were still coming to Palestine, the Jewish Agency was collaboring with the British, the Declaration of Sympathy was passed and the Balfour Declaration was alive and well.   Hence, discouraged Arab-Americans were confronted with a fait accompli.   For them, as for Arabs everywhere, there existed a compelling desire to turn the clock back and stop it at the instant of Allenby's triumphal march into Jerusalem.[44]

With the emergence of a new cause in 1929, the Arab-Americans were refreshed.   In the intervening years, the Anglo-Syrian press recorded the Jews' deleterious influence on "Syria" but organiza-

---

[41] *Hearings... Committee on Foreign Affairs... on H. Con. Res. 52*, pp. 136-144, 154-170.

[42] Fuad I. Shatara, "Mr. Lodge, Syria and Zion," *The New York Times*, December 16, 1922, p. 14; Harry N. Howard, *The American Inquiry*, p. 312n.

[43] "Between Ourselves" (editorial), *Editor and Publisher*, 55 (December 9, 1922), 30; "Our Turkey Supplement," *Editor and Publisher*, 55 (December 2, 1922), 1.

[44] A good example is "Famous Cities of Syria: Jerusalem," *The Syrian World*, I (April 1927), 39-45.

tional response was lacking.[45] The formation of an Enlarged Jewish Agency in 1929 meant, to *Meraat-Ul-Ghaarb*, that the Syrians "must conquer their own resources before the Zionists do."[46] All the spent force, however, did not coalesce into an explosive brew until August, when the J.A.P. held its first session and the blood-letting in Palestine resuscitated what many Arabs thought and Jews hoped was a dead issue.

Arab-American groups sedulously petitioned notables after the riots had begun. On August 30, 1929, a protest meeting was held in New York City and was presided over by Fuad Shatara, President of the Palestine National League (P.N.L.), Abbas M. Abushakra, General Secretary of the New Syria Party (N.S.P.) and Abd M. Kateeb, Secretary of the Young Men's Moslem Association (Y.M. M.A.). Abushakra carefully pointed out that the Arab attacks on Jews were not "religious" but politically and economically moti-vated. Besides underplaying the spiritual issue, which was primary in 1917, the Balfour Declaration was assailed with heretofore unprecedented ferocity. Messages indicting the Zionists were sent to President Hoover, Ramsay MacDonald, Senator Borah, Cardinal Hayes of New York, Secretary of State Stimson and Pope Pius XI; missives of encouragement and solidarity went to an array of Near Eastern rulers, including Faisal, then King of Iraq, the Imam Yaya of Yemen, King Riza Khan of Persia and Ibn Saud of the Hejaz.[47] A week later, Ameen Rihani headed a delegation, representing the N.S.P., the Y.M.M.A. and the P.N.L., which was received by Stimson at the Capitol. As with most of these visits, nothing was accomplished. If anything, the Secretary of State may have been less amenable to the Arabs than he was to the Zionists, simply because Arab-Americans sought a more activist position from the American Government than did the Jews. The latter desired that the President

[45] "Spirit of the Syrian Press," *The Syrian World*, II (October 1927), 53-56; "Spirit of the Syrian Press," *The Syrian World*, II (December 1927), 50-52; "Spirit of the Syrian Press," *The Syrian World*, II (May 1928), 44-48.

[46] "Spirit of the Syrian Press," *The Syrian World*, III (March 1929), 41-44.

[47] "Arab Sympathizers Petition Hoover on Palestine Trouble," *The World*, August 29, 1929, p. 2; "Arabs Here Assail Jewish Riot Views," *The New York Times*, August 29, 1929, p. 2. "Arabs Here Appeal to MacDonald for Aid," *The New York Times*, September 8, 1929, p. 22; "Borah to Speak at Garden Rally of Jews Tonight," *New York Herald Tribune*, August 29, 1929, p. 12; "Arabian Citizens in America Protest Against Unfairness," *The Jewish World*, XVI (August 31, 1929), 8.

stand by the Balfour Declaration and the Mandate. Since these were
established policies, nothing was demanded of the President save
that he be mildly agreeable, though uncommitted. What the Arabs
wanted was American intervention to overturn the Balfour Declaration, censure of England, and revision of the Mandate, all of which
required action.[48] If they had not already done so, Arab-Americans
learned, in 1929, that the isolationist position precluded any such
affirmative response.

The nationalist Syrian press in the United States was unsatisfied
with the outcome.[49] Salloum Mokarzel, editor of the *Syrian World*,
journeyed to Palestine, was there during the violence and reported
Arab helplessness to resist Zionist pressures. Tenant farmers, he
said, had been dispossessed when wealthy Arab landowners sold out
to Jewish nationalists.[50] Ameen Rihani toured the United States in
late 1929 and early 1930, trying to arouse popular sympathy for the
Shaw Commission. Zionist Jews, he claimed, were expansionist
and the Arabs would fight political Zionism to the end. Jewish
nationalists, he wrote in *Nation*, would be responsible for provoking
a pan-Islamic revolt and, appealing to the isolationist impulse, asked
whether Americans would care to be drawn in.[51] The Zionists
regarded him as too important a figure to ignore and, therefore, on
January 20, 1930, engaged him in debate. His opponent was Jacob

---

[48] Stimson to Paul Knabenshue, September 6, 1929, 867N.404 Wailing Wall/190
telegram, United States Department of State, *USFR:1929*, III, 56; "Arabs Ask
Stimson to Aid Palestine," *The New York Times*, September 7, 1929, p. 3; Albert
Howe.Lvbver, "The Conflict Between Jews and Arabs in Palestine," *Current
History*, XXXI (October 1929), 193; "Arab Interest Asks America to Assist in
Palestine Area," *The United States Daily*, September 7, 1929, p. 3; "Palestine
Riots Blamed on Jews by Arabs Here," *New York Herald Tribune*, August 29,
1929, p. 12; "Arabs Ask America For Its Good Offices," *The Springfield Daily
Republican*, September 7, 1929, p. 2; "Arabic Delegations Ask Stimson Aid," *The
World*, September 7, 1929, p. 2.

[49] Joshua Finkel to Cyrus Adler, August 30, 1929, AJC; "Spirit of the Syrian
Press," *The Syrian World*, II (January 1930), 45-47.

[50] Salloum A. Mokarzel, "Through Palestine During the Recent Uprising," *The
Syrian World*, IV (September 1929), 33.

[51] Ameen Rihani, "Palestine Arabs Claim To Be Fighting For National Existence," *Current History*, XXXI (November 1929), 274, 277-278; Ameen Rihani,
Zionism and the Peace of the World," *The Nation* CXXIX (October 2, 1929), 346-
347; Louis I. Newman, "Palestine Inquiry Report — Anti-Jewish Fellowship,"
Jewish Journal, III (April 16, 1930), 12. The Shaw Commission was a British-
sponsored inquiry into the reasons behind the Wailing Wall riots.

de Haas, whom Julian Mack said was "too philosophical for his audience."[52]   Carolin Flexner gave Herbert Lehman a slightly different review: first of all, she mentioned, the meeting was sponsored by the Foreign Policy Association and "never before in my life have I felt or seen anti-Semitism in mass." Playing for the sympathies of all those present, Rihani recommended "burning the Balfour Declaration" and suggested that, if the 1929 stalemate was not broken, "there would be general uprising... throughout Palestine, Transjordania, Syria, Arabia and India that would make the Western World realize the strength of the East." As for de Haas, she thought his speech "controlled and scholarly" but "as far as the meeting was concerned, did not equal the emotional appeal" of Rihani.[53]

As-Sayeh, Al-Bayan and *Ash-Shaab* were plainly anti-American in the following months. They also lashed out at Stephen Wise, British imperialism and the "rich... American Jews" who had invested in the J.A.P. It appeared to Arab journalists that Palestinians were "foreigners in their own country"; one paper tartly insinuated that New York become the Jewish national home. *Al-Bayan's* caustic rebuttal of Zionism was that it would be "easier for the Jews to reach the moon than to take possession of Palestine."[54]

As a result of the 1929 disturbances and subsequent British investigations, a new organization, the Friends of Palestine Arabs, was formed in the law offices of Selim Totah.[55] With this as with succeeding groups, there were three foci of discontent: the Balfour Declaration, land sales to Jews in Palestine and immigration.[56]
At the moment, though, the key was the Balfour Declaration and, in

[52] Julian Mack to Brandeis, January 20, 1930, LDB.

[53] Carolin Flexner to Herbert Lehman, January 20, 1930, HL.

[54] "Spirit of the Syrian Press," *The Syrian World*, IV (November 1929), 43-44; "Spirit of the Syrian Press," *Syrian World*, IV (December 1929), 45-49; "Spirit of the Syrian Press," *The Syrian World*, IV (October 1929), 47, 49; "Spirit of the Syrian Press," *The Syrian World*, IV (February 1930), 48.

[55] " 'Arab Friends' Conduct Anti-Zion Drive in U.S.," *The Jewish Review and Observer*, LVI (January 3, 1930), 1, 4.

[56] "Spirit of the Syrian Press," *The Syrian World*, IV (June 1930), 45-46; Fuad I. Shatara, "Defining New British Policy in Palestine," *The Syrian World*, V (November 1930), 9; George F. Hourani and Nabih A. Faris, "Jewish Immigration into Palestine," *Commonweal*, XXIX (November 11, 1938), 72-73.

anticipation of its abrogation by the Shaw Commission, the Arab press prematurely complimented itself on "successfully turning the Zionist tide."[57] When the Shaw findings disappointed, the Arabs took the initiative in trying to restore good relations with those Jews who opposed political Zionism and sterile British pronouncements.[58] For those "disillusioned" Jews, Arab-Americans talked of implanting religio-cultural Judaism in Palestine and implementing the Magnes plan.[59] In the 1930s, this particular approach was never really abandoned, although it was, at times, preempted.

The White Paper of 1930 and its subsequent reversal by Ramsay MacDonald aroused Arab American ire and electrified an already heavily charged atmosphere. Peter George, a lawyer and spokesman for New York Arabs, released a cautious statement on their behalf accepting the White Paper, though "not totally satisfactory," as a "starting point towards a fuller measure of (Arab) self-government and independence (in Palestine)."[60] His words were barely uttered when MacDonald recanted, thus igniting a new wave of Arab cynicism. That past June, quite a commotion had been stirred among Arab-Americans by the execution of three Palestinians who had participated in the Wailing Wall outbreaks. Additional accusations were leveled against Jews after the sentence was carried out, with special emphasis on the Jewish Labor Party which, newspapers

[57] "Spirit of the Syrian Press," *The Syrian World*, IV (February 1930), 49-50; "Political Developments in Syria," *The Syrian World*, IV (February 1930), 51-52.

[58] "Spirit of the Syrian Press," *The Syrian World*, IV (January 1930) 45-46; "The Palestine Issue" (editorial), *The Syrian World*, V (November 1930), 44. Testifying before the Shaw Commission, Hajj Amin El Husseini affirmed his belief in the veracity of the Protocols of the Elders of Zion. "Palestine Testimony Contradictory," *The Jewish Monitor*, XVI (November 22, 1929), 1, 6; Pierre Crabites, "A Jewish Political State in Palestine," *Current History*, XXXI (January 1930), 749-754; "Mufti's Testimony Shows Him to be Believer in 'Protocols of Elders of Zion' " *The Jewish Review and Observer*, LVI (December 13, 1929), 1, 4.

[59] "Spirit of the Syrian Press," *The Syrian World*, IV (January 1930), 48; "Spirit of the Syrian Press," *The Syrian World*, IV (December 1929), 50-51; "Objectives" (editorial), *The Syrian World*, VII (February 2, 1934), 4; "Correspondence," *The American Jewish World*, XIX (July 31, 1931), 7-8; Ameen Rihani, "Is Palestine Safe for Zionism," *Palestine and Transjordan*, I (November 21, 1936), 6-7.

[60] Fuad I. Shatara, "Defining New British Policy in Palestine," *The Syrian World*, V, (November 1930), 8; "Political Developments in Syria," *The Syrian World*, V (February 1931), 49-50.

declared, showed no inclination to ease the antagonism by hiring Arab workmen.[61] To the collection of combustible materials was added a new element. Quite unexpectedly, when it seemed as if the Arab-American offensive had been blunted by the Zionists, inspired help arrived. Twice, in 1931 and 1939, Mahatma Gandhi, a famous Hindu and a Moslem supporter who was also at odds with England, stiffened Arab resistance with his anti-Zionist declarations.[62]

Arab-Americans of long-standing were, by the mid-1930s, entertaining a wider audience. For one thing, a Syrian-Lebanese, Christian migration to the United States, occurring between 1930 and 1938, increased their numbers to a quarter of a million. For another, their national cause and plight, highlighted by the 1929 affray, attracted self-styled anti-imperialists like Professor William Ernest Hocking of Harvard University, Elihu Grant, professor of Biblical literature at Haverford College, and assorted Protestant ministers to their camp.[63] The world, in the 1930s was polarized by political ideologies and, accommodating the times, Arab-Americans pressed their abhorrence of "political Zionism," meaning the Balfour Declaration, immigration and land sales.

In November, 1932, the *Annals of the American Academy of Political and Social Science* devoted its entire issue to an overview and progress report on Palestine. Twenty articles covered the diverse aspects of Palestinian life; five were written by American Christians, seven by Jews and eight by Arabs. While the Gentile and Jewish contributors were exploring problems related to colonization, education, sanitation, medicine and economics, the Arab writers were distinctly political. Arab articles were more aggressive; at least five of them impugned the Balfour Declaration. Fuad Shatara,

---

[61] "Palestine," *The Syrian World*, IV (June 1930), 51-52; "Spirit of the Syrian Press, *The Syrian World*, IV (June 1930), 45; "Grave Situation in Palestine," *The Syrian World*, V (January 1931), 38.

[62] "Gandhi Gives Views on Zionism" *The New York Times*, October 2, 1931, p. 11; "Palestine Belongs to Arabs Says Gandhi In Word To Jews," *Christian Science Monitor*, March 3, 1939, p. 3.

[63] Elkholy, *The Arab-Americans*, p. 4. Arab-Americans, whose national visibility and influence increased after the 1929 disturbances, were closely allied with the American academic community. Harvard, Yale, Brown, Columbia and smaller universities were staffed with pro-Arab scholars, many of whom had journeyed to Palestine. The best known and most vociferous of these were Hocking, Grant, Harry N. Howard of Miami University in Ohio and Albert H. Lybyer of the University of Illinois.

heavily pro-Magnes, discussed the King-Crane Report, quoted freely from anti-Zionist Reform Jews and offered a program for Arab-Jewish cooperation. He proposed that a representative government be established in Palestine "along the lines of the White Paper," that Jews be guaranteed "their minority rights," that immigration be controlled by the principle of "economic absorptive capacity" set forth in the Churchill Memorandum of 1922, that development and conservation of natural resources be conducted for the benefit of the entire population, not a single element as had been done with the Rutenberg project, that Arab farmers, through relief, tariffs and farm credits, be protected "from the cause whereby he sells his land" and that social, medical, cultural, communal and business relationships be fostered among Jews and Arabs.[64] Habib I. Katibah, then editor of the *Syrian World*, praised the articles mightily.[65]

Shatara had said that Arab opposition to Zionism "is not religious." But, by all indications it was and continued to be from the year 1917 onward. In 1937, Habib I. Katibah incautiously stated that Arabs "must fear religious Jews most," since it was upon their "dogma" that Zionists fed.[66] Shatara would have been on safer ground had he stressed a change in priorities which permitted only occasional references to religious or "racial" Judaism. In actuality, his and Katibah's statements are not contradictory; there is a dichotomy in thought but it was a relative rather than an absolute difference which separated them and other Arab-American nationalists during the totalitarian decade of the 1930s. After the onset of Hitler, Arabs in the United States had, for obvious reasons, super-

---

[64] Fuad I. Shatara, "Arab Jewish Unity in Palestine," *AAAPSS* 164 (November 1932), 178-183; Khalil Totah, "Education in Palestine," *AAAPSS*, 164 (November 1932), 162; Ameen Rihani, *AAAPSS*, 164, 65, 67; George Antonius, "The Machinery of Government in Palestine," *AAAPSS*, 164 (November 1932), 55-61; Mogannem E. Mogannem, "Palestine Legislation Under the British," *AAAPSS*, 164 (November 1932), 54; Omar Bey Salih Al-Barguthi, "Local Self-Government Past and Present," *AAAPSS*, 164 (November 1932), 38; Jamaal Bey Husseini, "The Proposed Palestine Constitution," *AAAPSS* (November 1932), 22-26; Aouni Bey Abdul Hadi, "The Balfour Declaration," *AAAPSS*, 164 (November 1932), 14-15, 19-21.

[65] Habib I. Katibah, "A Book A Week," *The Syrian World*, VII (September 1, 1933), 4.

[66] Habib I. Katibah, "The Palestine Arab Case," *Palestine and Transjordan*, I (May 8, 1937), 5-6; Shatara, *AAAPSS*, 164, 179.

seded but never quite dispensed with the anti-Zionist religious argument. They were at great pains to dissociate themselves from the sort of anti-Semitism, primarily racial and religious, in which Nazi Germany was taking part. Thus they claimed incorrectly, but from necessity, that their Zionist position was purely political and in no way harbored a religious element.[67] The policy defined by this course of action, that is defense of German Jews and condemnation of Hitler, was, in the long run, insupportable. It was too easy to slip back into comfortable habits, as Katibah's assertions show. By virtue of this policy, however, and because they lived in the United States, Arab-Americans were at first enabled to resist Fascism, even after the Reich had begun to propaganidze in the Near East.[68] After 1939, though, accumulated setbacks for Arab nationalism and the increased strength of the Nazi Bund in the United States rendered the finely etched distinctions irrelevant and set Arab-American leaders, at least those that remained, upon a pro-Axis path.

By 1934, the Arab-American press was nearly unanimous in its advocacy of the political argument but nevertheless was often placed in an untenable position. While claiming to be anti-Fascist, it would not countenance the settling of dispossessed Jews in Palestine or anywhere else in the Middle East and displayed little concern for the fate of Jewry in general. The Zionists, having managed to stay on friendly terms with Faisal's son Abdullah, were contracting with him to buy Transjordanian land for the purpose of providing homes for refugees. The same procedure was being inaugurated in Lebanon, much to the displeasure, stated *Syrian World*, of native Arabs. When Zionists purchased from the Arabs the forbidding, marshlike tract of Huleh, on the Palestine-Syrian border, the same paper feared Jewish expansionism into Syria. In September, 1934, Fuad Shatara and an American Revisionist debated inconclusively on the aggressive nature of Zionism and its imperial ramifications.[69]

As the "creature" of Great Britain, political Zionism was daily vilified by the Arab press. After the Wailing Wall riots and MacDonald's failure to enforce the White Paper, Arabs throughout

---

[67] Fuad I. Shatara, "Affairs in Palestine," *The New York Times*, November 15, 1933, p. 20; "Fate Blinds Zionists" (editorial), *The Syrian World*, VII (June 23, 1933), 4; Habib I. Katibah, "The Nazis Goose-Step Before Their Gods," *The Syrian World*, VII (February 16, 1934), 5.

[68] Max Freedman, ed., *Roosevelt and Frankfurter: Their Correspondence 1928-1945* (Boston, 1967), p. 213.

the world became estranged from England. Greatly spurred by what most Palestinians interpreted as the negative consequences of British rule, Arab nationalism grew. In 1934, Near East Arabs asserted what the *Syrian World* termed their "progressive" nationalism by staging a commercial exposition to which Syrians, Lebanese, Egyptians and Iraqis contributed. Neither Zionists nor British officials were invited and later, the former were to anger the Arabs by holding a counter-exhibition which was said to have been encouraged by the Mandatory.[70] It followed that the Arabs would be affronted by the "collusion" and in the ensuing months, Arab-Americans projected a mystique of "unstoppable" Arab nationalism flying in the face of hated colonialism, its Zionist twin and Jewish Communism.[71] The *Syrian World* was jubilant over a minor confrontation between Palestinian Arabs and Jews in November, 1933. The Arabs, Katibah asseverated, bore no malice toward cultural Zionism, just toward the Zionism that bred "detestable nationalism as displayed by Hitlerism in Germany." Another commentator, a correspondent for *Al-Hoda*, stated that if the Zionists were allowed to establish a state in "another people's country" then the Arabs had the same prerogative in Spain. The changing times and injured sensibilities of Arabs were pungently portrayed by the *Syrian World*: in June, 1933, prior to his departure for London, Arabs thronged to greet King Faisal of Iraq

[69] "A Bad Bargain" (editorial), *The Syrian World*, VIII (April 27, 1934), 4; "Zionism Seeks to Invade Lebanon and Syria," *The Syrian World*, VII (June 23, 1933), 1, 2; "Zionists Set Foot in Lebanon," *The Syrian World*, VII (August 4, 1933), 1; "Syrians in Egypt Resent Conditions in Palestine Today," *The Syrian World*, VII (May 26, 1933), 6; Zeidan D. Zeidan, "130 Killed in Arab Warfare," *The Syrian World*, VIII (April 27, 1934), 1; "More Syrian Land to Pass into Jewish Hands," *The Syrian World*, VIII (January 3, 1935), 1; "Rich Plains Pass From Hands of Arabs to Jews," *The Syrian World*, VIII (December 6, 1934), 1; "Plan Three Zionist Colonies in Lebanon," *The Syrian World*, VIII (January 24, 1935), 1; "Buying Resort Hotels," *The Syrian World*, VIII (January 31, 1935), 1; "To Debate on Zionism," *The Syrian World*, VIII (September 21, 1934), 2; "Heated Arguments at Zionist Debate," *The Syrian World*, VIII (September 28, 1934, 2.

[70] "Arab Exposition in Palestine Rallies Opposition in Palestine," *The Syrian World*, VII (August 4, 1933), 1; "The Great Day of Araby" (editorial), *The Syrian World*, VII (August 4, 1933), 4; "The Mandate's Pet," *The Syrian World*, VII (January 26, 1934), 4.

[71] Khalil Totah, "An Arab Federation — Permanent Solution to the Palestine Problem," *Palestine and Transjordan*, I (December 12, 1936), 5-6; "Readers' Letters," *Palestine and Transjordan*, I (October 31, 1936), 9-10; "Communist Paper in Palestine," *The Syrian World*, VIII (January 10, 1936), 1.

and laid their complaints before him, including Jewish nationalism and British deception; a month before, General Allenby arrived in Palestine for a visit and none save Zionists welcomed him.[72]

Quickening the Arab-American national conscience was accomplished in the press and over the airways. Fuad Shatara became active in the latter medium with his frequent radio broadcasts. As a result, Syrian-Americans were well-informed on Near Eastern events and were also presented with a challenging point of view. They responded in kind. In 1934, Syrian committees were established in Worcester, New Kensington, Kansas City, Scranton, Syracuse, Richmond, New London, Akron, Waco, Shreveport, Paterson, Chicago, Cleveland, St. Petersburg and Wilkes-Barre.[73] Boston, traditionally a center of Arab-American settlement, gave birth to the New England Confederation whose objective was to organize the Syrian-Lebanese community locally and nationally. The Federation had, before 1941, reached a firm decision "that Zionism was a danger not only to the Arabs but also to American-Arab relations and to the best interests of the United States in that part of the world." On various occasions in the interwar period, "the Federation appointed committees to confer with high officials of the United States Government for the purpose of supporting... the independence of Lebanon and Syria from the Mandate power...." It also requested blanket support of all other legitimate Arab World causes.[74]

Mounting disillusionment with Britain played a decisive part in the events of 1936 to 1941. With Axis backing, the Arab Higher Committee was established in the midst of the 1936 general strike. Interestingly, a member of the Committee was Amil Ghori, a graduate of the University of Cincinnati.[75] By August, the Arab

[72] "Mr. Milkie Says," *The Syrian World*, VII (November 3, 1933), 1; "Thirty Lose Lives in Palestine Riots," *The Syrian World*, VII (November 3, 1933), 1; "Dr. Shatara Says," *The Syrian World*, VII (November 3, 1933), 1; Habib I. Katibah, "From East and West," *The Syrian World*, VII (November 3, 1933), 4; "All Palestine Greets Faisal," *The Syrian World*, VII (June 30, 1933), 1; "Allenby Visits Holy Land," *The Syrian World*, (May 19, 1933), 1.

[73] "Shatara Flays Zionism on Air," *The Syrian World*, VII (August 4, 1933), 2; "New Committees Formed," *The Syrian World*, VII (May 11, 1934), 3.

[74] Elaine C. Hagopian, "The Institutional Development of the Arab-American Community of Boston; A Sketch," *The Arab-Americans: Studies in Assimilation*, edd. Elaine C. Hagopian and Ann Paden (Wilmette, Ill., 1969), pp. 73, 75-76.

[75] Sumner Welles to Franklin Roosevelt, January 9, 1939, 867N.01/1365 *USFR: 1939*, IV, 694-696; Sachar, *The Course of Modern Jewish History*, 389.

National League (A.N.L.), under Fuad Shatara's leadership, was founded in New York City for the dual purpose of fund-raising and publicizing the Palestinian position. The League, in one of its publications compared Arabs to American revolutionaries and exhibited an uncommon familiarity with the anti-Zionist works of Vincent Sheean and William Ernest Hocking. Shatara's demands, though more strongly stated, merely reiterated the post-1930 objectives of Arab nationalists. In a poor but predictive choice of words, Shatara expressed his conviction that the Arabs would eventually take their place beside non-Arabs as "honorable members of a new world order."[76]

Arab-Americans felt that the time was ripe and their own sense of self developed sufficiently to take on the task of educating the American public on the Balfour Declaration and British "incompetence."[77] Until partition, individuals and organizations attempted to enlighten on several issues, among them the Copeland Commission, the Jewish Labor Party in Palestine and the necessity for a Jewish immigration ban. In an open letter to President Roosevelt, Shatara beseeched him to "apply the great principles of democracy" he used America to the Arabs in Palestine.[78] Another thought was injected by Peter George in December, 1936. George, a Socialist and an A.N.L. member had formed an Arab-Jewish committee, in which he had interested some prominent Jews. He favored a large Jewish immigration into Palestine on condition that Zionists would relinquish political nationalism.[79] His plan was to be of some help in subsequent discussions between Jews and Arabs but, at the moment, both ethnic minorities were preoccupied with the Peel investigation.

---

[76] Arab National League, *Whither Palestine?* (New York, 1936), pp. 7-35, 38-42; "Arab Support in America," *Palestine and Transjordan*, I (August 22, 1936), 3; Jacob Coleman Hurewitz, *The Struggle for Palestine* (New York, 1968), pp. 85-86; De Novo, p. 343.

[77] Nabih A. Faris, "The Need for Arab Publicity," *Palestine and Transjordan*, I (August 29, 1936), 5; "Arab vs. Jew," *Literary Digest* 121 (June 20, 1936), 16.

[78] "The American Senatorial Investigation," *Palestine and Transjordan*, I (October 10, 1936), 4; Albert Viton, "Can There Be Peace in Palestine?" *Christian Century*, LIII (September 9, 1936), 1195; "Protest Ignored," *Palestine and Transjordan*, I (November 28, 1936), 11; "Arab Activity in America," *Palestine and Transjordan*, I (November 7, 1936), 4; "The Arab National League," *Palestine and Transjordan*, I (December 26, 1936), 4.

[79] Max Rhoade to Louis Brandeis, December 9 and December 11, 1936, LDB.

Some American citizens of Arab descent, Khalil Totah for one, testified before the British commission in early 1937. The American Arabs were counting on Christian support and may have even anticipated some aid from Agudath Yisroel.[80] The A.N.L., whose powers of persuasion with American Presidents and cabinet officials had yet to be tested, hoped for better luck in this endeavor than its predecessor organizations had experienced. Knowing the terms of the Anglo-American Agreement of 1924 and the sections pertaining to possible United States action in the event of a Mandate change, the A.N.L. petitioned Hull not to "discriminate between one group and another group of citizens" with reference to the Holy Land. The document was presented to Hull presonally by Ameen Rihani, who had just returned from Palestine, the moderate Peter George and the Reverend Benjamin Hofiz, all of whom lived in New York. The State Secretary made no comment to the delegates' avowal that "the Arabs are not against the Jews, they are against political Zionism." Shatara, himself, borrowing from George's calm, considered evaluation, retracted some of his harsher anti-Jewish statements. For a brief time he too supported the Magnes formula and glowingly described the Palestinian desideratum: Arab-Jewish amity and the inauguration of a "Semitic Renaissance" that would embrace not only the Holy Land but "the entire Arab World."[81] The arrival in the United States of Dr. Izzat Tannous, a Palestinian representative of the Arab Supreme Council, arrested the somewhat milder, hopeful tone that had possessed Arabs in recent months. The first week in June was marked by a resurgence of anti-Balfourism with Hocking and Rihani broadcasting their feelings over New York radio.[82]

---

[80] "Arabs Heard, Ending Inquiry on Palestine," *The New York Times*, January 19, 1937, p. 11; "Palestine Royal Commission Returns Home," *The American Hebrew*, 140 (January 29, 1937), 823; "Readers' Letters," *Palestine and Transjordan*, I (February 29, 1937), 9; "Religion vs. Zionism," *Palestine and Transjordan*, I (February 13, 1937), 5-6. Khalil Totah was an Arab Quaker and principal of the Friends' Boys' High School at Ramallah, Palestine.

[81] "Hull Hears Arab Plea," *The New York Times*, February 2, 1937, p. 12; "Memorandum of Arab National League," *Palestine and Transjordan*, I (March 6, 1937), 719; Fuad I. Shatara, "The Palestine Question," *Palestine and Transjordan*, I (May 15, 1937) 5, 7.

[82] "Arab Delegate Warns on Palestine," *The New York Times*, May 30, 1937, p. 17; Harry Schneiderman, "Review of the Year 5697," *AJYB*, XXXIX, 241; "Cackling Geese," *The Reform Advocate*, XCIII (June 25, 1937), 3-4; "Zionism Decried By Arab Leaders," *The New York Times*, June 6, 1937 , p. 37.

Partition was as ominous for the Arabs as it had been for American Zionists. Shatara and the A.N.L. were aghast. Habib I. Katibah, Secretary of the League, bluntly declared that no Arab would agree to a Jewish state in Palestine and demanded an immediate halt on land sales.[83] At this point, a series of meetings occurred in New York City between Arabs and non-Zionists, probably convened upon the latter's initiative. The Jewish discussants, George Backer, Morris Waldman and Lewis Strauss were arrayed against their Arab opposite numbers, Tannous and the two Americans, Rihani and Shatara. The goal of the talks was twofold: to present Britain with a united Arab-Jewish front against partition and inform the League of Nations Mandates Commission that an alternate plan was being devised.   The presence of deep seated resentments among the negotiators did not augur well. "The Arab leaders placed the entire responsibility for the situation now existing upon the Zionist leaders, especially Jabotinsky and Weizman (sic)."   The Arabs further contended that all the events had been carefully staged to arouse support for political Zionism throughout the world.   "Finally, the Arabs blamed the non-Zionists for keeping silent and allowing Zionists to turn a simple problem into a catastrophe." As an absolute minimum, Shatara requested that Arabs remain in the majority and the political ambitions of Zionism be abandoned. The Shatara plan had incorporated sections of the George and Magnes outlines. The main feature was that Jewish immigration was not to be stopped, simply curbed, so that the Jewish population would never exceed forty per cent of the total.[84]

Habib Katibah and Khalil Totah regarded the initial reaction to the modified Magnes proposal as distinctly favorable.[85] But the urgency to implement bi-nationalism dissipated when Britain showed

[83] "Palestine Division Protested Here," *The New York Times*, July 9, 1937, p. 10; "Betrayal: Aroused Leaders Hit 'Jewish State' Idea," *The Jewish Transcript*, XIV (July 16, 1937) 5; Habib I. Katibah "Can Jews and Arabs Live Together?" *Philadelphia Jewish World*, XXIV (July 19, 1937), 8; "Palestine Division Arouses World-Wide Interest, Arab Leaders Protest and Jews Seen Divided," *Philadelphia Jewish World*, XXIV (July 10, 1937), 8; Berkowitz, pp. 460-461; Habib I. Katibah, "Conditions in Palestine," *The New York Times*, October 1, 1938, p. 20; "Letters to the Editor of the Times on Issues of Current Interest," *The New York Times* August 14, 1937, Sec. 4, p. 9.

[84] *Confidential Report on Exchange of Views Between Arab Leaders and Group of Jewish Gentlemen*, July 14, 1937, AJC: Wise to Brandeis, July 16, 1937 and Z.O.A. cable to Weizmann, July 16, 1937, LDB; Susan Lee Hattis, *The Bi-National Idea in Palestine During Mandatory Times* (Haifa, 1970), p. 185.

no interest. Thereafter, Arab-Americans resumed an uncomplicated anti-partition, anti-Zionist offensive. In January, 1938, Arabs picketed a Zionist conference in Washington, D.C. The signs, held high, blended anti-Zionism and anti-Judaism all too closely: "Arabs demand they shall no longer be victims of Jewish... Zionism", "Is there a Jewish problem? Then Madagascar"; "Zionists claim Palestine as reward for influencing America to enter World War.... Is that Americanism?"[86]

Before the year was out, the Peel partition plan had been crushed and Arabs had played no small part in the outcome. Two weeks before partition was revoked, the A.N.L. and the Arab press implored Americans not to lose sight of the Arab cause; they appealed to Roosevelt and Hull to isolate themselves from the Palestine tangle. Fund-raising committees to aid non-Jewish Palestinians were established in New York City and even Syrian Catholics were represented. In an optimistic climate, then, Shatara had begun to expect Zionism's defeat at the British Round Table discussions.[87]

In November, 1938, the A.N.L. invited two prominent Palestinians, one of them Amil Ghori, to the United States with the purpose of introducing them to State Department officials. The Arabs, escorted by Peter George, were received by J. Rives Childs of the Near Eastern Division. They tried to impress upon him the importance of ending Jewish immigration into Palestine, stopping land sales and abrogating the Balfour Declaration. Besides this return to the pre-Magnes position, they wished the help of England in the erection of an Arab federation to include Palestine. Above all, said the group, they had come to the conclusion that Arab nationalism and

---

[85] Khalil Totah, "The Palestine Triangle," *Asia*, XXXVII (November 1937), 748-750; "Arabs Here Offer A Palestine Plan," *The New York Times*, August 7, 1937, Sec. 4, p. 5; "The Will to Unity Spells A Happier Year" (editorial), *The American Hebrew*, 141, (September 3, 1937), 5; Khalil Totah, "The Palestine Triangle," *Palestine and Transjordan*, II (February 5, 1938), 5-6.

[86] "Arabs Versus Zionists in the United States," *Palestine and Transjordan*, II (May 7, 1938), 4, 7.

[87] "Arab Congress Hostile," *The New York Times*, October 8, 1938, p. 8; "U.S. Studies Plea in Behalf of Jews," *The New York Times*, October 13, 1938, p. 16; "Ask U.S. to Keep Out of Palestine's Affairs," *Brooklyn Daily Eagle*, November 9, 1938, p. 25; "Arab Protest Appeals," *The New York Times*, October 16, 1938, p. 33; "Syrians Aid Palestine Relief," *The New York Times*, January 9, 1939, p. 5; "Leaders Here Hail Palestine Parley," *The New York Times*, November 10, 1939, p. 5.

Zionism were incompatible. They "hoped" that America would remain "steadfast in the face of Zionist pressure" and stand by "those principles enunciated in the State Department announcement of October 26, 1938. What impressions they made is not recorded but it was apparently satisfactory.[88]

No one invited George Antonius. He just came and created a sensation in New York's Arab community, which now numbered fifty thousand. The ostensible reason for Antonius' arrival in the United States was to publicize his new book, *The Arab Awakening*.[89] This he did and during his stay, traveled to Columbia University to see an old friend, Nicholas Murray Butler.[90] It was certainly not Antonius's first trip to America, nor his first association with American institutions. He was, like Rihani, a scholar, a Lebanese Christian to whom Arab nationalism had become paramount. After having served as a high official in the Mandatory administration, he joined the Near East Institute of Current World Affairs, an American-endowed body. His work prevented him from taking a Columbia teaching post offered by Butler in 1936 but he nonetheless kept his friendship with the College President viable.[91]

Timely is the word for Antonius's appearance in January, 1939. He was in the United States to mobilize the important Arab-American community behind anti-Zionism. Apparently, the Round Table discussions were snared in a cul-de-sac and, if possible, Antonius wished to avoid another bout with partition or something equally unsatisfying. His book, more propaganda than history, is not well-documented, considering the depth with which he treats his topic. He talked of Palestine as if it were an immense property, the most important spot to the Arabs in the world. He discussed the Husain-McMahon correspondence, the British design behind the Balfour Declaration, the inability of Jewish nationalism to cope with anti-Semitism and the economic failures of Zionism in Palestine. He treated the Nazi outrages upon Jews as a purely Western problem, a

---

[88] Memorandum of Conversation by J. Rives Childs with Peter George, Jamil Beyhum, Amil Ghori, Wallace Murray and Paul Alling in Washington, January 30, 1939, 867N.01/1402, *USFR:1939*, IV, 701-703; "Arabs Here Warn of Boycott of United States," *The New York Times*, November 12, 1938, p. 30.

[89] "Palestine," *Time*, XXXIII (January 30, 1939), 17; Paul Novick, *Solution for Palestine: The Chamberlain White Paper* (New York, 1939), p. 30.

[90] George Antonius to Nicholas Murray Butler, January 16, 1939 and Butler to Antonius, January 17, 1939, Butler Papers.

situation for which Arabs should neither be held accountable nor responsible.[92]   The dedication was to Charles R. Crane, who subsidized the writing; he was dubbed "affectionately... Harun Al-Rashid."[93]

Before the contents of the White Paper were divulged, the Foreign Policy Association staged another debate, this time between Shatara, Sir Ronald Storrs and Robert Szold. It was evident that the American Arab leader detested the Briton more than the Jew.[94] And this was a pattern that, once set in motion, was not easily reversed. It was a short step from revulsion with Britain to utter despondency and revulsion with the United States, the step itself facilitated by the close bond existing between the two countries. A hint of things to come was found in the words of Habib I. Katibah. In May, 1940, the editor of the *Syrian World* expressed a half-hearted hope for an Allied triumph, but he spared them no sympathy: "Should the Totalitarian States come out victorious, all... is not lost.... Out of the jaws of ruthless tyranny," he intoned, "the sweetness of... peace will come forth."[95]

---

[91] Esco Foundation, I, 552; "Palestine Royal Commission Returns Home," *The American Hebrew*, 140 (January 29, 1937), 823; At Columbia, in 1936, Butler took advantage of the favorable anti-Semitic atmosphere and the recent demise of Professor Richard Gottheil to nominate George Antonius for the position of visiting lecturer in Semitics and Near Eastern Affairs. Antonius was competent, knowledgeable but an anti-Zionist and, pointedly, an Arab. Butler had asked William Westermann what he thought of Antonius' appointment; Westermann responded positively. Stephen Wise was informed by another Columbia professor and also by Mrs. Gottheil, whose shocked letter of protest reached President Butler's desk on September 12, 1936. Butler responded that, personally, he saw nothing amiss with Antonius, who had been recommended by "competent scholars," was "an outstanding layman of the Greek Orthodox Church," was friendly with Jews, Moslems, Catholics and Protestants and was known to be "deeply concerned to find a solution for the Palestinian problem." See Nicholas Murray Butler to Mrs. Richard Gottheil, September 12, 1936, Mrs. Gottheil to Butler, September 12, 1936, and Wise to Brandeis, Frankfurter and Mack, September 21, 1936, LDB; Nicholas Murray Butler to William Linn Westermann, October 5 and October 12, 1936, WLW, Box 1.

[92] George Antonius, *The Arab Awakening* (New York, 1965), pp. 177, 262-274, 285-298, 313, 387-398, 403-412.

[93] Memorandum by Westermann, December 5, 1938, WLW, Box 2. Harun Al-Rashid means "Aaron the Rightly Guided."

[94] "Palestine Forum Hears Three Opinions," *The New York Times*, April 2, 1939, p. 28.

By 1941, the Grand Mufti was leading the pro-Axis Arab revolt in Iraq and was in the pay of the Reich. In the United States, the anti-Zionist feeling among Arabs was considerable.[96] The State Department conducted an Arab-American attitudes survey in April, 1943, which revealed that the A.N.L. "favored the development of an independent, federated Arab state in the Near East." The man who conducted the poll, Harold Hoskins of the Division of Foreign Activities Correlation, found that most Arabs were loyal to the United States and their modest request was that America not become allied to either the Zionists or the Arabs in Palestine. The only fear expressed by any of the Syrians interviewed, he emphasized, was that Britain, by being too pro-Zionist in Palestine, "would antagonize the seventy million people of the Arab-speaking world and would thus give German propaganda its opportunity to gain support it could not otherwise obtain."[97]

Hoskins's conclusions were not altogether borne out by the facts. The disappointments proved too great for American Arab nationalist leaders and the A.N.L., their principal political organization. In 1941, the League received the endorsement of the Nazi-run *World Service* and American Bund National Secretary, James Wheeler Hill. After Pearl Harbor, the A.N.L. was dissolved. In the same year, Habib I. Katibah distributed some of the writings of Ahmed Hussein, founder of the Fascist Green Shirts and Young Egypt Party; the suicide of Fuad I. Shatara threw American Arabs into confusion and left a leadership gap in the community that would not immediately be filled.[98]

The Arab-American attempt to thwart a Jewish state in Palestine was not successful. The sort of leadership that emerged, fundamentally drawn from the professional and intellectual classes of the Eastern seaboard, was tenacious and aggressive, but not sufficiently in touch with Arab Americans in far-flung communities throughout the United States. At crucial times, for example in 1919, 1929 and

[95] Katibah, *The New Spirit*, p. 292.

[96] "Arab Anti-Zionist Activities in the United States," *Palestine Affairs*, I (February 1946), 8-9; Sachar, p. 461.

[97] Memorandum by Wallace Murray, April 10, 1941, 867N.01/ 1740, *USFR: 1941*, III, 594-597.

[98] John Roy Carlson, *Cairo to Damascus* (New York, 1952), p. 55; "Arab Anti-Zionist Activities in the United States," *Palestine Affairs*, I, (February 1946), 9.

the late 1930s, theses small elites could not count on strong, united support from their own people. Naturally, this made their appeal to Government less effective and diminished their total impact on American foreign policy. Significantly, though, the anti-Zionist campaign of two decades duration served to develop a formidable set of historic, political, economic and social arguments against a Jewish state, many of which endured beyond 1941 and are widely utilized today. If one measures success by the durability of an idea, the old leadership's contribution cannot be gainsaid.

IX

Conclusions

Two significant conclusions emerge from this study. First, with the exceptions of some A.J.C. members, the American Council for Judaism and the Agudath Yisroel, there were by 1942 practically no Jewish critics of Zionism in the United States; second, the non-Jewish opposition, from lack of unity and loss of cause, crumbled into angry fragments. Along the way, it has been learned that certain dates were important to all the critics; 1917, 1919, 1921, 1924, 1929, 1933, 1937 and 1939. These years, themselves, tell a story: one of rise, decline, revival and eclipse of Zionist criticism in the United States.

The year 1917, via the Balfour Declaration, launched Zionism upon its political career, which was not nearly as ambitious as some of the critics made it appear.[1] A source of unity for Reform Jews, missionaries, intellectuals and Arabs was the assumption that "state" and "national home" were synonymous. Secretary of State Lansing and Colonel House joined them at the outset in leveling the state accusation against Brandeis and Weizmann. Their suspicions, however, find no justification in either of these two Zionists' writings or correspondence. The limit of commitment was to a Jewish commonwealth which might, sometime in the future, become

---

[1] If Zionism were truly political, the Jews could have gone anywhere. The fact that they did not indicates that Palestine was, for most Zionists, endowed with a religio-historical significance as well.

self-governing. Whatever plans existed were certainly not immediate nor were they well-defined. The door to Arab conciliation was left ajar. Either the first critics knew something about Jewish nationalism that Zionists themselves were not yet aware of or, for their own reasons, wished to mislead others as to Zionism's implications.

Many Christian writers during the interwar period charged American Zionists with dual nationality, dual allegiance and hyphenism. There were several other ideas to choose from as well. Perhaps a Zionist "state" would become a theocracy, a regression to a primitive past welcomed by Orthodox Jews. Or, quite the contrary: Palestine would attract the radical, Bolshevist Jewish element yearnint to establish an atheistic workers' state. A major concern of many was the issue of anti-Semitism and its inevitable upturn should Zionism prevail. But, it was neither a new story nor their story; they had gleaned their knowledge from America's liberal Jews, who had been developing an effective anti-nationalist platform since 1898. A good deal of anti-Zionist information was filtered into the Government by America's Reform Jews, principally Morgenthau, Edelman and Elkus. Thus, liberal Jews were influential in anti-Zionism. Only the missionaries, perhaps, were as ardent as they.

By the Peace Conference, further divisions among Jews occurred. The A.J.C. experienced such a division as anti-Zionists and non-Zionists split. The former were opposed to Jewish migration to Palestine and a Jewish cultural renaissance; the latter, only objecting to the possibility of a Jewish political structure, were not. American Jews further differentiated themselves into distinct factions when Louis Brandeis issued the proclamation of Zionist aims in 1918. In that year, the United States had five Jewish nationalist organizations, all cutting across religious lines: anti-Zionists, non-Zionists, Zionists who differed from Weizmann, Zionists who agreed with Weizmann and apathetic bystanders. With the exception of the Poale Zion, Socialists were subsumed with non-Zionists; later, Communists were to be classed with anti-Zionists.

The segmentation of American Judaism was completed in 1919. February through May were the high-water months of anti-Zionism. Then, it seemed to all Zionists, European and American, as if the opposition forces were poised on the brink of union.[2] In truth, the proponents of anti-Zionism were never more powerful nor more

[2] Israel Friedlaender to Julian Mack, January 28, 1919, IF.

threatening to the Jewish national home than at that time. Anti-Zionist statements from Arab-Americans, liberal Jews, mission-aries, professors and State Department officials desired that a special commission proceed to the Holy Land to ascertain the wishes of the people.   Charles R. Crane was an ideal candidate as was the theologian Henry Chruchill King to lead the group. The makeup of the commission with its strong missionary character testified to the power of anti-nationalism at Versailles.

Fortunately for the Zionists, the loose confederation of interests failed to cooperate with one another after the departure of the King-Crane Commission. No sooner were the Zionists unburdened than internal pressures began to mount. Brandeis's visit to Palestine in August, 1919, his presentation of an antithetical plan to Weizmann's and his fall from grace in 1921 created another crisis for the national home. Ironically, though, this occurrence was a disguised blessing for the Z.O.A. and W.Z.O. Zionists and the American Jewish community as a whole began to reverse the 1917-1921 trend toward division. Talking of American Zionism, Stephen Wise said that, in the twenties, "we were a movement. Then we became an avalanche and we tumbled along with many a boulder of Jewish respectabi-lity."[3] His hyperbole notwithstanding, Rabbi Wise had a point. Although the Jewish world was "still firmly divided into Zionists and (critics) in the 1920s," some events tended to draw American Jews of all Zionist persuasion together.[4]   But the process was laborious and slow. The irreversible transformation was a long time coming. The arrival of Hitler in 1933 muffled but did not scotch debate. Various reservations lingered until America's second in-volvement in a world war necessitated a truce. This laying down of arms was the forerunner of American Jewry's permanent peace on Palestine.

American Jewish communal leaders had been attempting to mediate their differences since the passage of the National Origins Act. It disturbed Louis Marshall and Stephen Wise to the extent that both their attempts to free Zionism from real and imagined restraints took on new meaning. Marshall had been discussing the possibility of joining the Jewish Agency with Weizmann but never lost his admiration for Brandeis's methods. During Zionism's five-year

[3] Eric Goldman, *Rendezvous with Destiny* (New York, 1955), p. 232.

[4] Robert Weltsch, "Yesterday's Youth Rebellion," *The Jewish Spectator*, XXXVI (April 1971), 12.

"slow period," 1923-1927, Marshall was often more cordial to the deposed Z.O.A. President than he was to the European with whom he was bargaining. Thus, the split in Zionism, occurring when it did, was possibly the most fortunate Zionist event of the first postwar decade. It offered Jewish Zionist critics the option of chastening Weizmann without denying the movement as a whole. Since Wise and Marshall opposed and lobbied against exclusion, the Brandeis-non-Zionist link was firmed. With the quota systems established in Europe and the Untied States, Jews who maintained a cultural and religious link with their past, like Marshall, Adler, Lehman and Warburg, were wont to regard Palestine as the only avenue of escape. Brandeis's economic program was one with which they could comply because it had no political overtones; as far back as 1920, Julian Mack had declared against the concept of "diaspora nationalism." Through Brandeis, then, a portion of the American Jewish community, an important minority even to Weizmann, was inexorably drawn toward Palestinian renovation in cooperation with Zionism.

The period 1929 to 1933 was a watershed for America's liberal Jews. In those years, they proceeded to abandon one course for another. Both non- and anti-nationalists were attracted to the Zionist orbit through the Jewish Agency for Palestine, which became a Jewish meeting ground. In it, anti-Zionists became non-Zionists and non-Zionists were found midway between their old position and Zionism.[5] Recalling the compromise in 1940, Morris Waldman said "When the non-Zionists entered into the enlarged Agency in 1929, it was clearly implied if not expressed that they recognized the ultimate objective of the Zionist movement, namely a state and though... they made it clear that they would not endorse the idea of a state, it was assumed they would not combat it."[6] By 1930, though not committed to what they considered the climax of Jewish national-ism, non-Zionists were bound to the Balfour Declaration.

The Agency was also an irresistible magnet for Brandeis. It was he and not Weizmann who had the trust and individual support of the non-Zionists; it was he and not Weizmann who had cracked the anti-Zionist armor with his pleas for economic equality and civil liberties for Palestine's Jewish population. Again, the word "state" was

---

[5] Oscar I. Janowsky, "Zionism Today," *The Menorah Journal*, XXXI (Autumn 1943), 233.

[6] Morris Waldman to Edward S. Greenbaum, March 7, 1940, AJC.

never employed by either Brandeis or Weizmann.   But, as was shown above, the non-Zionists believed this to be a Zionist goal, and anti-nationalists were no less suspicious.   American Jews, however, were always more wary of Weizmann's socio-educational than Brandeis's economic plans.   Weizmann, cognizant of his limited appeal to Jewish-Americans and the reality that large sums of money were necessary to support his refugee program was instrumental in returning Brandeis, the man he had unseated in 1921, to leadership in 1929-1930.

Stephen Wise, Felix Frankfurter, Julian Mack and Robert Szold did not mellow during the nine-year Lipsky regime.   But, over the same span, American Zionism's loss in prestige made a crucial difference to Weizmann: by 1929, he was prepared to tolerate, even welcome, the return of Brandeis because he could no longer do without him.   During the "interregnum," as some Brandeis-associates called their exile, the skills of the one-time leaders sharpened.   Zionism was not ready for a Western model after World War I, but the Brandeis people were not discouraged.   Not only did they bring wealthy and prominent American Jews into the Agency fold but the time was fortuitously ripe for their second coming. Weizmann's faith in England as Jewish protector in Palestine was, after the Wailing Wall incident, unfounded.   He was repudiated in the United States, and tacitly acknowledged his defeat by with-drawing his support from Louis Lipsky.   After 1929, the entire debate concerning Great Britain's ability and desire to establish a Jewish national home was reopened, except on much broader terms. Enter Brandeis and most importantly, Stephen Wise and Jacob de Haas, who were skeptical of Britain's promises since the mid-1920s, the time of Revisionism's de facto break with Weizmann's "gradu-alism.   Questions that had not been raised could, by 1930, no longer be hidden.

What were these questions?   They originated in 1924, when American quota laws blocked Jewish migration from Eastern Europe.   They were aggravated by the riots of 1929 and the White Paper of the following year: they had to do with the acknowledged responsibility of the Western, Christian world toward its Jews.   Was there, indeed, ever such a responsibility and, if there was, had the Jews been relying too heavily upon it?   Had Weizmann relied too heavily upon it?   From the Brandeis legions, there issued a resound-ing "yes" on both points. The Z.O.A. under Brandeis had brought Herzl's philosophy to maturity.   Aside from its contribution to Palestinian economic theory, American Zionism, as distinguished from Weizmann and the Lipsky-run Z.O.A., fervently desired that

Jews disentangle themselves from the favors of an alternately guilty-hostile Christian world. Weizmann denied in 1920 and 1921, that Zionism was a Western or American concern, at least in terms of ideological contribution. He thought Americans were useful fundraisers but hopeless, naive thinkers. At that time, Jewish anti-Zionists would have readily concurred with him. Rabbis Schulman, Landman, Rosenau, Levi, Hirsch and Philipson publicly denied that the problem of Jews, East or West, was an American affair. The insecurity wrought by the 1924 immigration legislation, compounded by the 1929 riots and Hitler's accession to power four years later, placed a great strain upon America's "liberal" Jews. By the time the Jewish Agency for Palestine was founded, they may have been ready to condone Palestinian Jewish life, but it still would have seemed vaguely disloyal to treat with Weizmann. Brandeis, however, presented an American, if Zionist, point of view which could be borne with few qualms. Even among non-Zionists, this was so. After six years of tedious negotiation with Weizmann, the enlarged J.A.P. was formed but Marshall and Warburg always looked to Brandeis as a mediator between themselves and the Europeans.

The year 1929 was pivotal for America's Jews, not only because they found themselves striving toward unity within the Jewish Agency for Palestine but also because they confronted new foes. The critics of Zionism were experiencing what may loosely be termed an "escalator effect," that is they were not coordinated because some were on the rise and others on the decline. The influential Jewish and Christian anti-Zionists of 1919 were relatively silent a decade later. The missionaries were content after the 1924 Anglo-American Convention; by 1930, the sensation they had helped to create at Versailles was forgotten. Some remained determined anti-Zionists and their State Department connections were still valuable but they lost their militant flair.

The non-Jewish critics on the ascendent were the Communists, both Stalinist and Trotskyite, and Arab-Americans. Each group pursued its individual avenue of Zionist attack. The Hitler years played havoc with both sets of criticism: by 1942, the Jewish Communists and their Gentile associates were urged to make peace with the Zionists, at least for the duration, and the Arab-Americans had few leaders and no organizational machinery left. Hence, anti-Zionism lapsed.

What of the anti-nationalist Reform Judaism after 1929? Did it progress beyond reluctant inclusion in the Agency with Zionists and non-Zionists? Most definitely, it did. By November, 1937, the *American Hebrew* had, at last, fallen into line with the C.C.A.R.

proclamations of 1935 and May, 1937. This, in itself, marked the end of an era. The journal announced the failure of Reform Judaism and the Reformed Jewish Temple to attract and keep younger people. Actually, it was more an admission of failure for the Jewish religion in general whether Reform, Conservative or Orthodox. Jews who felt their Judaism differently, the editorial said, could no longer look to the synagogue. Those who were disillusioned by the burial of the liberal dream in Germany, the paper complained, found an outlet, not in spiritual Judaism but in secularization and Zionism.[7] But this confession of discontent was no more than that. it was not an attempt to stem the Zionist tide, merely a plaintive cry to understand it. American Jewish liberals and their hopeful philosophy were also "victims" of German fascism; as the world into which their ideology was born slowly crumpled, so did their resistance. Brandeis had, in 1929, been favorably disposed to the seating of Rabbi Samuel Schulman on the J.A.P. Executive. In a decade, with the minor exceptions of Rabbi Lazaron, Lessing Rosenwald and the soon-to-be established American Council for Judaism, Palestinian Jewish immigration was the desideratum for which all American Jews fought. In 1941, former distinctions, like anti-Zionist, non-Zionist, Brandeis Zionist and Weizmann Zionist were hardly applicable. There were no Jewish critics of Zionism to speak of. When they lost their Jewish adherents, the Gentile critics lost a great deal. As a direct consequence of Hitler's regime and the Evian conference, non-Jewish liberals and intellectual journals began to speak out in favor of transporting Jewish refugees to the Holy Land. After Munich and the British White Paper of 1939 there were probably as many Christian Zionists as anti-Zionists in the United States. Non-Jewish critics were diffuse and the Arab-Americans had faltered. Disunity reigned as it had since 1919 when, very briefly, the anti-Zionist coalition verged on deposing Jewish nationalism. The State Department, in the past a rather enthusiastic receptacle for anti-Zionism, could only be relied upon to support the missionary interest.

By way of summary, then, interwar Zionist criticism compartmentalizes into three phases: the first, 1917 to 1919, was a time of growth and peak strength; 1920 to 1928 was a period of Jewish infighting and Zionist decline but not of intense criticism from without; 1929 to 1941 saw a resurgence of non-Jewish anti-Zionism

---

[7] "Judaism and Secularism" (editorial), *The American Hebrew*, 142 (November 19, 1937), 3.

under the leadership of new groups. The revival however, was short lived. At the time of Roosevelt's war declaration, a failure to coalesce on anti-Zionism and its consummate unpopularity as an anti-Jewish mode of expression presaged its speedy demise.

The anti-Zionists never had enough in common. Besides anti-nationalism or anti-Judaism, they were hard put to blend any other of their interests. For instance, the powerful 1919 alliance of intel-lectuals, missionaries, Arabs and Reform Jews were gratified that they had participated in a campaign that had led to the selection of King and Crane. After the Commission departed, the interests did not really fall into quarreling; they drifted apart, naturally. The Arabs and missionaries, James Barton for one, were not the best of friends. The Reform Jews hastily returned to the United States and became embroiled with Jewish concerns: the Weizmann-Brandeis melee, Zangwill's speech and a defense of their own stand before non-Zionists. Non-Jewish professors like Westermann and Yale, former State Department officials turned academics, were formid-able but scattered.

One reason that the critics never fully meshed was confusion on the nature of Jewish nationalism. Some opposed a "state" (mission-aries, anti-Zionists and non-Zionist Jews and Arab-Americans after 1930), some opposed a religious revival (liberal Jews, Arab-Ameri-cans at Versailles and missionaries), some the economic motives of the Zionists (Brandeis, the Arabs, the Socialists and the Commu-nists, all from different aspects) and some the very thought of Jewish migration to Palestine (especially liberal Jews, Communists and King and Crane). Some changed arguments in midstream and lost their chance to achieve credibility.

A transformation of the latter sort occurred among Arab-Ameri-cans.. From an historical viewpoint, they and their Palestinian kinsmen had the best anti-Zionist arguments. But, they damaged their chances for success by indecision. Arab-Americans, generally, were not anti-Semitic, the latter phrase being used to connote an anti-Jewish bias prevalent in the United States. The type of rhetoric they employed until 1920 was closest in style and content to that of the liberal rabbinate and non-Jewish scholars. Arab-Americans had few thoughts of a political entity when they reluctantly approved the national home idea in July, 1917. With America at war and patriotism at its height, the dual allegiance-hyphenism construct made headway. Ameen Rihani feigned indifference to Palestine. His pressing concerns, inferred in his articles, were for Jewish assimilation and its success in a superheated climate.

Following the 1929 riots, the Arab-Americans did an about-face.

Their reliable friends were still Gentile academics, but their major appeal altered to fit the times. In the 1930s, Arab writers asserted that a Jewish political state had been the perpetual bone of contention between Zionists and Arabs. The Jewish religion, they maintained, had never been an issue; it was always welcome in Palestine. Also present was a tinge of anti-Jewish anti-Semitism. Due to the exigencies of the time, however, the political argument was fast losing ground. Excluding Jewish Communists, the Orthodox Agudah and Lazaron, non-Jewish Americans, Moslems and the State. Department had no organized Jewish opinion to present in defense of anti-Zionism: even Jewish Socialists and the C.C.A.R. after 1935 were advocating a Palestine refuge for Jews.

Only after disunity among Zionist critics was complete did the "Jewish state" idea come into being. And it was not Brandeis or Wise but Weizmann who first enunciated it. After the partition fracas and the White Paper, Weizmann proved more receptive to the lessons being taught by Wise, Szold and Mack: that the Jewish home was as much a Western, American concern as it was East European. No Jew could rightfully claim a monopoly on Palestinian life and its development. With Weizmann's assistance, the American Zionists wrested the so-called "Jewish question" from the hands of the Christian nations and advanced a solution which was uniquely their own. Under Brandeis and Wise, the American Zionists accomplished far more than their economic innovations in Palestine would indicate. They reoriented centuries of Jewish thought; they taught their co-religionists to look East rather than West for the redress of past indignities. In essence, the creation of industry and independent agriculture rung the curtain down upon Weizmann's philanthropic approach.   Whereas the European preached Palestinian Jewish reliance upon world Jewry and Great Britain, the Americans' message was self-help, independence. The Jews of the Holy Land would have to learn to rely on themselves, place confidence in their own talents, if they were to survive.

By the end of 1941, the Jewish Agency Executive, combining the wisdom and energy of former anti-nationalists and non-nationalists with those of Weizmann and Wise, felt that it was necessary to formulate the ultimate aims of Zionism before the war ended. A comprehensive solution to the Jewish problem demanded the transfer of substantial portions of European Jewry to Palestine and such an undertaking required a large-scale development of Palestine's resources, which could be achieved only by endowing the Jewish national home with the independence of a state. This view, assumed by Zionist critics since 1917 to be an accurate one, was publicly expounded for the first time by Zionists in January, 1942. Writing in *Foreign Affairs* at that time, Chaim Weizmann stated that Jews should be "able to achieve their freedom and self-government by establishing a State of their own and ceasing to be a minority dependent on the will and pleasure of other nations." This was hardly the Weizmann who sought the olive branch as late as September, 1937. After Munich and the British White Paper of May, 1939, even he had lost his confidence in England. His article was given formal endorsement and general publicity at a conference of all Zionist parties and organizations held in May, 1942, at the Biltmore Hotel in New York City. There, a resolution was adopted demanding the opening of Palestine to Jewish immigration to be controlled by the Jewish Agency, in whom "should be vested the authority to develop the country in such a way as to establish it as a Jewish land integrated in the structure of a new democratic world."[8] Thunderous applause, an affirmation of unity, stirred the assembly and closed an age of Zionist criticism in America.

[8] Israel Cohen, *A Short History of Zionism*, pp. 181-182.

Bibliography

Manuscripts and Archival Materials

As Cited in Text

AJC   American Jewish Committee Archives, New York City.

JB   Joseph Barondess Papers, New York Public Library.

           Eleanor Robson Belmont Collection, Columbia University
New York City

           Sol Bloom Papers, New York Public Library.

LDB   Louis D. Brandeis Papers, Zionist Archives, New York City

Butler PapersNicholas Murray Butler Papers, Columbia University, New
York City.

CEIP   Carneigie Endowment for International Peace, Manuscript
Collection, Columbia University, New York City.

JHF   John Huston Finley Papers, New York Public Library.

IF   Israel Friedlaender Papers, Jewish Theological Seminary,
New York City.

GRDS:RG59 *General Records of the Department of State, Record Group
59, Decimal File 1910-1929*, Zionist Archives, New York
City.

MH   Morris Hillquit Papers, Tamiment Institute, New York City.

HL   Herbert Lehman Papers, Columbia University, New York
City.

ALD   Albert Lybyer Diary in Albert Lybyer Papers, University of
Illinois Library, Urbana, Illinois.

JGMcD   James G. McDonald Papers, Columbia University, New York City.

ERAS   Edwin R.A. Seligman Papers, Columbia University, New York City.

Albert Shaw Papers, New York Public Library.

BCV   Baruch Charney Vladeck Papers, Tamiment Institute, New York City.

Frank P. Walsh Papers, New York Public Library.

WLW   William Linn Westermann Papers, Columbia University, New York City.

Henry White Papers, Columbia University, New York City

WYP,EMHC William Yale Papers, Edward M. House Collection, Yale University Library, New Haven, Connecticut.

WYPLC   William Yale Collection, Acquisition 2206, Library of Congress.

Public Documents

Congressional Record, 1919, 1922, 1929, 1932, 1936-1939, 1941-1942.

U.S. Congress, House of Representatives, *Hearings Before the Committee on Foreign Affairs, United States House of Representatives, Sixty-Seventh Congress, Second Session, on H. Con. Res. 52 Expressing Satisfaction at the Re-creation of Palestine as the National Home of the Jewish Race.* Washington, Government Printing Office, 1922.

USFR: U.S. Department of State. *Papers Relating to the Foreign Relations of the United States,* 1917, 1921-1925, 1929, 1932, 1936-1941. Washington, Government Printing Office, 1932, 1936-1940, 1947, 1953-1955, 1958-1959.

USFR: Lansing Papers   U.S. Department of State. *Papers Relating to the Foreign Relations of the United States: The Lansing Papers* 1914-1920, 2 vols. Washington, Government Printing Office, 1940.

USFR:PPC   U.S. Department of State. *Papers Relating to the Foreign Relations of the United States: The Paris Peace Conference 1919,* 13 vols. Washington, Government Printing Office, 1946.

Personal Interview

Mrs. May Bromberg, at Bund Archives, New York City, September 13, 1972.

Yaakov Shalom Hertz, Bund Archives, New York City, September 11, 1972.

Emanuel Scherer, at Bund Archives, New York City, September 12, 1972.

Newspapers

American Jewish Tribune, 1929
Brooklyn Daily Eagle, 1917, 1929, 1937-1938.
Christian Science Monitor, 1917, 1921-1922, 1929-1930, 1936-1937, 1939.
Day (Yiddish), 1937.
Dearborn Independent, 1920-1922.
Die Naye Welt (Yiddish), 1917-1918.
Evening Mail, 1923.
Freiheit (Yiddish), 1922, 1929-1930, 1937.
Hadoar (Hebrew), 1937.
Jewish Week, 1972.
New Leader, 1929, 1938-1939.
New York Daily News, 1929.
New York Herald, 1917, 1919.
New York Herald Tribune, 1929-1930, 1939.
New York Sun, 1936.
New York Telegram, 1929.
New York Times, 1917-1941, 1972.
New York Tribune, 1919.
Socialist Call, 1936, 1939.
Springfield Daily Republican, 1929.
United States Daily, 1929.
Washington Post, 1917, 1919.
Western Worker, 1936-1937.
Workers' Age, 1934, 1936, 1938-1939.
World, 1921, 1929.

Periodicals

American Hebrew, 1917-1926, 1928-1930, 1936-1941.

American Jewish Chronicle, 1940.

American Jewish Historical Quarterly, 1968, 1970.

American Jewish Times, 1936-1938.

American Jewish World, 1917-1923, 1930-1931, 1937.

American Scholar, 1933.

American Socialist Monthly, 1936.

Annals of the American Academy of Political and Social Science, 1932,
1972.

Asia, 1922, 1929-1930, 1937-1938, 1941.

B'nai B'rith Messenger, 1922, 1925, 1936-1939.

Bookman, 1917.

Buffalo Jewish Review, 1930, 1937.

Century Magazine, 1919.

Christian Century, 1923, 1929-1930, 1935-1939, 1941.

Commonweal, 1929-1930, 1932, 1937-1939.

Council News, 1957.

Current History, 1921, 1925, 1927-1931, 1933, 1937.

Current Opinion, 1918-1919, 1921.

Daily Worker, 1929, 1936-1937, 1939.

Denver Jewish News, 1919-1924.

Editor and Publisher, 1922.

Emanu-El, 1917-1918, 1920-1923, 1925, 1930, 1937.

Forum, 1921.

Globe and Commercial Advertiser, 1920-1921.

Hadassah Newsletter, 1941-1942.

Harper's Magazine, 1930, 1938.

Hebrew Standard, 1919, 1921, 1922.

Herzl Year Book, 1963.

Hibbert Journal, 1918.

Independent, 1919.

Industrial Unionist, 1939.

Intermountain Jewish News, 1928, 1936, 1939.

Jewish Advocate, 1921-1922, 1930, 1937.

Jewish Chronicle (Brooklyn), 1923, 1925.

Jewish Chronicle (Chicago), 1936-1937.

Jewish Chronicle (Detroit), 1929-1930, 1935-1936.

Jewish Comment, 1917-1918.

Jewish Community Press, 1936-1938.

Jewish Criterion, 1917, 1921.

Jewish Examiner, 1937-1939.

Jewish Forum, 1939.

Jewish Guardian, 1929.

Jewish Independent, 1930.

Jewish Journal, 1930.
Jewish Ledger, 1937-1939.
Jewish Life, 1937-1938.
Jewish Monitor, 1929
Jewish Press, 1930.
Jewish Quarterly Review, 1936.
Jewish Review and Observer, 1917, 1919-1921, 1928-1930.
Jewish Social Studies, 1948, 1967, 1970.
Jewish Spectator, 1937.
Jewish Spectator, 1971.
Jewish Standard, 1937, 1939.
Jewish Transcript, 1926-1927, 1929-1930, 1936-1938.
Jewish Tribune, 1917, 1921-1925, 1928, 1930.
Jewish Voice, 1917-1918.
Jewish Voice (Communist), 1941-1942.
Jewish World, 1929, 1937.
Journal of Contemporary History, 1971.
Journal of Religion, 1933.
Literary Digest, 1919-1923, 1925-1926, 1929-1931, 1933, 1936.
Menorah Journal, 1926, 1929-1931, 1938, 1943.
Midstream, 1971.
Militant, 1929.
Missionary Review of the World, 1929, 1936.
Modern View, 1917-1923, 1928-1930, 1937.
Moslem World, 1932, 1935, 1942.
Nation, 1929, 1936-1938.
New International, 1938-1939.
New Jewish Chronicle, 1918-1920.
New Liberation, 1937.
New Masses, 1934-1936, 1939.
New Republic, 1919, 1929-1930, 1937, 1938.
North American Review, 1919-1920.
Opinion, 1937-1938.
Outlook, 1916, 1930.
Palestine, 1944-1946.
Palestine and Transjordan, 1936-1938.
Political Science Quarterly, 1919.
Reform Advocate, 1917, 1919, 1921-1923, 1925, 1928-1930, 1937.
Reformed Church Review, 1920.
Review of Reviews, 1918, 1929.
Revolutionary Age, 1930-1931.
Scribe, 1920-1923, 1929-1930, 1937.
Sentinel, 1924.

Southwest Jewish Chronicle, 1937.
Spectator, 1939.
Syrian World, 1927-1931, 1933-1935.
Texas Jewish Herald, 1937.
Time, 1939.
Union Bulletin, 1918, 1921.
Weekly People, 1939.
Westchester Jewish Weekly, 1937-1938.
Workers' Council, 1921.
World Tomorrow, 1929-1930.
World Unity, 1930.
Yale Review, 1920
Youngstown Jewish Times, 1937.

Reports

Conference on the Perpetuation of Judaism. Cleveland, Union of American Hebrew Congregations, 1927.
Jewish Press Abstracts (cited as JPA), 84 Reports, March-June, 1921.
Non-Zionist Conference Concerning Palestine: Verbatim Report of Proceedings, October 20-21, 1928. New York, 1928.
American Jewish Committee: Twelfth Annual Report 1919-1920. Philadelphia, Jewish Publication Society of America, 1926.
American Jewish Committee: Nineteenth Annual Report 1926-1927. Philadelphia, Jewish Publication Society of America, 1926.
American Jewish Committee: Twentieth Annual Report 1927-1928. Philadelphia, Jewish Publication Society of America, 1927.
American Jewish Committee: Twenty-First Annual Report 1928-1929. Philadelphia, Jewish Publication Society of America, 1928.
American Jewish Committee: Twenty-Second Annual Report 1929-1930. Philadelphia, Jewish Publication Society of America, 1929.
American Jewish Committee: Twenty-Third Annual Report 1930-1931. Philadelphia, Jewish Publication Society of America, 1930.
American Jewish Committee: Twenty-Fourth Annual Report 1931-1932. Philadelphia, Jewish Publication Society of America, 1931.
American Jewish Committee: Twenty-Ninth Annual Report 1936-1937. Philadelphia, Jewish Publication Society of America, 1936.
American Jewish Committee: Thirtieth Annual Report 1937-1938. Philadelphia, Jewish Publication Society of America, 1937.
American Jewish Committee: Thirty-First Annual Report 1938-1939. Philadelphia, Jewish Publication Society of America, 1938.
Central Conference of American Rabbis: Twenty-Eighth Annual Convention

June 28-July 4, 1917, Cincinnati, C.J. Krehbiel Co., 1917.
Central Conference of American Rabbis: Twenty-Ninth Annual Convention June 28-July 4, 1918. Cincinnati, Bacharach Press, 1918.
Central Conference of American Rabbis: thirty-Second Annual Convention April 13-17, 1921. Richmond, Old Dominion Press, 1921.
Central Conference of American Rabbis: Thirty-Fourth Annual Convention June 27-July 2, 1923. Richmond, Old Dominion Press, 1923.
Central Conference of American Rabbis: Thirty-Fifth Annual Convention June 26-30, 1924. Richmond, Old Dominion Press, 1924.
Central Conference of American Rabbis: Fifty-First Annual Convention June 18-23, 1940. Philadelphia, Jewish Publication Society Press, 1940.

Pamphlets

Adler, Cyrus. *Observations on the Report of the Palestine Royal Commission.* n.p., 1938.
Adler, Felix. *Nationalism and Zionism.* New York, The American Ethical Union, 1919.
American Jewish Committee. *Digest of American Editorial Opinion on Topics of Interest to the Jews.* Pamphlet no. 13. New York, 1938.
American Jewish Committee. *In Vigilant Brotherhood.* New York, Institute of Human Relations, 1965.
American Jewish Committee. *Jewish Post-War Problems: A Study Course Unit VI Palestine in the New World.* New York, The American Jewish Committee, 1943.
Arab National League. *Whither Palestine: A Statement of Facts and Causes of the Arab-Jewish Conflict in the Holy Land.* New York, the Arab National League, 1936.
Bernheim, Isaac Wolfe. *An Open Letter to Rabbi Stephen S. Wise.* Louisville, 1922.
Browder, Earl. *the Jewish People and the War.* New York,. Workers Library Publishers, 1940.
Glazer, Simon. *The Palestine Resolution: A Record of Its Origin.* Kansas City, Mo., Cline Publishing Co., 1922.
Grant, Elihu. *Palestine Today.* Baltimore, J.H. Furst Co., 1938.
            . *Palestine: Our Holy Land.* Baltimore, J.H. Furst Co., 1940.
Hefter, Joseph Otmar. *Room For The Jew.* New York, The Otmar Press, 1939.
Jewish National Fund of America. *Acts and Pronouncements of the American Federation of Labor on Palestine and the Jewish Race.* n.p. 1938.
Mack, Harold L. *The Problem of the Jews.* Del Monte, Calif., The Hacienda, 193_.

Novick, Paul. *Palestine: The Communist Position*. New York, Jewish Bureau of the Central Committee of the Communist Party of the United States of America, 1936.

  Solution for Palestine: The Chamberlain White Paper. New York, National Council of Jewish Communists, 1939.

  Zionism Today. New York, Central Bureau of the Communist Party of the United States of America, 1936.

Pritchett, Henry S. *Egypt, Palestine and Greece: A Report*. Pamphlet no. 225. New York, Carnegie Endowment for International Peace *(International Conciliation)*, 1926.

Revolutionary Workers League. *Where Shall the Jewish Masses Turn?* Chicago, Demos Press, 1939.

Szold, Robert. *The Proposed Partition of Palestine*. New York. 1937.

Wise, Stephen S. *The Partition of Palestine*. n.p., n.d.

Zionist Organization of America. *Summary of the Position of the Zionist Organization of America in Conference with Dr. Weizmann and Associates,* n.p., n.d.

Unpublished Works

Berkowitz, Simcha, "Felix Frankfurter's Zionist Activities." Unpublished D.H.L. dissertation, Jewish Theological Seminary, 1971.

Eisner, Joan. "American Policy Toward Palestine 1916-1948." Unpublished Master's thesis, New York University, 1955.

Jonas, Franklin. "The Early Life and Career of B. Charney Vladeck 1886-1921: The Emergence of an Immigrant Spokesman." Unpublished Ph.D. dissertation, New York University, 1972.

Personal Diary of William Linn Westermann Kept on Board the S.S. George Washington from December 4, 1918 to ca. July 4, 1919, (cited as *PDWLW*) Unpublished, microfilmed at Columbia University, 1937.

Articles

Cohen, Naomi Wiener. "The Reaction of Reform Judaism in America to Political Zionism 1897-1922." *The Jewish Experience in America*. ed. Abraham J. Karp. New York, Ktav Publishing Co., 1969, pp. 154-182.

De Sola Pool, David. "Henry Pereira Mendes." *American Jewish Year Book*, XL (1939), 41-60.

Elkholy, Abdo A. "The Arab-Americans: Nationalism and Traditional Preservations." *The Arab-Americans: Studies in Assimilation*, edd. Elaine C. Hagopian and Ann Paden. Wilmette, Ill., The Medina University Press International, 1969, pp. 3-17.

"Events in 5679." *American Jewish Year Book*, XXI (1919), 175-207.

Fine, Morris. "Review of the Year 5699." *American Jewish Year Book*, XLI (1939), 189-237.

Friedman, Elisha M. "America and the Israel of Tomorrow," *Israel of Tomorrow*, ed. Leo Jung, 2 vols. New York, Herald Square Press, 1949, II, 471-541.

Golomb, Abraham I. "Jewish Self-Hatred." *Yivo Annual of Jewish Social Science*, I (1946), 250-259.

Grob, Gerald N., and Robert N. Beck. "Morris Raphael Cohen." *American Ideas*, edd. Gerald N. Grob and Robert N. Beck, 2 vols., New York, The Free Press, 1963, II, 429-435.

Hagopian, Elaine C. "The Institutional Development of the Arab-American Community of Boston: A Sketch." *The Arab-Americans: Studies in Assimilation*, edd. Elaine C. Hagopian and Ann Paden. Wilmette, Ill. The Media University Press International, 1969, pp. 67-83.

Kessler, Lawton. "American Jews and the Paris Peace Conference." *Yivo Annual of Jewish Social Science*, II (1947/1948), 222-241.

Lipset, Seymour Martin and Everett Carll Ladd, Jr. "Jewish Academics in the United States." *American Jewish Year Book Reprint, 1971*, pp. 89-128.

Nathanson, Nathaniel L. "Mr. Justice Brandeis: A Law Clerk's Recollections of the October Term, 1934." *Critical Studies in American Jewish History*, ed. Jacob R. Marcus, 3 vols. New York, Ktav Publishing House, 1971, III, 107-117.

Nolte, Richard H. "United States Policy and the Middle East." *The United States and the Middle East*, ed. Georgiana G. Stevens. Englewood Cliffs, N.J., Prentice-Hall, Inc., 1964, pp. 148-182.

Philipson, David. "Central Conference of American Rabbis 1889-1939." *American Jewish Year Book*, XLII (1940), 179-214.

Rich, Louis. "Adolph S. Ochs." *American Jewish Year Book*, XXXVII (1935), 27-55.

Sapir, Boris, and Leon Shapiro. "The Joint Distribution Committee in Jewish Life." *Israel of Tomorrow*, ed. Leo Jung. 2 vols. New York. Herald Square Press, 1949, I. 101-136.

Schneiderman, Harry. 'Julius Kahn." *American Jewish Year Book,* XXVII (1925), 238-246.

          "Review of the Year 5696." *American Jewish Year Book*, XXXVIII (1936) 175-394.

          . "Review of the Year 5697." *American Jewish Year Book.* XXXIX (1937), 203-503.

          and Melvin M. Fagen. "Review of the Year 5695." *American Jewish Year Book*, XXXVII (1935), 123-297.

Schwartz, S.D. "Emil Gustave Hirsch." *American Jewish Year Book*, XXVII (1925), 230-237.

Stevens, Georgiana G. "Middle East Perspectives." *The United States and the Middle East*, ed. Georgiana G. Stevens. Englewood Cliffs, N.J. Prentice-Hall, Inc. 1964, pp. 1-9.

Stevens, Richard P. "Colonization by Proxy: Two Franchising Ventures of the Home Office." *The Arab World*, XVIII (March-April 1972), 18-25.

Szajkowski, Zosa. "Concord and Discord in American Jewish Overseas Relief 1914-1924." *Yivo Annual of Jewish Social Science*, XVI (1969), 99-159.

Tenzer, Morton. "The Jews." *The Immigrants' Influence on Wilson's Peace Policies*, ed. Joseph P. O'Grady, n.p., The University of Kentucky Press, 1967, pp. 287-317.

Autobiographies, Memoirs and Published Collections Of Letters, Documents, Addresses and Sermons

Address of Sol M. Stroock Introducing a Resolution on the Partition of Palestine. n.p., the American Jewish Committee, 1938.

Adler, Cyrus, *Jacob H. Schiff: His Life and Letters*, 2 vols. Garden City, N.Y., Doubleday, Doran and Co., 1929.

American Council for Judaism. *Christian Opinion on Jewish Nationalism and a Jewish State*. n.p., 1944.

Berkowitz, Henry. *Intimate Glimpses of a Rabbi's Career*. Cincinnati, Hebrew Union College Press, 1921.

Bernheim, Isaac Wolfe. *The Closing Chapters of a Busy Life*. Denver 1929.
    . *The Reform Church of American Israelites*. Buffalo, 1921.

Bloom, Sol. *Autobiography*. New York, G.P. Putnam's Sons, 1948.

De Wolfe, Mark (ed.) *Holmes-Laski Letters*, 2 vols. Cambridge, Harvard University Press, 1953.

Enelow, H.G. *The Allied Countries and the Jews: A Series of Addresses*. New York, Temple Emanu-El, 1918.

Feuchtwanger, Lion. *Nationalism and Judaism: An Address*. New York, 1933.

Finley, John Huston. *A Pilgrim in Palestine*. New York, Charles Scribner's Sons, 1919.

Freedman, Max. *Roosevelt and Frankfurter: Their Correspondence 1928-1945*. Boston, Little, Brown and Co. 1967.

Goldenson, Samuel H. *The Present Status and Future Outlook of Reform Judaism*. Reprint from the Central Conference of American Rabbis' Yearbook XXXIV (1924).

Haber, Julius. *The Odyssey of an American Zionist: Fifty Years of Zionist History*. New York, Twayne Publishers, 1956.

Hendrick, Burton J. *The Life And Letters of Walter H. Page*, 3 vols. New York, Doubleday, Page and Co., 1923.

Holmes, John Haynes. *Palestine Today and Tomorrow*. New York, The Macmillan Co., 1929.

Ingrams, Doreen. *Palestine Papers 1917-1922: Seeds of Conflict*. New York, George Braziller, 1973.

Lowenthal, Marvin. *Henrietta Szold: Life and Letters*. New York, Viking Press, 1942.

Magnes, Judah L. *War-Time Addresses 1917-1921*. New York, Thomas Seltzer, 1923.

Miller, David Hunter. *My Diary At The Conference of Paris*, 21 vols. New York, Appeal Printing Co., 1924.

Morgenthau, Henry, in collaboration with French Strother. *All In A Lifetime*. Garden City, N.Y., Doubleday, Page and Co., 1922.

Philipson, David. *Centenary Papers and Others*. Cincinnati, Ark Publishing Co., 1919.

        . *Israel The International People: A Sermon Delivered Before the Convention of the Union of American Hebrew Congregations at Baltimore January 15, 1917*. n.p., 1917.

        . *My Life As An American Jew: An Autobiography*. Cincinnati, John G. Kidd and Son, Inc., 1941.

Reichert, Irving Frederick. *One Reform Rabbi Replies to Ludwig Lewisohn: Sermon Delivered Before Congregation Emanu-El, San Francisco, January 11, 1936*. n.p., 1936.

        Judaism and the American Jew: Selected Sermons and Addresses. San Francisco, The Grabhorn Press, 1953.

Reznikoff, Charles (ed.). *Louis Marshall: Champion of Liberty Selected Papers and Addresses*, 2 vols. Philadelphia, Jewish Publication Society of America; 1927.

Schulman, Samuel. *The Challenge, The Heritage and The Environment: An Address*. New York, 1939.

        . *Judaism, Jesus and the Decadence of the Reform Jewish Pulpit: A Sermon Delivered At Temple Beth-El, New York City, on January 3, 1926*. New York, 1926.

        . *The Non-Zionist and the New Palestine: A Sermon Delivered on Sunday, March 8, 1925*. New York, 1925.

        . *The University in Jerusalem: A Symbol of the Secular Palestine: A Sermon Delivered at Temple Beth-El, New York City, on April 12, 1925*. New York, 1925.

Sheean, Vincent. *Personal History*. Boston, Houghton Mifflin Co., 1969.

Voss, Carl Hermann (ed.). *Stephen S. Wise: Servant of the People Selected Letters*. Philadelphia, Jewish Publication Society of America, 1969.

Wise, James Waterman, and Justine Wise Polier (edd.). *Personal Letters of Stephen Wise*. Boston, The Beacon Press, 1956.

Monographs and Biographies

Abelow, Samuel P. *History of Brooklyn Jewry*. Brooklyn, Scheba Publishing Co., 1937.

Antonius, George. *The Arab Awakening*. New York, Capricorn Books, 1965.

Bailey, Thomas A. *Woodrow Wilson and the Lost Peace*. Chicago, Quadrangle Books, 1963.

Boustany, W.F. *The Palestine Mandate: Invalid and Impracticable*. Beirut, The American Press, 1936.

Bregstone, Philip P. *Chicago and Its Jews*. n.p., privately published, 1933.

Cauman, Samuel. *Jonah Bondi Wise*. New York. Crown Publishers, 1966.

Cohen, Israel. *A Short History of Zionism*. London, Frederick Muller Ltd. 1951.

⸺. *The Zionist Movement*. London, 1945.

Cohen, Naomi Wiener. *A Dual Heritage: The Public Career of Oscar S. Straus*. Philadelphia, Jewish Publication Society of America, 1969.

⸺. *Not Free to Desist: A History of the American Jewish Committee 1906-1966*. Philadelphia, Jewish Publication Society of America, 1972.

Coit, Margaret L. *Mr. Baruch*. Boston, Houghton Mifflin Co., 1957.

Cole, Wayne S. *America First: The Battle Against Intervention 1940-1941*. Madison, University of Wisconsin Press, 1953.

DeHaas, Jacob. *Louis D. Brandeis: A Biographical Sketch*. New York, Bloch Publishing Co., 1929.

DeNovo, John. *American Interests and Policies in the Middle East 1900-1930*. Minneapolis, The University of Minnesota Press, 1963.

Druks, Herbert. *The Failure to Rescue*. New York. Robert Speller and Sons, 1977.

Epstein, Melech. *The Jew and Communism 1919-1941*. New York, Union Sponsoring Committee, 1959.

Esco Foundation for Palestine, Inc. *Palestine: A Study of Jewish, Arab and British Policies*, 2 vols. New Haven, Yale University Press, 1947.

Evans, Laurence. *United States Policy and the Partition of Turkey 1914-1924*. Baltimore, Johns Hopkins Press, 1965.

Fein, Isaac M. *The Making of an American Jewish Community: A History of*

Baltimore Jewry from 1773 to 1920. Philadelphia, Jewish Publication Society of America, 1971.

Feingold, Henry L. *The Politics of Rescue: A Study of American Diplomacy and Politics Related to the Rescue of Refugees 1938-1944*. Ph.D. dissertation completed at New York University, 1966.

Fleischman, Harry. *Norman Thomas: A Biography*. New York, W.W. Norton and Co. 1969.

Friedman, Elisha M. *Survival or Extinction*. New York, Thomas Seltzer, 1924.

Friedrich, Carl J. *American Policy Toward Palestine*. Washington, D.C. Foreign Affairs Press, 1944.

Gersh, Harry. *These Are My People*. New York. Behrman House, Inc., 1959.

Glazer, Nathan. *American Judaism*. Chicago, University of Chicago Press, 1957.

Goren, Arthur A. *New York Jews and the Quest for Community: The Kehillah Experiment 1908-1922*. New York, Columbia University Press, 1970.

Grabill, Joseph L. *Protestant Diplomacy and the Near East: Missionary Influence on American Policy 1810-1927*. Minneapolis, University of Minnesota Press, 1971.

Halperin, Samuel. *The Political World of American Zionism*. Detroit, Wayne State University Press. 1961.

Halpern, Ben. *The Idea of a Jewish State*. Cambridge, Harvard University Press, 1961.

Hattis, Susan Lee. *The Bi-National Idea in Palestine During Mandatory Times*. Haifa, Shikmona Press, 1970.

Hirsch, Emil Gustav. *My Religion*. New York, The Macmillan Co, 1925.

Howard, Harry N. *The American Inquiry into the Middle East: The King-Crane Commission*. Beirut, Khayats, 1963.

        . *The Partition of Turkey*. New York, Howard Fertig, 1966.

Hurewitz, Jacob Coleman. *The Struggle for Palestine*. New York, Greenwood Press, 1968.

Janowsky, Oscar I. *The Jews and Minority Rights 1898-1919*. New York, Columbia University Press, 1933.

Jastrow, Morris. *Zionism and the Future of Palestine: The Fallacies and Dangers of Political Zionism*. New York, The Macmillan Co., 1919.

Johnson, Gerald W. *An Honorable Titan: A Biographical Study of Adolph S. Ochs*. New York, Harper and Brothers Publishers, 1946.

Kallen, Horace M. *Judaism At Bay*. New York, Bloch Publishing Co., 1932.

Katibah, Habib I. *The Case Against Zionism* New York, Syrian-American

Press, 1922.

———. *The New Spirit in the Arab Lands*. New York, privately printed, 1940.

Koestler, Arthur, *Promise and Fulfillment: Palestine 1917-1949*. New York, The Macmillan Co., 1949.

Laqueur, Walter. *A History of Zionism*. New York, Holt, Rinehart and Winston, 1972.

Lipsky, Louis. *Thirty Years of American Zionism*. n.p., Nesher Publishing Co., 1927.

Love, Donald M. *Henry Churchill King of Oberlin*. New Haven, Yale University Press, 1956.

Manuel, Frank E. *The Realities of American-Palestine Relations*. Washington, D.C., Public Affairs Press, 1949.

Mason, Alpheus Thomas. *Brandeis: A Free Man's Life*. New York, The Viking Press, 1956.

Mousa, Suleiman. *T.E. Lawrence: An Arab View*, trans. Albert Butros. London, Oxford University Press, 1966.

Neuman, Abraham. *Cyrus Adler: A Biographical Sketch*. Philadelphia, Jewish Publication Society of America, 1942.

Philipson, David. *The Reform Movement in Judaism*, 2nd ed. n.p., Ktav Publishing House, Inc., 1967.

Rabinowitz, Ezekiel. *Justice Louis D. Brandeis: The Zionist Chapter of His Life*. New York. The Philosophical Library, 1968.

Rihbany, Abraham Mitrie. *America Save the Near East*. Boston, The Beacon Press, 1918.

Rogoff, Harry. *An East Side Epic: The Life and Work of Meyer London*. New York, The Vanguard Press, 1930.

Rosenstock, Morton. *Louis Marshall: Defender of Jewish Rights*. Detroit, Wayne State University Press, 1965.

Safran, Nadav. *The United States and Israel*. Cambridge, Harvard University Press, 1963.

Schechtman, Joseph B. *The United States and the Jewish State Movement: The Crucial Decade 1939-1949*. New York, Herzl Press, 1966.

Shannon, David A. *The Socialist Party of America: A History*. Chicago, Quadrangle Books, 1967.

Shapiro, Yonathan. *Leadership of the American Zionist Organization 1897-1930*. Urbana, University of Illinois Press, 1971.

Stein, Leonard. *The Balfour Declaration*. New York, Simon and Schuster, 1961.

Stevens, Richard P. *American Zionism and United States Foreign Policy 1942-1947*. New York, Pageant Press, 1962.

Storrs, Ronald. *Orientations*. London, Ivor, Nicholson and Watson, Ltd., 1937.

Teller, Judd L. *Strangers and Natives: The Evolution of the American Jew from 1921 to the Present*. New York, The Delacorte Press, 1968.

Urofsky, Melvin I. *A Mind of One Piece: Brandeis and American Reform*. New York, Charles Scribner's Sons, 1971.

. *American Zionism from Herzl to the Holocaust*. Garden City, New York, Doubleday, 1975.

Werner, M.R. *Julius Rosenwald: The Life of a Practical Humanitarian*. New York, Harper and Brothers Publishers, 1939.

Yale, William. *The Near East*. Ann Arbor, The University of Michigan Press, 1968.

Zeine, Zeine N. *The Struggle for Arab Independence*. Beirut, Khayats, 1960.

Miscellaneous Secondary Works

Baker, Ray Stannard. *Woodrow Wilson and World Settlement*, 2 vols. Garden City, N.Y., Doubleday, Page and Co., 1923.

Barton, James L. *The Story of Near Eastern Relief 1915-1930*. New York, The Macmillan Co., 1930.

Berger, Elmer. *The Jewish Dilemma*. New York, The Devin-Adair Co., 1945.

. *Judaism or Jewish Nationalism: The Alternative to Zionism*. New York, Bookman Association, 1957.

Brown, Bernard J. *From Pharoh to Hitler*. Chicago, Consolidated Book Co., 1933.

Carlson, John Roy. *Cairo to Damascus*. New York, Alfred A. Knopf, 1952.

Chambers, Frank P. *This Age of Conflict*. New York, Harcourt, Brace and World, 1962.

Ellis, William T. *Bible Lands To-Day*. New York, D. Appleton and Co. 1927.

Fink, Reuben. *America and Palestine*. New York, American Zionist Emergency Council, 1944.

Fisher, Sydney Nettleton. *the Middle East: A History*. New York, Alfred A. Knopf, 1959.

Goldberg, Israel (pseud. Rufus Learsi). *Fulfillment: The Epic Story of Zionism*. New York, The World Publishing Co., 1951.

. *The Jews in America: A History*. New York, The World Publishing Co., 1954.

Goldman, Eric F. *Rendezvous With Destiny*. New York, Vintage Books, 1955.

Higham, John. *Strangers in the Land*. New York, Atheneum, 1970.

Hull, William L. *The Fall and the Rise of Israel*. Grand Rapids, Mich. Zondervan Publishing Co., 1954.

Jerusalem: Its Redemption and Future. New York, The Christian Herald, 1918.

Johnson, Julia E. (ed.). *Palestine: Jewish Homeland?* New York, The H.W. Wilson Co., 1946.

Kedourie, Elie. *The Chatham House Version and Other Middle Eastern Studies*. New York, Praeger Publishers, 1970.

Lazaron, Morris. *Common Ground: A Plea for Intelligent Americanism*. New York, Liveright Publishing Co., 1930.

McCrackan, William D. *The New Palestine*. Boston, The Page Co., 1922.

Martin, James J. *American Liberalism and World Politics 1931-1941*, 2 vols. New York, The Devin-Adair Co., 1964.

Rubin, Jacob A. *Partners in State-Building: American Jewry and Israel*. New York, The M.P. Press, Inc. 1969.

Sachar, Howard Morley. *the Course of Modern Jewish History*. New York, Delta Books, 1958.

    . *The Emergence of the Middle East 1914-1924*. New York, Alfred A. Knopf, 1969.

Selden, Harry Louis. *Five Million Jews Without a Country: What Is The Answer?* (A Digest of *The Rape of Palestine* by William B. Ziff). New York, The American Friends of a Jewish Palestine, 1940.

Selzer, Michael (ed.). *Zionism Reconsidered: The Rejection of Jewish Normalcy*. London, The Macmillan Co., 1970.

Sheean, Vincent. *The Eleventh Hour*. London, Hamish Hamilton, 1939.

    . *Not Peace, But A Sword*. New York, Doubleday, Doran and Co., 1939.

Waldman, Morris D. *Nor By Power*. New York, International Universities Press, 1953.

Foreign Language Sources

Deinard, Ephraim. *Aruchas Bas Ami* (Hebrew). St. Louis, Moinester Printing Co., 1920.

    . *Cherpas Brittania* (Hebrew). New York 1929.

    . *Machaas Sofrim* (Hebrew). St Louis, Morningstar, 1918.

    . *Pachdu B'Tzion Chatoim* (Hebrew). Arlington, N.J. 1917.

    . *Tzion B'Ad Mi?* (Hebrew). Arlington, N.J., 1918.

. *Tzelem B'Haichal* (Hebrew). New Orleans, 1926.

Hertz, Yaakov Shalom. *The Jewish Labor Bund* (Yiddish). New York, Farlag Unser Tsait, 1958.

The Jewish Socialist Movement in America. (Yiddish). New York, Der Wecker, 1954.

Shub, David. *The Revolving Stage of History: Memoirs*, 2 vols. New York, Cyco, 1970.

Index